The New Chosen People

The New Chosen People

A Corporate View of Election

William W. Klein

Academie Books Grand Rapids, Michigan
Zondervan Publishing House

ACADEMIE BOOKS is an imprint of Zondervan Publishing House,
1415 Lake Drive, S.E., Grand Rapids, Michigan 49506.

Library of Congress Cataloging in Publication Data

Klein, William W. (William Wade)
    The new chosen people : a corporate view of election / William W.
Klein.
      p.   cm.
    Includes bibliographical references.
    ISBN 0-310-51251-4
    1. Election (Theology)—Biblical teaching.   2. Bible.   N.T.—
Theology.   3. People of God—Biblical teaching.   4. Church—
Biblical teaching.   Title.
BS2545.E44   1990
234–dc20   89-49594
                                        CIP

Edited by Leonard G. Goss and Tom Raabe

Printed in the United States of America

90 91 92 93 94 / AK / 10 9 8 7 6 5 4 3 2 1

To my parents
William C. and Eleanor Klein.
As faithful servants of God
They made known to me the Holy Scriptures.
They are "chosen in the Lord."

CONTENTS

Abbreviations 11
Preface 17
Introduction 19

I. BACKGROUNDS TO ELECTION IN THE NEW TESTAMENT
1. Old Testament Background 25
   Introduction 25
   The Biblical Data 26
     God's Choice of Individuals 27
     God's Choice of Israel 28
   Purpose of Election 33
   Conclusion: Corporate Nature of Election 35
   The Concept of Corporate Solidarity 36
   Response to Objections to
         "Corporate Personality" 40
     Summary 42
2. Qumran 45
3. Apocrypha and Pseudepigrapha 53
4. The Rabbis 57

II. THE NEW TESTAMENT DOCUMENTS
   Introduction 63
5. The Synoptic Gospels 65
   God's Election of His People 65
   God's Role in the Acquisition/Application
         of Salvation 70
   The Role of God's Will in
         Applying Salvation 80

God's Knowledge of His People 87
Jesus' Choice of Individuals 90
God's Choice of Christ 92
Summary 101
6. The Acts of the Apostles 104
God's Determination of Events or
    States of Affairs 104
God's Elective Role with Corporate Groups 107
God's Elective Role with Individuals 111
   Jesus' Choice of the Twelve Apostles 112
   God's Choice of the Patriarchs
     of Israel 113
   God's Call to Mission 113
   The Salvation of Lydia 114
   God's Appointment of Overseers 114
   God's Choice of Paul as an Apostle 115
God's Choice of Christ and His Career 117
Summary 120
7. The Johannine Literature 124
God's Love for People 124
God's Knowledge of His People 127
The Election of Individuals 128
The Task of the Only Son 132
   Mongenēs 133
   Thelēma 135
   John 6:69 135
An Elect Local Congregation 136
The Role of God's Will in Attaining Salvation 136
God's Role in Applying Salvation 139
Summary 154
8. The Pauline Literature 158
God Foreknows People 161
God Purposes 165
   God's Purposes and Will Concerning the
     Plan of Salvation 165
   God's Purposes and Will Concerning Events 171
   God's Will Concerning His People 172
God Elects 172
   God's Election of Corporate Israel 173

God's Election of Christians 176
God's Election of Angels 184
God Predestines 184
God Appoints 188
God Appoints Jesus 189
God Appoints Paul to His Role
as Apostle 191
God Appoints Individuals (Besides Paul)
to a Position or Task 197
God Calls 199
God Calls Corporate Israel 200
God Calls Christians 200
Summary 209
9. Hebrews 213
God Determines Dates 213
God's Appointment of Individuals 214
God's Role in Applying Salvation 214
God's Appointment of Christ 216
Summary 219
10. The Epistles of James, Peter, and Jude 222
James 222
God's Will in the Circumstances of Life 222
God's Will in Providing Salvation 223
God Calls People to Salvation 224
God's Election of People 226
Summary 228
1 Peter 229
God's Will in the Circumstances of Life 229
God Calls People to Salvation 230
God's Choice of Christ 233
God's Election of People 236
Summary 245
2 Peter 247
God's Will for People's Salvation 247
God Calls People to Salvation 249
God's Choice of Christ 251
God's Election of People 252
Summary 253
Jude 254

III. CONCLUSIONS
   1. The Corporate Nature of Election
      to Salvation 257
       Implications of a Corporate View
          of Election 263
   2. Individual Election to a Task 268
       The Election of Christ 269
       The Election of the Twelve Apostles 270
       The Election of Paul 271
       The Election of Other Christians 272
       Implications for Individual Election
          to Ministry 272
   3. God's Call to Salvation 274
       Implications of the Call of God 276
   4. God's Foreknowledge 277
   5. God's Predestination 278
       Implications of God's Foreknowledge and
          Predestination 279
   6. The Place of God's Will 280
       Implications of God's Will 282

   Bibliography 285
   Index 301

ABBREVIATIONS

1. Old Testament

Ge	Genesis	Ecc	Ecclesiastes
Ex	Exodus	S	Song of Songs
Lev	Leviticus	Isa	Isaiah
Nu	Numbers	Jer	Jeremiah
Dt	Deuteronomy	La	Lamentations
Jos	Joshua	Eze	Ezekiel
Jdg	Judges	Da	Daniel
Ru	Ruth	Hos	Hosea
1Sa	1 Samuel	Joel	Joel
2Sa	2 Samuel	Amos	Amos
1Ki	1 Kings	Obadiah	Obadiah
2Ki	2 Kings	Jnh	Jonah
1Ch	1 Chronicles	Mic	Micah
2Ch	2 Chronicles	Na	Nahum
Ez	Ezra	Hab	Habakkuk
Ne	Nehemiah	Zep	Zephaniah
Es	Esther	Hag	Haggai
J	Job	Zec	Zechariah
Ps	Psalm(s)	Mal	Malachi
Pr	Proverbs		

2. New Testament

Mt	Matthew	Col	Colossians
Mk	Mark	1Th	1 Thessalonians
Lk	Luke	2Th	2 Thessalonians
Jn	John	1Ti	1 Timothy
Ac	Acts	2Ti	2 Timothy
Ro	Romans	Tit	Titus
1Co	1 Corinthians	Phm	Philemon
2Co	2 Corinthians	Heb	Hebrews
Gal	Galatians	Jas	James
Eph	Ephesians	1Pe	1 Peter
Php	Philippians	2Pe	2 Peter

1Jn	1 John	3Jn	3 John
2Jn	2 John	Rev	Revelation

3. Old Testament Apocrypha and Pseudepigrapha

Apoc Abr	Apocalypse of Abraham	PJ	Paralipomena of Jeremiah
Bar	1 Baruch	PS	Psalms of Solomon
1Es	1 Esdras	RE	Rest of Esther
2Es	2 Esdras	Sir	Sirach or Ecclesiasticus
Jub	Book of Jubilees		
Jth	Judith	Sib	Sibylline Oracles
1Mc	1 Maccabees	Tb	Tobit
2Mc	2 Maccabees	WS	Wisdom of Solomon

4. Josephus

Ant	*Jewish Antiquities*	*Life*	*Life*
Ap	*Contra Apionem*	*War*	*The Jewish War*

5. Qumran Writings, Dead Sea Scrolls

CD	Damascus Document
1QH	Thanksgiving Hymns, Hodayot
1QM	War Scroll
1QS	Community Rule or Manual of Discipline
1QSb	The Blessings (originally an appendix to 1QS)
1QGenAp	Genesis Apocryphon
1QpHab	Commentary (Pesher) on Habakkuk
1QpMic	Commentary (Pesher) on Micah
4QFl	Florilegium (Eschatological Midrashim)
4QpPs37	Commentary (Pesher) on Psalm 37

6. Early Christian Writings

Barn	Barnabas	Did	Didache
1 Clem	1 Clement	Euseb	Eusebius
2 Clem	2 Clement	*HE*	*Ecclesiastical History*

7. Rabbinic Writings

Ex. Rabba	Exodus Rabba (midrash)
Lev. Rabba	Leviticus Rabba (midrash)
Num. Rabba	Numbers Rabba (midrash)
Pes R	Pesikta Rabbati (homiletic midrash)

Sifre   "writing"; Midrashim on Numbers and
         Deuteronomy

8. Bible Translations and Paraphrases

GNB   Good News Bible (1966; 1976)
KJV   King James Version (1611) = AV
NASB   New American Standard Bible (1963)
NEB   New English Bible (1961; 1970)
NIV   New International Version (1978)
Phillips J. B. Phillips, New Testament in Modern English
          (1959)
RSV   Revised Standard Version (1946; 1952; Apocrypha
          1957)

9. Reference Works, Journals, and Serials

AB   Anchor Bible
BAGD   W. Bauer, *A Greek-English Lexicon of the New
          Testament and Other Early Christian Literature*,
          trans. and adapted by W. Arndt and F. W.
          Gingrich; 2d ed. rev. by F. W. Gingrich and
          F. W. Danker (1979)
BDF   F. Blass, A. Debrunner, and R. W. Funk, *A
          Greek Grammar of the New Testament* (1961)
Bib   *Biblica*
BibSac   *Bibliotheca Sacra*
BJRL   *Bulletin of the John Rylands Library*
BNTC   Black's New Testament Commentary series, ed.
          H. Chadwick (also called *Harpers New
          Testament Commentary*)
CBQ   *Catholic Biblical Quarterly*
CGTC   *Cambridge Greek Testament Commentary*
EvQ   *Evangelical Quarterly*
ExpT   *Expository Times*
HTR   *Harvard Theological Review*
HUCA   *Hebrew Union College Annual*
ICC   International Critical Commentary series, ed. S.
          R. Driver, A. Plummer, C. A. Briggs, J. A.
          Emerton, C. E. B. Cranfield
Int   *Interpretation*
ITQ   *Irish Theological Quarterly*
JAAR   *Journal of the American Academy of Religion*
JBL   *Journal of Biblical Literature*
JETS   *Journal of the Evangelical Theological Society*
JR   *Journal of Religion*
JSNT   *Journal for the Study of the New Testament*

JSOT	*Journal for the Study of the Old Testament*
JTS	*Journal of Theological Studies*
MNTC	Moffatt New Testament Commentary
Moulton-Turner	J. H. Moulton, *A Grammar of New Testament Greek*, vol. III, "Syntax," by N. Turner.
NCB	New Century Bible (new series), ed. R. E. Clements and M. Black
Nestle	Nestle-Aland et al., eds., *Novum Testament Graece*, 26th edition (1979)
NICNT	New International Commentary on the New Testament series, ed. F. F. Bruce (also called the New London Commentary on the New Testament)
NIDNTT	C. Brown, ed., *New International Dictionary of New Testament Theology*, 3 vols. (1975–78)
NIGTC	New International Greek Testament Commentary series, ed. W. W. Gasque and I. H. Marshall
NovT	*Novum Testamentum*
NTS	*New Testament Studies*
RB	*Revue biblique*
SBT	Studies in Biblical Theology
SJT	*Scottish Journal of Theology*
SNTS	Society for New Testament Studies
TBT	*The Bible Translator*
TDNT	G. Kittel and G. Friedrich, eds., *Theological Dictionary of the New Testament*, 10 vols. (ET, 1964–76)
TDOT	G. J. Botterweck and H. Ringgren, eds., *Theological Dictionary of the Old Testament*, I– (ET, 1974–)
THAT	E. Jenni and C. Westermann, eds., *Theologisches Handwörterbuch zum Alten Testament*, 2 vols. (1978).
TNTC	Tyndale New Testament Commentary series, ed. R. V. G. Tasker
TynB	*Tyndale Bulletin*
UBS	*The United Bible Societies Greek New Testament*, ed. K. Aland et al.
WBC	Word Biblical Commentary series, ed. D. A. Hubbard, G. W. Barker, J. D. W. Watts, and R. P. Martin
WTJ	*Westminster Theological Journal*
ZNW	*Zeitschrift für die neutestamentliche Wissenschaft*

10. General Abbreviations

Apoc.	Apocrypha	MS(S)	manuscript(s)
c.	*circa*, about	MT	Masoretic Text of the Old Testament
cf.	*confer*, compare		
chap(s).	chapter(s)		
comm.	commentary	n.d.	no date
DSS	Dead Sea Scrolls	NT	New Testament
eds.	edited by, editor(s)	OT	Old Testament
e.g.	*exempli gratia*, for example	p., pp.	page, pages
		pace	differing from
et al.	*et alii*, and others	par.	parallel(s)
ET	English translation	R	Rabbi
ff.	following verse	sec./§	section
Gk.	Greek	Suppl.	Supplementary
Heb.	Hebrew	v., vv.	verse, verses
ibid.	*ibidem*, in the same place	v.l.	*varia lectio*, other reading
i.e.	*id est*, that is	viz.	*videlicet*, namely
inscr.	inscription(s)	vol.	volume
LXX	Septuagint		

PREFACE

Like many budding theologues, I first learned theology from a Reformed position. I read the requisite volumes and studied the appropriate passages. But I also read the Wesleyans, Arminians, Lutherans, and Barth, to name some others. Instead of finding a consensus based on the biblical evidence, I discovered conflicting claims and mutually exclusive positions. Others who have had a similar experience can understand how puzzling and unsettling this was. I decided to pursue my own study of the theology of election. What does the Bible mean when it affirms that God chose us to be his people? How do the biblical writers use the key election terminology? This volume presents my analysis of the biblical data, but especially the New Testament theology of election.

Several key people merit acknowledgment here. My Calvinist friend and colleague, Gordon Lewis, first stimulated my thinking in theology. Though I didn't find Donald Burdick's more Arminian alternative totally convincing, he spurred me on to careful study and biblically defensible options. He has been a faithful example in both life and exegesis. During my doctoral work in Aberdeen, Scotland, I fell in with a Calvinist mentor—Professor R. A. S. Barbour—and an Arminian professor—Dr. I. H. Marshall. I acknowledge the challenge and encouragement provided by both. My Old Testament colleague at Denver, Robert Hubbard, carefully read and submitted helpful comments on the first chapter, though I alone am responsible for what is written. I wish to thank numerous students in my New Testament classes at Denver Seminary who have helped sharpen my thinking and encouraged me to bring this project to completion.

I express my gratitude to the trustees of Denver

Conservative Baptist Seminary for granting me sabbatical leaves in 1985 and 1989 for research and writing. Thanks to the Tyndale House Council for making available to me the excellent library facilities of Tyndale House in Cambridge, where much of this book was written. The Denver Seminary Library staff provided efficient and courteous service. The proficient people in the word processing department deserve recognition; Doris Haslam and Kris Smith managed that department during the course of this book. Special thanks to Denise Duke, who transformed several chapters of handwritten script onto floppy diskettes for later rewriting.

My daughters Alison and Sarah are constant reminders of the truly important matters in this life. I'm grateful for the balance, perspective, and joy they bring to me, particularly during an extended project like this. But I reserve my principal thanks for my wife, Phyllis, whose constant encouragement, patience, and sacrifices I gratefully acknowledge. Her literary skills are evident in several places in this manuscript. Concerning these three dear ones I affirm, "How can we thank God enough for you?" (1Th 3:9).

Above all, "To him be the glory forever! Amen."

INTRODUCTION

Election—to some, an embarrassment; to others, an important rallying point; and to most of us, a cause of bewilderment or frustration. Election embarrasses some Christians. They are reluctant to say, "God chose me," when he apparently passed by many others. Such a claim makes them uncomfortable; it seems so arrogant, so exclusive. God's choice of the few strikes them as unfair or unjust.

Yet others argue we cannot deny election or turn it around to say that "we chose God." They insist the Bible affirms that God has chosen to save certain people. To dilute its meaning, they believe, takes away from the biblical view of a sovereign God who alone is responsible for extending salvation to unworthy and depraved sinners.

Frustration or bewilderment comes, at times, because one side accuses the other of affirming what it claims to deny and denying what it claims to affirm. The Calvinist accuses the Arminian of making faith a "work" so that humans are responsible for their salvation. The Arminian vehemently rejects the charge and accuses the Calvinist of denying human free will, making people into robots, and turning God into a despot who arbitrarily consigns some to heaven and others to hell. The Calvinists resent what they feel is a misrepresentation of their position.

In spite of a long history of interpretation, no consensus about election has emerged. Some of the greatest theologians in the church's history have thought and written extensively about this issue. Theological luminaries such as Pelagius, Augustine, Aquinas, Luther, Calvin, Arminius, and more recently, Hodge, Warfield, and Barth stand out, at least in part, because of their contributions to the ongoing controversy. Can we simply call a truce and avoid the topic? Because of the uncertainty that surrounds this issue, many

Christians do just that. They think, "If these theologians can't agree, then who am I to venture an opinion?" Others see that election inevitably involves heated arguments and want no part in such strife. They would rather talk about issues that draw Christians together or that have more personal significance. So they avoid talking about election.

However, the theme of election in the Bible is too important to dismiss. Whether bewildering, embarrassing, or controversial, election occupies so prominent a place in the biblical revelation that the modern Christian cannot simply avoid it. The Old Testament writers repeatedly affirm that Israel exists because of God's choice. The Deuteronomist asserts, "The LORD your God has chosen you out of all the peoples on the face of the earth to be his people, his treasured possession" (Dt 7:6). We cannot understand Israel's position and mission apart from her election. Likewise, the prophets, priests, and kings of Israel served as God's chosen instruments.

Correspondingly, the New Testament writers devote much attention to God's choosing. Jesus is God's Elect One; Jesus chose disciples; Paul was chosen prior to his birth; and Christians are God's chosen ones. Ephesians 1:4 asserts that God chose Christians in Christ before the creation of the world. Using terminology that once applied to the nation Israel, 1 Pe 2:9 labels the church "a chosen people." In both Testaments God chooses people, they become the objects of his special care and concern, and he uses them to accomplish his purposes in the world. According to the Bible, election lies at the very foundation of God's relationship with people. To evade the subject is irresponsible.

Obviously, any valid understanding of election must derive from the Scriptures. Nevertheless, all too often the discussion has gone awry because the participants have been more concerned to formulate a systematic position than to understand the meaning and intent of the biblical authors.

Our goal, therefore, is to conduct an analysis of election in the New Testament—to take a biblical rather than a systematic approach. In other words, our concern will *not* be to set out in a systematic fashion what the Calvinists and Arminians believe and then to see which position better matches the evidence of the New Testament. Nor will we formulate a systematic explanation of election. Rather, after surveying the Old Testament and Jewish backgrounds, we will evaluate the New Testament evidence, seeking to understand how the writers themselves presented the reality of God's choosing.

A paradigm for understanding election does emerge from the New Testament. We believe the New Testament writers do share a basic understanding of God as a choosing or electing God. *They present "election to salvation" as corporate.* Rooted in their Hebrew heritage, the earliest Christians believed that they comprised a new chosen people. Whereas God had formerly chosen Israel, in the messianic era he has chosen the church—in Christ.

This corporate understanding of election to salvation avoids some of the pitfalls, frustrations, and embarrassments of many discussions of election. The typical Calvinist and Arminian formulations focus on God's choice of individuals for salvation. They debate about what motivated God to select certain individuals for salvation. Was he motivated simply by his own loving and sovereign purposes? Or, given his foreknowledge, did he select those who he knew would eventually believe? From the biblical perspective, however, such debates may be beside the point. Election concerns the church—the corporate body of Christians. The church finds her election in her union with Christ. On this point both the Arminian and the Calvinist deviate from the biblical perspective when they try to explain salvific election as God's choice of individuals. The biblical perspective is corporate. God has chosen a people to save.

In these pages we hope to unveil and illuminate that perspective. The writer hopes that the result will be an enhanced understanding and appreciation of God's gracious provision in Christ. Election ought to fill us with praise and thanksgiving, not embarrassment or misgiving. When we comprehend God's gracious provision, we will celebrate it as Peter did:

> But you are a chosen people, a royal priesthood, a holy nation, a people belonging to God, that you may declare the praises of him who called you out of darkness into his wonderful light. Once you were not a people, but now you are the people of God; once you had not received mercy, but now you have received mercy (1 Pe 2:9–10).

I

BACKGROUNDS TO ELECTION IN THE NEW TESTAMENT

1

OLD TESTAMENT BACKGROUND

INTRODUCTION

Old Testament theology stands firmly on the bedrock of God's election of Israel. Election is presumed and pervasive, and finds explicit expression in many ways and places. The Old Testament writers unashamedly exclaim that Yahweh, the one true God, has chosen Israel out of all the nations of the world to be his own people. They call him the God of Israel, and in their Scriptures he calls himself the God of Abraham, Isaac, and Jacob. G. E. Wright asserts,

> The Old Testament doctrine of a chosen people, one selected by God "for his own possession above all the people that are on the face of the earth" (Deut 7:6), is the chief clue for the understanding of the meaning and significance of Israel.[1]

Can such a claim be supported? How do the Old Testament documents employ this concept of God's choice or election?[2]

---

[1]G. E. Wright, *The Old Testament Against Its Environment* (London: SCM, 1957), 47.

[2]Several helpful treatments of election in the Old Testament are H. H. Rowley, *The Biblical Doctrine of Election* (London: Lutterworth, 1950); H. Seebass et al., *"bāchar," TDOT*, 2:73–87; J. Jocz, *A Theology of Election*

The following discussion attempts to unpack the essential dimensions of the concept of election in the Old Testament. To do that requires an assessment of the key terms the writers employ when they present Yahweh as an electing God. Beyond simply noting key words, we need to identify and understand the theme of election wherever it occurs. Our study will begin with the study of several words and concepts that seem to convey the theme of election— God's choice of people, of course, comprises our central concern. We will seek to understand what the authors present as the purpose of election: Why did God choose? We will focus our efforts on understanding the basic or essential nature of election in the Old Testament documents.

THE BIBLICAL DATA

The basic Hebrew word for "choose," *bāchar*, means "a careful choice occasioned by actual needs, and thus a very conscious choice."[3] "To choose" occurs in very ordinary situations. David *chose* stones for his sling (1Sa 17:40); a carpenter *selects* wood suitable for a project (Isa 40:20). Moving to the realm of religion, people may choose God (Jos 24:22), his law or his way (Pss 25:12; 119:173; Pr 3:31). Likewise, they may choose other people for marriage, as leaders, and as warriors, for example (Ge 6:2; Ex 18:25; Jdg 20:15).

The God who chooses stands at the heart of the Old Testament concept of election.[4] A survey of the uses of the verb *bāchar* (to choose) with God as subject, reveals two broad categories: God's choice of specific individuals and God's choice of groups or peoples.[5]

(London: SPCK, 1958); H. Wildberger, *"bḥr,"* THAT, 1:275–300; and G. Quell, *"eklegomai,"* TDNT, 4:144–68.

   [3]Seebass, *TDOT*, 2:74.

   [4]According to Wildberger's tabulation, theologically significant uses with God as subject constitute 67 percent of the occurrences of the *bḥr* (choose) group of words (*THAT*, 1:277).

   [5]Though some texts may be questioned, the locations where God is subject, using the verbal forms of *bāchar* only, may be divided roughly as follows.

   a. *Individuals*: Dt 17:15; 1Sa 2:28; 10:24; 16:8, 9, 10; 2Sa 6:21; 1Ki 8:16; 11:34; 14:21; 1Ch 28:4, 5, 6, 10; 29:1; 2Ch 6:5, 6; Ne 9:7.; Pss 65:4; 78:70; 89:3; 105:26; 106:23; Hag 2:23.

God's Choice of Individuals

God's choice of individuals is the less common use of the concept of election. God chose the heroes of the nation: Abraham (Ne 9:7), Jacob (Ps 135:4; Mal 1:2), Moses (Nu 16:5,7; Ps 106:23), David (1Sa 13:13–14; 2Sa 6:21; Ps 78:70), and Zerubbabel (Hag 2:23). The prophets, too, are objects of God's election. Admittedly, in the explicit statements of God's call of Jeremiah (1:4–8) and Amos (7:14–15), the word *bāchar* (choose) does not occur. Nevertheless, the prophets' "calling" often was equivalent to election, despite the omission of explicit election terminology. The word *yāda'*, "know," which Jeremiah uses (1:5), highlights the prophet's personal relation to the God who chose and commissioned him. Unquestionably, God selected certain prophets to speak for him (also see Eze 2:1–3; Am 7:14–15).

The priesthood also exists by virtue of God's election. According to 1Sa 2:27ff., God chose Eli's family to serve as priests forever (2:20), but their unfaithfulness nullified their election. God determined to raise up another priest who would be faithful (2:35). Election terminology later applies to the Levites (1Ch 15:2; 2Ch 29:11; Dt 18:5; 21:5). The corporate priesthood was elect, though God disqualified individual priests from their position when they proved unsuitable. Indeed, God struck down Korah the Levite when he instigated a rebellion against Moses and Aaron (Nu 16).

The election of kings is a borderline category. Though God selected the king individually, his calling and mission were bound up with the entire nation and its election to be God's people. Samuel applied the term *bāchar* (choose) to Saul, referring to him as "the man the Lord has *chosen*" (1Sa 10:24). In places the OT writers stress the special election of David's dynasty (e.g., 2Sa 7; Pss 110; 132:11–12). David himself insisted that God chose him to be king (2Sa 6:21; cf. 1Sa 16:8–10; 1Ki 8:16; 11:34; 1Ch 28:4; 2Ch 6:6). David affirmed Solomon as God's chosen successor to his reign (1Ch 28:5; 29:1). The Deuteronomic instructions warned

---

b. *Corporate* (many references to Zion and Jerusalem are corporate, standing for the nation; most are not included here): Dt 4:37–38; 7:6, 7; 10:15; 14:2; 18:5; 21:5; 1 Ki 3:8; 1Ch 15:2; 16:13; 28:4; 2Ch 29:11; Pss 33:12; 78:67, 68; 105:6, 43; 106:5; 135:4; Isa 14:1; 41:8, 9; 43:10, 20–21; 44:1, 2; 49:7; 65:9, 15, 22; Jer 33:24; Eze 20:5; Zec 1:17; 2:12; 3:2.

Israel to appoint as king only one whom the Lord chose (Dt 17:15). In a nation belonging to God, the monarch rules in God's place. His role transcends the political, for he leads the very people of God (Pss 28:8; 72:1–2).

God's Choice of Israel

The dominant use of election terminology applies to the people as a body or nation. Israel considered herself the very special people of God (Ex 19:5; Jdg 5:11). Several key texts epitomize this self-consciousness of Israel's election:

> For you are a people holy to the LORD your God. The LORD your God has *chosen* you out of all the peoples on the face of the earth to be his people, his treasured possession (Dt 7:6).

> Yet the LORD set his affection on your forefathers and loved them, and he *chose* you, their descendants, above all the nations, as it is today (Deut. 10:15).

> Out of all the peoples on the face of the earth, the LORD has *chosen* you to be his treasured possession (Dt 14:2).

> But you, O Israel, my servant, Jacob, whom I have *chosen*, you descendants of Abraham my friend, I took you from the ends of the earth, from its farthest corners I called you. I said, "You are my servant"; I have *chosen* you and have not rejected you" (Isa 41:8–9).

> For the LORD has chosen Zion, he has desired it for his dwelling: "This is my resting place for ever and ever; here I will sit enthroned for I have desired it . . ." (Ps 132:13–14).

Though this listing could continue, these examples sufficiently advance Israel's unequivocal claim to be God's chosen nation.[6] Her "most favored nation" status never comes under question. Election brings together two critical concepts: Israel is God's holy people and his treasured possession (Dt 7:6).[7]

---

[6]The listing of texts asserting God's choice of Israel could be considerably lengthened beyond these representative texts. Others include 1 Ki 3:8; 1Ch 16:13; Dt 4:37–38; Pss 105:6, 43; 106:5; Isa 43:20–21; 44:1–2; 49:7; 65:9, 15, 22; and Eze 20:5. In Eze 16:4–14 the prophet paints a graphic picture of God's unmerited choice of Jerusalem (the city stands for the people of Israel). Clearly it was not motivated by anything in Israel herself.

[7]Wildberger makes this point, *THAT*, 1:285.

Yet God calls her to account for the responsibilities inherent in that status. Prophets like Amos (3:2; 9:7) continually reminded Israel that her election implied righteous conduct—the fulfillment of God's will and the display of godly virtues like obedience, justice, and compassion. Election gave no blanket approval to all Israel did, nor could it guarantee political success.

The Deuteronomic code emphasized this accountability. The writer of Dt 10:16 followed up the affirmation of election with this urgent exhortation: "Circumcise your hearts, therefore, and do not be stiff-necked any longer." God chose Israel; therefore her actions had to correspond with her standing. Similarly Dt 7:6–12, 19–20 make clear that God's election and covenant entailed specific responsibilities and would have distinct results. Obedience secured blessing; forgetting the Lord brought destruction. Though election meant that God sided with Israel (Dt 4:37–38), he refused to ignore her disobedience (4:39–40). Election did not shield Israel against misfortune, political defeat, or the judgment of God. In the same vein, Ezekiel follows his depiction of God's sovereign choice of Jerusalem—standing for the nation (Eze 16:4–14), with a catalog of her unfaithfulness (16:15–34) and God's judgment (16:35–58).

In sum, God called his elect people to live holy lives. In Ex 19 God spoke in elective terms when he reviewed Israel's deliverance from Egypt. Then he affirmed his covenant with them:

> Now if you obey me fully and keep my covenant, then out of all nations you will be my treasured possession. Although the whole earth is mine, you will be for me a kingdom of priests and a *holy nation* (Ex 19:5–6).

To be God's people—his treasured possession—demanded a separation from the gods and the practices of the pagans.

What motivated God to choose Israel? The Old Testament writers overwhelmingly assert that Israel could not attribute her election to anything within the nation herself. Beginning with God's selection of the patriarch Abraham (Ge 18:18–19; cf. 12:1–4; 17:1–8; Dt 4:37), Israel owes its existence as God's people solely to his gracious, unmerited choice. The writer of Deuteronomy makes this clear:

> The LORD did not set his affection on you and choose you because you were more numerous than other peoples, for you were the fewest of all peoples. But it was because the LORD loved you and kept the oath he swore to your forefathers that he brought you out with a mighty hand and redeemed you from the land of slavery. . . . (Dt 7:7–8)

Israel's strength, numbers, virtue, or winsomeness did not merit God's notice and selection. How could they, when Israel did not even exist before God elected her? God's lovingkindness alone can explain his choice.

Consideration of election terminology in the Old Testament must include *yāda'*, the Hebrew word meaning "to know." Like the corresponding Greek and English words, the Hebrew word *yāda'* (know) has a wide range of meaning. The basic meaning involves knowledge gained through the senses. Thus "know" can mean to experience, to distinguish between, to know by learning, a relationship based on familiarity, to know how to do something, or to know a person face to face.[8]

New Testament theologian R. Bultmann boldly asserts:

> The element of will in *yāda'* emerges with particular emphasis when it is used of God, whose knowing establishes the significance of what is known. In this connection *yāda'* can mean "to elect," i.e. to make an object of concern and acknowledgment.[9]

Is Bultmann correct? First, what does *yāda'*, "know," mean when the Old Testament writers use it to describe God's relationship to people? Bultmann contends that *yāda'* includes more of the sense of detecting or learning by experience than its Greek counterparts and thus governs objects not found with the Greek verb *ginōskō*.[10] This experiential aspect helps explain the common use of know for sexual intercourse. Hence Bultmann deduces, "This means that knowledge is not thought of in terms of the

---

[8]For the basic meanings of *yāda'*, see W. Schottroff, "*yd'*," *THAT*, I (1978): 682–702; R. Bultmann, "*ginōskō*, et al.," *TDNT*, 1:689–716; and E. D. Schmitz, "Knowledge—*ginōskō*, et al.," *NIDNTT*, 2:392–406.

[9]R. Bultmann, *TDNT*, I (1964): 698.

[10]Examples include: to know blows (1Sa 14:12), to know childlessness (Isa 47:8), to know sickness (Isa 53:3), and to know divine punishment (Jer 16:21; Eze 25:14).

possession of information. It is possessed only in its exercise or actualization."[11] Bultmann concludes that when God is the "knower," election is inevitable.

Is *yāda'* itself "elective," or does it have elective significance only when used in certain contexts? The prophet Amos uses the term *yāda'* with elective significance. He quotes Yahweh, who says, literally, "I have *known* only you from all the families of the earth" (Amos 3:2). Though *know* is used here in the sense of appropriation, this component of meaning is in fact expressed by the *combination* of *yāda'* (know) with *raq* (only) and *min* (the partitive indicating separation: "from . . ."). In this combination of terms *yāda'* has the sense of a "free and efficacious act of will."[12] This clarifies the issue that Bultmann leaves muddled. To know does not by itself imply election, though it can mark the intimate and special relationship God has with certain people. It may have elective significance when used with other elements.

The use of *yāda'*, "know," in Jeremiah 1:5 also illustrates this point. There God says to the prophet:

> Before I formed you in the womb I knew you,
> before you were born I set you apart;
> I appointed you as a prophet to the nations.

Here the addition of "I *set you apart*" and "I *appointed* you as a prophet" gives elective significance to this verse and, particularly, to *yāda'*.[13]

To summarize, God's knowledge of people is personal, experiential, and intimate. Although the component "to choose" is not intrinsic to "to know," the context may suggest this idea in certain uses. In such cases, God's knowledge of a prophet (Jer 1:5) or a people (Am 3:2) may indeed connote his special choice of them.

This elective sense of *yāda'*, "to know," seems to parallel the findings for *bāchar*, "to choose." As God chooses, so he chooses to know a prophet whom he appoints for his task (Jer 1:5; also Ge 18:19 of Abraham; Ex 33:12 of Moses; and perhaps 2Sa 7:20 of David). As with "choose," God also "knows" the nation as a people (Am 3:2). In reference to

---

[11]Bultmann, *TDNT*, 1:698.
[12]G. Quell, *TDNT*, 4:147.
[13]Ibid., *TDNT*, 4:148.

individuals, the election-knowing involves a function or task and does not necessarily imply their salvation. Of course, individuals like Abraham, Moses, David, and Jeremiah were among the faithful Jews, the remnant whom God would save. Yet God "knows" them primarily so that they might fulfill leadership roles in his program. This knowledge means choice for a task, not election to what we might call eternal salvation.[14]

God's elective knowledge of Israel does not guarantee the salvation of all Israelites. What holds for *bāchar*, "choose," also applies here. Certainly God has made Israel the "object of his concern and acknowledgment," but in no way can this mean that God chose all or even specific individual Israelites for eternal salvation. This election-knowing denotes an enabling, liberating choice, but one that still requires the personal response of the individual. Isaiah's appointment shows, in his case, how the prophet "volunteered" to serve God (Isa 6:1–13).

This requirement of individual responsibility finds parallels in the concept of *covenant* in the Old Testament. God unilaterally initiated his covenant(s), *berîth*, with the nation Israel, but the covenants did not determine the "eternal destinies" of specific individuals. Temporal blessing and prosperity depended upon keeping the terms of the covenant. Covenant did not guarantee salvation. This inability explains Jeremiah's prophecy of the coming of a "new covenant" that would provide for salvation: "For I will forgive their wickedness and will remember their sins no more" (Jer 31:34).

The Old Testament writers use the word *love* with elective significance. The word *love* occurs most commonly in the sphere of human relationships. More pertinent, however, are the less common uses where the writers speak of God's love for people. The prophets extol God's love which motivated his salvation of his unworthy people Israel (Jer 31:3; Hos 2:19–20, 23; 11:1, 4; 14:4; Mal 1:2).[15] Though love originally meant an emotion, the writers of the Old Testament saw it as an activity. Wallis says, "Yahweh's love

---

[14]Election to a task might presuppose their eternal salvation, but we argue they are separate issues. In these texts the choice for tasks is central.

[15]God's love for his people finds expression in many places (e.g., Dt 7:8; 10:15, 18; 23:5; 1 Ki 10:9; 2Ch 2:11; 9:8; Ps 146:8; Pr 3:12; and Ne 13:26).

expressed itself in action in behalf of his chosen people."[16] Because of this action,[17] God's people were commanded to love God (Dt 6:5) and their neighbors (Lev 19:18, 34; Dt 10:18–19).

Does the phrase "God loves" mean "God elects"? The evidence does not seem to warrant this conclusion. More accurately, God's love stands behind and explains his choice of Israel. As Quell puts it, "because He loved Israel He bound himself to it (Dt 7:6ff.)."[18] Because God loves, and for no other reason, he chose his people (Dt 7:8).

God's love as expressed in the Old Testament is almost exclusively corporate. "What the Old Testament has to say about the love of God moves for the most part in national trains of thought, where it finds its natural soil."[19] Certainly God loves individual people. The writer of Ne 13:26 describes Solomon, king of Israel, as "loved by his God" (see also 2Sa 12:24–25), and Pr 3:12 could certainly apply to an individual. When the issue is God's saving, electing love, however, the corporate sense predominates. God most often reveals his love in his covenant relationship to his people.

PURPOSE OF ELECTION

What is the purpose of God's choosing? The Old Testament writers do not paint a picture of election as a self-serving or self-aggrandizing doctrine. Israel dare not become proud of her status, for election does not come without strings. Rooted in God's initial promise to Abram (Ge 12:1–3), God's choice put Israel under a distinct burden while promising the highest blessing to the obedient. He promised, "Now if you obey me fully and keep my covenant, then out of all nations you will be my treasured possession" (Ex 19:5). Thus election was a call to serve God in the world. Rowley has stressed this point: "Election is for service. And if God chose Israel, it was not alone that He might reveal

---

[16]G. Wallis, *TDOT*, 1:115.

[17]An allied term, *ḥesed*, loving-kindness or steadfast love, as it is variously translated, also expresses this active, concrete, and practical understanding of love. God's covenant faithfulness to his people implies his practical, tangible care for them.

[18]Quell, *TDNT*, 1:33.

[19]Ibid., *TDNT*, 1:31.

Himself to her, but that He might claim her for service."[20] Again, "it is never primarily for the privilege but for the service that the elect are chosen."[21] Rowley is correct.

Though we readily observe this focus of service in the election of individuals (prophets, priests, and kings), God's choice of his people had this goal too. The terms of God's unilateral covenant placed the people under an obligation to obedience and service. Failure to keep its demands meant forfeiture of its promises. This duty continued with each succeeding generation. The Deuteronomist asserts that the generation of the Exodus could not stand on the merits of the patriarchs (Dt 5:2–3). Each generation had to renew God's covenant for itself.

God brought into existence a people to serve him. This is election. Israel exists as a people because of God's choice. He did not find a people and select them; God's election created Israel. Yet God insisted that each Israelite keep the terms he set up. Sutcliffe correctly observes that

> this divine choice of the nation was no guarantee that individual members would always continue to enjoy its special privileges. On the contrary, those guilty of serious transgressions of the divine law were to be cut off from the people (Ex 12:19; Num 19:13, etc.).[22]

God, in election, brought the people into existence and established his covenant with the nation. Israel's survival attests to the truth of her election. God proved his sovereign faithfulness to his people, preserving them in spite of their unfaithfulness. But discipline went hand in hand with election.[23] Those who failed to keep the terms of the covenant forfeited their individual places in this elect body. When individuals (or even a mass of Israelites) fail to give to God the loyalty and obedient service he demands, then in love he chastens them. Amos 3:2 clearly connects election and discipline: "You only have I chosen of all the families of the earth; therefore I will punish you for all your sins." God will prove faithful; he will not abandon his people, nor will

---

[20]H. H. Rowley, *The Biblical Doctrine of Election* (London: Lutterworth, 1950), 43.

[21]Ibid., 45.

[22]E. F. Sutcliffe, "Many Are Called but Few Are Chosen," *ITQ* 28 (1961): 127.

[23]Rowley, *Biblical Doctrine of Election*, 53.

they fail to arrive at their appointed destiny (Eze 16:59–60). Yet the writers make a distinction between God's choice of a corporate people and his choice of individuals who may or may not ultimately benefit from that corporate choice.

CONCLUSION: CORPORATE NATURE OF ELECTION

The Old Testament data concerning God's election naturally leads to a major conclusion—*election is primarily a corporate concept*. The election of the priesthood puts this in bold relief. God chose the priests as a category, but individual Levites could be disqualified. The Davidic dynasty certainly follows this pattern. Though "election" can apply to individuals, more frequently it applies to the election of corporate groups.[24] In fact, the scattered references to elect individuals find their significance in the context of the election of the community.

Surely the evidence does not warrant dismissing the significant references to God's choice of individuals, for they are neither few nor isolated. God specifically selected individuals to assume special roles or tasks. But in that an individual may fail to perform the task and so forfeit election, we may distinguish between individual and corporate election. God chose Saul as king (1Sa 10:24), but because of Saul's sins, God rejected his kingship (13:13–14; 15:10–11, 23, 26–29). In distinction, God will not revoke his choice of his people, nor forget his promises to her (1Sa 12:22; Jer 31:27–28 Eze 16:59–60). The corporate "people of God" is an abiding grouping. God alone has brought it into existence, and it owes everything to his mercy and love. Only this people shares in God's benefits and blessings. Those from this body who rebel lose what God has provided. Accordingly, this essential principle of election of the corporate people of Israel has application to individuals. God selects individuals to perform his bidding. If they accept his call and

---

[24]A. Richardson, *Introduction to the Theology of the New Testament* (London: SCM, 1958), may take this too far, but his main assertion is valid: "Election in the Bible is a social conception, since it is comparatively rarely that we meet with the idea of the election of the individual, such as a prophet, for a special task (e.g., Jer 1:4–5; contrast Isa 44:2, 24; 49:1; Ps 22:9–10; 71:6, 271)."

faithfully discharge their duties, they find his favor and blessing. He calls them to serve, as he called the entire nation. Individuals do not merit their standing as chosen ones any more than did the nation.

Therefore, in its essence election is corporate. Election terminology in the Old Testament asserts the astounding conviction that God has chosen a people, Israel. Daane urges, "Divine election in its basic Old Testament form is collective, corporate, national. It encompasses a community of which the individual Israelite is an integral part."[25] When God elected, Israel came into existence. Isaiah makes this explicit: "But now listen, O Jacob, my servant, Israel, whom I have chosen. This is what the LORD says—he who made you, who formed you in the womb, and who will help you" (Isa 44:1–2; cf. 43:20–21). An extended quote from Pannenberg seems fitting:

> The act of election was identified in ancient Israel in different ways, but it was always understood as a unique act constituting the entire course of Israel's subsequent history. This uniqueness of the elective act did not preclude, however, the possibility of particular persons' or groups' being chosen in a particular way and to a particular function in the service of the people within the encompassing context of the history constituted once in the election of the people itself.[26]

THE CONCEPT OF CORPORATE SOLIDARITY

The essentially corporate nature of election finds considerable support in the abundant corporate concepts and terms in the Old Testament. Eissfeldt notes:

> To Israelite thought, which in this connection is quite in harmony with Semitic thought in general and also has parallels outside the Semitic world, unity is prior to diversity, the community prior to the individual; the real entity is the community, and the individuals belonging to it have their origin therein.[27]

---

[25]J. Daane, *The Freedom of God* (Grand Rapids: Eerdmans, 1973), 104.

[26]W. Pannenburg, *Human Nature, Election and History* (Philadelphia: Westminster, 1977), 90.

[27]"The *Ebed-Jahwe* in Isaiah xl.–lv. in the Light of the Israelite Conceptions of the Community and the Individual, the Ideal and the Real," *Expository Times* 44 (1933): 264.

He argues that this applies particularly to blood-communities who owe their being and destiny to a particular ancestor. In his book *Man in Community*,[28] R. P. Shedd convincingly marshals six kinds of data that show the extent of corporateness in the Old Testament. His points merit a careful examination. (1) The personality of the group transcended time and space so a family could be identified with its ancestor (Ge 13:15–17; Isa 41:8; Hos 11:1; Mal 1:3–4). (2) Punishment and blessing extended beyond the specific individual responsible. As for punishment see the account of Achan's sin (Jos 7) or Korah's rebellion (Nu 16), as well as the statements in Ex 20:5–6. As for blessing note Ge 12:3 and Ex 32:13. (3) Regarding the covenant Shedd states, "All the members of a covenantal community are subordinate to the whole. To sever oneself from the group is to be cut off from the covenant and thereby from the covenant-making God."[29] (4) The high priests, on the Day of Atonement, sacrificed for the sins of the people (Lev 16:15, 19, 21). The sins of the community, seen as a unity, could be transferred to the scapegoat. (5) Certain prayers expressed the intercessor's sense of corporate guilt (Ne 9:33; Da 9:5–19). (6) Some situations evidence a kind of "oscillation," where the individual embodies the group and the group appears as an individual (Ex 34:15; Nu 21:22; Dt 7:25; 8:19; 14:21).

In parallel to Shedd's points, any reader notices that the writers of the Old Testament commonly treat the entire people of Israel as a unit (Isa 5:1–7; Jer 12:10). E. Best adds, "The people of Israel do not merely form a unit; they form a unit which is related to God. They are a temple in which he dwells (Lev 26:12; Ezek 37:27; Isa 60:19; Zech 2:10–13)."[30]

Furthermore, the Old Testament writers routinely apply to Israel a variety of corporate terms. Israel was the *bride* of Yahweh, selected and loved by God, though often adulterous (Isa 54:1–8; Hos 1–3; 61:10; 62:4–5; Jer 3:8; Eze 16, where Jerusalem represents the nation, and Eze 23). The term *congregation* of Israel expressed Israel's collective unity. The metaphor of Israel as the *flock* of Yahweh, its shepherd,

---

[28]R. P. Shedd, *Man in Community* (London: Epworth, 1958), 3–41.

[29]Ibid., 26.

[30]E. Best, *One Body in Christ* (London: SPCK, 1955), 204. See his Appendix A, "Corporate Personality and Racial Solidarity," 203ff., for his fuller explanation.

occurs repeatedly (for example, Pss 23; 78:52; 80:1; 95:7; 100:3; Jer 13:17; 23:1; Hos 4:16; Mic 7:14). The Messiah stands as the shepherd of the flock (1Sa 17:34–36; Ps 78:70–72; Isa 40:11; 63:11; Jer 23:4–5; Eze 34:15–16, 23). Old Testament writers often use the term *house* to portray Israel's collective unity. They describe the Israelites collectively as the "house of Israel" or, sometimes, as the place where God dwells (e.g., Ex 16:31; Lev 10:6; Ru 4:11; 19:3; 1Sa 7:2–3; 2Sa 12:8; Isa 2:5; Jer 2:4; 5:15).

Of course the term *people* itself, as a collective term for Israel, pervades the Old Testament. "For you are a people holy to the LORD your God. The LORD your God has chosen you out of all the peoples on the face of the earth to be his people" (e.g., Dt 7:6; cf. 14:2; 21:8; 1Sa 2:24; 1 Ki 8:30, 33–34; Isa 43:20). *Vine* also occurs commonly as a concept embodying all the people (Ps 80:8–16; Isa 5:2; Jer 2:21; Eze 15; Hos 10:1). The failure of some (perhaps most) Israelites to tithe was judged so comprehensively by God (Mal 3:8–12) because God considered this sin to exceed an individual's stewardship. It had collective importance; the people had sinned. Their stinginess demonstrated a national shortcoming. In summary, Old Testament writers conceived of Israel as a people, a corporate entity. But what exactly does corporateness mean or include?

In describing the Old Testament doctrine of humanity, H. Wheeler Robinson refers to "the idea of corporate personality,"[31] a consciousness that sees people together as part of a larger unit. He argues that this outlook characterized preexilic Jewish thinking before the rise of more individualistic conceptions.[32] Robinson cites the narrative of 2Sa 21:1–14 to illustrate this corporate viewpoint in Israel.[33] God explained to David that he had allowed a famine in Israel because of Saul's unavenged, unwarranted slaughter of the Gibeonites. Yahweh stopped the famine only when David allowed the Gibeonites to kill two of Saul's sons and five of his grandsons. No one appears to have considered the rights of the innocent who "paid" for Saul's sins by dying.

---

[31]H. Wheeler Robinson, *The Christian Doctrine of Man*, 2d ed. (Edinburgh: T. & T. Clark, 1913), 8.

[32]Ibid., 27ff.

[33]Ibid., 28.

Saul's *family* bore the guilt and therefore suffered the punishment. In Robinson's words,

> Corporate personality means for us the treatment of the family, the clan, or the nation, as the unit in place of the individual. It does not mean that no individual life is recognized, but simply that in a number of realms in which we have come to think individualistically, and to treat the single man as the unit, e.g., for punishment or reward, ancient thought envisaged the whole group of which he was part.[34]

Robinson argues that the pervasive corporate perspective in the Old Testament reflects a pattern of thought, or a way of structuring reality. The Western focus is atomistic and individualistic, but the ancient Hebrews viewed reality in more holistic and integrated patterns. Wheeler Robinson did not say that the ancients could not recognize individuals and individual reward or punishment, or that they were unable to conceive of diversity or multiplicity. Nor did Robinson mean that Israelites could not distinguish between an individual and his group—that by punishing an offspring they thought they were really punishing his ancestor. Rather, Robinson suggests they viewed a people together as a corporate personality, or perhaps more accurately, in terms of racial solidarity.

Robinson's formulation has attracted followers and, recently, critics. E. Best, in *One Body in Christ*, finds the concept very useful, as we have seen above. R. P. Shedd, in his *Man in Community*, makes frequent and favorable use of Robinson's concept of corporate personality.[35] Other New Testament scholars also adopt its basic idea, notably C. H. Dodd,[36] A. Nygren,[37] and H. Ridderbos.[38] We will have cause

---

[34]"Hebrew Psychology," in *The People and the Book*, ed. A. S. Peake (Oxford: Clarendon, 1925), 376. For Robinson's further explanation of corporate personality see his *The Cross of the Servant*, (London: SCM, 1926), 32–37, and the booklet that embodies two previously published articles, *Corporate Personality in Ancient Israel* (Philadelphia: Fortress, 1964).

[35]See, for example, 4, 10, 26, 37, 41, 87, 103.

[36]C. H. Dodd, *Epistle of Paul to the Romans* (London: Hodder & Stoughton, 1932), 79–80, 86.

[37]A. Nygren, *Commentary on Romans*, trans. C. C. Rasmussen (London: SCM, 1952), 213.

[38]H. Ridderbos, *Paul: An Outline of His Theology* (Grand Rapids: Eerdmans, 1975). See, e.g., 38 and 61–62. Though recognizing the limitations of the

to return to them at a later point in our study. The Old Testament scholar Th. C. Vriezen refers favorably to the conception.[39] He suggests explaining the plurals of Ge 1:26 ("Let us make man in our image") and 3:22 as a "corporate personality."[40]

RESPONSE TO OBJECTIONS TO "CORPORATE PERSONALITY"

Since 1960 several scholars have expressed doubts about the notion of "corporate solidarity." Initially G. E. Mendenhall openly questioned its existence, calling it a cliché and probably a myth.[41] He did concede the "solidarity of the local community" but went on to insist that this "does not by any means exclude a very considerable individualism and diversity within."[42] Then J. R. Porter urged caution in the widespread use of "corporate personality" and proposed limits, particularly in its usage within the realm of Hebrew legal practice.[43] Finally, in two places J. W. Rogerson has issued the most scathing attack on "corporate personality."[44] He faults H. W. Robinson, who popularized the notion, and Lévy-Bruhl, who was a source for its development. We must

---

term "corporate personality," Ridderbos says, ". . . yet the idea one intends to typify with the aid of this expression is undoubtedly of great significance for insight into the fundamental structures of Paul's preaching" (p. 38). Ridderbos himself prefers to call this idea "all-in-one."

[39]Th. C. Vriezen, *An Outline of Old Testament Theology*, 2d ed. (Oxford: Basil Blackwell, 1970), 327, n. 1.

[40]Vriezen also uses H. W. Robinson's term "corporate personality" again on 387, explaining the basic concept of solidarity on 382–87. We will simply note here in passing that E. P. Sanders (*Paul and Palestinian Judaism* [London: SCM, 1977], 237) observes: "Rabbinic religion, while personal and individual, was also corporate and collective." We discuss, in brief, the Tannaitic period below.

[41]G. E. Mendenhall, "The Relation of the Individual to Political Society in Ancient Israel," in *Biblical Studies in Memory of C. C. Allemann*, ed. J. M. Myers, et al (Locust Valley, N.Y.: Augustin, 1960), 91.

[42]Ibid.

[43]J. R. Porter, "The Legal Aspects of the Concept of 'Corporate Personality' in the Old Testament," *Vetus Testamentum* 15 (1965): 361–80.

[44]J. W. Rogerson, "The Hebrew Conception of Corporate Personality: A Re-examination," *JTS*, 21 (1970): 1–16; and *Anthropology and the Old Testament* (Oxford: Blackwell, 1978), 55–59.

assess these objections and their implications for retaining the concept of corporate personality.[45]

We need to summarize briefly the objections these men present. Mendenhall objects to corporate personality defined as a "group in which individual personality was of no importance or unrecognized."[46] Porter argues that Robinson's examples are all exceptions or special cases. They involve the breaking of ancient religious taboos or prohibitions, or are sins, like murder, adultery, or apostasy, concerning which the law "provided no machinery."[47]

Rogerson argues that H. W. Robinson's use of "corporate personality" ambiguously denoted two things—corporate responsibility and psychical unity among members of a group (to such an extent as to obscure the limits of an individual's personality). Robinson erred, says Rogerson, when he did not distinguish these two separate issues but oscillated between one and the other in explaining various biblical phenomena. Finally, Rogerson wants to abandon *both* as incompatible with modern anthropological theory. He denies that Robinson proved there existed a Hebrew mental notion of a corporate personality that did not clearly distinguish between a person's individual identity and that of the larger group to which he belonged.[48] Rogerson has no desire to deny "that parts of the Old Testament appear to imply what might be called a 'corporate' sense of an individual figure or speaker."[49] But he objects to positing, from such observations, a special theory of a Hebrew mentality, when we can only construct such theories out of our own very different worldview.

These men score several noteworthy points. We must not infer that the Israelites obliterated individual personality. Rogerson rightly argues that we cannot assume that the Hebrews *thought* differently from us. We must not think they didn't distinguish individuals from groups. But the concept of corporate personality does not necessarily commit these errors. Indeed, we must dispute Porter's case. He cannot

---

[45]No doubt others have criticized Robinson's formulation of "corporate personality." But the three critics we survey present the major objections.
[46]Mendenhall, 91.
[47]Porter, 367.
[48]Rogerson, *Anthropology and the Old Testament*, 55–56.
[49]Ibid., 56.

simply dismiss the evidence as he does. Whether or not these sins violate ancient taboos, they plainly do reflect a consciousness of corporate responsibility for sins of individuals. Porter admits that some sense of corporate personality "may well be found in the Old Testament outside the legal sphere and may play a vital part there."[50] But he has not succeeded in refuting its presence even in the legal sphere. Porter may rightly question that the Israelites thought of themselves as a "psychic unity"—not distinguishing between individual and group—but he cannot ignore the definite awareness of corporate responsibility or solidarity. "Corporate personality" does not imply that typical Israelites of David's time thought that the Gibeonites' murder of Saul's sons and grandsons literally punished Saul, who was long dead. It does imply a sense of group identity.

These important points have not overturned the basic concept of corporate solidarity. The widespread use of corporate concepts and terminology may not simply be dismissed.[51]

SUMMARY

Has this been a long tangent, peripheral to the main concern of this chapter? Not at all. At its core, election in the Old Testament is corporate—the election of a people to bear the name of God. Yet this fact does not deny God's choice of individuals (the patriarchs, priests, kings, prophets) for specific tasks or ministries. We have demonstrated this claim in two ways, direct and indirect. Many texts show directly God's election of the nation or people. Then, indirectly, we saw the pervasiveness of corporate concepts and terminology in the Old Testament. God frequently relates to Israel in national and corporate terms. The covenant and the blessing or cursing that follow for the *nation* attest to this truth. The Day of Atonement, group responsibility for certain (though not all) sins, and the repeated references to the people as a unit in corporate terms all combine to depict Israel as a corporate entity. Though individuals are important, recog-

---

[50]Porter, 379.

[51]We will return to this issue of "corporate personality" when we come to our discussion of Paul, particularly concerning what it means to be "in Adam" and "in Christ."

nized, and prominent, God's foremost choice encompasses a people or nation. The discussion of "corporate personality" clarified the pervasive nature of corporate "thinking" and showed how the Old Testament writers expressed that thinking in various ways and circumstances. Yet the cautions explained above alert us to beware of reading too much into the Israelites' supposed mind-set.

By way of summary, the Old Testament writers present two types of election. First, God chooses individuals to perform certain tasks. The second and dominant motif is his election of the people Israel. The choice of individuals does not necessarily involve their personal salvation. Saul's election by God to the role of king and then his later forfeiture of that position, did not directly concern his eternal destiny. Similarly, the choice of the Aaronic priesthood did not necessarily guarantee the salvation of every priest. Therefore, election of individuals to tasks and their eternal salvation are separate (though related) issues.

God's love alone stands as the motive for his choice of the people of Israel to be his own. Never do the biblical writers describe election as a reward. It does not come in response to any attribute or action of Israel. His election did not give Israel a privileged position among the nations so she might gloat. Rather, God chose Israel to serve him and reflect his character and ways to the other nations—"that they may proclaim [His] praise" (Isa 43:21). In this sense God's election of Israel parallels his election of individuals—he has called her into existence to serve him in the world. Thus Israel's election does not mean God has rejected the other nations. Rather, election creates for Israel the task of representing God among the nations so salvation might come to them.[52]

Election essentially means that God called Israel to serve him and to reflect his character. Similar to God's choice of individuals, election does not guarantee to every Israelite eternal salvation. God's election of the people Israel and his imposition of the covenant are one issue. But Israel's faithfulness to keeping the terms of her election and the covenant is quite another issue. This explains why God can cast away Israel and judge her unfaithful, while yet recogniz-

---

[52]This point is stressed by A. Richardson, *Introduction to the Theology of the New Testament*, 271, and H. H. Rowley, *The Biblical Doctrine of Election*, 60–68.

ing the faithful remnant which does please him and will attain salvation.[53] Election of the nation did not guarantee God's continuous blessing or eternal salvation for all Israelites (though later rabbis did so interpret it, as we shall see). God chose the nation, and thus all of Jacob's descendants are under that umbrella. But as a first-century descendant of Jacob put it: "not all who are descended from Israel are Israel" (Ro 9:6). Again, election and salvation are separate issues.

---

[53]The Old Testament hope concerning a faithful remnant points to another criterion that determines an Israelite's status apart from his membership in Israel. "I will surely bring together the remnant of Israel" (Mic 2:12). With the returning exiles from Babylon Jeremiah saw the future hope for Israel. God would impose a new covenant (Jer 31:33; 32:37–40; 50:5; cf. Isa 55:3). Isaiah gives us the criterion plainly:

> This is what the LORD says:
> "As when juice is still found in a cluster of grapes
> and men say, 'Don't destroy it,
>   'there is yet some good in it,'
> so will I do in behalf of my servants;
>   I will not destroy them all.
> I will bring forth descendants from Jacob,
>   and from Judah those who will possess my mountains;
> my chosen people will inherit them,
>   and there will my servants live.
> Sharon will become a pasture for flocks,
>   and the Valley of Achor a resting place for herds,
> for my people who seek me" (Isa 65:8–10).

These blessings are solely for God's servants who seek him.

2

QUMRAN

Several recent studies have illuminated the phenomena of election and predestination in the Qumran documents.[1] Our purpose will not be to treat these scrolls in any in-depth fashion. It will be useful to our appraisal of the New Testament evidence, however, if we take a brief look at how these Jewish sectarians at Qumran wrote about election issues close to the first century. Our basic approach will be to investigate the occurrences of *bāchar* and its derivative *bāchîr*, and then to note other "predestinarian" and "free-will" concepts.

The verb *bāchar* (to choose) occurs about twenty-eight times in the scrolls as we have them, not counting the

---

[1]E. H. Merrill, *Qumran and Predestination* (Leiden: Brill, 1975), focuses mostly on the Hymns (1 QH), though his discussion sometimes ranges more widely. See also Holm-Nielsen, *Hodayot. Psalms from Qumran* (Aarhus: Universitetsforlaget, 1960), 274–300; Dombkowski Hopkins, "The Qumran Community and 1 Q Hodayot: A Reassessment," *Revue de Qumran* 10 (1981): 323–64; and E. P. Sanders, *Paul and Palestinian Judaism* (London: SCM, 1977), 257–70. For a wider survey of the Qumran literature and its relationship to the issue of predestination, see H. Braun, *Qumran und das Neue Testament* (Tübingen: Mohr, 1966), 2:243–50. Braun discusses the various authors who treat the issue and includes a section on the similarities and differences between the Qumran literature and Paul (247–48).

fragments.[2] One-half of these are human choices.[3] Of the remaining fourteen God chooses things or places in six locations,[4] and people eight times.[5] The substantive *bāchîr* occurs about seventeen times, and with one exception,[6] it refers to God's elect, those whom he has chosen.[7] If we total all the uses, God's choice of people makes up twenty-four of the forty-five occurrences of these two terms. The scrolls show that the Qumran authors considered God's election of people an important topic. The concept of God's choosing or predestining goes beyond the occurrences of these specific terms. We observe passages like the following:[8]

> Thou alone didst [create] the just and establish him from the womb . . . that he might hearken to Thy Covenant and walk in all (Thy ways), . . . and enlarge his straitened soul to eternal salvation. . . . But the wicked Thou didst create for [the time] of Thy [wrath],[9] and Thou didst vow them from the womb for the Day of Massacre. (1QH 15,15–17)

> Thou [hast redeemed us] for Thyself, [O God], that we may be an everlasting people. Thou hast decreed for us a destiny of light according to Thy truth. And the Prince of Light Thou hast appointed from ancient times to come to our support. (1QM 13,9–10)

> [God] has appointed for [man] two spirits in which to walk until the time of His visitation: the spirits of truth and falsehood. Those born of truth spring from a fountain

---

[2]The sources for the word occurrences are K. G. Kuhn, *Konkordanz zu den Qumrantexten* (Göttingen: Vandenhoeck und Ruprecht, 1960); Kuhn, "Nachträge zur *Konkordanz zu den Qumrantexten,*" *Revue de Qumran* 4 (1963): 163–234; and H. Lignée, "Concordance de *1 Q Genesis Apocryphon,*" *Revue de Qumran* 1 (1958): 163–86. Our statistics and investigations have been limited to these sources and the scrolls they reflect. We have ignored the more recently published finds with the presumption that their data would not seriously conflict with the major scrolls.

[3]1QS 9,17; 10,12; 1QM 2,7; 1QH 9,10; 15,19; 16,10; CD 1,18; 1,19; 2,15; 3,2; 3,11; 8,8; 19,20; 1QGenAP 22,6.

[4]1QS 1,4; 1QH 4,4; 15,23; 16,13; 17,21(?); 1QSb 3,25.

[5]1QS 4,22; 11,7; 1QM 10,9; 1QSb 1,2; 3,2; 3,23; 4,22; CD 2,7.

[6]1QGenAp 22,6.

[7]1QpHab 5,4; 9,12; 10,13; 1QS 8,6; 9,14; 11,16; 1QM 12,1; 12, 4; 12,5; 1QH 2,13; 14,15; 4QpPs37 1,5; 2,5; 4QF1 1,19; CD 4,3.

[8]All quotations, unless otherwise noted, are from G. Vermes, *The Dead Sea Scrolls in English* (Harmondsworth: Penguin, 1962).

[9]For this lacuna Holm-Nielsen, *Hodayot,* 228, reads "[choosing]" rather than Vermes' "[wrath]."

of light, but those born of falsehood spring from a source of darkness. All the children of righteousness are ruled by the Prince of light and walk in the ways of light, but all the children of falsehood are ruled by the Angel of Darkness and walk in the ways of darkness. . . . for it is [God] who created the spirits of Light and Darkness and founded every action upon them and established every deed [upon] their [ways]. (1QS 3:18ff.)

In addition, Sanders[10] notes several other passages that point to a belief that God was responsible for everything that happened: 1QM 17, 4–5; 1QS 3, 15; 11, 11; 11, 17–18; 1QH 1, 7–8; 1, 19–20; 10, 9–10. According to scholarly consensus, the Qumran covenanters held to a strong predestinarian belief. The elect were chosen by God from all eternity. God assigned to all persons their "lot" or "way." Merrill says, "God has created all things and has predetermined their functions and destinies for eternity."[11]

Before we consider how they understood "election," we need to add some contrasting data to round out the picture. Virtually as strongly as they affirm predestination, the Qumran writers emphasize the free will of people to join the company of the righteous. In the Commentary on Micah we read,

[Interpreted, this concerns] the Teacher of Righteousness Who [expounded the law to] his [Council] and to all who freely pledged themselves to join the elect of [God to keep the law] in the Council of the Community; who shall be saved on the Day [of Judgment]. (1QpMic 7–8)

According to the Hymn Scroll, uniting with the covenant is a matter of free choice (1QH 4,24). The covenant comes to those who seek it (5,9). The writers stress the need for repentance (4,6). A person may make the choice to love God freely (14, 26) and must make a choice to become pure (16, 10). In several places they speak of the need to "turn" from the former way of life to enter the covenant and join the community (1QS 5,14; 10,20–21; 1QH 14,24; CD 15,7).

On the other side, the wicked have only themselves to blame for their dismal fate. The Hymn Scroll quoted above (1QH 15,15–17) continues,

[10]Sanders, *Paul and Palestinian Judaism*, 259.
[11]Merrill, *Qumran and Predestination*, 51.

> But the wicked Thou didst create . . . *for*[12] they walk in the way which is not good. They have despised [Thy Covenant] and their souls have loathed Thy [truth]; they have taken no delight in all Thy commandments and have chosen that which Thou hatest. (1QH 15,18–19)

This is no isolated text. People miss God's salvation because they refuse to seek him, they reject his commands, and they shun the invitation to enter the covenant.

> They have neither inquired nor sought after Him concerning His laws that they might know the hidden things in which they have sinfully erred. (1QS 5,11–12)

> He shall not be counted among the upright for he has not persisted in the conversion of his life. (1QS 3,1)

> For as long as he despises the precepts of God he shall receive no instruction in the Community of His counsel. For it is through the spirit of true counsel concerning the ways of man that all his sins shall be expiated that he may contemplate the light of life. (1QS 3,5–6)

> [Thou art a merciful God] and rich in [favours], pardoning those who repent of their sin and visiting the iniquity of the wicked. (1QH 14,24)

Though we could cite more passages, it must suffice to give a summary statement offered by Sanders:

> All these passages suppose that membership in the covenant is subject to a man's own will, intention and success in fulfilling the commandments. . . . His sinning, on the other hand, is what puts him into the "lot" of the cursed: it is by his own deeds rather than by the predestination of God.[13]

Merrill attempts some synthesis with the prior data when he says, in answer to the question, why the wicked?: "The wicked man was so because of his own free will even though, in some mysterious sense, he had been allotted by God to the realm of darkness from the womb."[14]

The Qumran writers appear to maintain a paradoxical position. They affirm with vehemence both God's sovereign predestination of eternal destinations and human free will to

---

[12]The Hebrew word here is *kî*, indicating reason.

[13]Sanders, *Paul and Palestinian Judaism*, 264.

[14]Merrill, *Qumran and Predestination*, 43.

choose heaven or hell. Can we explain this apparent paradox? Apparently they did not perceive it as a problem. It presented no difficulty to their thinking.

Sanders confirms this explanation. He suggests that the Qumran covenanters were not concerned with systematizing their beliefs in the manner of a methodical theologian. They never felt the need to ask whether answers to various questions cohered with one another.[15] Their problem was why some Israelites seemed to be part of the covenant and not others. They responded with two answers. First, God decides upon some and, second, God chooses those who choose his way and rejects those who despise his commands.

They explained the relationship between these two perspectives in several ways. Merrill says of their view of God:

> In His prescience He knows who among men will react favorably to beneficent influences and who will spurn them and continue in wickedness. The former He causes to be influenced by His Holy Spirit, resulting in a thirst for knowledge of righteousness on the part of the one chosen. . . . As for the wicked, they are rejected from the womb even unto death because their tendency is to do evil always.[16]

So, in the Hymns Merrill finds a strong and rigid determinism, but not one that is arbitrary. Rather, God's foreknowledge of whether people will accept or reject the truth provides the basis for his allotment of their eternal destinies (see 1QSb 1,2; CD 2,7).

Sanders would have us go back to the crucial issue for the covenanters—why they were chosen and not other Jews—for the explanation of the stress on both predestination and free will. According to Sanders, the answer in the Dead Sea Scrolls was *not* that they, the Qumran covenanters, were the faithful remnant,[17] while the other Israelites were rebellious or disobedient. Rather, they viewed themselves as

---

[15]Sanders, *Paul and Palestinian Judaism*, 265.

[16]Merrill, *Qumran and Predestination*, 51.

[17]Sanders overlooks that at times the Covenanters did view themselves as the remnant as in this part of a Hymn: "as Thou raisest up a lively few among Thy people and a remnant among Thine inheritance," (from 1QH 6, 8 as translated by Holm-Nielsen, *Hodayot*, 101).

recipients of a new covenant. They had been enlightened. Hence when they contemplated their own situation and status, they could only exult in God's graciousness in choosing them. On this side, they stressed predestination; it was God's doing alone. They were unworthy benefactors of his covenant.

When they addressed outsiders—other Jews or Gentiles—or backsliders, then they focused on human free will and responsibility. With such people they focused on the demands of the covenant—repentance, forgiveness, and obedience. Sanders summarizes: "Both the statement that God determines the fate of every man and the affirmation that each man may choose his own lot are required for the sect, depending on what problem is being addressed."[18] Whether these two perspectives were logically or philosophically coherent was not their concern.

It remains for us to comment on how the Qumran writings viewed the elect. M. Burrows was among the first to suggest that the Qumran writers made a shift from the Old Testament pattern of the election of the entire nation.[19] He says,

> Such a division of individuals into groups is quite different from the old Hebrew conception of the whole nation as God's elect. The way had been prepared for a belief in individual election, however, by the Old Testament ideas of the righteous remnant and the new covenant.[20]

According to this view, to be in the elect at Qumran required more than membership in the chosen people by birth. Individuals choose by an act of their wills to join.[21]

We have reason to question, though, whether the Qumran writers had really abandoned a concept of corporate election in favor of election of individuals. We noted above that God's choice of people comprises a significant percentage of the total occurrences of the terms *bāchar* (choose) and *bāchîr* (the elect). In addition, God's choice of people in

---

[18]Sanders, *Paul and Palestinian Judaism*, 269.
[19]M. Burrows, *Dead Sea Scrolls* (New York: Viking, 1955), 263.
[20]Ibid.
[21]This point is made by Sanders, *Paul and Palestinian Judaism*, 270, and J. T. Milik, *Ten Years of Discovery in the Wilderness of Judea* (London: SCM, 1959), 114.

Qumran is invariably corporate. The substantive *bāchîr* is always used corporately. The writers regard the elect in their totality and view them as a group (1QS 9,14), host (1QM 12,4), holy people (1QM 12,1), congregation (4QpPs37 1,5; 2,5), and the elect of Israel (CD 4,3; 4QF1 1,19). Uses of the verb *bāchar* also focus on the people as God's corporate elect group. The writers may affirm that God has chosen them, the Qumran community (1QS 4,22; 11,7; 1QSb 1,2), and has not chosen the wicked (CD 2:7). In three places in the Blessings, the priests as a group are the objects of God's choosing (1QSb 3,2; 3,22; 4,22). In one place the people of Israel were chosen by God (1QM 10,9). In fact, in no instance is an individual singled out as elect.

Thus it is doubtful that we can dismiss the Old Testament stress on corporate election too readily. The question "Who is like Thy people Israel which Thou hast chosen for Thyself from all the peoples of the lands?" (1QM 10,9) recalls the characteristic Old Testament emphasis. Undoubtedly a new issue has emerged: some Israelites were elect—the Qumran sect—while other Israelites were not. Though this belief distinguished between Jews, it did not necessarily imply individual election. Though salvation required the voluntary exercise of an individual's will, this fails to confirm that God chose specific individuals. We recall again 1QM 13,9–10: "Thou [has redeemed us] for Thyself, [O God,], that we may be an everlasting people. Thou hast decreed for us a destiny of Light according to thy truth." We advise caution in proposing too great a split between the Old Testament doctrine of the election of Israel and the Qumran election of a select number of Israelites. They viewed themselves as the elect community—ones whom God had graciously chosen—in contrast to the wicked (other Jews and Gentiles) not under the covenant. That other Jews were also sons of Abraham mattered little.

In conclusion, though the Qumran covenanters still spoke in corporate terms, they had taken a crucial step. Election of Israel and salvation are not coterminous. For the Qumran sectarians, the elect equal the saved ones, that is, their community. Election was no longer a description of the entire nation. The elect are members of their spiritual community of holy ones, in distinction to the wicked. God chose the elect, and they attain salvation no matter what their race. Jews, too, have to repent and maintain a disciplined regimen of fidelity to the principles of the covenant. None are elect or saved by birth. This seems to be the crucial development.

The evidence does not show that for the Qumran sectarians election had become individualistic. God would save individuals, and they are among the elect. But we fail to find confirmation that they believed God chose specific individuals to enter the Covenant. Rather, the election terms point to a corporate sense, or realization of membership in a chosen community.[22] This corporate self-consciousness may even be more pronounced than that expressed in the Old Testament.

---

[22]Certainly the sense of being God's people pervades the Hymns—1QH 4,6; 4,11; 4,16; 4,26; 6,8; 14,1. See also 1QpHab 2,10; 5,3; 5,5; 1QM 1,5; 1,12; 3,13; 6,6; 10,9; 10,10; 12,1; 13,7; 13,9; 14,5; 14,12; 16,1; 18,7; 19,7; 1QSb 3,23; 4QFl 1,16; CD 5,16; 6,16. The Qumran writers apply many of the other corporate terms found in the Old Testament to the sect: *congregation, saints, nation, assembly,* et al.

3

APOCRYPHA AND PSEUDEPIGRAPHA

The period "between the Testaments" spawned not only the Qumran sect, which penned the Dead Sea Scrolls, but also "mainstream" Jews who generated the literature we call the Apocrypha and Pseudepigrapha. Our sole, briefly pursued, aim here will be to see if we find deviations from the patterns observed to this point. As with the Qumran literature, our study will make no attempt to be exhaustive. We simply desire an awareness of the essential data.[1]

In the main this body of literature reflects the Old Testament patterns. We discover, first, many examples of God's choice of things or places—like Jerusalem or the Temple—which are not integral to our investigation. Second, as with the Old Testament, the writers refer, upon a few occasions, to God's choice of individuals, and these occur mostly in Sirach (also called Ecclesiasticus). God chose Moses out of all mankind to serve him (Sir 45:4–5, 16). God

---

[1]Sources mainly consulted include R. H. Charles, *Apocrypha and Pseudepigrapha of the Old Testament*, 2 vols. (Oxford: Clarendon, 1913); J. H. Charlesworth, *The Old Testament Pseudepigrapha*, vol. 1: *Apocalyptic Literature and Testaments* (Garden City, NY: Doubleday, 1983); H. Wace, ed., *Holy Bible Apocrypha*, 2 vols. (London: John Murray, 1888); and H. G. May and B. M. Metzger, eds., *The New Oxford Annotated Bible with the Apocrypha* (RSV) (New York: Oxford University Press, 1973, 1977).

chose Aaron to serve him as priest (45:15–16). Of Jacob, it is written, the Lord "will never blot out the descendants of his chosen one" (47:22).[2] David was selected from the sons of Israel (47:2). God chose Solomon to be king of Israel (WS 9:7). The prophet Jeremiah was the object of God's choice (PJ 1:5, 8; 3:5, 7; 7:9).

In addition to these, in the Ethiopic Book of Enoch we find a new individual who is explicitly and repeatedly called the Elect One.[3] R. H. Charles has no doubts that these point to the Messiah (48:10; 52:4), also called the Righteous One (38:2; 43:6) and the Son of Man (46:1–8; 48:2).[4] God chose this messianic Son of Man for his task (46:3; 48:6). Thus, parallel to what we discovered in the Old Testament, this literature employs election language to designate an individual chosen by God to accomplish his appointed mission.

We find, by far, the most dominant use of election terminology in a third area—the election of Israel as a corporate body. A rehearsing of the prominent examples will demonstrate the range of usage. In Sirach, "Israel is the Lord's own portion" (17:17b), and she receives God's special inheritance (24:8). The nation is called God's elect (Sir 46:1). The writer of Sirach appears to view the entire nation as elect (see also Bar 3:26–28; and RE 10:10–12). In several places the writers speak of the people of God as his elect or chosen ones (Tb 8:15; WS 3:9; 4:15).

However, a crucial new dimension appears. In place of the completely unmerited ground of election in the Old Testament, a theology of merit develops. God chose Israel because of her righteousness (2 Ba 48:20). Israel, unlike the other nations (2 Ba 7:23–24, 72), assented to God's offer of the law.[5]

Do all Israelites attain salvation? The answer must be no. Sanders observes, "The question of a 'true Israel,' of those

[2]Unless otherwise noted, quotations of the Apocrypha are from the RSV.
[3]The Ethiopic Book of Enoch 39:6a; 40:5; 45:3–4; 49:2, 4; 51:3, 5; 52:6, 9; 53:6; 55:4; 61:5, 8, 10; 62:1. See also Apoc Abr II, 31.
[4]R. H. Charles, *The Book of Enoch* (Oxford: Clarendon, 1893), 112 (on 38:2); 119 (on 40:5); 127–29 (on 46:2–3).
[5]D. A. Carson makes the best case for this "merit theology" in the intertestamental Jewish writings. See his *Divine Sovereignty and Human Responsibility* (Atlanta: John Knox; London: Marshall, Morgan & Scott, 1981), 68–69.

who are *really* among the elect, does not arise."[6] But the Book
of Jubilees (1:29 and 2:20) gives the impression that though
all Israel is elect, a Jew could forfeit a place in Israel by failing
to keep God's Law. Thus, as in the Old Testament, physical
descent from Jacob is not tantamount to eternal salvation
(Jub 15:26–34). God chose the seed of Abraham before all
nations (PS 9:16–19). However, as Sanders urges, this does
not imply all Israel will be saved. He says, "God's covenant
is the basis of salvation, and the elect remain in the covenant
unless they sin in such a way as to be removed."[7]

This phenomenon is particularly visible in the Ethiopic
Book of Enoch where the descriptions "the elect" or "the
elect and righteous" occur repeatedly,[8] and where the
righteous do elect works (38:2) and seek an elect life (94:4).
Yet the writers of the Ethiopic Book of Enoch do not see
election as God's blanket, uncritical acceptance of Israel. We
find the elect must obey God's Law and maintain their
loyalty to him. Only thus do they prove they are really God's
elect. The truly elect obtain salvation. Not all Israelites will
share in this salvation, for some of them are guilty of
apostasy.

A possibly ambiguous reference occurs at 2 Mc 1:25—
God made the fathers his chosen ones. Rawlinson is
probably correct in saying that this refers to the patriarchs
and thus includes God's choice of Israel out of all other
nations.[9] This point is made specifically in 2 Ba 48:20: "This is
the nation which Thou hast chosen" (see also 2 Es 5:23–30).
Likewise, Israel is God's firstborn, only begotten and most
dear (2 Es 6:58).

In summary, Israel as the chosen people or nation
emerges as the dominant use of election.[10] They are the seed

---

[6]E. P. Sanders, *Paul and Palestinian Judaism*, (London: SCM, 1977) 333; his
emphasis.

[7]Sanders, *Paul and Palestinian Judaism*, 408.

[8]"The elect": 1:3, 8; 5:7–8; 25:5; 40:5; 41:2; 45:5; 48:9; 50:1; 51:5; 56:6, 8;
58:3; 60:6; 61:4, 12; 62:7–8, 11; 93:2. "The elect and righteous": 1:1; 38:2–4;
39:6–7; 48:1; 58:1–2; 61:13; 62:12–13,15; 70:3; 93:10 (elect righteous). Carson
sees the references to the elect as "righteous" as further evidence of a shift
toward "merit theology." God saw in Israel a righteous and holy people and
so chose her (*Divine Sovereignty and Human Responsibility*, 68).

[9]In H. Wace, ed., *Holy Bible Apocrypha*, 2:553.

[10]D. A. Carson agrees. He says, "As a rule . . . election pertains to the
Jews as a whole, rather than to the individual" (*Divine Sovereignty and Human
Responsibility*, 48).

of Abraham or Jacob (Jub 2:20), chosen in the patriarchs. Nevertheless, membership in this elect body by itself does not guarantee salvation, for there is another way of speaking of election that may cut across the first way. When the authors label the elect God's righteous ones, as occurs so often in the Ethiopic Book of Enoch, they imply that salvation comes only to those who meet the entrance requirements. These include: loyalty to God, obedience to his commands, and faithfulness to his will. Thus, though the nation may be elect in the first sense, not all individual Israelites are "elect unto salvation," or elect in the second sense. When viewed among the nations, Israel is certainly God's chosen people. But when the writers discuss the righteous versus the wicked, then election only embraces God's faithful ones. Not all Israelites were faithful, and some Israelites occupy the class of "the wicked."

As to individual election, its dominant usage involves key figures chosen by God to perform his bidding. In addition to the patriarchs and kings, the Ethiopic Book of Enoch has introduced a messianic figure who was chosen by God: God's Elect One. In none of these instances, though, do we find God's choice of individuals for salvation. God has chosen key figures to perform special tasks. These individuals' eternal salvation does not concern the authors of the Apocrypha and Pseudepigrapha when they employ election terminology.

4

THE RABBIS

J. Neusner rightly warns about the possible dangers in using third-to-fifth-century A.D. rabbinic sources to describe the Jewish religion of the first century.[1] At the same time, E. P. Sanders argues, "it would be surprising if there were no connections."[2] Thus, this brief foray into the Tannaitic literature (c. A.D. 70–200), and perhaps the Amoraitic (A.D. 220–500), cannot presume to describe fully Jewish beliefs about election in the first century. We only hope to investigate, in secondary sources, what a few representative scholars say about the rabbis' teaching on this topic.[3] Our

---

[1]J. Neusner, "The Use of Later Rabbinic Evidence for the Study of First-Century Pharisaism, " in *Approaches to Ancient Judaism—I*, ed. W. S. Green (Missoula: Scholars, 1978), 219. At the same time he dismisses as absurd any view that states that a later source by definition does not tell us anything about an earlier period.

[2]E. P. Sanders, *Paul and Palestinian Judaism* (London: SCM, 1977), 60.

[3]The sources from which we have drawn our observations include: F. C. Grant, *Ancient Judaism and the New Testament* (Edinburgh and London: Oliver and Boyd, 1960); B. W. Helfgott, *The Doctrine of Election in Tannaitic Literature* (New York: Columbia University King's Crown, 1954); E. P. Sanders, *Paul and Palestinian Judaism*; S. Schechter, *Some Aspects of Rabbinic Theology* (London: A. & C. Black, 1909); and E. E. Urbach, *The Sages. Their Concepts and Beliefs*, trans. I. Abrahams (Jerusalem: Magnes, Hebrew University, 1979).

primary goal will be to see whether the picture that emerges confirms or diverges from the conclusions we have already reached.

The developing theology of the Christian church confronted the rabbis with a rival claim to God's electing grace. Christian writers, both in the New Testament and the early Fathers, declared that the church had inherited the promises made to Israel of old. Due to her unfaithfulness, Israel had lost her position. Now the title of the New Israel belonged to the church. Understandably, the rabbis endorsed no such forfeiture. The rabbis consistently maintained that Israel, though judged and chastened, was still God's chosen people. God would restore her again if she displayed repentance and good deeds.

To some rabbis Israel's election had been predestined before the world's creation. For whatever reason—often foreknowledge of her obedience (Ex. Rabba, 15:17)—God chose Israel. For other rabbis Israel actually merited God's choice, continuing the merit theology of the intertestamental period. For example, some rabbis pointed to Israel's declaration of God as King at the Red Sea when they said, "The LORD will reign forever" (Ex 15:18). Other rabbis detected merit in Israel's agreement to adopt God's Law at Sinai when all the other nations refused to do so (Num. Rabba, 14:10; Pes R. 21). Some taught that Israel's humility and meekness or proneness to suffering motivated her election (Lev. Rabba, 27:6). Or, it was Israel's foreseen holiness (Sifre 94a [§ 97]) or good works (Num. Rabba, 3:2). D. A. Carson puts it this way: "The blessings of election demonstrate moral superiority."[4]

Yet even when these rabbis suggest some merit, they consistently add confessions of Israel's unworthiness and God's freely lavished love. So, in the end, we discover a mixed message. While admitting a role for Israel's merit, the rabbis cannot deny the dominant position of God's grace. Thus Schechter states, "The great majority of Rabbis are silent about merits and attribute the election to a mere act of grace (or love) on the part of God."[5] Helfgott catalogues rabbi

---

[4]D. A. Carson, *Divine Sovereignty and Human Responsibility* (Atlanta: John Knox; London: Marshall, Morgan & Scott, 1981), 105.

[5]Schechter, *Some Aspects of Rabbinic Theology*, 61. We need not decide whether or not "merit theology" played a dominant role in rabbinic

after rabbi to confirm the Jews' continuing and staunch insistence that Israel was God's elect.[6]

Though the rabbis offer us several conclusions about election,[7] for our study it is striking that "Rabbinic religion, while personal and individual, was also corporate and collective."[8] E. E. Urbach echoes this same point: "The election was of one entire people and the covenant was made on condition that 'all Israel be sureties for one another.'"[9] Both Sanders and Urbach connect the election of the nation with the resulting responsibility placed upon all individuals to keep God's commandments.[10] But this individual responsibility implied a collective accountability so that sin could bring punishment on all Israel.[11] Urbach states,

> The punishment of the whole people of Israel is a consequence of their mutual responsibility and is inherent in the act of election, which made Israel one nation upon earth. The very concept of election implies mutual responsibility and consequently also collective punishment.[12]

For the rabbis, the sectarianism of Qumran had disappeared. The nation was elect, and those who were a part of

---

theology. Our conclusions about the corporate nature of their view of election does not depend upon the answer to this question.

[6]Helfgott, *The Doctrine of Election in Tannaitic Literature*. For another catalog of rabbinic teachings concerning election, see E. E. Urbach, *The Sages*, 525–54.

[7]The rabbis displayed sensitivity to charges of favoritism and often expressed their surprise that God should choose Israel. In *Midrash Rabbah* on Song of Songs VI:12, R. Hiyya told the parable of a king who was riding in his carriage and passed a field of workers. When he recognized his daughter among the workers, he took her with him, much to the surprise of her fellow workers. They said, "Yesterday you were gathering sheaves and today you sit in a carriage with the king!" She responded, "Just as you are astonished at me, so I am astonished at myself." Likewise, the Rabbi concluded, Israel was enslaved in Egypt, and God rescued her and set her as his own. In response to the astonishment of the nations Israel said, "Just as you are astonished at us, so we are astonished at ourselves" (H. Freedman and M. Simon, eds. *Midrash Rabbah: Esther and Song of Songs* [London: Soncino, 1939], 273).

[8]Sanders, *Paul and Palestinian Judaism*, 237.

[9]Urbach, *The Sages*, 539.

[10]See Sanders, *Paul and Palestinian Judaism*, 237–38 and Urbach, *The Sages*, 539–40.

[11]Recall our discussion above about corporate personality and corporate responsibility in the Old Testament.

[12]Urbach, *The Sages*, 540.

Israel would attain salvation.[13] Sanders can detect virtually no individual quest for salvation in the teaching of the rabbis. The worst fate for an Israelite was to be "cut off" from his people. "On the other hand, simple heredity did not ensure salvation." One must be part of the elect nation to be saved, though not all ethnic Jews qualify for salvation. Salvation "came to all Israelites who were faithful."[14] The rabbis are much closer to Old Testament theology than to the sectarian developments at Qumran. For the rabbis, as in the Old Testament, all Israel was elect, but not all Israelites would be saved. Election was corporate. We detect little movement from that position.

---

[13]Schechter argues that this does not mean that the rabbis took God's election of Israel in an exclusive sense as if he were not concerned for the other nations too. They affirmed his lordship over all the nations (see S. Schechter, *Some Aspects of Rabbinic Theology*, 62–64). But they limited election to God's choice of Israel.

[14]Sanders, *Paul and Palestinian Judaism*, 237–38.

II

THE NEW TESTAMENT DOCUMENTS

INTRODUCTION

Having discussed the Old Testament and Jewish perspectives on the concept of election, we can now move from this background to our primary objective. We will proceed through the New Testament to discover how each writer or section presents election/predestination concepts. We will limit our investigation to the realm of salvation and its outworking. Thus, we will bypass some of the larger philosophical issues of determinism and free will as beyond our scope. Likewise God's sovereignty versus human freedom, as a philosophical issue in itself, cannot concern us. Instead, we focus on how God chooses, determines, appoints and purposes in relation to people, all under the overarching rubric of salvation.

Immediately we encounter the question of methodology. What will be our approach as we investigate how each author discusses these concepts? First, we will divide our study into six sections that will comprise the six chapters of this division of the book: (1) the Synoptic Gospels, (2) the Acts, (3) the Johannine literature, (4) the Pauline literature, (5) Hebrews, and (6) the letters of Peter, James, and Jude. Thus we can see how the various parts of the New Testament introduce election issues.

Second, we must explain the strategy of study for the documents themselves. Our approach has been both intuitive and systematic. In reading through each section intuition led us to list certain verses or passages as being relevant and worthy of detailed study. What ideas would intuition suggest are pertinent? As suggested above, ideas include: God's choosing or appointing people; God's foreknowing or determining events that impinge on people's salvation; God's willing or purposing, again, with some reference to the salvation of people; and God's involvement in the acquisition or application of salvation to people. These are meant to be suggestive. We attempted to investigate all passages that gave some hint of possible value.

We also proceeded more systematically. Obviously, certain key concepts are conveyed by technical terms, other words, or their synonyms and equivalents. Thus, after discovering a term that is important in one context, we sought, through concordance and synonym searches, to discover other possibly fruitful passages and words for study. We investigated collocates of key words as well as antonyms and words etymologically related.

Once we located crucial passages, in each instance we sought the basic intention of the biblical author. We drew conclusions and organized the results. In the pages that follow, we rearranged these steps to present the results in an understandable and useful way. In each chapter we will present our findings topically. We organize the results of our exegeses under certain headings, under which we then discuss the passages that fit. At the end of each section we then draw conclusions in more detail. Thus we will have, in each chapter, an outline of the nature and extent of each author's (or section's) position on the issues of our study.

5

THE SYNOPTIC GOSPELS

The Synoptic Gospels present a multifaceted picture of the topic of election without developing their teachings from some of the key terms for election. The verb *eklegomai*, "to choose," occurs only three times with any elective significance,[1] and these uses signal three different actions (choice of believers, the Twelve, and Jesus). The synoptists apply the substantive *eklektoi*, "the chosen ones," to Christians eight times, though six of those occur in the context of a few sentences in the Olivet Discourse.[2] Once, Jesus' taunters call him "the Chosen One" (Lk 23:35). These occurrences show that God's electing activity was commonly assumed and taught. We will return to the Twelve and Jesus below. First let us consider God's deliberative choice of a people.

GOD'S ELECTION OF HIS PEOPLE

Luke 18:7

When Jesus applies his point in the parable of the unjust judge and the widow, he mentions God's "chosen ones,"

---

[1]Mk 13:20; Lk 6:13; 9:35.
[2]Mt 24:22, 24, 31; Mk 13:20, 22, 27.

eklektoi. In contrast to the judge who cares not a bit for the widow and her plight, God will certainly and readily come to the aid of the *ones he has chosen*. Neither Matthew nor Jesus develops the meaning of election here, yet no doubt exists. The elect ones belong to God; he cares about them even though they may undergo suffering and injustice in the world. In fact, perhaps election and suffering are related, for, as we saw in the Old Testament, election often denotes service and suffering, not privilege.[3] As we will shortly see, the other uses of *eklektos* (chosen), when used of believers, occur in eschatological contexts. Thus the synoptists do not stress God's act of choosing, nor whom he has chosen. Rather they emphasize that those who are God's chosen ones will experience his preservation, vindication, and final salvation.[4] Jesus assures all the elect of God's attention if they "cry out to him day and night" (18:7). The question in 18:8 raises an important issue: "When the Son of Man comes, will he find faith on the earth?" The elect ones rest in the assurance that God will save them, but Jesus' question issues a warning to the elect ones. God desires people who believe. The Son of Man longs to find faith.

Matthew 24:22, 24, 31 (= Mark 13:20, 22, 27)

In these verses the plural *eklektous* (elect ones) refers to believers during the time of great tribulation. The authors take for granted, in keeping with the uses of Mt 22:14 and Lk 18:7, that the readers recognized the import of the reference. The "elect" here are genuine disciples[5]—God's people, those he has chosen and whom he will save at the Parousia (Mt

---

[3]G. B. Caird develops this point and says, "The elect are those who are specially called to serve God through suffering for their faith at the hands of an ungodly world" (*The Gospel of St. Luke* [London: A. & C. Black, 1968], 201).

[4]Marshall says of *eklektos* in Luke 18:7, "The use of the term implies that eschatological vindication is in view, and not a purely this-worldly answer to prayer" (I. H. Marshall, *The Gospel of Luke*, NIGTC [Grand Rapids: Eerdmans, 1978], 674). However we dare not dismiss the this-worldly dimension. For Luke, this is a parable encouraging unflagging prayer (18:1).

[5]Taylor calls them "the members of the Christian community" (V. Taylor, *The Gospel According to St. Mark*, 2d ed. [London: Macmillan, 1966], 514), while Swete suggests they are "probably the faithful members of the church of Jerusalem" (H. B. Swete, *The Gospel According to St. Mark* [London: Macmillan, 1909], 309).

24:27, 37, 39). The elect are viewed as a group, the people of God, and they are *all* gathered. The same group that suffers in the tribulation finds release from it when the trumpet of the Parousia sounds.[6] God acts to aid his people in the eschatological drama, first to shorten its days so they can survive, and then to gather his elect to himself.

Matthew 22:14

This perplexing saying merits a detailed discussion. In Matthew's presentation Jesus refers to God's people in corporate terms. Initially we note the saved character of the *eklektoi* (chosen ones). We will see in the epistles that the "called" stands for the believers in Christ. However, here Jesus distinguishes between the larger group—the called—to whom the invitation goes, and the smaller group—the chosen—who are saved. Jesus sets these chosen ones in contrast to those who suffer eternal punishment (22:13). Apart from its one application to Jesus (Lk 23:35), *eklektos* (chosen) applies to believers. Very significantly, in this context we also discover the criterion that distinguishes the elect from the nonelect. If Jesus furnishes any explanation why some are elect and others are not, here it is.

This difficult saying concludes the parable of the wedding banquet (Mt 22:1–14). In 22:3 the king sends out his slaves to invite or call those whom he invited. Likewise in 22:9 the invitation goes out to all. But the chosen ones are marked out because they alone responded to the invitation *in the proper way.* The key elements in the story that differentiate those who enjoy the banquet from those who do not are the response to the invitation and the wearing of the prescribed wedding garment. Failure to enjoy the feast lies not with the king, but solely with those invited. As the final scene makes abundantly clear, even being in the banquet hall itself does not suffice. Presumably, the guilty man had defiantly refused to dress himself in a fitting fashion, as had

---

[6]The theme of the elect in tribulation permeates 1 Enoch: "The elect shall be saved on that day" (see 1En 1:1; 28:2–4; 48:9; 62:8, 11–13). We see the image of a trumpet gathering the elect in PS 11:1–3 and Isa 27:12–13. The gathering of God's people is a familiar concept in the Old Testament, Apocrypha, and Pseudepigrapha.

all his fellow banqueters.[7] The consequence for the ill-clad guest was severe: eschatological judgment. Jesus injects reality into the parable, using some of the synoptics' distinctive imagery for the judgment of eternal punishment (see Mt 8:12; 13:42, 50; 24:51; 25:30; Lk 13:28).[8]

The redactional setting in which Matthew locates the parable makes it likely that its *Sitz im Leben* is the opposition of opponents—chief priests, Pharisees, and Sadducees (21:45–46; 22:15, 23). As leaders of the Jewish nation, they typified a rebellious people who, in rejecting Jesus, were spurning God's invitation to his messianic banquet (22:2: "a wedding banquet for his son"). Like the preceding parables of the tenants (21:33–44) and the two sons (21:28–32), the parable of the wedding banquet underscores the Jews' refusal to come to God on *his* terms. At times they devised their own terms—like the improperly dressed banqueter— but usually they simply refused God's invitation altogether.

On the other hand, those whom the Pharisees considered unclean were responding to God's invitation; they would enjoy his banquet. *They are the chosen ones.* Parallel to the other uses of *eklektos*, here, too, "chosen" means saved ones. The criterion for being among this chosen group jumps out from this parable: a positive response to Jesus and his message.[9] Hill says, "It is behavior and action which indicate whether a man is among the chosen or not."[10] From the parable we understand that people acquire "chosenness" at

---

[7]Perhaps they had gone home to put on their finest, but this seems unlikely due to their situation (22:9). More likely the king provided the requisite robes, as God provides salvation. But this controversy need not detain us. The point is that while the other guests had complied with the king's expectations, one did not.

[8]The judgment against the initial spurners of the king's invitation was also severe—they were destroyed and their city was burned (22:7)—but it remained within the confines of the parable.

[9]We detect no hint here of any prior elective choice of this group of banqueters. Hendriksen simply has no basis for drawing as a conclusion from this verse: "In comparison with those many that are lost there are but few that are saved, that is, few that are chosen from eternity to inherit life everlasting" (W. Hendriksen, *The Gospel of Matthew* [Grand Rapids: Baker, 1973], 798). Beyschlag is more to the mark: "The notion of being elected, therefore, does not contain the result of a onesided decree of God, but a mutual working of human and divine conduct. God chooses those who make it possible for Him to choose them" (W. Beyschlag, *New Testament Theology*, 2d ed., 2 vols. [Edinburgh: T. & T. Clark, 1899], 1:138).

[10]David Hill, *The Gospel of Matthew*, NCB (London: Oliphants, 1972), 303.

some point in their lives. The Jews had every opportunity to enter the sphere of the elect, but they refused God's invitations. The disciples accepted the invitation and are therefore among the chosen few.

In drawing conclusions about election from this passage we must be wary of reading into it Pauline theology[11] or other preconceived notions. For Matthew a distinction exists between those many[12] called (or invited) and a smaller group, the chosen, even though for other writers the terms describe the same group (see, for example, Ro 8:28–33; 2Pe 1:10; Rev 17:14). In Jesus' disputations with the Pharisees he presses the point that no one may presume upon a relationship with God. Because one has heard God's invitation (or however else we may describe the Jews' privileged position), carries no guarantee of eternal life. Sutcliffe puts this point well:

> The parable makes it plain that if the others were not among the chosen, it was solely because they themselves refused the call. It was in their power to be among the chosen but they preferred to remain aloof. This was pointed out long ago by Theophylact: "The call depends on God; to become elect (or chosen ones) depends on ourselves."[13]

By appending the logion of Mt 22:14 to this parable (and this group of parables [21:28–22:13]), the synoptic writer makes plain his approach to election. The elect follow Jesus.[14]

---

[11]Schweizer succumbs to this temptation when he says, concerning Mt 22:3, "The word for 'invite' also means 'call.' Paul uses the same word to describe the power of the gospel, which 'calls' people to God. The point therefore is God's call to salvation" (E. Schweizer, *The Good News According to Matthew* [London: SPCK, 1976], 420).

[12]J. Jeremias surveys the uses of *polloi* (many) (TDNT, 4:542). It can have an inclusive meaning—"all." He cites the parallel of 4Es 8:3: "There are many created, but few shall be saved." Obviously *many* here means "all." Thus, he continues, "If 4 Esdr 8:3 contrasts the totality of those created with the small number of the saved, Matthew 22:14 contrasts the totality of those invited with the small number of the chosen" (ibid.).

[13]E. F. Sutcliffe, "Many Are Called But Few Are Chosen," *ITQ* 28 (1961): 130. According to Sutcliffe, the Theophylact quotes are from *Enarration im Evangelium Matthaei*; PG. 123:388C.

[14]This conclusion is preferable to Schmidt's (*TDNT*, 3:494–96) who explains Mt 22:14 in a dialectical sense: "Many are called and yet few are called; many are elected and yet few are elected" (p. 495). For Schmidt Jesus simply warns against taking spiritual realities for granted. This

GOD'S ROLE IN THE ACQUISITION/APPLICATION OF SALVATION

A second group of texts that provides insight for our quest concerns God's role in applying salvation to people. This section includes many passages, and they vary in significance. Our tactic will be to move through the list in canonical order, though treating synoptic parallels together.

Matthew 5:9

This text affirms that peacemakers will be called or given the name "sons of God." Kingdom subjects demonstrate God's concern for peace; they reflect God's character, and he names them his children. Manson observes, "The peacemakers are the true Israel and acknowledged by God as his children."[15] The Old Testament and Jewish writings enunciated the concept of being a "son of God" (see Hos 1:10; Dt 14:1; Sir 4:1–10; WS 2:18; Jub 1:23–25; PS 17:30). Matthew's use of the future tense of the verb "to call" implies an eschatological act. R. Gundry suggests that it means "acknowledged by God as his sons at the last judgment."[16] Thus, at the final judgment the corporate body of kingdom subjects will bear the title "sons of God." As to the basis for God's action, the requisite criterion is to be a peacemaker, though the context of the Beatitudes and beyond assume the basic requirement of having entered the kingdom. Hence we conclude that God will name kingdom subjects as his children.

---

assessment fails to take the context sufficiently into account. Surely the context distinguishes between the called and chosen. Likewise we find Schweizer's interpretation deficient. It is inconsistent with the parable to conclude, as he does, that " 'called' means taking up the initial invitation (vss. 3–8), 'chosen' means persevering to the end (24:22, 24, 31)" (Schweizer, *Good News According to Matthew*, 421). In fact, the initial invitation of vv. 3–8 was not taken up. The ones initially invited spurned the king's invitation. Only in v. 10 do some heed the invitation, and even among this group one disqualified himself.

[15]T. W. Manson, *The Sayings of Jesus* (London: SCM, 1937), 151.

[16]R. H. Gundry, *Matthew. A Commentary on His Literary and Theological Art* (Grand Rapids: Eerdmans, 1982), 72. Schweizer comes to a similar conclusion—transformation into sons of God occurs at the Last Judgment (Schweizer, *Good News According to Matthew*), 95.

Matthew 9:13; Mark 2:17; Luke 5:32

In this triple-tradition pericope we encounter another use of the verb *to call*. The passages describe a scene from Matthew's postconversion dinner party. Jesus was there and also many people whom the Pharisees considered unsuitable company for an alleged religious teacher. So Mt 9:11 records their outrage, and in response Jesus defended his ministry to outcasts.

Only Matthew's account includes Hos 6:6 as part of Jesus' rebuttal[17] (again cited at 12:7): God desires mercy, not sacrifice. The Hebrew word translated as "mercy" is *ḥesed* and refers to Israel's covenant obligation or loyalty to God. Though Israel dutifully performed the prescribed rituals, the people's hearts did not belong to God. As Hosea called Israel back to her covenantal responsibilities, so Jesus asserts what God desires from people in the first century. As Hill puts it, God wants "not sacrifice . . . but the compassionate attitude and merciful action which give concrete expression to one's faithful adherence to and love for God."[18] Jesus pinpoints the Pharisees' error—they exhibited concern only for external matters of ritualism, such as with whom Jesus ate.

Jesus follows with a succinct depiction of his mission— to call sinners, and Luke adds "to repentance." Unlike the Pharisees, Jesus acts in keeping with his covenantal responsibilities, and so he extends love and compassion to sinners. Probably using irony, Jesus claims he has come to call sinners not the righteous (that is, the Pharisees who believe themselves to be righteous).[19] By his addition of *eis metanoian* (to repentance), Luke makes explicit what is implicit in Jesus'

---

[17]It appears that Matthew's statement of the quote is directly from the Hebrew since most LXX versions read *eleos thelō hē thysian* (I desire mercy or sacrifice).

[18]D. Hill, "On the Use and Meaning of Hosea VI.6 in Matthew's Gospel," *NTS* 24 (1978): 110.

[19]Commentators who opt for irony include V. Taylor, *The Gospel According to St. Mark*, 207; W. L. Lane, *The Gospel According to Mark*, NICNT (Grand Rapids: Eerdmans, 1974), 105; L. Morris, *The Gospel According to St. Luke*, TNTC (London: Inter-Varsity, 1974), 120; and J. M. Creed, *The Gospel According to St. Luke* (London: Macmillan, 1942), 82. This seems more likely than Gould's view that Jesus admitted that the Pharisees were righteous, from their point of view (E. Gould, *Gospel According to St. Mark*, ICC [Edinburgh: T. & T. Clark, 1896], 43). As evident elsewhere, Jesus did not believe that the Pharisees were righteous.

use of *call*. Jesus calls or invites people to repentance and salvation. Luke's addition shows repentance to be a central element of his understanding of the kerygma.[20] The Pharisees project complacency, hypocrisy, and self-satisfaction. Thus, according to Jesus, salvation in fact eludes them but comes rather to those who respond to Jesus' invitation to conversion.[21] Jesus calls sinners to salvation, and he requires a willing response. To so call sinners embraces the essence of Jesus' ministry.

Matthew 13:11; Mark 4:11; Luke 8:10

One can hardly find in the Gospels verses—and the pericopes of which they are part—that are more perplexing or that have generated more debate than these. We must understand them, for here Jesus gives his disciples an explicit explanation of the acquisition of the mysteries of the kingdom. First, we take the phrase "mysteries of the kingdom" (KJV) to be those truths about the in-breaking of the reign of God that Jesus reveals in his person and preaching. The kingdom and its promise of salvation have arrived for all those willing to submit to the reign of God.[22] That we take to be clear from the wealth of references to the kingdom in the synoptics. Much more problematic is the way Jesus appears to distribute the kingdom's secrets (mysteries):

Matthew:	to you it has been given (*dedotai*) to know . . . but to them it has not been given.
Mark:	to you has been given . . . but for those outside everything is in parables.

---

[20]Luke's use of *metanoia* (repentance) and *metanoein* (to repent) far exceeds that of Matthew and Mark. Luke's total use of these terms is fourteen (plus eleven in Acts), whereas Matthew has seven and Mark has three occurrences.

[21]We ought not read *metanoia* as only negative sorrow and turning from sin. Surely it includes the positive turning to God in faith and a holy life. Hendriksen makes this point well in his *The Gospel of Luke* (Grand Rapids: Baker, 1978), 306.

[22]We cannot afford to stop at this point, for it has been repeatedly developed. A quick perusal of a story like that of the rich young man (Mt 19:16–30, par.) will illustrate how the narrator moves easily among undoubtedly synonymous terms: eternal life (vv. 16, 29); kingdom of heaven (v. 23; cf. kingdom of God, Mk 10:23 and Lk 18:24); kingdom of God (v. 24); saved (v. 25); and the new world (v. 28).

Luke: to you it has been given to know . . . but for
               others they are in parables.

Jesus implies that some selective principle operates so
that some *are given to know* while others are not given this
insight, or only receive enigmatic parables. The passive
verbal phrase *dedotai (gnōnai)*—"it is given (to know)"—
clearly implies the divine agent. Only God can be the source
of revelation about the mysteries of the kingdom.[23] Does this
mean that God specifically chooses some to enlighten, while
he withholds that light from others? And, noting Mk 4:12
and Luke 8:10b, does God purpose to darken the minds of
some and so keep them from coming to the truth?

In this pericope Jesus answers his disciples' question
concerning why he speaks to the crowds in parables (Mt
13:10). Mark frames the question more in terms of the
meaning of the parables, while in Luke the issue is the
meaning of the parable of the sower. In response Jesus
divides his hearers into two groups: (1) the disciples to
whom the mysteries of the kingdom are given, and (2) those
outside (Mark: *ekeinois tois exō*) or the others, the rest (Luke:
tois loipois), to whom the mysteries are not given. So, God
reveals mysteries to some but not to others. The question
naturally rises: Does Jesus convey some principle or criterion
that marks the basis for God's enlightening some and not
others? In fact, all three do give further explanation, but their
answers do not appear univocal. Matthew appears to give a
"palatable" explanation while the other two go another,
more difficult, way.

Matthew 13:12–16 provides an explanation of Jesus'
intent in employing parables in his teaching. Specifically, in
13:13 Jesus characterizes outsiders as ones who do not see,
hear, nor understand. He quotes Isa 6:9–10 to describe their
condition.[24] They typify many "enlightened" people whose

---

[23]See J. D. Kingsbury, *The Parables in Matthew 13*(London: SPCK, 1969), 43;
J. Jeremias, *The Parables of Jesus* (New York: Scribner 1963), 15; C. E. B.
Cranfield, *The Gospel According to Saint Mark* (Cambridge: University Press,
1959), 157–58; and Cranfield, "St. Mark 4.1–34," *SJT* 5 (1952): 61.

[24]Matthew quotes from the LXX not the Hebrew MT. Whereas in Hebrew
the first three verbs in v. 15 are imperatives, in the LXX and for Matthew
they are aorist indicatives. Thus, in Matthew, these peoples' hearts have
become calloused (*epachonthē*), their ears do not hear (*ēkousan*), and their
eyes are closed (*ekammysan*). Eakin discusses the passage Isa 6:9–13 and sees
a cause-effect relation between the people's insensitivity to God's message

hearts are hard and who refuse to act on what they have heard. Parables allow people to accept or reject what they have heard. Thus, according to Matthew's account, those outside have themselves to blame, as the *hoti* (because) that introduces the Isa 6:9–10 quote in v. 13 shows. These hard-hearted rejecters have brought their judgment on them-selves—*because*, (although) seeing, they do not see and (although) hearing they do not hear nor do they understand. They alone bear responsibility for their failure to perceive the mysteries. Divine rejection has followed human rejection.[25] In fact, if they had opened their eyes, ears, and hearts to God, he would have healed them (last line of v. 15). This reaffirms God's basic stance toward his creatures, to welcome all who come to him on his terms (cf. Mt 11:28–30).

In many ways 13:12 provides a key to understanding Jesus' teaching in Matthew's version. For those who have responded to the truth already granted, more truth and enlightenment follow. But those who refuse to hear can never expect understanding. Kingsbury has it right when he says,

> Matthew . . . does not say that Jesus speaks to the crowds in parables *in order to* make them blind, etc., but *because* they are blind, deaf and without understanding. For Matthew, the fact that Jesus speaks to the crowds in parables substantiates the circumstance that they have already proved themselves to be hardened toward the Word of Revelation.[26]

---

and their "hardening." "The people have lived in their insensitivity, now they are left to exult in it" (F. E. Eakin, "Spiritual Obduracy and Parable Purpose," in *The Use of the Old Testament in the New and Other Essays*, ed. J. M. Efird [Durham, NC: Duke University Press, 1972], 91). He says Eichrodt and Von Rad agree and summarizes their positions: "Israel had refused for so long to be attuned to the word of Yahweh that ultimately her 'will not' became her 'cannot' " (ibid., 94). Taylor takes a different approach. He understands Isa 6:9–10 to be a command that "ironically describes what in fact would be *the result* of Isaiah's ministry" (Taylor, *The Gospel According to St. Mark*, 256; his emphasis). In both cases, however, clearly Israel bears responsibility for her judgment by God. As Moule says, "It is difficult to believe that, in its original context in Isaiah 6, it was intended as an instruction to the prophet to make sure that his message was unintelligible" (C. F. D. Moule, "Mk 4:1–20 Yet Once More," in *Neotestamentica et Semitica*, ed. E. E. Ellis and M. Wilcox [Edinburgh: T. & T. Clark, 1969], 100).

[25]Gundry says, ". . . people have refused to understand, and the parables will obscure the truth judgmentally" (*Matthew*, 256).

[26]Kingsbury, *Parables*, 49.

So, we ought not interpret "it is given" as some divine decree of election, as if God has chosen to enlighten some and to darken the minds of others. Since the disciples have responded to the kingdom message, they are privileged (or blessed, Mt 13:16–17) to obtain more knowledge. Those outside have rejected the message, and parables serve to obscure further insight from them.[27]

In place of the *hoti* (because) in Mt 13:13 to introduce the Isaiah quote, Mark and Luke use *hina* (Mk 4:12; Lk 8:10b). The conjunction *hina* usually has a final sense, denoting purpose,[28] but the "harshness" that results from saying that Jesus' *purpose* was to obscure his message has caused many interpreters to search for alternatives. Let us set out the major options that scholars defend.

1. The *hina* must be taken in its common sense of purpose. Evans says,

> The best understanding of the *hina/mēpote* construction in Mark 4:12 is that it is telic or final in meaning. According to the logion Jesus tells his disciples that all things are given in parables to those outside in order that they may not understand, not repent, and not be forgiven.[29]

Baird's research supports this conclusion.[30] Likewise Cranfield concludes that according to Mark the message of the kingdom is a secret understandable only by those to whom God gives faith.[31] He puts it concisely: "There are

---

[27]Van Elderen paraphrases the intent well: "To you disciples in me (Jesus the Messiah) has been given a new knowledge of and full insight into the hidden things regarding the kingdom in the Old Testament revelation; but to them this new knowledge and insight has not been given, because they do not accept me as the Messiah" (B. Van Elderen, "The Purpose of the Parables According to Matthew 13:10–17," in *New Dimensions in New Testament Study*, ed. R. Longenecker and M. Tenney [Grand Rapids: Zondervan, 1974], 185).

[28]BAGD, 376ff.

[29]C. A. Evans, "The Function of Isaiah 6:9–10 in Mark and John," *Novum Testamentum* 24 (1982), 132; his emphasis).

[30]J. A. Baird, "A Pragmatic Approach to Parable Exegesis: Some New Evidence on Mark 4:11, 33–34," *JBL* 76 (1957): 201–207.

[31]Cranfield, *The Gospel According to Saint Mark*, 157–58. However Cranfield softens the seeming harshness of this when he says, "While the eyes of faith see through the veil and grasp the secret, for the unbeliever, so long as he remains an unbeliever, the veil is unpenetrated, and everything is still simply *en parabolais*," that is, obscure as in a riddle (ibid., 157). E. Schweizer (*The Good News According to Mark* [London: SPCK, 1971], 92) also sees the

those to whom God has given the secret. For the rest it remains a closed secret."[32]

2. Mark has mistakenly used *hina*, for surely Jesus never intended to veil truth or to prevent people from coming for forgiveness. Possibly Mark missed what Jesus intended as irony and simply too mechanically used *hina* and neglected to leave out the *mēpote* (otherwise) clause from the Isaiah quote.[33]

3. The *hina* should be taken in a causal sense equivalent in meaning to *hoti*. Yet it is difficult to explain why Mark and Luke should use *hina* if they meant *hoti*.

4. The *hina* is an introductory formula meaning "that it might be fulfilled." It introduces the quote, but ought not be taken to express Jesus' purpose for employing parables. Concerning Mark 4 Lane argues:

> In verse 11 Jesus called attention to the contemporary situation of belief and unbelief, of repentance and veil-edness; in verse 12 he cites the text from Isaiah, not to explain why he speaks in parables, but as a commentary on the contemporary situation in which the purpose of God was coming to fulfillment.[34]

This removes the stumbling block. Jesus does not exclude any from the opportunity or possibility of belief.

5. The *hina* is both explanatory and an introductory formula. Kirkland argues that the consecutive sense of *hina* fits better than the final sense. Thus, for Kirkland the *hina* functions in both a consecutive (or explanatory) way *and* to introduce the following prophecy. The sense is thus ". . . hence [it is as the scriptures say]: they indeed see but do not perceive . . . ."[35] So, unless the hearers decide to perceive and understand (and receive God's forgiveness) the result is precisely what Isa 6:9–10 prophesies.

---

parables as riddles. Taylor retains the harshness: "Mark's meaning must be that for those who are not disciples the purpose of the parables is to conceal the truth and to prevent repentance and forgiveness" (*The Gospel According to St. Mark*, 257).

[32]Cranfield, "St. Mark 4.1–34," (1952): 61.

[33]Gould (*Gospel According to St. Mark*, 73) adopts this view.

[34]Lane, *The Gospel According to Mark*, 159. Jeremias, *The Parables of Jesus* (New York: Scribner 1963), 17, and Marshall, *The Gospel of Luke*, 323, also speak positively of this option.

[35]J. R. Kirkland, "The Earliest Understanding of Jesus' Use of Parables: Mark IV.10–12 in Context," *NovT* 19 (1977): 7.

6. For C. F. D. Moule, the *hina* is "a vigorous way of stating the inevitable."[36] From his appraisal of the entire tenor of Jesus' ministry he finds it inconceivable that Jesus had as his purpose to conceal truth. Parables are not "designed to conceal a secret, nor yet, on the other hand, as merely illustrative, but as provocative and dynamic and creative."[37] Thus, Moule continues, "those inside" and "those outside" do not represent two fixed groups: those elected to be enlightened and those "permanently underprivileged."[38] Rather, these describe how people respond to Jesus' teaching. Moule is emphatic: "There seems to be no trace, elsewhere in the New Testament, of a theory that the effect of preaching the Gospel is to harden all hearers except the elect."[39] Thus, Moule and Marshall see the *hina* as simple realism.[40] Since people do in fact reject the message, in one sense the purpose of the message is to induce them to reject it. At the same time, the hearers bear total responsibility for their rejection.

7. The *hina* denotes both purpose and result. Most commentators take this option.[41] This explanation differs little from options (5) and (6) on the result side. But, in contrast to them, this option also gives *hina* its common force and sees a divine purpose in hardening those who reject the truth. The hardening of God only results as the consequence of these outsiders' own refusal to accept the truth. The operative key to this interpretation resides in Mk 4:25 and Lk 8:18, which Matthew puts between the statement of the revelation (13:11) and the Isaiah quote (13:13–15). Plummer says,

---

[36]Moule, "Mk 4:1–20 Yet Once More," 100.

[37]Ibid., 98.

[38]Ibid., 99.

[39]Ibid., 105.

[40]Marshall (*The Gospel of Luke*, 323) follows Moule here and concludes, "By his method of teaching in parables Jesus not only invited his audiences to penetrate below the surface and find the real meaning; at the same time he allowed them the opportunity—which many of them took—of turning a blind eye and a deaf ear to the real point at issue."

[41]Significant examples include: E. E. Ellis, *The Gospel of Luke*, NCB, 128; W. Hendriksen, *The Gospel of Luke* (Grand Rapids: Baker, 1978), 425; L. Morris, *The Gospel According to St. Luke*, 152; A. Plummer, *Gospel According to Luke*, ICC, 219; G. B. Stevens, *The Theology of the New Testament*, 2d ed. (Edinburgh: T. & T. Clark, 1911), 121; and H. B. Swete, *The Gospel According to St. Mark*, 76.

> At first sight it might seem as if the *hina* of Luke and Mark was very different from the *hoti* of Matthew. But the principle that he who hath shall receive more, while he who hath not shall be deprived of what he seemeth to have, explains both the *hina* and the *hoti*.[42]

Several lines from Ellis elaborate this further:

> It is difficult to avoid the conclusion that Christ connects parabolic teaching . . . with the citation from Isaiah 6:9ff. precisely because he views the arcane parables as judgment upon unbelief. . . . It is clear, in any case, that God's rejection is viewed as a response to man's prior rejection.[43]

By way of conclusion several points emerge. It is difficult to escape the final sense of *hina*—purpose is implied in the Isaiah quote. To dismiss Mark and Luke as mistaken seems unlikely, as does the suggestion that *hina* is only an introductory formula. Yet to say that Jesus purposed to exclude some and to prevent their comprehension of his message is inconsistent with his entire ministry. Jesus' goal was to seek and save the lost. As we saw above, Jesus depicted his ministry as "to call . . . sinners to repentance" (Lk 5:32).

So we must follow a position similar to (7) above, while admitting the cogency of Moule's arguments. Through a variety of means, including parables, Jesus tried to reach sinners with the gospel. Indeed, on some occasions Jesus explained his parables to outsiders—as if he wanted them to understand his message.[44] We find that outsiders did understand some of Jesus' parables (e.g., Mt 21:45, par.). Grammarians find great difficulty at times in distinguishing between *hina* denoting purpose or result,[45] and there is no inherent problem in allowing Mark and Luke the fluidity (or ambiguity) of including both. However, this point must be underscored—Jesus does not veil the truth to keep people from coming to faith. Rather, the parables allow hearers to seal their own fate. The parables give people the opportunity

---

[42]Plummer, *Gospel According to Luke*, 219.

[43]Ellis, *The Gospel of Luke*, 128.

[44]According to Baird's findings ("A Pragmatic Approach," 205ff.), out of Jesus' twenty-eight parables told to outsiders, he explained thirteen of them, although, of these, only two concern the kingdom.

[45]See BAGD, 378, II.2; and BDF, 187, Sec. 369 (2).

to believe in Jesus, or, if they choose, the occasion to reject him and to be judged for their unbelief.

In the short pericopes that closely follow the Isaiah quotes, both Mark and Luke emphasize the essential revelatory purpose of Jesus' teaching (Mk 4:21–25; Lk 8:16–18).

> "Do you bring in a lamp to put it under a bowl or a bed? Instead, don't you put it on its stand? For whatever is hidden is meant to be disclosed, and whatever is concealed is meant to be brought out into the open. If anyone has ears to hear, let him hear." (Mk 4:21–23)

Unquestionably, Mark and Luke do not teach that God selects out some to enlighten and hides the truth from the rest. "Rather what is meant is that a wise and discerning person will see the truth hidden in 'parables,' while the dull and unperceptive will not."[46] The outsiders could only blame themselves for rejecting, denying, and misconstruing the truth in the parables, for by their nature and *design* (*hina*), parables give people just such an opportunity. The parables' uncertainty provides the occasion for a person to reject the truth and bring down God's judgment.

Hence, what Mark and Luke give us does not hopelessly conflict with Matthew's meaning. Matthew gives explicitly (*hoti*) what is more implicit in Mark and Luke. Mark and Luke show that God purposed to give people the freedom to reject the gospel of God's healing forgiveness. The result of Jesus' teaching was precisely as Isaiah prophesied. People have turned a blind eye and deaf ear and as a result have forfeited their only hope for forgiveness. In God's purpose those who reject the truth in Jesus will not find forgiveness or healing. Parables reveal truth to those with ears to hear; they conceal it from those with dull or calloused hearts.

Matthew 25:32

A word that occurs with elective significance in Paul's letters is *aphorizein*. It has two basic senses: "to separate, take away," and "to set apart, appoint."[47] Paul employs the verb to indicate that God separated or appointed him to his apostolic role (Ro 1:1; Gal 1:15). Matthew uses the verb twice,

---

[46]Kirkland, "Mark IV:10–12 in Context," 13.
[47]BAGD, 127.

once to indicate that the angels will "separate" the wicked from the righteous at the judgment (13:49) and then at 25:32. In the scene of the Last Judgment the Son of Man (25:31)— the King (25:34)—*separates* the people before him into two groups, one for eternal punishment, the other to eternal life. Is this an instance of appointment, like Paul's to his apostleship?

The answer must be no, for the criterion the King employs for determining people's ends is whether or not they have exhibited an active social concern "for one of the least of these brothers of mine" (25:40, 45). The separation occurs at the time of judgment (cf. 13:49); it was not pretemporally predetermined. The possession of a living faith establishes one's eternal destination in heaven.[48]

THE ROLE OF GOD'S WILL IN APPLYING SALVATION

In places the function or role of God's will figures significantly in the New Testament doctrine of election. The synoptic writers employ several of the key terms that denote "will, wish, purpose," and so we must evaluate these texts and related passages for the insight they might provide. How does God's will in applying salvation function in the Synoptic Gospels?

Matthew 6:10

Matthew's first use of the term *God's will* occurs in the Lord's Prayer when Jesus instructs his disciples to pray that God's will (*thelēma*) be done on earth as it is in heaven. Frequently the New Testament writers use *thelēma* for God's will; five of Matthew's six uses of this noun refer to God's will. By its use in instructions about prayer we see that *will* here refers to that which God desires. We can clarify that even more. First, the probable Hebrew parallelism inherent in this Jewish prayer suggests that "thy will be done" develops or explains the previous line "thy kingdom

---

[48]The criterion of lifestyle is present in Ro 2:6–10; Ja 2:14–17; and Rev 20:12–13. A genuine faith will demonstrate its existence and reality by "good works."

come."[49] Thus God's will probably concerns the coming of the kingdom, and the disciples were to pray that people would submit to the reign of God in their lives, as God reigns in heaven. Hill reminds us of another perspective about God's will in Mt: it usually has ethical connotations (see 7:21; 12:50; 18:15; 21:31).[50] Thus prayer for God's will involves submission to his reign, not only for salvation, but in the practical, ethical dimensions of life.[51] God wills that people submit to his reign and act in keeping with his character.

Matthew 9:13 (12:7)

We have already considered this verse in the previous section, though there we focused on the word *call*. Matthew alone quotes Hos 6:6, which explains what God desires or wills (*thelō*). According to Hosea, sinful Israel had disobeyed God's will. Manifestly, this was Jesus' indictment of the Pharisees both times he quotes Hos 6:6: they were neglecting God's will, even in their scrupulous Sabbath observance (Mt 12:2).

Matthew 11:25–27; Luke 10:21–22

Though Matthew and Luke locate this pericope in different places in their narratives, their wording is virtually identical. In this short section Jesus employs two key words: *eudokia* (good pleasure, pleasurable will) and *boulomai* (to will, desire, resolve). At the time of the New Testament there was no essential difference in meaning between *thelō* and *boulomai*.[52] It is interesting, however, that when the New Testament writers use *boulomai* for God's will, the sense is often strong, rather than mere wishing or desiring. Müller

---

[49]In fact, in the Lucan parallel the specific petition about God's will is not present (Lk 10:2).

[50]Hill, *The Gospel of Matthew*, 137.

[51]B. Gerhardsson makes the point that even the third-person form of the imperative (*genēthētō*—let be done) demands a suitable human response ("The Matthaean Version of the Lord's Prayer [Matthew 6:9b–13]: Some Observations," in *The New Testament Age*, ed. W. C. Weinrich [Macon, Ga.: Mercer University Press, 1984], vol. 1, p. 213).

[52]"The terms are almost entirely interchangeable," says D. Müller (*NIDNTT*, 3:1016). G. Schrenk concurs (*TDNT*, 1:629–37).

goes so far as to say, "It is always a case of an irrefragable determination."[53]

Employing *eudokia*,[54] Jesus states that it was his Father's *pleasurable will* to reveal "these things" to little children while keeping them hidden from the wise and learned. We must understand what is God's "pleasurable will" before we can see to whom Jesus "wills" to reveal the Father. We agree with Hunter that the phrase "these things" refers to knowledge, "complete knowledge of God's saving purpose."[55] So, the truth of salvation comes to children, not the wise.

What differentiates the two? Surely Jesus uses "wise and learned" in a perjorative way to refer to those who appear wise in their own eyes; they are proud and self-satisfied. Both Evangelists previously reported the unrepentant condition of the people of Korazin, Bethsaida, and Capernaum (Mt 11:20–24; Lk 10:13–15). These Jews typify this intellectual complacency. They presume they know God. They are doing what he requires, and so Jesus is irrelevant. On the other hand, in Mt "children" exemplify the humble disciples, poor in spirit and meek (5:3, 5). They enter the kingdom humbly like children (18:3–4). Hence, God pleasurably wills to reveal himself and enter into an intimate relationship with those who come to him humbly, as children. To these alone God reveals his saving truth.

This leads to the second question: to whom does the *Son* will to reveal the Father? Now the answer is clear—only through the Son can a person know God, and the Son wills to reveal God only to such children. This involves two issues: (1) the reciprocal knowledge between Father and Son that Jesus, in some sense, passes on; and (2) Jesus' will to reveal God only to childlike believers. Though the reciprocal knowledge between Father and Son is a fascinating topic,[56] it

---

[53] Müller, *NIDNTT*; 3:1017.

[54] *Eudokia* is found only in Jewish and Christian literature and translates *rāṣôn* in the Old Testament and Sirach. Of God, it refers to his favor or pleasure. In Sirach we encounter the sense "divine ordination or resolve" (Schrenk, *TDNT*, 2:744). The Rabbis retained both these senses in their writings: divine good pleasure or favorable will of God.

[55] A. M. Hunter, "Crux Criticarum—Mathew XI. 25–30—A Reappraisal," *NTS* 8 (1961–62): 246.

[56] The literature on this ranges far. Among the most helpful are: Gundry, *Matthew*, 216–17; Schweizer, *Good News According to Matthew*, 270–71; F. C.

lies beyond the scope of our study. In the immediate context of both accounts, including the report of the unrepentant Galilean cities, the writers emphasize the response to Jesus' message and person. In fact, Matthew follows this pericope with Jesus' famous invitation for all to come to him.[57] One's response to Jesus determines whether one is a "child" or is "wise and learned." Hunter's statement seems warranted: "The power Christ claims to give is not the power to know the Father *as he did*, but rather the power to know the Father *in him*."[58] Though "in Christ" is a decidedly Pauline formulation,[59] this passage provides a parallel idea. In coming to Jesus (11:28) one enters the sphere of divine knowledge that brings salvation. By rejecting Jesus the "wise" Jews had bypassed the way to salvation.

We detect here no evidence that in the secret counsels of the divine will the Father and the Son chose only some to whom to reveal the truth about salvation.[60] Rather, the Son wishes to reveal salvation and rest to all who will come as little children. Surely Matthew could not propose in 11:27 that Jesus only chooses a select group to know the truth, and then in 11:28 announce that Jesus invites all (*pantes*) to find rest in him. Müller puts it well:

> It is one's attitude to the Humiliated and Crucified One which now decides to whom the revelation will be disclosed. "To whom the Son will reveal him" (Lk. 10:22)

Burkitt, "On Matthew XI.27, Luke X.22," *JTS* 12 (1911), 296–97; A. M. Hunter, "Crux Criticarum," *NTS* 8 (1961–62), 246; B. M. F. van Iersel, *"Der Sohn in den Synoptischen Jesusworten"* [Suppl. to *NovT* 3] (Leiden: Brill, 1961), 151–57; 180–83; Ellis, *The Gospel of Luke*, 157; and I. H. Marshall, *The Gospel of Luke*, 437.

[57]The context in Luke is also "evangelistic." Luke records, in chapter 10, the mission of the Seventy-two (10:1–20), the receptivity of the disciples to God's truth (10:23–24), and the inquiry of the lawyer (10:25ff.).

[58]A. M. Hunter, "Crux Criticarum," 246; his emphasis.

[59]We find interesting Johannine parallels to Mt 11:27: mutual knowledge of Father and Son (Jn 10:14–15; 17:25, 7:28–29); Father giving all things into the Son's hands (3:35; 13:3; 17:2, 7); and the union between Father and Son (10:30, 38; 14:7, 9; 16:15; 17:10–12). Though some suggest that John was the source for this unique synoptic occurrence of this idea, M. Sabbe surveys and evaluates the evidence and shows that Mt 11:27/Lk 10:22 represent an original saying of Jesus ("Can Matthew 11,27 and Luke 10,22 Be Called a Johannine Logion?", in *Logia*, ed. J. Delobel [Leuven: University Press, 1982]).

[60]Some, like Hendriksen, *The Gospel of Matthew*, 502–3, assert such a position, but it is clearly dogmatically motivated.

means, therefore, first, that with respect to knowledge of God, all human willing here reaches its limits; and secondly, here is no rule of arbitrary predestination, but rather, in the encounter with the message of Jesus the decision about the revealed will of God is made.[61]

Matthew 18:14

Matthew records a saying of Jesus that specifies God's will (*thelēma*) concerning salvation. The expression concludes a pericope about the "little ones who believe in me" (18:6, 10, 14). One must become like a child to enter the kingdom (18:3). Such "little ones," that is, kingdom subjects or believers in Jesus, are precious to God. The parable of the lost sheep shows Jesus' point: if one of these believers should wander from the fold, his fellow believers ought to seek to win or reclaim him. Jesus confirms his intent with a reference to God's will: God wills that no little ones perish.[62] Schweizer sums it up: "If God is unwilling to lose a single one of these little ones, someone in the band of his disciples must get up and go after the one going astray."[63] The saying is clear-cut. Literally it reads, "It is not your Father in heaven's will that one of these little ones perish." We seem to have clear evidence that God wills the salvation of all his little ones.

This proves embarrassing to Hendriksen, who feels compelled to define *thelēma* (will) here as God's revealed will, not his secret or decretive will. In the *open* God wills to save all, but *secretly* he wills to save only some. So, according to Hendriksen, "it is God's revealed will that not a single one should perish but that all should be saved, that is his *delight*."[64] But in his secret elective counsels, God's delight did not move him to elect all.

Surely our text gives no warrant for such a bifurcation of the divine will. God does not say one thing in public, but decide otherwise in secret. Jesus flatly states that God wills

---

[61]Müller, *NIDNTT*, 3:1017–18.

[62]God's concern for wayward Israel is a common Old Testament motif. As the following samples show, God longs for the repentance and willing return of his people: Ps 81:13; Isa 45:22; Eze 18:23, 32; 33:11 (cf. Mt 11:28–29; Jn 7:37; 2Pe 3:9; Rev 22:17).

[63]Schweizer, *The Good News According to Matthew*, 369.

[64]Hendriksen, *The Gospel of Matthew*, 696–97; his emphasis.

that not one perish. Hence the disciples need to show active concern for lost sheep. If some do perish, then God's will is obstructed, but this is no different from the use of *thelēma* in Mt 6:10.

Matthew 23:37; Luke 13:34

This saying expresses Jesus' heartfelt desire for his fellow Jews. After his extended tirade against the hypocritical Pharisees, Jesus cries out with great longing to Jerusalem—"How often I had willed [wished, desired] to gather your children" (author's translation). Jesus uses the verb *thelō* to express his frustrated desire or will that the Jews come to him. Nevertheless, they refused (literally: "you willed it not," using the same tense of the verb *thelō*). Jesus was willing to receive and welcome them, as a hen does her chicks, but the Jews would have none of him. Thus, their fate lay in their own hands. They will experience judgment, but will have only themselves to blame (Mt 23:38–39).

Luke 2:14

In his infancy narrative Luke records the angelic choir promising, through the newborn Savior, peace to people of *eudokia* (good pleasure). More precisely, the promise is for peace to people with whom God is pleased; that is, to people who are objects of his pleasurable will. As we noted above, *eudokia* can refer either to good pleasure or to pleasurable will. Thus when we come upon the phrase *anthrōpoi eudokias* (literally, "people of good pleasure"), we have several options. The meaning could be, first, "people of good will," that is, those who have somehow found favor with God, perhaps because of their openness to salvation. But this understanding of *eudokia* is alien to the LXX, Rabbis, Sirach, and the rest of the New Testament.[65] Second, the phrase could mean "people who give God pleasure." However, the context surely highlights God's provision of salvation rather than any thought that people generate pleasure in God. Most likely, here is a reference to "people whom God favors or chooses." Fitzmyer agrees, after assessing Qumran parallels,

---

[65]See G. Schrenk, *TDNT*, 2:750.

that "the *eudokia* and *rāṣôn* express God's will in electing and predestining men rather than his pleasure in man's goodness."[66]

For Luke peace refers to the well-being of God's salvation (cf. Lk 1:79; 19:42). Marshall says peace "is used to indicate the full sum of the blessings associated with the coming of the Messiah (Isa 9:5–f.; Mic 5:4)."[67] The angels affirm that the newly arrived Messiah will bestow salvation on those whom God has chosen, that is, on the objects of his favorable will.[68] If we ask, second, whom does God choose, or on what basis, we get no answer from this text. It merely makes an assertion. J. M. Creed does make a connection between "people of good pleasure" here and "all the people" (*panti tō laō*) in 2:10.[69] The good news will come to all the people (v. 10), and the peace of salvation comes to those on whom his favor rests (v. 14). The text could mean this, though we wonder how the angel could call salvation good news for all people if God selects only some to receive it. Or it could mean that the message is good news for all (because all are invited), but God bestows his favor only on those whom he has chosen. We cannot draw conclusions from this text beyond this.

Luke 12:32

Like the noun *eudokia*, the verb *eudokeō* occurs with two basic senses: (1) object *pleases* person (or person *is pleased by* object); and (2) person *is pleased to* do something (or person *wills* something). In the Bible both senses occur with God as the "person."[70] We see the first use in a text to which we will

---

[66]J. A. Fitzmyer, "'Peace upon Earth Among Men of His Good Will' (Lk 2:14)," in *Essays on the Semitic Background of the New Testament* (London: Geoffrey Chapman, 1971), 101. Ellis sees both senses and suggests that peace is to "those upon whom God's redemptive mercy has been bestowed and with whom he is well pleased" (*The Gospel of Luke*, 80).

[67]Marshall, *The Gospel of Luke*, 112.

[68]T. W. Manson phrases it like this: "men as objects of God's goodwill" (*The Gospel of Luke*, MNTC [London: Hodder & Stoughton, 1930], 19).

[69]J. M. Creed, *The Gospel According to St. Luke* (London: Macmillan, 1942), 35.

[70]For "to take pleasure or delight in" see the LXX of Pss 43:4 (44:3); 149:4; Isa 62:4; Mal 2:17; and 2Th 2:12; 2Co 12:10; Heb 10:6, 8. The purposive "to decide or will or select" occurs in the LXX of Ps 39:14 (40:13); Hab 2:4; and in 2Co 5:8; Gal 1:15; Col 1:19 1Th 3:1.

return, "with him I am well pleased" (Mt 3:17). The Son pleases the Father. The Lukan text is an example of the second use: "Your Father has been pleased to give you the kingdom." This is determinative, willful resolve. The agent, God, wills an action—that he give the kingdom to Jesus' little flock of disciples.

The context of Jesus' promise incorporates instruction on kingdom values and priorities. The disciples were to trust God, who would care for them, and to seek his kingdom and its values rather than earthly possessions or treasures (v. 31). Such devoted abandon to God was not reckless, Jesus assured them, for God had pleasurably willed to give the kingdom to them. Those who seek God's kingdom— both his rule over their lives now and his eternal rule in the age to come—will indeed find what they seek. The grammar yields either God "is pleased" (timeless aorist: they have it) or God "has been pleased" (past sense: he gave it to them already) to grant to them the kingdom. With either option, as Plummer notes, "He gives the kingdom to those who seek it, and with it gives the necessities of life."[71] This describes God's pleasurable will. We find no hint here of any selection of only some to whom to grant salvation.

GOD'S KNOWLEDGE OF HIS PEOPLE

The elective significance of *yāda'* in Am 3:2—"You only have I *known* of all the families of the earth"—alerts us to the possible significance of the Greek words for *know* in the New Testament, *ginōskō* and *oida*. Though these terms occur frequently in the synoptics, only rarely do we find uses that have possible elective significance. In fact, we have only three passages to consider.

Matthew 7:21–23

In a scene from the Day of Judgment Jesus reveals the criterion for entrance into the kingdom of heaven. What counts on that day is not profession ("Lord, Lord . . . ," vv. 21–22) nor even the performance of miracles in Jesus' name (v. 22), but the practice of the Father's will. True kingdom

---

[71]Plummer, *Gospel According to Luke*, 329.

subjects will do what God desires, a reference, no doubt, to the instructions that preceded these verses in Matthew's account of the Sermon on the Mount. The Judge will indict those who fail this performance test with these words: "I have never *known* you" (v. 23, author's translation). In essence, there exists no real relationship between Jesus and these professors. Surely *ginōskō* (know) does not refer to cognition, the possession of information, nor to recognition. The omniscient Judge knows all. Rather, they share no real relationship with Jesus, or, as Schmitz puts it, Jesus says, "I never had anything to do with you."[72] Instead of doing God's will, they are "workers of lawlessness" (v. 23, author's translation). Hill suggests that Jesus' rejection goes even beyond the denial of any relationship:

> The rejection "I never knew you" corresponds to the mildest form of ban pronounced by the rabbis (SB IV, p. 293): it means "I have nothing to do with you," or "You mean nothing to me."[73]

We conclude that Jesus, in saying "I never knew you," denies any true relationship with those who fail to practice what God wills. He bans them from his presence as outsiders, regardless of their protests. We find no sense of pretemporal choice for *ginōskō* here. Jesus was not saying, "I have never elected you." That would be a depressing and hopeless taunt to those unfortunate nonelect. The issue is doing God's will, not election. Those who refuse to do God's will show that, professions notwithstanding, they have no relationship with Jesus. To know Jesus mandates practicing what God wills.

Matthew 25:12

Mt 25:1–13 also involves an eschatological drama. The parable of the ten virgins presents two kinds of people: the wise who were properly prepared and gain entrance to the banquet, and the foolish who miss out due to their irresponsibility. In verse 12 the real point of the parable intrudes into the story. Jesus says to the foolish five, in the words of the bridegroom, "I don't *know* [oida] you." The context of the

---

[72]E. D. Schmitz, *NIDNTT*, 2:398.
[73]Hill, *The Gospel of Matthew*, 152.

discourse in Mt 24–25 makes clear that people need to make careful preparation for the Lord's return. "Therefore keep watch, because you do not know the day or the hour" (25:13). Without proper vigilance a person might be unprepared for Jesus' return and so miss out on eternal life (25:34, 46). Jesus does not *know* those who are unprepared. *Know* must again refer to a genuine relationship. Though the virgins say, "Sir! Sir!" and beg, "Open the door for us," their pleas are insufficient and too late, for the Lord does not *know* them. Nothing else matters.

Certainly Seesemann is right when he argues that "in the absolute use in the *koine* it is hard to establish any distinction of meaning" between *ginōskō* and *oida*, the two words for "know" in Mt 7:23 and 25:12 respectively (cf. Lk 13:25).[74] In these two contexts the meanings are identical. In 7:21–23 Jesus rejects people for not doing God's will, while in the parable of 25:1–13 the rejected virgins have no oil. Those rejected clearly lack something that was in their power to perform.[75] Again I see no support for making *know* equal *elect*.[76]

Luke 13:25, 27

In a pericope unique to Luke (13:22–30),[77] Jesus responds to a question about the number of people who will be saved. Will there be only a few (v. 23)? Rather than answer the question, Jesus entreats his listeners to strive (make every effort, *agōnizesthe*, present tense) to attain salvation themselves (v. 24). Never mind how many; just be sure you are among that number! Then with eschatological imagery similar to that of the previous two passages, Jesus warns them that at some point the door of opportunity will close.

---

[74]H. Seesemann, *TDNT*, 5:116–19.

[75]K. Donfried thinks the oil is symbolic of something like "bearing fruit," equivalent to doing the will of God ("The Allegory of the Ten Virgins [Matthew 25:1–13] as a Summary of Matthean Theology," *JBL* 93 [1974]: 423).

[76]Thus Hendriksen can only be dogmatically motivated when he says, "By virtue of his sovereign grace the Lord from eternity acknowledged them as his own. Consequently in time he made them recipients of his special love and fellowship (in the Spirit)" (*The Gospel of Matthew*, 878).

[77]There are close parallels to parts of the passage in Mt 7:13–14, 22–23; 8:11–12; 19:30; 20:16; 25:10–12.

Then, no amount of pleading or argument will move the owner of the house to reopen the door. He will shut the door of salvation and say to the outsiders: "I don't know you or where you come from." They have no relationship with God and no part in the kingdom. These "workers of iniquity" ("evildoers") find themselves in the place of weeping and gnashing of teeth (v. 28; cf. Mt 8:12; 13:42, 50; 22:13; 24:51; 25:30).

Here the excluded ones claim only the most superficial acquaintance with God (v. 26); they lack a genuine relationship with him. So Jesus' listeners must take heed and *strive* to enter now while time remains. The earlier context, Lk 13:1–9 (especially v. 3: "Unless you repent, you too will all perish"), supplies crucial insight for our understanding of this saying. Repentance enables a person to go through the door. The hypocritical ruler of the synagogue provides the contrast (13:14). God excludes those like him, while he knows those who repent. We discover no hint here of any sense that knowing means choosing out some. Those who "make every effort" walk through the door of salvation.

JESUS' CHOICE OF INDIVIDUALS

Up to this point our exegeses have uncovered no particular stress on individuals, though the texts may involve individuals, as, for example, in the section just completed. Unless individuals make the necessary personal preparations for the coming Day of Judgment, they face the inevitable verdict "I never knew you." Having said this, however, we found no examples of God's specific choice of individuals. These last two sections consider this phenomenon. First we consider Jesus' choice of ambassadors.

Matthew 10:1

Mark (3:13–19) and Luke (6:12–16) locate Jesus' choice of the Twelve early in their narratives. Matthew records here Jesus' commissioning of the Twelve for their own ministries. This occasion probably does not involve election, though Matthew uses the verb *proskaleō* (call to oneself) to describe Jesus' summons to the disciples. They have already been chosen; this incident describes Jesus' subsequent bestowal (*didōmi*, give) of his authority for their ministries.

Mark 3:13–14; Luke 6:13

Here Mark and Luke appear to record a single incident, if we judge from the sequence of preceding material. Yet they clearly tell the incident separately using different vocabulary. Jesus called or summoned (Mk: *proskaleō*; Lk: *prosphōneō*) to himself whom he *willed* (*hous ēthelen autos*; Mk 3:13). Jesus' will determined a special, select group. This group may be the Twelve, but Lk 6:13 suggests the likelihood that this initial group of disciples was a larger body. Then from this body Jesus *appointed* (*poieō*, to make; Mk 3:14) or *chose* (*eklegomai*; Lk 6:13) twelve. Though Luke calls the larger group disciples, only the Twelve are apostles (Lk 6:13).[78] The verb *poieō* as "appoint" occurs on several occasions.[79] Luke uses the technical term for election, which he later applies to Jesus (9:35; cf. 23:35). He also uses *eklegomai* (choose) of the apostles in Ac 1:2, 24.

In Mk 3:14 the appointment of the Twelve has two elements. First Jesus appoints them to be with him, and then to preach (*kēryssein*) and have authority to exorcise demons. "Their relationship to Jesus explains their existence and their authority," says Lane.[80] Luke furnishes no explicit purpose for Jesus' selection of the Twelve. Yet in Luke's addition— "whom he also designated apostles"—we discover the clue to their role. They would serve as Jesus' apostles, representing him and acting on his authority.[81] Thus Jesus' selection of these individuals, who already believe in him, is for a task— to serve him as apostles. This election parallels the election of special individuals in the Old Testament, as we saw. We find no trace of election to salvation here.

---

[78]Luke prefers the term *apostle* for the Twelve, much more so than the other Evangelists. See Mt 10:2; Mk 3:14; 6:30; Jn 13:13 (nontechnical); but Lk 9:10; 11:49; 17:5; 22:14; 24:10. K. H. Rengstorf, *TDNT* 1:398–447, staunchly defended the position that the term *apostle* goes back to Jesus himself. Though that position has come under attack, Marshall feels it is still defensible (*The Gospel of Luke*, 238–39).

[79]See, for example, 1Sa 12:6; 1Ki 12:31; 13:33; 2Ch 2:18; Ac 2:36; Heb 3:2; and Rev 5:10.

[80]Lane, *The Gospel According to Mark*, 133.

[81]For the probable significance of the meaning of *apostle* see L. Goppelt, *Apostolic and Post-Apostolic Times* (London: A. & C. Black, 1970), 178ff.; E. Schweizer, *Church Order in the New Testament* (London: SCM, 1961), 194–97; R. Bultmann, *Theology of the New Testament* (London: SCM, 1955), 2:105; and the Rengstorf article in *TDNT*, 1:398–447.

Luke 10:1

Luke alone states that Jesus "appointed" (*anadeiknymi*) seventy-two (or seventy) others and sent them out as evangelists. The verb occurs only here and in Ac 1:24 (in the sense of "show"), but occurs regularly in the LXX. The most frequent sense of the verb—"to appoint to some public office"—occurs in Josephus (*Ant.* 20:227) and the LXX (Da 1:11; 2 Mc 9:23, 25; 10:11; 14:12, 26; 1 Es 1:34; 8:23; et al.). Luke's use fits this sense. Schlier says, "In Luke 10:1, therefore, the word is taken from the political sphere and the institution of the seventy has the character of a public and official action."[82] The appointment or election is strictly to a task—election for service.

GOD'S CHOICE OF CHRIST

This second group of individual-election passages concerns God's choice of a special Individual, his Son. The synoptic writers employ a variety of elective terms to discuss God's choice, predestination, and purpose for his sending the Christ to earth. This is a prominent concept, and thus we have several passages and terms to investigate.

Matthew 3:17; Mark 1:11; Luke 3:22

In their account of Jesus' baptism the three synoptists record a voice from heaven that identifies Jesus as God's beloved Son, the One with whom he is well pleased. This citation includes two key elements—the word *beloved* and the phrase *to be well pleased*—and thus requires our analysis.[83] Unquestionably, the voice (*phōnē*) out of the heavens (also heard at the Transfiguration [Mt 17:5, par.] and just before Jesus' death [Jn 12:28]) belongs to God. Several questions require answers. First, what is the source of the saying? Are there allusions to Ps 2:7 or to Isa 42:1 or both? The commentaries give much space to this issue.

---

[82]H. Schlier, *TDNT* 2:30.

[83]Of course, there is a verbal contrast between Matthew, who reads, "*This* is my son . . . ; with *whom* I am well pleased," and Mark/Luke who have, "*You* are my son . . . ; with *you* I am well pleased." Though this redactional phenomenon may require evaluation in some discussions, it has little relevance for this analysis.

Jeremias goes to great lengths to show that Isa 42:1 is the only basis for the quotation.[84] Cranfield agrees, arguing that the ambiguous *pais* (servant, slave, child) is sufficient to explain the origin of *hyios* (son).[85] The vast majority, though, see the joint influence of both passages, and this proves the better explanation. The manuscript reading of some Western scribes shows the connection to Ps 2:7 in their minds. In place of the accepted reading for Lk 3:22, these Western texts have *hyios mou ei su, egō sēmeron gegennēka se* (you are my son, today I have begotten you).[86] If the quote does allude to both Old Testament passages, then we learn from both. First, from Ps 2:7 we see the connection to the Davidic monarchy. As D. Hill puts it, "The point is 'Messianic (royal and Davidic) enthronement,' for Ps 2:7 is the coronation formula of Israel's Messianic king."[87] Second, from Isa 42:1 we discern the appointment of the servant who comes to suffer and die.

These Old Testament texts, then, provide the background for Jesus' upcoming ministry. The conflation of these sources on the occasion of Jesus' baptism implies that God recognizes and affirms Jesus to be the Davidic successor who has come to fulfill the mission of the Servant of the Lord. Here is the coronation and ordination of the Spirit-endowed, messianic servant.

A second question concerns the importance of the title "Son" here. Schweizer seems to argue that only here at his baptism did Jesus begin "to exercise his sonship."[88] Though in theological discussion we might argue that before his incarnation Jesus already held divine status, his baptism officially proclaimed his sonship for all (or Jesus) to hear. As Cranfield says, "It confirms his already existing filial con-

---

[84]J. Jeremias, *TDNT*, 5:701–2.

[85]C. E. B. Cranfield, "The Baptism of Our Lord—A Study of St. Mark 1.9–11," *SJT* 8 (1955): 59–60.

[86]This reading is found in D it a, b, c, d, ff, l, r plus some fathers. The commentators opting for a reference to both OT texts include Hill (*The Gospel of Matthew*, 97–98), J. D. Kingsbury (*Matthew: Structure, Christology, Kingdom* [Philadelphia: Fortress, 1975], 50), Caird (*The Gospel of St. Luke*), Plummer (*Gospel According to Luke*, 100), A. R. C. Leaney (*A Commentary on the Gospel According to Luke*, BNTC [London: A. & C. Black, 1958], 110–11), and I. H. Marshall (*The Gospel of Luke*, 155).

[87]Hill, *The Gospel of Matthew*, 97–98.

[88]Schweizer, *The Good News According to Mark*, 41 and *TDNT*, 8:367–68.

sciousness."[89] Kingsbury goes farther in arguing that the title "Son" here implies that Jesus is the One who comes from God. "The idiom 'my Son,' in view of chs. 1–2, is unambiguous in meaning: for Matthew, it identifies Jesus as the Son whose origin is in God."[90]

A third question surrounds the meaning of *agapētos*. Though literally meaning "beloved" when used of a son or daughter, it also connotes "only" or "unique," parallel to *monogenēs*—"only-begotten."[91] Thus the heavenly voice emphasizes Jesus as *the* unique Son; he shares a unique filial, loving relationship with God. He is *the* beloved One.

We have already discussed the verb *eudokeō*, which can mean "to be pleased" or "to pleasurably choose." This could refer simply to the pleasure God feels in the person of his Son. More likely, seeing the allusion to Isa 42:1 on this occasion of Jesus' formal "ordination,"[92] we find here the elective sense. Although the aorist tense could refer to some past choice,[93] probably it is timeless.[94] In either case,

> what is meant is God's decree of election, namely the election of the Son, which includes His mission and His appointment to the kingly office of Messiah. As *hyios ho agapētos* Jesus is the Recipient of this elective good-pleasure.[95]

Likewise Bietenhard has no doubts about the elective significance of *eudokeō* here: "It is a case of God's choice and determination, by which he has installed Jesus as Messiah."[96] Jesus is God's "pleasurably chosen One" who stands in a

---

[89]Cranfield, *The Gospel According to Saint Mark*, 55. See also Marshall, *The Gospel of Luke*, 155, and Taylor, *The Gospel According to St. Mark*, 162.

[90]Kingsbury, *Matthew: Structure*, 50.

[91]This position is convincingly presented by C. H. Turner ("HO HYIOS MOU HO AGAPETOS," *JTS* 27 (1926): 113–29). He says, "From Homer to Athanasius the history of the Greek language bears out, I venture to think, the argument of this paper, that *agapētos hyios* is rightly rendered 'Only Son'," 129. V. Taylor agrees (*The Gospel According to St. Mark*, 161).

[92]See Mt 12:18 where he quotes Isa 42:1 again. We discuss that passage below.

[93]Lane, *The Gospel According to Mark*, 58.

[94]Those who concur include Taylor, *The Gospel According to St. Mark*, 161–62; Hendriksen, *The Gospel of Mark*, 44; Cranfield, *The Gospel According to Saint Mark*, 56; and Plummer, *Gospel According to Luke*, 100.

[95]Schrenk,*TDNT*, 2:740.

[96]H. Bietenhard, *NIDNTT*, 2:819.

unique relationship to God as the Son of God.[97] At this baptismal event the Father affirms these realities and appoints him to take up the ministry of the Servant-Messiah. Here we have individual election, the election of the Son to serve God as Servant-Messiah.[98]

Matthew 11:27; Luke 10:22

We discussed these verses above in section C in connection with God's will. Here we examine, briefly, the expression of the relationship of knowing (Mt: *epiginōskō*; Lk: *ginōskō*) between Father and Son. Might this be elective in nature? The answer must be negative. Nothing in the inherent sense of the verbs nor in the context would suggest that knowing here equals choosing. Schweizer argues for such an equation, but offers no defense except to say that "in the Old Testament [knowledge] refers to election."[99] Surely this is an overstatement, given the data. If *know* equals *elect*, then not only did God elect the Son, but the Son also elected God, according to the reciprocal statements. But the idea of the Son choosing the Father is unparalleled and strange.[100] We conclude that these verses offer no insight about God's election of the Son.

Matthew 12:18

In this pericope (Mt 12:15–21) Jesus withdrew to a safer place following an explosive confrontation with the Pharisees (12:1–14). The crowds followed Jesus, and while he healed their sick he warned them not to make him known. This spurs Matthew to quote, in typical fashion, from the Old

---

[97]The present tenses "you are" (Mark and Luke) and "this is" (Matthew) suggest an eternal and essential relationship (Lane, *The Gospel According to Mark*, 58).

[98]Lane advances an intriguing possibility. He discusses the possible meanings of the descent of the dove, and concludes, from rabbinic parallels that the dove is a symbol of the Israel community. Thus, "At the moment of his baptism Jesus is the one true Israelite, in whom the election of God is concentrated. The descent of the Spirit 'as a dove' indicates that he is the unique representative of the new Israel created through the Spirit" (*The Gospel According to Mark*, 57).

[99]Schweizer, *The Good News According to Matthew*, 270.

[100]See Gundry, *Matthew*, 217, and Marshall, *The Gospel of Luke*, 437.

Testament, claiming fulfillment of Isa 42:1–4 in Jesus' desire for anonymity. Only Mt 12:18 (Isa 42:1) concerns us, for it contains several key terms: *pais* (servant/child), *hairetizō* (choose), *agapētos*, and *eudokeō*. Matthew's uses of the Old Testament make a fascinating study,[101] and particularly here where he departs in various ways from both the Hebrew and LXX. For the Hebrew *'ebed* (servant) Mt has not *doulos* (slave, servant) but, like the LXX, *pais* (son, child). Instead of the Hebrew "whom I uphold," Matthew independently has "whom I have chosen" (*hēretisa*). Instead of the Hebrew and LXX "my chosen one," Matthew has "my beloved" (RSV) (*ho agapētos mou*). And in place of the Hebrew "my soul delights," Matthew, independent of the LXX says, "my soul is well pleased" (RSV) (*eudokēsen hē psychē mou*). What does Matthew's version accomplish?

First, by quoting from Isa 42:1–4 Matthew leaves no doubt that he identifies Jesus as the Isaianic servant of the Lord.[102] Jesus' desire for anonymity coincides perfectly with this servant role. He is "my servant," a phrase Luke uses in Acts to identify Jesus' role in accomplishing salvation—from his humiliation to his triumphant session (Ac 3:13, 26; 4:27, 30). The verb *hairetizō*, a *hapax legomenon*, occurs in the LXX with the sense of choosing or election (1Ch 28:6; Hag 2:23). Matthew's translation shows that Jesus is God's chosen one. As in the baptismal formulation in Matthew God again calls Jesus "the one I love" (NIV). This translates the Hebrew *bāḥîr*, which is the main word for choose in the Old Testament. Because he has already described Jesus as one whom God has chosen, Matthew makes this odd departure, perhaps even under the influence of the baptismal (and Transfiguration) utterance. What we discovered about the meaning of "beloved" at Mt 3:17 applies here. Jesus manifests the status of *the* uniquely beloved One, even in the midst of the suffering he undergoes.

Finally we note Matthew's use, again, of *eudokeō*. Probably this, too, signifies God's pleasurable choice of the Servant-Messiah. In departing from the Hebrew and the LXX, perhaps again under the influence of the heavenly

---

[101]A classic study is R. H. Gundry, *The Use of the Old Testament in St. Matthew's Gospel*, Suppl. to *NovT*, 18 (Leiden: Brill, 1967).

[102]The servant songs of Isaiah are found at 42:1–4; 49:1–9a; 50:4–9; and 52:13–53:12.

quotations, Matthew brings in this favorite idea. Rather than seeking to stand out as a prominent miracle-worker, Jesus fulfills the role for which God chose him. Only he qualifies as God's beloved One, the Servant of the Lord. God chose Jesus to be the servant. Election of this individual is for service.

Matthew 17:5; Mark 9:7; Luke 9:35

All the synoptists record a second utterance from heaven, this time out of a (bright) cloud at the occasion of Jesus' Transfiguration.[103] For Matthew the heavenly words duplicate what the voice said at Jesus' baptism (3:17), with the addition here of the exhortation "Listen to him." God reaffirms the commission that came at the threshold of Jesus' ministry. Hendriksen puts it well:

> It was the Father who, in his great love for the Son, clothed him with glory and encouraged him with a bracing re-affirmation of continued delight, in order that this might sustain him in his fast approaching agony.[104]

God confirms his status and calling as God's unique, chosen Son.

Mark renders the quotation in the fewest words. This time he does not use the second person "you are" as at Mk 1:11, but, like Matthew, he writes, "This is . . . ," a public declaration for the disciples. However, Mark includes only the statement "This is my beloved Son; listen to him" (RSV) omitting Matthew's clause, "with whom I am well pleased" (RSV). Thus Mark omits the explicit elective component to the utterance; for him *agapētos* (beloved) bears all the freight. To Mark, God affirms Jesus' status as *the* uniquely beloved Son at the threshold of Jesus' supreme suffering and rejection.

Luke also differs. Like Matthew and Mark he quotes the voice saying, "This is . . . ." But in place of the *ho agapētos* (beloved),[105] Luke has *ho eklelegmenos*, making very explicit

---

[103]A cloud as a symbol of God's presence is common in the Old Testament theophanies of the Exodus (e.g., Ex 16:10; 19:9, 16; 40:35; Lev 16:2; Nu 11:25), the dedication of the first temple (1Ki 8:10–11), apocalyptic visions (Eze 1:4) and were expected to reappear in the Messianic period (2Mc 2:8). See W. C. Allen, *Gospel According to St. Matthew*, ICC (Edinburgh: T. & T. Clark, 1907), 185.

[104]W. Hendriksen, *The Gospel of Matthew*, 668.

[105]In fact many MSS do read *agapētos* here, but this seems to be a clear case of assimilation to Mk 9:7; Mt 17:5; Lk 3:22. The external evidence also favors

Jesus' status as "the one who has been chosen" by God (perfect tense). Like Mark, Luke omits the final clause, "with whom I am well pleased." Except where it occurs on the lips of taunters at Luke 23:35, only here in the synoptics does this term *elect* describe Jesus.[106] Following the path of suffering and eventual death, Jesus is God's chosen One.

In summary, these verses, in a fashion similar to the baptismal utterance, affirm (or reaffirm) Jesus' status as God's chosen One. The emphases of the synoptists vary, but clearly, in spite of the impending events (Lk 9:31), Jesus enjoys God's favor and goes forth as his elect One. Again, this Individual is elect to serve God in the path of suffering. The heavenly voice urges the disciples to "listen to him," which may mean to follow in the path of suffering with him.[107]

Matthew 26:24; Mark 14:21; Luke 22:22

At the occasion of the Last Supper all three synoptic writers attribute to Jesus a saying that has a very predestinarian ring to it. This marks Jesus' affirmation that God purposefully planned the course of events of his life, including the upcoming atrocities of Calvary. In the words recorded in Matthew and Mark the Son of Man is going "just as it is *written* about him." By using this imagery Jesus asserts that in his life he executes the prophesied scenario— doing what God had in mind all along, and what he revealed to the prophets long ago. Swete adds an important point:

> The saying has no flavour of Pharisaic fatalism; it is not a blind *anagkē*, but a Personal Will, long revealed and accepted, which the Son of Man consciously obeys (Phil. ii:8).[108]

Luke replaces the word *gegraptai* (written) with *hōrismenon* (destined). The basic sense of *horizein* is "to set the limit" and so can mean to fix, appoint or determine. The New Testament uses it to mean fixing times and locations

---

the reading we have included. See *UBS*, 3d. ed. (Stuttgart: United Bible Societies, 1983).

[106]Here at Luke 9:35 we find the verb *eklegomai* (choose), while at 23:35 Luke employs the adjective *eklektos* (chosen).

[107]So suggests I. H. Marshall, *The Gospel of Luke*, 388.

[108]Swete, *The Gospel According to St. Mark*, 333.

(Ac 17:26; Heb 4:7) as well as appointing people to positions (Ac 10:42; 17:31). Here in Lk 22:22 Jesus affirms that God has determined or decreed that his life should take a certain course—including his betrayal and crucifixion.[109]

All three writers record Jesus' statement of "woe" to Judas. The divine decree concerning these events in no way diminishes Judas' personal culpability for his actions. God's purpose in history did not excuse Judas' actions; he was no blind, oblivious, or unwilling pawn of higher forces. So Jesus expresses profound sorrow and pity for his betrayer: *woe*, which means "alas" or "too bad."

So we discover again an election of Jesus, or more accurately, the predestination of the course of his redemptive career. God decreed (and prophesied) Jesus' betrayal and death,[110] without being responsible for Judas' sin. Judas was no reluctant antagonist. He will suffer judgment for his sin. Jesus is certainly God's elect One, the course of whose life God marked out for him. God chose Jesus for service.

Luke 2:34

When Mary and Joseph brought the infant Jesus into the temple precincts, they encountered a man named Simeon (Lk 2:21–38). In his prophecy to Mary he asserted that Jesus was set or destined (*keitai*) to cause many in Israel to fall and to rise. The verb *keimai* means "to set something," but extends to mean "appoint," the sense here.[111] Thus Simeon claims that a specific feature of Jesus' career has been set or destined. In response to him many would rise and fall.

The phrase "the falling and rising of many in Israel" is ambiguous and can be understood in two ways. First, the

---

[109]It is difficult to know, presuming Luke has Mark or Matthew before him as he wrote, why he changed *gegraptai* to *hōrismenon*. Leaney (*A Commentary on the Gospel According to Luke*, 269) argues that Luke switched *written* since he knew of no direct prophesies of the betrayal. But this is unlikely given what Luke records at 24:25–26, that it was prophetically necessary that the Christ should suffer these things. More likely *decreed* just brings out the force of *written* for his readers. What was prophesied has been determined, and must happen.

[110]G. B. Caird observes, "The Cross was the preordained price of friendship with the outcast" (*The Gospel of St. Luke*, 238).

[111]See F. Büchsel, *TDNT*, 3:654. The idea of appoint or destine occurs at Php 1:16 and 1Th 3:3.

inevitable result of Jesus' ministry will be to divide the Jews, some for and some against him. As Morris puts it, "Those who reject Him will in the end *fall* (cf. Is. 8:14f.). Those who accept Him will rise, they will enter salvation."[112] Or, second, a group of Jews will *both* rise and fall. This embraces the remnant who believe. They must repent (fall, die) before they come to new life (rising in salvation, resurrection).[113] If we adopt the first interpretation that Jesus would divide the Jews, we find no hint that God decreed which ones would rise or fall. In fact, Jesus states at 13:34 that he wished that all the Jews would come to him, but they were not willing. If we go with the second option, we still find no hint that God determined the identity of those who would fall and rise.

Thus God affirms through the lips of Simeon that Jesus is God's appointed ambassador to bring salvation to many in Israel. God appointed him to his evangelistic and painful (2:35) ministry.

Luke 23:35

The synoptists record the mockery of the Jewish leaders as Jesus hung on the cross. In their derision of Jesus, they use various titles. They proclaim Jesus to be "King of Israel" (Mt 27:42); "this Christ, this King of Israel" (Mk 15:32); and "the Christ of God, the Chosen One" (Lk 23:35). Luke alone records this final title. We know that as a rule Jesus avoided applying terms like Messiah (Christ) and Chosen One to himself, so it is curious why the taunting Jews should use the terms. Two possibilities suggest themselves. First, the title *ho eklektos* (the Chosen One) may be due to Luke's redaction, for only he used the term at 9:35, par. Though the Christian community is made up of the elect ones (plural), only Christ merits the singular title of God's Chosen One. J. M. Creed says, "The Messiah of the new Israel is 'the elect one' *par excellence*."[114] Thus Luke affirms that even in the face of his

---

[112]Morris, *The Gospel According to St. Luke*, TNTC, 89.

[113]Those who prefer option (1) include Creed (*The Gospel According to St. Luke*, 42), Plummer (*Gospel According to Luke*, ICC, 70), and Hendriksen (*The Gospel of Luke*, 170). Both Caird (*The Gospel of St. Luke*, 64) and Marshall (*The Gospel of Luke*, 122) prefer option (2), while Morris (*The Gospel According to St. Luke*, 89) and Leaney (*A Commentary on the Gospel According to Luke*, 100) see both as possible.

[114]Creed, *The Gospel According to St. Luke*, 287.

greatest crisis and under the thumb of his persecutors, Jesus was God's Chosen One.

The other possibility is that this is a genuine Jewish title, as Jeremias argues.[115] He notes that Christian influence here is unlikely for only at Jn 1:34 is *ho eklektos* used elsewhere as a Christological predicate. Thus, knowing Jesus, his teachings, and signs, the Jews applied the titles king, Messiah and Chosen One. Many first-century Jews would associate messiahship with Jesus' activities, even though he himself did not use or encourage the titles. Luke certainly would agree that *ho eklektos* is appropriate.

In either case the title stands as a witness to Jesus' status as an individual—indeed, the only individual—to whom the description "elect" is applied. God has chosen him. He is God's Chosen One, even in the jaws of death. Suffering is not incompatible with election.

SUMMARY

The data we have considered from the Synoptic Gospels leads to several fairly pronounced conclusions. Though certain details may be debatable, the writers establish some well-defined contours. First, they identify a class of people whom they call the elect or chosen. These people are clearly saved. They are God's own people whom he will care for through suffering (Lk 18:7) and whom he will rescue at the Parousia (Mt 24:22, 24, 31, par.). While the "called" are invited, they may or may not obtain salvation. The "elect," however, have responded to God's invitation on God's terms (Mt 22:14). People become (or shows themselves to be) chosen by responding to God's invitation.

It is fair to ask, are people elect because they respond to God's invitation, or do they respond because they are elect? Can we discover an answer in the saying of Mt 22:14 and the preceding parable of the wedding supper? It may be that the parable gives the details which the saying then summarizes. In other words, some come to be included among the elect because they respond to God's invitation. Or perhaps Mt 22:14 explains why some responded in the parable (because God had previously chosen them to respond). Our exegesis

---

[115]Jeremias, *TDNT*, 5:689.

above endorsed the former option. We discovered no hint in the synoptics that God enables (or causes) some to respond to Jesus' invitation. In fact, the active or causative component in *eklegomai* and *eklektos* as applied to believers is decidedly toned down. We see believers called "the chosen ones" (*eklektos*) without any implication that God chose or selected them out of a larger group. The "elect" clearly constitute the saved group, but we don't find "elect" in the sense that God has chosen these ones, and not the others, to be saved.

A second point is also well-defined: to attain salvation one must respond to God's invitation and come to him on the terms he specifies. This requirement of response pervades the passages dealing with how or when salvation comes to people. Jesus came to call sinners to repentance (Lk 5:32). Only those who submit to the reign of God are named "sons of God" (Mt 5:9). God excludes from his healing forgiveness those who reject the truth as presented in Jesus' life and ministry. They have only themselves to blame (Mt 13:11, par.). The texts that explain God's will in applying salvation and its benefits provide important perspective. There we find nothing restrictive about God's will; he wills to save all (Mt 18:14). Though Jesus reveals the Father only to those to whom he so wills, in fact he wills not to limit this revelation but to reveal God to all who come as children (Mt 11:25–27, par.). Significantly, Jesus follows this teaching with his open invitation for all to come (11:28–30). How inconceivable that Jesus (and Matthew) would issue an open appeal to *all*, knowing that in his secret counsels God in fact only enables *some*. Rather, Jesus makes it clear that he wills all (the Jews) to come. The fault was with them—they would not (Mt 23:37, par.). Though God desires that people submit to his reign in their lives (Mt 6:10), sinners can reject God's will and go their own way (Mt 13:11, par.). The elect experience God's peace (Lk 2:14) and God's kingdom (Lk 12:32). Lacking is any teaching that God wills only some to be saved and that he chooses them alone to accept his invitation.

Nor did we find any elective significance in the few instances where the synoptists speak of God's knowledge of people. All the uses are negative. The writers deny that Jesus *knows* anyone who fails to do God's will (Mt 7:21–23), who is unprepared for Jesus' coming (Mt 25:12), or who failed to repent (Lk 13:5, 25, 27). The Evangelists place the onus for a relationship with God squarely on these "professors." God has made himself available to all who will come to him; he wants to be known by them. But people must come to God in the manner he has prescribed. Some disqualify themselves by failing to meet God's terms. We have found no justification for saying that "I don't know you" means "I have not chosen you."

The above conclusions argue that the synoptic writers address people largely in corporate terms. Certainly an individual must repent or come to God as a child, but we have not discovered passages that specifically speak of God's or Jesus' choice of a specific individual for salvation. Indeed, apart from the few references to God's choice of Jesus, and Jesus' appointment of the apostles, individual election does not occur in the Synoptic Gospels. The Evangelists inform us that Jesus chose and appointed his twelve apostles (Mk 3:13–14; Lk 6:13). Later he appointed seventy-two (or seventy) disciples. In both instances the choosing was for mission, not for salvation. They were chosen to preach and to exorcise demons; they were not chosen to become believers or to enter the kingdom.

Though more complex, God's election and appointment of Jesus was for mission. At his baptism God inaugurated Jesus' ministry by affirming his status as Son and the One chosen to undertake God's mission in the world (Mt 3:17, par.). He is the Chosen One, uniquely loved and pleasurably selected to fulfill the role of the Servant of Yahweh (Mt 12:18). As uniquely Chosen Son (Mt 17:5, par.) he must tread the path divinely marked out, a life of service to the point of death (Mt 26:24, par.). Only by this way, the way of death, can the Chosen One (Lk 23:35) bring salvation to God's people (Lk 2:34). In Jesus' life we come closest to any idea of predestination in the Synoptic Gospels. His life—especially his passion—fulfills his prophetic destiny.

6

THE ACTS OF
THE APOSTLES

Few scholars deny that the third Evangelist also wrote the Acts, and so we move from the Synoptic Gospels to Acts before considering the Johannine literature. Our procedure will follow that developed in the previous chapter. We have isolated four broad categories into which the election occurrences fit. We will start with the most general and end with the most specific. In the Acts Luke uses several of the terms that occur in the third Gospel. He also introduces several new terms and ideas.

GOD'S DETERMINATION OF EVENTS OR
STATES OF AFFAIRS

In the first few texts of this section Luke affirms that God has some role or control in either events that occur or certain states of affairs in this world. We deliberately exclude several texts that could fit here.[1] Because they allude to God's determination of aspects of Christ's career, we will include them with the other texts referring to Christ in a separate section (as in the previous chapter).

---

[1]These include Ac 2:23; 4:28; 13:29, 33.

Acts 1:7

In response to their inquiry about the timing of the coming kingdom, Jesus informed his disciples that they were not to be privy to "the times or dates the Father *has set* [*etheto*] by his own authority." This NIV translation reflects the literal sense of *tithēmi*, which means "to lay, place or put," and by extension, "to establish, institute, appoint." The verb occurs twenty-three times in Acts, and three of these appear with some elective sense.[2] Thus Jesus asserts that the Father has determined the timetable of eschatological events.

Acts 17:26

Parallel to the preceding text we find this use of *horizō*. Affirming God's sovereignty over the world and human affairs, Paul states that God "determined" (*horisas*)[3] the times and the locations of the nations on this planet. Following Dibelius, F. F. Bruce[4] and E. Haenchen[5] take Paul to mean that God determined the habitable zones on the earth and the annual seasons of the year. I. H. Marshall[6] and Lake and Cadbury[7] understand "times" to denote divinely appointed periods for individual nations to flourish, and "exact places" to refer to national boundaries. Both options are defensible and have Old Testament support, but we need not settle this. Significantly, for Paul this personal God has taken pains to *determine* a state of affairs that will benefit his creatures.

Acts 15:7

In his address at the Jerusalem council Peter employs the verb *eklegomai* (elect, choose). He argues that God chose a

[2]The others are Ac 13:47 and 20:28.

[3]The verb *horizō* is a favorite of Luke. We saw it at Lk 22:22, and it occurs five times in Acts (2:23; 10:42; 11:29; 17:26, 31) but elsewhere only at Ro 1:4 and Heb 4:7.

[4]F. F. Bruce, *Commentary on the Book of the Acts*, NICNT (Grand Rapids: Eerdmans, 1956), 358.

[5]E. Haenchen, *The Acts of the Apostles* (Oxford: Blackwell, 1971), 523–24.

[6]I. H. Marshall, *The Acts of the Apostles*, TNTC (Leicester: Inter-Varsity; Grand Rapids: Eerdmans, 1980), 288.

[7]K. Lake and H. J. Cadbury, *The Beginnings of Christianity*, part 1, "The Acts of the Apostles," ed. F. J. Foakes-Jackson and K. Lake, vol. 4, English Translation and Commentary (London: Macmillan, 1933), 216.

certain course of action—that through Peter's mouth the Gentiles would hear the gospel and believe. The salvation of the Gentiles as Gentiles is no travesty of the divine plan; indeed, God determined this strategy. Peter affirms not that God selected him to be God's mouthpiece,[8] but that God chose a course of action. Hence, following Bruce,[9] the NIV renders it, "God made a choice among you that the Gentiles might hear."

Acts 18:21

The last two texts in this section refer to God's will, the first employing the verb *thelō* (I will). Though Luke used this verb twenty-eight times in the third gospel, it occurs only fourteen times in Acts. Only here does it occur with the divine subject. Paul promised the Ephesians he would return to them, *tou theou thelontos* ("if it is God's will"). Paul had his own plans to return to Ephesus, but he admitted they were always contingent on God's sovereign will.[10] Thus, without any defense or further development, Paul voices a presupposition that underlies his planning: "if God wills."[11] He affirms that God's will is definitive. Thus we must set this in contrast to statements that seem to express more of God's desire or wish—which may or may not occur (recall Mt 6:10; 9:13; 23:37 above and 1Ti 2:4; 2Pe 3:9).

Acts 21:14

The sentiment Luke expresses here, through the words of the Caesarean Christians, parallels the previous text. The noun *thelēma* (will) occurs with no difference in meaning from the verb *thelō* (I will). When the believers could not dissuade Paul from proceeding on to Jerusalem—in spite of

---

[8]F. J. Foakes-Jackson places the emphasis on God's choice of Peter to preach (*The Acts of the Apostles* [London: Hodder & Stoughton, 1931], 136), but this cannot be sustained.

[9]F. F. Bruce, *The Acts of the Apostles* (London: Tyndale Press, 1951), 292.

[10]The contingency of human plans is made more explicit at Jas 4:15. See our discussion of this text below.

[11]Many commentators note that the phrase "if God wills" is not a Jewish formula but comes from pagan sources. There is no evidence that the Jews employed this concept in biblical or tannaitic times (see, e.g., Lake/Cadbury, *Beginnings of Christianity*, part 1, "The Acts of the Apostles," 231).

the dire prophecy about his fate there—they could only entrust him to the Lord's good and sovereign keeping. "The Lord's will be done," they announced. Their response raises several questions. Were they praying that God would overrule Paul's obstinate foolishness? Or had they come to agree with Paul that what he insisted on doing was indeed God's will? Were they convinced that God's will would be done anyway, so it would be futile for them to protest against Paul? Or did they believe that what God wills is good and the wisest course, so they ought to seek it too? To tie up Paul and send him away in another direction might go contrary to God's will and thwart his intentions. In any case, salvation is not in view. Here God wills a state of affairs.

GOD'S ELECTIVE ROLE
WITH CORPORATE GROUPS

In this section we have four texts with four different terms that have some elective sense. Two are etymologically related and share a common component of meaning, so we will consider those first.

Acts 2:39

In the final statement of Peter's Pentecost sermon he assures his hearers that God promises forgiveness of sins and the gift of the Holy Spirit (2:38) to both Jews and all those who are far off—perhaps the Gentiles. Avoiding universalism, Peter restricts the application of salvation to "all whom the Lord our God will *call*." We encountered this verb, translated "call" (*proskaleomai*) in the Gospels, when Jesus *summoned* the disciples before appointing the Twelve (Mt 10:1; Mk 3:13). There the verb had no elective significance. However, in three of its ten occurrences in Acts it does merit our attention. Luke employs what we shall see is the technical sense of *kalein*[12]—God's call to salvation— which Paul particularly prefers. In "calling," God definitively applies salvation and grants people the status of "Christian."[13] So while the appeal of salvation is universal—

---

[12]K. L. Schmidt agrees; see *TDNT*, 3:501.

[13]Our full development of the significance of this sense of "call" must await our consideration of Paul, who develops the technical sense of the *kalein* terms.

Jews and all (*pasin*) those far off—salvation comes only to those God calls.

People must call upon the Lord. His quotation of Joel in Ac 2:21 shows that Peter views the appeal and opportunity as universal and unrestricted. So we have two necessary calls: people must call on God, and God must call people. Further elaboration must await additional data. We discover no component of choice evident in the meaning of the verb *call* itself. It specifies God's naming of people to be his own (recall Mt 5:9: "they will be called sons of God"; see the next text).

Acts 15:17

In a quote from Am 9:11–12, James uses the verb *epikaleō*, "to call upon." Literally, James says that the name of God is called upon the Gentiles. A clear-cut "naming" sense occurs here and derives from the Old Testament. Schmidt explains that this reflects "the common Old Testament practice of naming the name of God over a man, who is in this way God's possession, because God has revealed and made Himself known to him."[14] Lacking any component of choice, this text affirms that to be one of God's people, one has to bear the name of God (see NIV: "Gentiles who bear my name"). The focus is on the application of the status "Christian."

Acts 13:48

Luke devotes 13:14–52 to the ministry of Paul and Barnabas at Pisidian Antioch. On the second Sabbath (vv. 44–45), when almost the entire city appeared to hear the preachers, the jealous Jews heaped verbal abuse upon Paul and his message. This evoked a response from the apostles that had two elements. First, since the Jews rejected the message of eternal life, Paul and Barnabas would offer it to Gentiles (v. 46). Second, they defended their ministry to Gentiles from Isa 49:6, saying that God had appointed them to minister to Gentiles (v. 47). Luke records two results from this change of strategy: the Gentiles rejoiced and honored

---

[14]Schmidt, *TDNT*, 3:498.

the word of the Lord, and "all who were appointed for eternal life believed" (v. 48).[15] What does Luke mean by the Gentiles' appointment (using the verb *tassō*) for eternal life? What is the meaning and significance of this appointment?

Though the apostles' preaching impressed some Jews and some Jewish proselytes (v. 43), the Jewish power structure obviously felt threatened by the popularity of the visitors. The Gentiles who were listening may not have followed the intricacies of Old Testament theology. Yet when Paul directed his message to them, and they understood that eternal life was within their grasp, they declared their joy and praise to the Lord whose word they heard.

Luke sees the salvation of the Gentiles as a matter of appointment. The verb *tassō* has the basic sense of "to arrange, determine," "to appoint," or "to set up." All these senses occur in the Old Testament. F. F. Bruce sees a strong predestination taught here and opposes toning down the force of this appointment. He cites papyrus evidence that *tassō* can mean "inscribe" or "enroll." He understands the meaning in this way: "all, in fact, who had been enrolled for eternal life in the records of heaven."[16]

Though I. H. Marshall admits that a predestinarian interpretation is possible, he says,

> It could also refer to those who had already put their trust in God in accordance with the Old Testament revelation of his grace and were enrolled in his people, or perhaps it means that the Gentiles believed in virtue of the fact that God's plan of redemption included them.[17]

On this side Delling observes, "*hosoi* hardly means that a specific number was appointed but distinguishes converts from other hearers."[18]

Without question, the basic sense of *tassō* is to set or appoint. The passive voice seems to point to God as the agent. However, we question that Luke intends this to point to some pretemporal election of certain ones so that they,

---

[15]The clause reads: *kai episteusan hosoi ēsan tetagmenoi eis zōēn aiōnion.*

[16]Bruce, *Commentary on the Book of the Acts*, 283. He cites texts from the Old Testament, New Testament, Pseudepigrapha, and the Rabbis to defend the idea of enrollment in something like a book of life. See pp. 283–84 for his evidence. See also Lake/Cadbury, *The Beginnings of Christianity*, 160.

[17]Marshall, *The Acts of the Apostles*, 231.

[18]G. Delling, *TDNT*, 8:28.

and only they, come to believe. This would fit poorly in the context. The Jews' rejection of the Word of God accounted for their failure to gain eternal life. They did not consider themselves worthy of eternal life (v. 46).

What a contrast to the Gentiles who, upon hearing the good news, rejoice, honor the Word, and believe. Surely in this context Luke does not intend to restrict the application of salvation only to those appointed. Rather he shows that salvation's sphere of application must expand from only Jews to believing Gentiles. We believe that Bruce misread the context. The key issue concerns whether people accept or reject the word of the Lord. Those who reject disqualify themselves from eternal life. On the other side, Luke describes believers as "those who were appointed for eternal life." Neil says of our text:

> It is not in any sense narrowly predestinarian, as if some are scheduled for salvation and others for damnation; the Bible constantly stresses the element of free choice: we may accept or reject the Word of God. In this case the Jews of Antioch as a whole reject the offer of eternal life, while some—but by no means all—of the Gentiles accept it. Those who do accept the Gospel fulfil the purpose of God that all men shall be saved, and by their response they show that they are worthy to be numbered with the saints in heaven.[19]

Thus the believers are "the appointed ones," a title that has obvious parallels to "the chosen ones" we saw in Mk 13:20, 22, 27, par. As did the people of God in the Old Testament, so Christians also considered themselves "the elect." Perhaps we have here a parallel expression. The "appointed" believed. Luke views those who have been appointed as a corporate group; they, as believers, stand over against those who rejected the message.

Acts 14:27

Upon their return to Syrian Antioch after their missionary tour, Paul and Barnabas reported to the church that God had *opened* (*anoigō*) the door of faith to the Gentiles. Does this imply that God selected (certain) Gentiles and opened their

---

[19]W. Neil, *The Acts of the Apostles*, NCB (London: Oliphants, 1973), 161.

hearts so they were able to come to faith? Luke often uses the
metaphor of opening—of eyes (Lk 24:31; Ac 26:18), understanding (Lk 24:45), heart (Ac 16:14), and Scripture (Lk 24:32;
Ac 17:3).[20] What does he intend by this image in this text?

There is no warrant to read election or predestination
into this metaphor. By writing that God had "opened the
door of faith" Luke does not mean that God determined that
some Gentiles would believe. Rather, God creates the
possibilities for mission work and the potential for believing.[21] God appointed Paul to open the eyes of the Gentiles
(Ac 26:18), but not all Gentiles believed. In the gospel the
apostles proclaimed the opportunity of forgiveness and life
to those who would believe. When Luke says, "God . . .
opened the door of faith," he does not disavow the need for
human response (13:39). Though once directed to Israel,
now, Luke observes, the gospel appeals to all people.
Gentiles may now obtain salvation, and God himself has
opened the way. Does that mean this text is elective? Not in
the sense that God has chosen some to believe. It affirms that
God has chosen to throw open the doors of the kingdom to
Gentiles, if they will believe.

GOD'S ELECTIVE ROLE WITH INDIVIDUALS

By far God's choice of individuals accounts for the
largest number of election-related texts in Acts. We shall
discuss God's choice of people in this section, and then
consider God's election of Christ in the final section. Luke's
application of election concepts to individuals is diverse. He
employs a variety of terms, some common and some unique,
to delimit what we see as six kinds of "election." He
addresses several of these in multiple passages.

---

[20]Paul also employs the idea as part of his mission vocabulary to describe
opportunities for ministry (see 1Co 16:9; 2Co 2:12; Col 4:3; cf. Rev. 3:8). Note
that at 2Co 2:12 Paul chose not to go through the open door.

[21]J. Jeremias (*TDNT*, 3:174) says, "In relation to God the expression finds a
place in missionary usage in the two-fold sense that God opens a door for
the missionary . . . , through which he can enter, by giving him a field in
which to work . . . , and also that he opens a door of faith to those who
come to believe . . . by giving them the possibility of believing."

Jesus' Choice of the Twelve Apostles

Acts 1:2

We saw at Lk 6:13 that Luke used the verb *eklegomai* (choose) to specify Jesus' selection or appointment of the twelve. Here he again asserts that Jesus gave instrucion "to the apostles he had *chosen*." Clearly, for Luke, apostles owed their position to the Spirit-led choice of Jesus.[22]

Acts 1:24

Since Jesus had chosen the original twelve (Ac 1:2; Lk 6:13; cf. Jn 6:70), when the believers sought a replacement for the traitor Judas, they naturally prayed that Jesus might show them which person he had *chosen* (*eklegomai*).[23] Jesus alone chose apostles. So, after narrowing down the list of candidates to two, they prayed and cast lots, presuming that Jesus would make his selection.

Thus in the two preceding passages we learn of the divine choice of individuals to serve in the "apostolic ministry" (Ac 1:25). This is not election to salvation, but to a task.

Acts 10:41

In his talk to those in Cornelius' house Peter explained that not all people saw the resurrected Jesus, but only those witnesses *previously chosen* by God. Luke employs the verb *proxeirotoneō*, its only appearance in the New Testament. The verb has two possible senses: to choose or elect before; and to take a preliminary vote. Surely Liddell and Scott correctly see the first sense at Ac 10:41;[24] this is an instance of God's choice. The following phrase clearly identifies the chosen

---

[22]Both Haenchen, *The Acts of the Apostles*, 139, and Marshall, *The Acts of the Apostles*, 57, argue that the prepositional phrase "through the Holy Spirit" should modify "[whom] he had chosen." The Spirit was the source of guidance for Jesus' choice of the Twelve.

[23]Haenchen, *The Acts of the Apostles*, 162, takes God as the subject of the verb *choose*. But in light of the reference to Lord Jesus in 1:21 and Jesus' choosing in 1:2, more likely, *Lord* in 1:24 refers to Jesus.

[24]H. G. Liddell and R. Scott, *A Greek-English Lexicon*, rev. and augmented by H. S. Jones and R. McKenzie (Oxford: Clarendon, 1940), 2:1541.

ones: ". . . us who ate and drank with him after he rose from the dead." These are the apostles whom Christ commissioned to preach (10:42). So we have still a third instance of Jesus' choice of apostles to preach and testify concerning Christ.

God's Choice of the Patriarchs of Israel

Acts 13:17

In Acts Luke never employs the verb *eklegomai* (choose, elect) of God's choice of people for salvation. As noted above, it may refer to God's choice of a course of action (15:7), or to Jesus' choice of apostles (1:2, 24). Now here in 13:17 Paul affirms that God chose Israel's fathers. This corresponds to the usage of the Old Testament (for example, Ne 9:7; Ps 106:23). We do not find here election to salvation but God's choice of specific men to serve him as leaders of his people Israel. In Paul's word to these Antiochans he makes no movement from the Old Testament teaching about God's choice of Israel's national heroes.

God's Call to Mission

Acts 13:2

The Holy Spirit instructed the Antioch church to set apart Barnabas and Saul "for the work to which I have *called* them." If we unpack this clause it reads: the Holy Spirit called Barnabas and Saul to the work. This is the "missionary call." F. F. Bruce observes, "The church's responsibility was to recognize the divine appointment and act accordingly."[25] The verb translated "call" is *proskaleomai* , already discussed above concerning 2:39. God issues his call or summons to a missionary task, not salvation. Also, he chooses a work or ministry for the two men to do. We could have included this in our first section—God's determination of states of affairs. However, this work closely involves the two specific men. God called them to the work. Hence, we put it here in the section for God's elective role with individuals. He chose for them a specific task.

---

[25]Bruce, *The Acts of the Apostles* , 254.

Acts 16:10

Using the same verb for call, *proskaleomai*, Luke again identifies a missionary call. As a result of Paul's vision, he and his company concluded that God had *called* them to evangelize the Macedonians. Again we find God's call of his servants to perform a specific task.

The Salvation of Lydia

Acts 16:14

Many people received salvation in Acts, but Lydia's conversion warrants inclusion because of the language Luke employs: "The Lord opened [*dianoigō*] her heart." Luke also uses *dianoigō* at 17:3, where the NIV translates it "explaining." Paul engaged in this activity so the Jews would come to the truth. It occurs in Lk 24:32 regarding Christ's "explaining" the Scriptures to the disciples. Later in 24:45 Luke says "[Jesus] *opened* their minds" so they could understand the significance of the Old Testament messianic prophecies.

We saw at Ac 14:27 that Luke applied the picture of "opening" to the Gentiles corporately—God opened the door of faith. We noted there that Luke employed the language of mission: to say "God opens doors" means he provides opportunities to preach the gospel, and people can believe and receive salvation (cf. 1Co 16:9; 2Co 2:12; Col 4:3).

So here in 16:14 the open door symbolizes opportunity. As a result of Paul's preaching, God confronted Lydia with the truth. God opened her understanding so she could grasp or respond to the truth of the gospel. This text does not lessen the need for Lydia to exercise faith. The Lord presented her with an open door, and she could go through it or remain outside. Later, still at Philippi, Paul gave his jailor the same opportunity. Luke includes Paul's explicit invitation to the jailor to believe in Jesus (16:31).

God's Appointment of Overseers

Acts 20:28

According to the account in Acts Paul appointed elders (or had elders appointed) in the churches he founded (14:23;

cf. Php 1:1; Tit 1:5). Yet in his speech to the Ephesian elders (20:17–35), Paul reminds them, "The Holy Spirit has *made* [*etheto*] you overseers." We saw above that Jesus selected the Twelve for their ministry of apostleship. The appointment of elders parallels Jesus' action. Paul wants these Ephesian leaders to sense the gravity of their roles as Holy Spirit appointees.[26] God selected individuals for the task of overseeing local churches.

God's Choice of Paul as an Apostle

Acts 9:15

In Luke's account of Saul's conversion God gives instructions to a disciple named Ananias. Ananias must go to Saul, God says, for "This man is my *chosen* instrument to carry my name before the Gentiles and their kings and before the people of Israel." The word translated "chosen," *eklogē*, was common in secular Greek (though absent from the LXX). It referred to the act of selection or choice. Paul uses it five times,[27] but elsewhere in the New Testament it occurs only here and in 2Pe 1:10. The construction, literally, "instrument of choice," is a Hebraic genitive, implying a chosen instrument.[28] So, God had chosen Saul. The words that follow make clear that the context and purpose of God's election of Saul is mission. As Schrenk puts it, "Paul has an *eklogē* to apostolic tasks before nations, kings and the children of Israel."[29] Unquestionably, God chose Paul for ministry. God selected Paul to be his instrument of witness to Gentiles and Jews. Luke's use of *eklogē* emphasizes election to ministry, not election to salvation.

Acts 13:47

Paul and Barnabas quote Isa 49:6 to defend the change of their focus of ministry to Gentiles. Luke has already applied

---

[26]Bruce suggests a helpful clarification: "Probably the reference to the Holy Spirit here does not mean that their appointment to this sacred ministry had been commanded by prophetic utterance in the church, but rather that they were so appointed and recognized because they were manifestly men on whom the Holy Spirit had bestowed the requisite qualifications for their work" (*Commentary on the Book of the Acts*, 416).

[27]Ro 9:11; 11:5, 7, 28; 1Th 1:4.

[28]So Bruce, *The Acts of the Apostles*, 201.

[29]G. Schrenk, *TDNT*, 4:179.

this prophecy (of the Servant of Yahweh) to Jesus (Lk 2:32). Now he has Paul apply it to Jesus' ambassadors. The interesting phrase for us is: "I *have made* [*tetheika*] you a light for the Gentiles," using the same verb *tithēmi* that he used in speaking of the appointment of overseers (Ac 20:28). So we have a similar idea: Paul is conscious of his divine appointment. God appointed him for his apostolic ministry.

Acts 22:10

We discussed Luke's use of the verb *tassō* in Ac 13:48 where he says that people were "appointed for eternal life." The verb can mean appoint, arrange, or determine. In Paul's explanation of his Damascus road experience he uses *tassō*, not in relation to eternal life, but to his own apostolic work. Unpacked, the text says that God had *appointed* Paul to do certain things. Here is another reference to Paul's appointment to his role as an apostle. We must not take *tassō* in too deterministic a way. God did not predetermine every facet of Paul's future life. Paul affirms his divine appointment to ministry. Delling clarifies: "God has arranged the commission which results for Paul from his experience on the Damascus road."[30]

Acts 22:14

Continuing his personal defense before the crowd in Jerusalem, Paul quotes Ananias: "The God of our Fathers *has chosen* (emphasis mine) you to know his will and to see the Righteous One and to hear words from his mouth. You will be his witness to all men of what you have seen and heard" (22:14–15).

Luke uses the verb translated "has chosen," *proxeirizomai*,[31] for Christ's appointment (3:20; below) and again for Paul at 26:16. God's choice of Paul centers on what God will reveal to him. As the result of this insight, Paul will be a witness to

---

[30]G. Delling, *TDNT*, 8:28.

[31]The literal sense "to take into one's hand" when referring to people has the meaning of "choose" or "appoint." In the LXX it has the sense of "elect" or "name" (Jos 3:12; 2Mc 3:7; 8:9). The *pro*—is not a temporal prefix. The word comes from the adjective *proxeiros*, "to have readily to hand." Thus there is no inherent temporal sense—*pre*destination, only choice or appointment.

all people. So, with this scenario before him, Paul had to respond to Ananias' appeal (22:16). Paul needed to act. With profound language Ananias urges Paul to call on the name of the Lord (cf. Ac 2:21; Rom 10:13), to wash his sins away (cf. Ac 2:38), and be baptized (cf. Ac 16:31–33). Paul has an apostolic commission before him, but still he must heed the exhortation: "Get yourself baptized and get your sins washed away."[32] God chose to grant Paul revelation that he will proclaim to the world. The first step was to commit his life to Jesus the Christ.

Primarily, this marks Paul's apostolic appointment— appointment for service in the world. It may be difficult to separate Paul's salvation from his apostolic commission here, but the focus is surely on mission rather than on salvation. Paul had to apprehend God's salvation if he was to fulfill his commission. God's choice notwithstanding, Paul needed to act to bring himself in line with God's will.

Acts 26:16

This text virtually duplicates the previous one. Again Paul uses *proxeirizomai* to convey his *appointment* by Christ. The Lord says, "I have appeared to you to appoint you as a servant and as a witness." The text of 26:16–18 is an extended appointment to ministry, and in v. 19 Paul affirms that he responded positively to the Lord's instructions. This complements the previous text, 22:14–16. So we conclude that the appointment expresses God's will for Paul, marking the role and ministries God intended for him to undertake. Paul obeyed God's will for him. The texts clearly emphasize Paul's appointment to ministry or election to a task.

GOD'S CHOICE OF CHRIST AND HIS CAREER

God's choice of Christ demarcates the final category into which we have divided the Acts texts that have some elective significance. In our study of the synoptics we saw their treatment of the election of this special Individual. In Acts there are seven texts that employ election language that

---

[32]Bruce, *The Acts of the Apostles*, 403, thus brings out the force of the middle voices in *baptisai* and *apolousai* (baptize and wash).

merit analysis. The term *horizō* occurs in three texts, and so we will consider them together.

Acts 2:23

In Peter's Pentecost sermon he states that Jesus' crucifixion, though perpetrated by men, took place "by God's set purpose and foreknowledge" (*tē hōrismenē boulē kai prognōsei tou theou*). This instrumental phrase includes three important words: *horizō*, *boulē*, and *prognōsis*. God not only knew beforehand that the awful event of crucifixion would occur, but it happened by means of his determined will. *Boulē* usually specifies God's will in the New Testament; it implies his "counsel, intention or purpose." Thus God's *will* stands behind the Cross. Here *horizō* modifies *boulē*. Thus his will is *fixed* or determined (recall Ac 17:26 and Lk 22:22). No haphazard or accidental event, the Cross carefully worked out the purposes of God.

The third concept behind the Cross is God's foreknowledge. The noun *prognōsis* occurs only here and at 1Pe 1:2 in the New Testament. In 1Pe 1:2, election and God's foreknowledge work together (we will return to this text later). The verb *proginōskō* occurs five times in the New Testament,[33] including Ac 26:5, which exemplifies its basic sense, "to know beforehand." The Jews had previous knowledge of Paul; prior to the present time, they knew him. Likewise 2Pe 3:17 displays this basic sense.

Thus, if we adopt this face-value meaning, Luke insists that God not only determined the Cross, but he knew ahead of time precisely all that it would involve. Long before it occurred, God knew the awfulness of Calvary. The Cross had no unforeseen developments or an unanticipated outcome.

"Foreknown" might suggest a further nuance. As in Ac 26:5, the idea of prior knowledge might also be the intent here. Perhaps Peter intends that God has revealed through his prophets how the Christ would suffer these things and then enter his glory (Lk 24:25–26). The Cross has been foreknown in that God has prophesied that it should take

---

[33]Ac 26:5; Ro 8:29; 11:2; 1Pe 1:20; 2Pe 3:17. The terms *prognōsis* and *proginōskō* occur five times in the LXX, but only in the apocrypha: WS 6:13; 8:8; 18:6; Jth 9:6; 11:19.

place. If we adopt this interpretation, then this text parallels the synoptists' use of *graphō* (written) in Mt 26:24; Mk 14:21 and *horizō* in Lk 22:22. Either understanding of "foreknowledge" fits the context well.

Thus Jesus is God's chosen agent, the One whom he destined or appointed to die to accomplish God's purposes. All this coincided with God's eternal foreknowledge.

Acts 10:42

The second use of *horizō* to refer to Christ occurs in Peter's talk to Cornelius' household. Peter states that Jesus commissioned the apostles to preach and testify that God *appointed* Jesus to be judge. Again we find appointment for a mission—Jesus as God's chosen judge.

Acts 17:31

Before the Areopagites Paul affirmed that God had set a day when he would judge the world by a man whom he *appointed*. The man (*anēr*) appointed judge must be Jesus, as in 10:42. The aorist tense underscores the past appointment. God selected him to serve as judge of the world.

Acts 3:20

In Peter's second sermon he promises to those who repent that God will "send the Christ, who has been *appointed* for [them]." Here the NIV translates *proxeirizomai* as "appoint," as at 26:16, though at 22:14 the translators use "chosen," both very acceptable interpretations. Thus, as God appointed Paul to be an apostle to preach the gospel, so God appointed (perfect tense) Jesus to be Messiah, with all that entails.[34] Again Luke relates an election to a task or role. Jesus exists as the Appointed One.

---

[34]See Bruce, *The Acts of the Apostles*, 112, and Marshall, *The Acts of the Apostles*, 93–94. Both Haenchen, *The Acts of the Apostles*, 208, and Lake/Cadbury, *The Beginnings of Christianity*, 38, see the temporal idea—forechosen, but Bruce doubts it.

Acts 4:28

To a great extent this verse repeats the thought of 2:23. Discussing Jesus' crucifixion, Luke again asserts that God's *boulē* (will, purpose) stands behind the events. The believers confess in prayer that the violent acts against Jesus were precisely what God's hand and will (*boulē*) determined beforehand (*proorizō*). This is the only non-Pauline use of *proorizō*; Paul uses it five times. In 2:23 Luke wrote of God's *determined* (*horizō*) purpose; here he refers to God's *pre*determined plan. Jesus, a man under appointment, fulfilled God's mission, even to the point of death. He accomplished God's purposes that were worked out in advance.

Acts 13:29

This text continues the theme of Jesus' execution. Here Paul uses a different image to convey, again, that these acts against Jesus were in some sense predestined, or at least foreknown. He refers to "all that was *written* about him," an image we detected in the synoptics. Mt 26:24 and Mk 14:21 also suggested the idea of prophetic destiny as a possible interpretation of *prognōsis* in Ac 2:23. The need for Scripture to be fulfilled in Jn 19:28 might also complement this idea. Thus Jesus' career, especially his passion, was prophesied in advance. God appointed Jesus for his salvific mission.

SUMMARY

The book of the Acts presents a different picture than the Synoptic Gospels. Though employing many parallels in concepts and terminology, the Acts lays a greater stress on the place of individuals. It gives surprisingly little space to the idea that the emerging church is God's elect body. Luke orients his theology around mission, and that theme certainly controls his discussion of election.

Luke speaks of God's role in choosing or determining specific events or circumstances in the world (a category we did not discover in the synoptics). God alone determined eschatological timetables (1:7) and the times and places of habitation of the nations (17:26). He provided for peoples' welfare not merely in regulating where they would live but, specifically, by choosing a way for the Gentiles to hear the gospel (15:7). God's determinative will operates in human affairs such that people are fools to make plans apart from acknowledging his will (18:21; 21:14). These texts, though informing us somewhat about God's immanence in the affairs of this world, provide no illumination about the issue of salvation.

Several texts do point us to God's elective role with people. From Peter's Pentecost sermon we hear that God *calls* people (2:39). God's promise encompasses the Jews and the Gentiles, but it applies only to those whom God calls. We saw in Mt 22:14 that the "called" are invited but not necessarily saved, that is, "chosen." Luke's uses in Acts admit of no such explanation. They fit with the technical sense that Paul employs. The "called" are the saved; they have appropriated the promise (2:39) and bear God's name (15:17). This naming sense is critical for, we feel, it provides the key that explains what Paul understands by "calling." To be a Christian is to be called (cf. Mt 5:9).

Not only are people called, but they are appointed (13:48). Luke observes that God's appointed ones came to believe. We argued against seeing this as restrictive when the context is liberating. God has not restricted the gospel of salvation to Jews; he offers the good news to all. Those who are enrolled for eternal life are those who believe. The appointed ones are those who come to faith.

The text of Ac 13:48 is the closest Luke comes to suggesting that God might determine who will believe: those enrolled for eternal life believe. We noted that some interpreters do see this as God's election of some to salvation. However, though this describes God's appointment of believers, it does not necessarily imply a pretemporal election. In fact, there are no temporal elements in the context, only those that relate immediately to the historical situation at Antioch. The Jews rejected the gospel and disqualified themselves from salvation. The Gentiles believed and entered the category of the appointed ones. Luke's commentary at 14:27 is germane here. God determined to set before the Gentiles an open door. In contrast to previous days, now they have an unparalleled opportunity to hear and respond to the gospel. As our next point will show, God has raised up many spokesmen to accomplish this very thing—to proclaim salvation to the Gentiles (cf.

2:39; 15:7). Thus, "all who were appointed" seems to be a category similar to "the chosen ones" where Luke stresses their status as ones who belong to God and ones who owe all they are and have to God's provision. We regard it less likely that here Luke makes a theological affirmation that in some past eternity God selected specific Gentiles for salvation.[35]

Many texts operate more on the individual level. Our study in the Old Testament alerts us to expect God's choice of individuals to serve him in some task or function. Indeed, we find abundant instances of this. Luke describes Israel's patriarchs as chosen (13:17). The Acts recognizes Jesus' choice of the Twelve (1:2; 10:41), so much so that even Judas' replacement must be chosen by the Lord (1:24). God called Paul and Barnabas to specific missionary tasks (13:2; 16:10) and appointed overseers to serve the local congregation at Ephesus (20:28). Luke repeatedly emphasizes Paul's appointment as an apostle. He highlights the tasks God called Paul to perform, particularly the commission to carry God's name both to Gentiles and Jews (9:15; 13:47). God appoints Paul to be an apostle—one sent on God's behalf (22:10) to bear witness to what he had revealed to Paul (22:14; 26:16).

The one text not related to ministry concerned Lydia's conversion (16:14). God opened her heart to receive Paul's message. Is this an example of the "efficacious actions" mentioned above that accounts for the faith of those "who were appointed for eternal life"? After surveying the uses of the "open" metaphor elsewhere and the specific use at 14:27,

---

[35]What if "God's appointment to eternal life" does in some way stand as an explanation for the faith of those who believe? Then all those who come to believe have already been appointed or enrolled for eternal life. Yet, even this is not unambiguous. It could mean (1) that God's appointment implies God's efficacious actions to bring the person to the point of conversion. God appoints some people, and so he insures that they come to faith. This is the Calvinist explanation. However, the phase could mean (2) that the appointment exists in God's (fore)knowledge. Just as the events of Christ's crucifixion could be foreknown by God (2:23), so the names of those who would come to believe might be said to be enrolled in God's book (cf. Lk 10:20; Rev 13:8; 20:15; 21:27). But the fact of such foreknowledge need not imply causality (any more than God caused the Fall). Thus it might be argued that, knowing who will believe, metaphorically speaking, God has enrolled their names in the book of eternal life. This in no way diminishes the need for each person to exercise faith. Their appointment reflects their foreseen faith; it does not explain or determine it. This is more like the Arminian position. Again, the appointed are the chosen; they are God's special people.

we rejected that explanation. By being opened, Lydia had the gospel and its implications explained to her. When the missionaries confronted her with the truth of salvation, she had the chance to respond to Paul's message. In fact she did, and immediately submitted to baptism (16:15). Explaining the way of salvation, the gospel confronts people with the truth. When people hear this good news, they can respond (that is, believe).

In such a way the Lord opened Lydia's heart. We see here an important factor in the conversion of people—God's truth meets them head-on. Luke does not imply that God selected Lydia and specially enabled her to believe. Presumably Lydia had to do exactly what Paul told the jailor to do: "Believe in the Lord Jesus, and you will be saved" (16:31). Had she refused, she would have been in the condition of so many of the Jews reported in Acts (e.g., 13:46; 18:6–7).

The synoptics presented Jesus as God's Chosen One, and Acts shares this view. God appointed Jesus to be the Messiah (3:20). More specifically, God appointed Jesus for his salvific mission; the Crucifixion occurred by means of God's predetermined will (2:23; 4:28). Far from being an accident or a mission-gone-awry, Jesus' earthly career—including his death—followed the course that was foreknown and prophesied (2:23; 13:29). God also appointed Jesus for a task as yet unaccomplished: he will serve as judge of all people (10:42; 17:31). We readily see that the appointment of Jesus in Acts exists for service, following the pattern for other individuals noted above. God has chosen and appointed Jesus to accomplish his will. Jesus fulfilled his mission as the Messiah who died and who will come again to judge.

7

THE JOHANNINE
LITERATURE

Moving from the Synoptic Gospels and Acts, we turn to the fourth gospel. In addition, we consider here the remaining writings attributed to John since they share much in common and all seem to derive from the same source. The fourth gospel really provides the bulk of material to consider in this chapter, although the epistles and the Apocalypse add several interesting bits to the discussion. In analyzing the results of our exegeses of the applicable texts and passages, we discovered seven categories that capture the Johannine perspective. Several of these match what we observed in the synoptics or Acts, but several represent new directions. John travels his own route on some issues and formulates his positions in novel ways.

GOD'S LOVE FOR PEOPLE

In the synoptics we encountered the use of "beloved" (*agapētos*) as a description of Jesus, the Son. The Father's elective love laid hold of Jesus for his messianic task. As well, we noted in our survey of the Old Testament data that God's love explains his choice of Israel (Dt 7:6–9). With this backdrop we observe immediately John's use of love terms.

We need not consider every use of these words; several will give us the sense of the concept.

John 3:16

In this first occurrence of the verb *agapaō* (love),[1] Jesus asserts that God loved the world. He demonstrated this love by (or, this love consists of his) giving his Son. So, in brief, we cannot conclude that this "love" is elective in the sense that God has chosen some. Nor does this "love" imply a special relationship with some. The application of God's love is unlimited, for he has universally provided for the sins of the world (3:17–18). Though God's love is especially effective or operative in the lives of believers, we cannot dismiss here God's love for all humanity, including unbelievers.[2] Having said that, however, I also contend that John does not affirm universalism. People must decide to believe or they stand condemned (3:18). Love stands behind the costly step God took to make salvation available to the world. But God's love does not determine who will attain salvation; salvation is for *pas ho pisteuōn*—all who believe.

---

[1]This verb is clearly a favorite in the fourth gospel and the Johannine epistles. It occurs 37 times in the Gospel (cf. Mt, 8; Mk, 5; Lk, 13) and 28 times in 1 John, but only 34 times in the traditional Pauline corpus. In total, in the Johannine writings the verb occurs 72 out of its 143 times in the New Testament, more than 50 percent.

[2]Of course, this statement could be challenged. For example, C. R. Bowen, "Love in the Fourth Gospel," *JR* 13 (1933): 39–49, argues that Jn 3:16 cannot really mean that God loved the whole cosmos. Rather, he sees this divine love to be extended only to those "in the world" who were "his own"—that is, those who believe. Bowen says of those who did not believe and perished, "There is no hint that God loved them and yearned over them; they were simply not *his*" (46; his emphasis). The only way Bowen can reconcile what he sees as a Johannine exclusivistic love (only for Christians) with the synoptic sayings to love enemies or neighbors, is to posit different "Jesuses," coming out of different gospel milieux. Nor can John's "Jesus" be reconciled with Paul's exhortations to love outsiders, et al.

However, the problem turns out to be Bowen's "Jesuses," or, rather, his exegesis. Admittedly, the exhortations to love in the Johannine writings are mostly directed internally to members of the community. But the needs of the recipients determine this. The expressions of God's love often are directed to the world, though it has a special application to believers. This is evident in 1Jn 4:9–10. God's love is never exclusivistic or parochial; but it must be appropriated by faith. See also Jn 15:13.

John 17:23

Another possible instance of God's love for the world occurs in Jesus' prayer. Jesus prays for unity for his disciples so the world would know that God loves *them* (*autous*), as he loves Jesus. Lindars argues that *them* here refers to the world, so Jesus prays that the church's united life "displays and effects God's love for mankind."[3] If Lindars is right, like Jn 3:16 this verse affirms God's love for all people, though not specific individuals. But surely Lindars errs here. The thought of God's love for the disciples dominates the Johannine language of love. In addition, the context of Jn 14–17 concerns the Christian community in contrast to the world which hates the believers (cf. 14:30–31; 15:18–19; 16:8–11; 17:6, 9, 16, 25). Jesus intends that Christian unity demonstrate to the world that God loves Christians; his love explains their unity.[4]

1 John 4:9–11, 16, 19

These texts represent the large number of Johannine verses that affirm God's love—in sending his Son to die, and specifically, his love for believers. John characterizes God's nature and activity as love or loving. God is love (4:8), and he loved his own when he sent his Son (4:10–11). Though common for John, these expressions do not convey election in any partitive sense. God's love does not explain why only some become disciples. Rather, it reaches its fulfillment when Christians appropriate it and express love to him and one another (4:12). However, John does not say God has loved "us" but not "them." God loves all believers. Love characterizes all in God's family. Likewise, Christ's love for his children remains constant (Rev 1:5; present tense use of verb *to love*).

---

[3]B. Lindars, *The Gospel of John*, NCB (London: Oliphants, 1972), 531.

[4]L. Morris (*The Gospel According to John*, NICNT [Grand Rapids: Eerdmans, 1971], 736) and R. E. Brown (*The Gospel According to John*, AB, 2 vols. [Garden City, NY: Doubleday, 1966, 1970], 2:771) support this latter interpretation.

GOD'S KNOWLEDGE OF HIS PEOPLE

Though words that we translate "know" abound in the Johannine literature,[5] on surprisingly few occasions do we actually find references to God or Jesus "knowing" people, and specifically, disciples.

John 10:14, 27

Using the sheep/shepherd metaphor Jesus states, "I *know* my sheep," adding, "my sheep know me," and "they follow me." Schnackenburg explains,

> The term *ginōskein* does not denote knowledge of the theoretical-rational kind but, in an Old Testament-Semitic sense, a personal bond, a knowing that leads on to communion.[6]

He deduces from this that Jesus' knowing here conveys election "in overtones." Jesus' knowledge of them enables them to know him in turn. Though Schnackenburg explains *ginōskō* correctly, we question his use of the word *election* here. Jesus focuses on the mutual-knowing relationship between him and his sheep; it corresponds to the reciprocal knowing between Jesus and the Father (10:15). If by "election overtones" Schnackenburg simply means that the sheep are in some sense Jesus' chosen ones, enjoying that special status, we can agree. Yet Jesus gives no hint here that he selected these specific disciples to be his sheep. We fail to discover that concept in *know* here.[7]

---

[5]Just considering verbs, *ginōskō* (I know) occurs 56 times in the fourth gospel, 26 times in the Johannine epistles and four times in Revelation (cf. Mt, 20; Mk, 12; Lk, 28; and Paul, 50). The verb *oida* (I know) occurs eighty-five times in John, sixteen times in the epistles and twelve times in Revelation (Matthew, 25; Mark, 22; Luke, 25; and Paul, 103). For the sake of comparison, the total word count in John's gospel is slightly less than half that of the traditional Pauline corpus.

[6]R. Schnackenburg, *The Gospel According to St. John*, 3 vols. (New York: Herder and Herder; London: Burns & Oates, 1968, 1980, 1982), 2:297.

[7]Potterie nicely summarizes what we do find: "Il s'agit d'une connaissance mutuelle, comme celle qui existe entre amis: elle inclut sympathie réciproque, amour, communauté de nature" (I. de la Potterie, "*oida* et *ginōskō*. Les deux modes de la connaissance dans le quatrième évangile," *Biblica* 40 (1959): 714.

John 13:11, 18

Using a second word for know, *oida*, John explains that Jesus *knew* who was going to betray him (13:11). Further, Jesus says, "I *know* those I have chosen" (13:18). We must return to verse 18 below to learn the meaning of *chosen*, but for now we consider only *know*. Yet we find little to say. Jesus *knows* the caliber of his disciples—the type of men they all are, including Judas. The word *caliber* is suggested by *tinas* (those): "I know *what kind* I have chosen," even a man like Judas. But the sense of *know* here is surely less intimate or mutual than *know* at 10:14 and 27. The context here implies a more cognitive sense—recognition, possession of information. We can see no election here.

THE ELECTION OF INDIVIDUALS

Though the synoptic Evangelists refer to Jesus' choice or appointment of the Twelve in only one place (Mt 10:1; Mk 13:13–14; Lk 6:13), John mentions this action on four occasions, using the verb *eklegomai* (choose). The texts we locate here stress Jesus' appointment of the Twelve to be apostles. (In sections F and G below, we consider the texts that concern salvation.) First we appraise a text that identifies the Baptist's role.

John 3:27

John's disciples sensed a growing crisis in their ministry. Jesus was increasing in popularity. More and more people flocked to him, while John's cause was on the wane (3:26). In response John explained his own role as forerunner and the reason for Jesus' popularity with the crowds. Cryptically John affirmed that a person can only receive "what is given" to him from God. Brown takes the statement to mean that God dispenses the privilege of coming to John or Jesus. God gives people, so here he gives more followers to Jesus and fewer to John.[8] However, the context argues for a different understanding, that "what is given" refers not to converts but to roles. God is responsible for John's role as forerunner and Jesus' role as Messiah. God has given John to be the

---

[8]R. E. Brown, *The Gospel According to John*, AB, 1:155–56.

"friend" and Jesus to be the "bridegroom" (3:29). Since God has given, John is content with the role God assigned to him.[9] We find again that God appoints people to ministries: God has chosen that John be the forerunner, while Jesus is to be Messiah. This is election to a task or ministry.

John 6:70

Jesus' popularity did not last, for many of his disciples began to desert him (6:66). Would the Twelve abandon Jesus too? In response Peter affirmed their belief in Jesus as "the Holy One of God" (6:69), a clear statement of his deity.[10] They had found the giver of eternal life; why go elsewhere?

Jesus responded to this confession with something we might expect, but also something very puzzling. As expected, Jesus affirms their election. More suprising, he affirms the election of *all* twelve, including Judas whom he terms *diabolos*, a devil! We might expect Jesus to say, "I know you won't desert me, for you are my chosen ones." That is, "You are all saved." But in this text Jesus departs from the synoptic use of *eklektoi* (chosen ones), which referred exclusively to the "saved" (e.g., Mt 22:14; Mk 13:20; Lk 18:7). Here Jesus does not catalog those chosen *soteriologically*, but those individuals chosen *for a task or ministry* (as at Lk 6:13).[11]

Jesus knew that although Peter affirmed a corporate faith (6:69), in fact Judas did not share that belief. Jesus also

---

[9]Calvin correctly applies this to John's ministry (*The Gospel According to St. John, 1–10* [Edinburgh, London: Oliver & Boyd, 1959], 80). So does Schnackenburg, who says, "Jesus could not have attracted so many men to him if God had not given him the power to do so" (*The Gospel According to St. John,* I:415). Thus the appointment of roles determines the "prosperity" of their ministries.

[10]Procksch (*TDNT,* 1:102) shows how John consistently applies the adjective *hagios* (holy) to God in passages like John 17:11; Revelation 3:7. "Thus in all the passages adduced *hagios* is used to describe the deity of Christ." C. K. Barrett takes "Holy One of God" to be a messianic title. "Jesus is the emissary of God; in Jewish terms the Messiah, more generally, the Holy One of God, who comes from God and goes to God" (*The Gospel According to St. John,* 2d ed. [London: SPCK, 1978], 307). Likewise Morris says, "There can be not the slightest doubt that the title is meant to assign to Jesus the highest possible place. It stresses His consecration and His purity. It sets Him with God and not man" (*The Gospel According to John,* 390).

[11]Calvin also assigns the use of *chosen* here, not to the "eternal purpose of God" but rather choice to apostolic office (*The Gospel According to St. John, 1–10,* 1:179).

knew that his group of chosen ones included Judas (13:18). So Jesus was expressing again his reservations, parallel to 2:24–25: "But Jesus would not entrust himself to them, for he knew all men. He did not need man's testimony about man, for he knew what was in a man." In effect he says, "You say you all believe, but have I not chosen you twelve? I know that one of you is a devil." We get no hint here why Jesus chose one he knew to be *diabolos*, though an answer emerges in our next text (13:18). Whatever we say, this text affirms Judas as chosen. So either Judas was elect salvifically and forfeited his election—a unique instance of such a teaching—or this election parallels other examples of God's choice of individuals to a task (recall Saul forfeited his election as king). We say more on this in the next section.

John 13:18

We return to this verse, where the verb *eklegomai* (choose) occurs. The pericope preceding this verse includes Jesus' washing of the disciples' feet and his accompanying instructions for them. At this point his teaching had the ever-present backdrop of the betrayer (13:10–11). He taught them while aware that for Judas the teaching did not apply. John makes this explicit in 13:18: "I am not referring to all of you; I know those I have chosen." We could understand "chosen" here in either of two senses. Possibly Jesus means, "I know whom I have *really* chosen, and, of course, I would never choose a scoundrel like Judas." But Jesus' statement at 6:70—"Have I not chosen you, the Twelve?"—and the following quotation in 13:18 argue for another meaning. In fact, Jesus knows even Judas, who is one of the chosen apostles. Election includes the choice of one who was not clean (13:10–11), who would actively set himself against Jesus (13:18), and who was in league with Satan (13:27; cf. 6:70).

Barrett posits an ellipse between the word *chosen* and the following clause. The complete idea really is: "I know whom I have chosen: therefore I know that Judas is a traitor, but I have chosen him in order that . . ."[12] The quote from Ps 41:9 gives the reason Jesus selected Judas to be in his close

---

[12]Barrett, *The Gospel According to St. John*, 444.

fellowship, even though he knew what kind of person Judas was. This seems accurate. Though Judas was in no way required or forced to betray Jesus, he was allowed into Jesus' band of disciples where he would have the freedom and opportunity to rebel and thus fulfill his prophetic destiny.

Thus, we argue, Jesus chose Judas, not for salvation, but to perform a task. He had every opportunity, like the others, to receive salvation on God's terms—to believe and accept Jesus as Lord—but Judas refused. The Scriptures are clear that Judas bears full responsibility for his rebellious betrayal, as we have seen (Mt 26:24, par.; Lk 22:22). Jesus chose him to enter the apostolic band, and with full freedom Judas chose the path prophesied long ago. No doubt Jesus tolerated a traitor in his midst because he understood these prophecies. And so Judas exchanged the task of apostleship for the role of traitor.

Could it be that Judas was chosen in some salvific sense but failed to actualize his election, as the others did? If so, what would election mean? It would not mean choice or recognition of a special status at all. John does not write that all people are elect. The fourth gospel predicates election only upon the Twelve, and 2Jn 1 and 13 predicate it upon local congregations. The only forfeiture of election that makes sense is nonsalvific selection for a task. The uniform New Testament use of *salvific* election is that the elect are believers, the holy ones, the church. If Jesus calls Judas elect in some salvific sense and then calls him a devil, election has little meaning. But if he chose Judas for a task, Judas could either do it or not do it. This makes the best sense of the evidence. Even Judas' betrayal fulfilled the divine plan (Acts 2:23).

John 15:16

Still a third time Jesus uses choose (*eklegomai*), but here he adds the verb appoint (*tithēmi*). At the end of his vine/branches discourse to the eleven disciples, Jesus assured them that they were his friends (not simply servants) to whom he had revealed everything he had learned from his Father (15:15). He assured them, "I chose you" and added, "I [appointed] you." The initiative for the relationship between Jesus and the disciples lay with Jesus (emphatic *egō*,

I), not with them. He chose them. But more, he appointed[13] them to go and produce lasting fruit. The purpose for the election was mission.

Has John changed his meaning of *choose* now that Judas had departed? No, this is clearly appointment for ministry and probably parallels the synoptic sense in Mk 3:13–14, where Jesus "appoints" (*poieō*; Lk 6:13 says, "choose," *eklegomai*) the Twelve for ministry. Calvin agrees this is "election by which He appointed His disciples to the office of preaching the Gospel."[14] This is election of individuals to a task.

John 15:19

Immediately Jesus assures and reminds the Eleven that he *chose* (aorist) them out of the world, again employing the emphatic *egō*—*I* chose you. Since Jesus chose them, they possess values and affections distinct from those of the world. Thus, as they follow and serve him, they can expect the same treatment that the world gave to Jesus—hatred and persecution. No new insight about the nature of this choosing emerges here. We can only assume it reflects the previous uses, especially 15:16. The context of 15:18–16:4 is clearly ministry. This fits our previous assessment of election to service, not salvation.

THE TASK OF THE ONLY SON

The evidence of the synoptics and Acts established the pattern of God's choice of the Son as a special category within his choice of individuals for ministry. John also gives a special role for the appointment of the Son, revolving primarily around two words, *monogenēs* and *thelēma*. We will discuss them in that sequence and then add a text mentioned earlier.

---

[13]It is surprising that the NIV (1978) translators simply omitted *tithēmi* entirely. Most versions do render it "appoint" (e.g., RSV, NEB, PHILLIPS) or "ordain" (KJV).

[14]J. Calvin, *The Gospel According to St. John, 11–21 and the First Epistle of John* (Edinburgh & London: Oliver & Boyd, 1961), 2:102.

Monogenēs

This Greek word occurs nine times in the New Testament, four of which are outside of John's writings and either mean an "only child" (Lk 7:12; 8:42; 9:38), or imply someone "special" or "unique," as was Isaac, the "one and only son" of Abraham (Heb 11:17). Isaac was not Abraham's only-begotten son. The other five uses of *monogenēs* occur in the Johannine writings (Jn 1:14, 18; 3:16, 18; 1Jn 4:9). The background of the term in the LXX is perplexing. The word translates the Hebrew *yāhîd* to designate an only child (Judg 11:34) or means "sole" or "precious" (Pss 21:21 LXX; 24:16 LXX; 34:17 LXX). However, the Greek word *agapētos* (beloved) also translates *yāhîd* in the LXX (Gen 22:2, 12, 16; Jer 6:26; Am 8:10; Zec 12:10). Apparently, *monogenēs* and *agapētos* overlap in meaning,[15] though we cannot say they are synonyms.

In explaining what John means when he calls Jesus the *monogenēs*, there are two options, or schools of thought, both represented by able defenders. The first position holds that Jesus is the "only begotten Son"; he is an only child, the only one begotten by his Father.[16] Defenders point to the following: his relation to the Father in 1:14; the context of giving birth in 1:13; the frequent sense in both testaments (and Josephus [*Ant* V 264; XX 20]) of an only child; and the substitutability of *agapētos*, which often means beloved son. The use of "son" in 3:16 also points to begetting, they contend.

The alternate position is that *monogenēs* is a qualitative attribution of uniqueness. Jesus is special, "one of a kind," the "one and only" son.[17] Proponents note several points.

---

[15]It is often observed that an only child is particularly beloved by his or her parents (cf. Mk 12:6).

[16]Supporters include Barrett (*The Gospel According to St. John*, 166); F. Büchsel (*TDNT*, 4:740); R. Bultmann (*The Gospel of John. A Commentary* [Oxford: Blackwell, 1971], 72–74, n. 2); J. V. Dahms ("The Johannine Use of Monogenēs Reconsidered," *NTS* 29 [1983]:222–32); Lindars (*The Gospel of John*, 96); and Schnackenburg (*The Gospel According to St. John*, 1:271).

[17]The roll of supporters includes: A. E. Brooke (*Johannine Epistles*, ICC [Edinburgh: T. & T. Clark, 1912], 119); Brown (*The Gospel According to John*, 1:13–14); Th. C. de Kruijf "The Glory of the Only Son (John 1:14)," in *Studies in John* [Sevenster *Festschrift*], Suppl. *NovT* 24 [Leiden: Brill, 1970]); I. H. Marshall (*The Epistles of John*, NICNT [Grand Rapids: Eerdmans, 1978], 214, n. 8); Morris (*The Gospel According to John*, 105); D. Moody ("God's Only Son:

The etymology of *monogenēs* signifies "of a single (*monos*) kind (*genos*)" and has no connection with birth. The use at Heb 11:17 must mean unique or precious, as do some uses in the LXX. In the uses indicating only *child*, the "child" idea comes from the context and is not inherent to *monogenēs*. Finally, the lexica and dictionaries are virtually unanimous that *monogenēs* means only, unique, but *not* only begotten.[18] In our judgment the case is stronger for the second position, and most translations of this century reflect this conclusion (NIV: "the One and Only [Son]," [1:14]). However, it would not be prudent to be dogmatic. In any case, what does this contribute to our enterprise?

The five uses of *monogenēs* stress the uniqueness of Jesus as God's agent of revelation. God demonstrated his own love for people by sending an absolutely unique Person into the world to die (1Jn 4:9). *Monogenēs* underscores that, more than merely a unique person, Jesus was "the one and only Son who completely reproduces the nature and character of His Father."[19] Since the Word is God (Jn 1:1), the only Son—who is God (1:18)—is able to reveal God (1:18; 1:14).[20] Schnackenburg puts it concisely in commenting on 3:16:

> The only-begotten is also the uniquely loved. It is this Son, most intimately united to him and supremely loved,

The Translation of John 3:16 in the Revised Standard Version,"*JBL* 72 [1953]: 213–19); R. L. Roberts ("The Rendering 'Only Begotten' in John 3:16," *Restoration Quarterly* 16 [1973]: 2–22); J. R. W. Stott (*The Epistles of John*, [London: Tyndale, 1964], 162); and B. F. Westcott (*The Epistles of St. John* [London: Macmillan, 1909], 149).

[18]In his article (72:213–14) D. Moody traces the origin of the concept "only begotten" and how it came to be applied to *monogenēs*. He argues that for dogmatic reasons Jerome initially employed the Latin *unigenitus* (only begotten) for the word *unicus* (only), which originally translated *monogenēs*. Under the Latin tradition "only begotten" got into the KJV and most English versions up to this century. Dahms (29:222–32) attempts to refute Moody, and though he argues his case thoroughly, it is not altogether convincing.

[19]Brooke, *Johannine Epistles*, 119.

[20]There is a textual problem at Jn 1:18. Some texts read "the only Son" where others read "God the only Son." Both external evidence and transcriptional probabilities favor the second option, adopted by the *UBS*, 3d ed. and Nestle, 26th ed. Some commentators (e.g. Barrett, 169, Bultmann, 81–82, and Schnackenburg, 1:279–80) favor the first and easier reading based on what they think the author was more likely to have written. It is preferable to follow the superior evidence and adopt the second option (as do, e.g., Morris, 113; Lindars, 98–99; and R. E. Brown, 1:17).

his own and only Son, that God has given to the world to snatch it from destruction.[21]

Thus *monogenēs* takes up the concepts we saw in the synoptists' use of *agapētos* and *eudokeō* in the Baptism and Transfiguration accounts. Jesus is beloved and chosen; he is the Chosen One (Lk 9:35). John now tells us Jesus is the Unique One of God—the one and only Son whom the Father has sent to reveal God. From the Father's bosom (indicating affection and close communion) the Son comes to earth in his unique capacity as revealer and Savior.

Thelēma

Three uses of *thelēma*, "will" (Jn 4:34; 5:30; 6:38), establish that submission to God's will characterized Jesus' life. His sustenance came through accomplishing the task God set out for him to do. Here that task is to reap the harvest, spreading the news that God has made salvation available to those who believe (4:39, 41–42). He labors to secure for the day of resurrection all who believe in the Son (6:39–40). "He is so full of a sense of mission and so zealous for his Father's interests that worldly things and needs sink into insignificance," says Schnackenburg.[22] In a different way, then, John conveys Jesus' "appointment" to his task. John presents the perspective of Jesus as the appointee. Jesus knows and accepts that the Father's will governs all he does.[23] He never wavers or questions God's will.[24] Jesus never acts independently, or seeks to have his own way. He performs his task to accomplish everything that God desires for him to do.

John 6:69

We return to this text simply to note again that the disciples confess that Jesus is *ho hagios tou theou*, "the Holy

---

[21]Schnackenburg, *The Gospel According to St. John*, 1:400.

[22]Ibid., 1:448.

[23]We find a similar viewpoint in the synoptic accounts of Jesus in Gethsemane (Mt 26:39; Mk 14:36; Lk 22:42).

[24]G. B. Caird, "The Will of God: In the Fourth Gospel," *ExpT* 72 (1961): 115, makes a special note of the absence in John of temptation and Gethsemane accounts.

One of God."[25] We get a glimpse of Jesus as one on a mission. The One who comes from God has invaded this world to bring the "words of eternal life" to the likes of Simon Peter.

AN ELECT LOCAL CONGREGATION

In 2 John the elder refers to the recipient of his letter as the *eklektē kyria* ("chosen lady," v. 1) and sends greetings from the children of *tēs adelphēs sou tēs eklektēs* ("your chosen sister," v. 13). Though many of the older commentaries viewed these females as individual persons, now most see here a device that personifies two local congregations.[26] Their reasons include the following: (1) New Testament writers do speak of the church in figurative terms (*bride*: Eph 5; Rev 21:9–10; Gal 4:26; *elect* [woman]: 1Pe 5:13); (2) John probably wrote to a single local congregation under his care, and the children (*tekna*) in vv. 1 and 13 are its members; (3) the lack of personal references points to a congregation more than an individual; (4) John's exhortations to love better fit a church than an individual, vv. 5–6; (5) the letter's beginning befits a community more than an individual, vv. 1–3; and (6) the interchange of singular and plural terminology points to a community as recipient. The case is quite clear-cut.

Thus the elder describes a local congregation as chosen or elect. The term is purely descriptive; John does not unpack the elements of the attribution. "Elect" characterizes this local congregation. As Christians are the "elect" with no further elaboration or explanation, so John can call the church "elect." The term fittingly describes the church as a body, much as Israel was the elect people.

THE ROLE OF GOD'S WILL IN ATTAINING SALVATION

We briefly discussed above the place God's will has in Jesus' life. John also gives space to the relationship between

---

[25]In note 10 I maintained that this title denotes not only Jesus' role as Messiah but also his deity.

[26]M. M. Womack, in "The Elect Lady," *Restoration Quarterly* 1 (1957): 67–69, provides the handiest summary of the supporters of both views. W. Foerster (*TDNT*, 3:1095) and G. Schrenk (*TDNT*, 4:191) both view this as the personification of the church.

God's will and the acquisition of salvation. We discovered this topic in the synoptics as well.

John 5:21

In defending his special relationship to God, Jesus asserts that, like the Father, the Son gives life to whomever he *wills* to give it. It is Jesus' will that determines who are the recipients of life. Is this a statement of specific election: Jesus' will determines the precise ones whom he will save? Is Calvin correct when he says of this verse, "He means that He specially honours only certain men, the elect, with this grace"?[27]

Perhaps we ought to settle first that "life" here must refer to eternal life or salvation. The use of the noun *zōē* (life) in the fourth gospel makes that clear (e.g., Jn 3:15–16, 36; 4:14, 36; 5:24, 29, 39–40; 6:40, 54, 68; 10:28; 11:25). Here John uses a compound, *zōopoieō*, "to give life." There can be no doubt that the Father and the Son give eternal life.[28] Can we determine from this context any explanation of Jesus' will— to whom he wills to give salvation? Is it his sovereign choice that is in view here?

The context makes abundantly clear what the criterion is for attaining life or salvation. One must "honor the Son" (5:23), precisely what the Jews were *not* doing (5:16–18). One must accept John's testimony about Jesus "that you may be saved" (5:32–34). John's testimony about Jesus is recorded, in capsule, in the words "Look, the Lamb of God, who takes away the sin of the world!" (1:29), or in his statement "I testify that this is the Son of God" (1:34). "Whoever hears my word and believes him who sent me has eternal life," said Jesus (5:24). One must believe Jesus (5:38) and come to him for life (5:40). Faith in Jesus (5:46) is the key.

The way to obtain life is faith in Jesus. Jesus makes this clear in this passage (and elsewhere). The statement in 5:21, then, cannot mean that Jesus has some secret will, and gives life only to some select group whom he has chosen. Jesus

---

[27]Calvin, *The Gospel According to St. John, 1–10*, 127.

[28]The verb *zōopoieō* occurs in only one other place in John, 6:63, where the Spirit *gives life*. Salvation is clearly the issue there. Outside of John it occurs at Ro 4:17; 8:11; 1Co 15:22, 36, 45; 2Co 3:6; Gal 3:21; and 1Pe 3:18, with various senses.

wills to give life to those who believe in him. In this confrontation with the Jews, Jesus affirms that life is only available on the Father's and his terms; one must come to God as he wills people to come. And that way is through the Son. Jesus wills to give life only to believers in him.[29] The Son does not arbitrarily select out some to whom to give life. The fourth gospel give consistent witness that he gives life to those who believe (3:16, 18, 36; 4:42, 53; 6:40, 47, et al.).[30]

John 6:38–40

Jesus' mission involved accomplishing God's will (6:38; cf. 5:30). In 6:39–40 he gives some elaboration of what is God's will—that he raise up all whom the Father has given[31] him (v. 39), and that all who believe in the Son shall have eternal life and be raised up (v. 40). While our full explanation of this passage must await the next section, several things seem clear. First, in God's will Jesus loses *none* of those given to him. Second, Jesus states clearly in v. 40 that God wills to encompass all who believe in Jesus into a group whom he will raise to eternal life on the Day of Judgment. Far from being restrictive or selective, God's will is open. As v. 37 affirms, God will never drive away anyone who comes to him. So the Jews only have themselves to blame for their plight. Jesus comes to them as the bread of life (v. 35), but he also says, "You have seen me and still you do not believe" (v. 36). This text on God's will seems to parallel the previous one. God wills that his Son be the "continental divide" between two destinies. Those who look to the Son and believe attain resurrection to eternal life. To reject the

---

[29]It is interesting that several old Syriac MSS actually make this interpretation explicit. They read, ". . . the Son gives life to those who believe in him" (syr[s] and syr[c]). Clearly this reading is not original, but it points to the correct understanding of the verse.

[30]Bultmann agrees there is no elective sense to *thelei* here. Rather it shows that Jesus acts purposefully; "it is intended to stress the congruity of his purpose and his actions" (Bultmann, *The Gospel of John. A Commentary*, 256). Schnackenburg says, "The addition of *hous thelei*, 'to whom he will' . . . does not imply arbitrariness but authority, since the Son only carries out the will of the Father, who wishes to give eternal life to all *who believe* in the Son" (*The Gospel According to St. John*, 2:106; emphasis added).

[31]We will investigate this verb in the following section.

Son results in condemnation (3:18, 36; 5:24). This expresses God's will about securing salvation.

GOD'S ROLE IN APPLYING SALVATION

The final category we isolate in the Johannine literature has the most entries. In this rather broad classification we have placed a variety of texts that express God's actions that cause people to attain salvation. In the previous section we saw the expression of God's will for salvation. Now we investigate the texts that describe ways in which God seems to implement his will. We noted the synoptic treatment of this idea. John uses some parallel concepts, but goes his own way too.

John 6:37–40

In returning to this passage we add 6:37, the first of several places where John employs the verb *didōmi* (give) to render the Father's "giving" in some salvific sense.[32] In this passage Jesus asserts that the Father *gives* persons to Jesus, that these persons come to Jesus, and that Jesus will never reject those who come to him (v. 37). He adds that God wills that Jesus lose none the Father has *given* to him, but raise them all up at the Last Day (v. 39). What does it mean for God to "give" people to Jesus, and how does this fit together with what we have already said about God's will? If God wills to give salvation to those who believe in Jesus (v. 40), whom, then, does the Father "give" to Jesus? And when does this "giving" occur? Are they "given" so that they may believe?

Immediately we note the force of Jesus' statement in verse 37: "all that the Father gives [present tense] me will come to me." The first words are intriguing, for the terms translated "all that" are neuter not masculine. Barrett says,

> *pan ho* is used collectively where the masculine *pantes hous* would be expected. Cf. 3:6; 6:39; 10:29; 17:2, 24; see also 17:21. The effect of the neuter is to emphasize strongly the collective aspect of the Father's gift of believers.[33]

---

[32]The other locations that we will investigate are 6:39, 65; 17:2, 6, 9, 24.
[33]Barrett, *The Gospel According to St. John*, 294. On this point also see BDF, 138(1).

Barrett's comment immediately warns us against going down the wrong track in understanding *didōmi*.

Some interpreters find here the teaching that God only grants the capacity to come to Jesus to some, the elect. L. Morris, for example, comments, "Before men can come to Christ it is necessary that the Father give them to him."[34] So, he suggests, when some so-called disciples later decide to leave Jesus, it is because "they were not among those whom God gives Him."[35] According to Morris, then, a person cannot or will not truly believe unless God first "gives" that person to Christ. Morris despairs of reconciling this with the latter part of v. 37, which affirms that Jesus rejects none and welcomes all. Similarly, Calvin says,

> By these words He means that faith is not at men's disposal, so that this man or that may believe indiscriminately and by chance, but that God elects those whom he hands over, as it were, to His Son.[36]

But Barrett's comment and Morris's difficulty with 6:37 suggest another understanding, one that more adequately meshes with Jesus' statements about God's will (6:40). The affirmation that Jesus welcomes all, and the criterion of faith for anyone, both weigh against putting *didōmi* (give) into a predestinarian framework. Certainly God only "gives" one group (of people) to Christ. However, when Jesus supplies the basis or explanation for their place in that group, it turns out to be their faith. Lindars warns against reading out of 6:37 "a rigid doctrine of predestination," since "we know from 3:17 that it is the desire of God that all men should be saved."[37] He goes on,

> The point is that all those who *do* respond to the Father (or are "drawn" by him [verse 44]) come to *Jesus*, because of the unique prerogatives which he has from the Father (cf. 5:20–3).[38]

Jesus teaches that a group of people are en route to a grand and glorious destination—resurrection to life everlast-

---

[34]Morris, *The Gospel According to John*, 367.

[35]Ibid.

[36]J. Calvin, *The Gospel According to St. John 1–10* (Edinburgh: Oliver & Boyd, 1959), 160.

[37]Lindars, *The Gospel of John*, 260–61.

[38]Ibid., 261; his emphasis.

ing. The Father has them in his care, and he has entrusted them to Jesus. They come to Jesus, and he will not turn them away. Jesus assures his disciples that he will not lose any of these special ones; they will all attain to resurrection. This is assured and even (pre)destined in the sense that God's will has determined it all. But when we come to answer the question, Who is in this group? Jesus' response is *"everyone who looks to the Son and believes in him"* (v. 40). God gives to Jesus the company of believers. Jesus will *never*[39] reject one who comes to him in faith. This is God's will. He implements his will by giving to Jesus those who respond to God's gospel in faith.

John 17:2, 6, 9, 24

During his prayer to the Father on behalf of the disciples, Jesus referred to them several times as the ones whom the Father has *given* to him.[40] In various forms the idea recurs: the disciples are ones whom the Father gave to the Son. John does not develop this idea at this point; he simply assumes it.[41] My analysis of 6:37 and 39 above provides the interpretive key for these uses. First, we note a strong plea by those who find in the term *give* here, "the thought of divine predestination."[42] Barrett adds, " . . . prominence is given in this chapter to the idea of predestination."[43] Yet the evidence for this is meager. We noted, at Barrett's suggestion, a pointed collective sense to what is "given" to Jesus in 6:37 and 39. In a way, Jesus' use of the concept of the "given ones" in chapter 17 is also collective or corporate, especially

---

[39]The text of 6:37 is very strong at this point. Using two negatives, it reads *ou mē ekbalō exō*, "I will in *no* way cast out."

[40]We consider the uses of *didōmi* (give) in Jn 17 at this point, even though he uses the verb in a significant text in 6:65. First we have determined that 17:2, 6, 9, and 24 parallel closely the sense we have just described in 6:37 and 39. Second, it will be helpful to discuss 6:44–45 before we tackle 6:65. This breaks up our consideration of the uses of *didōmi*, but it has distinct advantages, we judge.

[41]C. Pinto de Oliveira performs a comprehensive analysis of the uses of *didōmi* in the fourth gospel and calls one category of uses: "Les disciples sont un 'don' du Père au Fils" ["Le verbe ΔΙΔΟΝΑΙ comme expression des rapports du père et du fils dans le IVe Evangile," *Revue des Sciences Philosophiques et Théologiques* 49 (1965), 95].

[42]Morris, *The Gospel According to John*, 719.

[43]Barrett, *The Gospel According to St. John*, 502.

in 17:24 when Jesus includes not only his immediate disciples, but also "those who will believe in me through their message" (17:20). As we saw in 6:37–40, both with *give* and God's *will*, faith in Jesus is the key to eternal life. Here Jesus gives no warrant to read in some pretemporal idea of predestination. In the context of John's gospel, the "given ones" are believers, in contrast to the unbelieving world out of which they have come. We agree with Lindars that "those whom you have given to me" equal "those who have been receptive, as explained in the prologue (1:12)."[44]

John 6:44–45

Here Jesus explains to the recalcitrant Jews the way to eternal life—they must come through Jesus. However, in their eyes Jesus hardly qualifies for the role of Savior (6:41–42). In response to their unbelieving grumbling, Jesus explains that apart from the Father's "drawing" (or "pulling") no one can come to Jesus. The Greek word *helkō/helkyō* occurs eight times in the New Testament with the sense of drag, draw, or tug. Peter *drew* his sword and severed Malchus' ear (Jn 18:10); the disciples could not *pull* or *haul in* the net full of fish (Jn 21:6); or only with difficulty Peter *dragged* the net ashore (21:11). It is used of people: Paul and Silas were *dragged* into the marketplace (Ac 16:19), and Paul was *dragged* from the temple (Ac 21:30; cf. Jas 2:6).

In the LXX the Lord assured the prophet: I have loved you with an eternal love; I have *drawn* you with compassion (Jer 38[31]:3). Oepke cites a use of *helkō* where one is "drawn" to a place of magic; another suggests the "attraction" of a magnet. He notes Plato's use referring to the inner influencing of the will.[45]

The evidence points to senses that are either literal or figurative: a net or person can be dragged literally or a person can be drawn or attracted to a place or outlook by nonliteral means. In the first instance a person can be (forcibly) dragged against his or her will. In the second we would usually say that the will participated. If we say, "I am attracted (or drawn) to that position (or that person)," usually there are reasons, arguments, or features of the

---

[44]Lindars, *The Gospel of John*, 521.
[45]A. Oepke, *TDNT*, 2:503.

position (or person) that have carried the day. Obviously some situations would involve more rational thought than others. But usually to be drawn or attracted (in the figurative sense) is not involuntary nor without criteria. Having said all that, however, we still must see how John uses *helkō* in 6:44 and then 12:32.

Jesus' statement in Jn 6:44, "No one can come to me unless the Father who sent me draws him," raises at least two pressing questions. Do we understand this pull or drawing as irresistible (almost literal)? Is this pull in some way selective—God only pulls some? L. Morris, for one, responds positively to both questions.[46] So does Calvin, who says, "It follows that not all are drawn, but that God honours with this grace those whom he has elected."[47] He adds, "All who are taught by God are effectually drawn so that they come."[48] We doubt such conclusions cannot be sustained. If any "selection" is going on in this context, the Jews are doing it. By persisting in unbelief, they disqualify themselves from participation in eternal life.

Jesus issues an invitation in 6:45 that clarifies the "drawing" of 6:44. Everyone (*pas*) who *listens* and *learns* from God comes to Jesus. God's drawing is not selective nor irresistible. The "drawing" stands right in their midst; in effect, Jesus is saying, "No one comes to the Father except through me" (14:6). The attraction, the reasons, arguments, and features are all there. The question is: will the Jews really listen and learn from God? In the synoptics Jesus explained the possibility of hearing without understanding and seeing without perceiving (Mt 13:11–16; Mk 4:11; Lk 8:10). Such was the state of the Jews.

Nothing here requires us to conclude that all whom God draws do in fact come to Jesus, particularly when we note 12:32 (but we will take that up shortly). It is one thing to say, "No one can come to Jesus apart from God's pull," but quite another to say, "God only pulls certain people, and all those he pulls do in fact come to Jesus." John only asserts the former. Thus we affirm with Barrett that here Jesus emphasizes that "salvation apart from the initiative of God is quite

[46]See Morris, *The Gospel According to John*, 371–72.
[47]Calvin, *The Gospel According to St. John, 1–10*, 1:164.
[48]Ibid.

impossible."[49] The text also affirms, by the addition of *pas ho akousas* and *mathōn* (everyone who listens and learns), that the one drawn must engage the "data" and make a positive response, which John everywhere calls faith or believing. We concur with Bultmann here:

> It is now perfectly clear what is meant when it is said that the Father "draws" men to him. The *pas* already indicates that it does not refer to the selection of a chosen few, but that any man is free to be among those drawn by the Father. . . . This "drawing" occurs when man abandons his own judgment and "hears" and "learns" from the Father, when he allows God to speak to him.[50]

The Jews were unwilling to listen and to learn. They refused to believe in Jesus the Messiah. Rather, they wondered what they had to *do* (6:28); they inquired after signs (6:30); they grumbled about his heavenly origin (6:41); and they argued about the literal meaning of Jesus' words (6:52). They needed to allow God to move them to faith in Jesus. Learning from the Father means "keeping oneself open to the word of the Father which leads men to follow Jesus."[51] The "drawing" was indeed there and available to *all* who would listen and learn. Those who responded in faith found salvation.

John 12:32

Before we return to a final text from chapter 6, we must complement the use of *helkō* in 6:44 with its use in 12:32. The verse occurs in a pericope in which Jesus was preparing the disciples for his impending death by crucifixion. His glorification drew near, Jesus said, and that required the prior step of dying (12:23–24). The hour to which his entire life had been pointing had arrived (12:27). He told them that his imminent death would effect judgment on Satan and his followers, and open up the way of salvation for all people. Jesus said, "But I, when I am lifted up from the earth, will *draw* all men to myself."

We have already discussed the background and range of

---

[49]Barrett, *The Gospel According to St. John*, 295.
[50]Bultmann, *The Gospel of John. A Commentary*, 231–32.
[51]D. Müller, *NIDNTT*, 1:486.

meaning for this word *helkō*, and we determined the best understanding of its significance at 6:44. In fact, that sense fits the use here very well. Jesus' death provides the objective basis upon which salvation becomes available to all people (*pantas*). Surely Morris cannot be right when he takes "draw" here to mean irresistibly drawn to salvation. (He does this because of his understanding of it at 6:45.) Then he is forced to do some fancy footwork to avoid an untenable conclusion. He says,

> In fact not every man is drawn to Christ, and this Gospel envisages the possibility that some will not be. We must take the expression accordingly to mean that all those who are to be drawn will be drawn.[52]

Who are *pantas* (all)? Morris denies Jesus intends to include all persons. He believes Jesus only includes all who are to be drawn. Why use "all," then? Morris answers, because the new covenant marks the end of particularism. Because of the Cross "all men," not only Jews, would be drawn to Christ.[53] Calvin also understands "all" to refer to the universal makeup of the church from Jews and Gentiles.[54]

However, the context will not admit of such an understanding of "all." The issue is not Jews and Gentiles and the universal makeup of the new community. Rather, Jesus addresses the universal availability of the gospel of a crucified Savior in the face of Jews who, "even after Jesus had done all these miraculous signs in their presence, . . . still would not believe in him" (12:37).

Such a universal "drawing" or "attracting" fits nicely with the previous text, 6:44–45. Jesus makes his saving message available to all; it remains for people to listen to, learn from, and believe in him. The drawing is there, God has provided the basis for salvation, and no one is excluded. Rejection and unbelief alone exclude one from salvation. Schnackenburg observes:

> The victorious character is reinforced by *pantas*: there is no limit to Jesus' saving power—except the resistance of

[52]Morris, *The Gospel According to John*, 598.

[53]Ibid., 598–99.

[54]Calvin, *The Gospel According to St. John 11–21 and the First Epistle of John*, 2:43.

> unbelief. In spite of the universalistic overtone and . . .
> intent of the statement, faith is still included as a
> condition (cf. 3:15, 16; 6:37 with 40; 6:45b with c).[55]

The *pantas* (all) must include "each and every person." Any other interpretation is unnatural and forced. We must agree with Caird, who says it is "God's will that all men should by the Cross be drawn into union with the Son, and so with the Father."[56] The Cross opens up the possibility of salvation to all, not only to some secretly selected few. God makes salvation available to all, but they must appropriate it by faith. God's "drawing" does not override the human will. All are drawn, but not all find salvation. People are attracted by the love of God demonstrated on the Cross, but the human will may spurn God's pull (recall Jesus' lament over Jerusalem: Mt 23:37; Lk 13:34).

John 6:65

Jesus' discourse about himself as the bread of life, with the requirement that people must eat his flesh and drink his blood, proved difficult for Jesus' disciples. His words are spirit and life (6:63), but the unwillingness of many to believe (6:64) disqualified them from these rewards. John records that Jesus added, "This is why I told you that no one can come to me unless it is granted him by the Father" (RSV).

Some interpret Jesus to mean that the disciples were to expect deserters. Some people are only disciples by their own resolve or strength, and this kind will never last. Only divinely given disciples truly believe and continue to the end (like Peter, 6:68–69). So, according to this interpretation, God only grants the capacity to believe to some, the elect. When a person does not continue with Jesus, this shows that God never granted that one the ability to believe. We might call this the particularist interpretation; God himself limits the capacity to believe to particular individuals. Apart from God's special work in the hearts of specific people, they will not believe.

Another interpretation commends itself. Here 6:65 func-

---

[55]Schnackenburg, *The Gospel According to St. John*, 2:393.

[56]G. B. Caird, "The Will of God: In the Fourth Gospel," *ExpT* 72 (1961): 116.

tions not as an explanation of why specific people respond but as the explanation of why anyone can respond. In 6:63 Jesus gives a crucial principle: "The Spirit gives life; the flesh counts for nothing." Lindars notes, "It is only if he is open to the influence of God, that he can perceive divine things."[57] By themselves people are unable to comprehend spiritual matters; the illumination of God is critical. In 6:63 Jesus affirms that he has spoken "spirit" words to them—he has exposed them to revelation, to the truth. "Yet there are some of you who do not believe" (6:64). Thus, as we have consistently seen in John, the failure lies in the rejection of the truth about Jesus. Their unwillingness to believe is the true explanation why many deserted Jesus. They refused to accept the demands and implications of following Jesus, so they "turned back and no longer followed him" (6:66).

It would seem that the second explanation fits better the total picture in John, and this context in particular. The former interpretation must import some alien concepts. How, then, do we understand the phrase in 6:64, *ex archēs*, "from the beginning"? Might this not imply some pretemporal foreknowledge and therefore election? The phrase itself is rare, only occurring in the New Testament at 6:64 and 16:4. The more typical construction is *ap' archēs* (8:44; 15:27; frequently in 1Jn, and elsewhere). At 16:4 the phrase *ex archēs* undoubtedly refers to the beginning of Jesus' association with the disciples, not to some eternal beginning. On the other hand, the more common *ap' archēs* does occur once in this present sense (15:27), but also of some pretemporal activity of Satan (8:44).

There really is no reason to assign a pretemporal sense to "from the beginning" here. Instead, right from the beginning of his association with these "disciples," Jesus knew who would prove to be unfaithful and even who would betray him.[58] John thus assures his readers that Jesus had made no mistake. He knew their spiritual status, but he did not determine it, nor would he foreclose on their opportunity to believe. Jesus had given them revelation— words of spirit and life—and the enablement of the Father.

---

[57]Lindars, *The Gospel of John*, 273.

[58]Both Barrett (*The Gospel According to St. John*, 305) and Brown (*The Gospel According to John*, 1:297) take "from the beginning" in this more natural sense.

Both are absolutely required if one is to come to genuine faith. Yet as John presents the picture in this pericope, Jesus' hearers could either desert him or say with Peter, "Lord, to whom shall we go? You have the words of eternal life" (6:68).[59]

To summarize, Jesus affirms here that no one can obtain salvation apart from divine enablement. That seems incontrovertible. It is less clear that Jesus intended his words in a particularistic sense. As we have noted, it is possible (and popular) to see this as a proof-text for particular election. If this was Jesus' intent, then his statement in 6:65 explains why some fell away; that is, God never granted them the capacity to believe in the first place. However, we have attempted to show that an alternative makes better sense. According to this other understanding, the phrase "it is given to him by the Father" is not the limiting factor, but the enabling capacity that explains why there are believers. Nevertheless, people can refuse to believe and so reject God's revelation in Christ, just as Jesus knew all along they would. Eternal life comes to those who, with God's enablement, respond in faith and accept Jesus' words of spirit and life.

John 12:37–40

John records a clash between Jesus and the Jews, part of which we have already discussed. We saw Jesus' statement that his crucifixion would serve to draw all people to himself (12:32). These words perplexed the crowds. In response he urged them to take hold of the light (literally, "believe in the light") while the light was still available, "so that you may become sons of light" (12:36). Evidently, Jesus was attempting to summon them to faith in him while there was still time. They needed to act immediately to become "sons of light." John comments that although Jesus had accomplished (perfect tense of *poieō*) many signs (*sēmeia*) among the Jews, they were not believing (imperfect) in him. The abiding results of Jesus' signs were there to see, but they persisted in

---

[59]Bultmann argues that 6:63 functions as a call to decision. Jesus does not alleviate the difficulty of his teaching (6:60) or its offense (6:61–62). Rather he tells them that he is giving them the opportunity of life if they will believe (Bultmann, *The Gospel of John: A Commentary*, 446–47).

unbelief (12:37). Next John says of this state of affairs: it was foreseen by the prophet Isaiah. In 12:38 John quotes Isa 53:1 to confirm the *fact* of the Jews' unbelief, and in 12:39–40 he cites Isa 6:10 to give the *reason* behind their unbelief.

In 12:38 John uses the formula *hina . . . plērōthē* (in order that it might be fulfilled) to introduce Isa 53:1.[60] The Jews' failure to believe Jesus fulfills Isaiah's prophecy of a lack of faith and an unwillingness to accept God's revelation. John shows that the ancient prophet aptly described Jesus' contemporaries.[61] The Evangelist goes beyond merely describing the fact of these Jews' unbelief. In 12:39–40 he asserts that in fact the Jews were not able to believe (present tense), because of God's work of hardening (as Isa 6:10 demonstrates).[62]

How ought we understand the quote from Isa 6:10? Does John mean that God prevented the Jews from responding to Jesus' message? Might this parallel one interpretation of the last text we considered (Jn 6:65)—that we attribute the lack of faith to God's own doing? Is it God's desire to keep some people from believing? Does he thus blind them from the truth?

We may understand John's intention in three possible ways, though these overlap somewhat. First, we may take this as teaching a kind of election to damnation. C. A. Evans argues we should not diminish the telic sense here. "Obduracy, then, is not merely the result of Jesus' ministry, but it is its very purpose."[63] According to Evans, this stance is due to John's *Tendenz* (intention) where he portrays Christology in terms of suffering, rejection, and cross. So in John's presentation Jesus must promote opposition. Jesus provokes antagonists to fulfill Scripture. Rejection is part of the divine plan, and therefore God purposed to produce unbelief.[64]

Most interpreters disagree with Evans. Even Morris, who takes a strong predestinarian stance throughout John, eschews "double predestination." And we must agree. A

---

[60]John uses it again at 13:18; 15:25; 17:12; 19:24, 36.

[61]Paul uses this same text to make this point about the Jews more widely (Ro 10:16). The Jews will not believe.

[62]Jesus also cites Isa 6:10 in the parallels Mt 13:14–15; Mk 4:12; Lk 8:10. Luke quotes Paul's citation of it in Acts 28:26–27.

[63]Evans, "The Function of Isaiah 6:9–10 in Mark and John," *NovT* 24 (1982): 136.

[64]Ibid., 138.

positive statement that God prevents faith would be totally out of character for this gospel and for Jesus' ministry.

A second option seeks to soften John's words. Barrett, for one, says we must not understand John in so crass a way. He points to 12:42 which shows that many Jews, even leaders, did believe in Jesus, as did Peter, John, and many other Jewish Christians. So in truth God has not hardened all Jews so they can't believe.[65] Brown gives his similar conclusion:

> The concept that people had to disbelieve ("could not believe" in vs. 39) Jesus' word and deed because the Old Testament said they would disbelieve must not be understood on a psychological plane. This is an explanation on the plane of salvific history. It does not destroy human freedom, for vs. 42 makes it quite clear that men were free to accept Jesus. John's summation is not a statement of determinism but an implicit appeal to believe.[66]

Thus we might have a statement that is broadly true in describing the response of many Jews to Jesus. As a people, the Jews rejected Jesus. Proponents insist the statement does not undercut human freedom to believe or prevent faith. This view avoids the harshness of the first view, but does it truly do justice to *ouk ēdynanto pisteuein* ("they were not able to believe")? Does it understand correctly the active verbs in the Isa 6:10 quote: he blinded, he deafened; and the *hina* clause (so that they cannot see)? I think not.

The context suggests a third possibility that is actually preferable. We noted in 12:37 that preceding his Isaiah quotes John informed his readers of the hard-heartedness of the Jews as a group: they were continually not believing in Jesus. Is it not the case, then, that God's hardening comes as a response to the adamant self-will of these Jews who reject Christ? This best expresses John's intention. He does not quote Isaiah to show that it *had* to be thus, but that it *was* this way. Isaiah provided a precedent for such a stubborn people. John states in 12:37 that the Jews refused to believe. John finds a paradigm for this refusal in Isa 53:1, where the prophet laments over the people who rejected God's word. To reject God's word inevitably incurs a divine response.

[65]Barrett, *The Gospel According to St. John*, 430–31.
[66]Brown, *The Gospel According to John*, 1:484–85.

Because they have spurned God's message (Jn 12:37–38), "for this reason they could not believe . . ." (39–40). God does not prevent the faith of any, but when people continually reject the truth, God may act to make faith an impossibility.[67]

This understanding does not prevent individuals from exercising faith. The principle that rejection often (or usually) produces hardening may apply generally to the nation (cf. 2Co 3:14; Ro 11:25). Yet this does not doom every Jew to unbelief, as Jn 12:42 shows. "God's general decision to harden, as expressed in Scripture, does not affect individual human beings in such a way that they cannot escape from the circle of darkness," says Schnackenburg.[68] As Jn 9:39–41 makes clear, God destines none to blindness if they are willing, like the man born blind, to trust Jesus. Those who may claim to see, like the Pharisees, will become blind, Jesus said, if they persist in their rejection of him. Significantly, after John records his quotations from Isaiah, he resumes Jesus' words of invitation for people to believe in him (12:44–50).

Thus I reject the interpretation that suggests that some specific group of people has forever been excluded from the realm of salvation. Nevertheless I insist that we must take these words seriously. The most acceptable solution suggests that continual rejection of Christ, both personal and national (though the national is not John's focus here), may incur God's hardening so that faith becomes impossible. This may explain the "impossibility of repentance" mentioned in Hebrews 6:4–6, and it may account for the obduracy of some to spiritual matters. Jesus insists it is never too early to believe in him. A willful and continual rejection of Christ may eventually consign a person to a state of intractable unbelief.

1 John 3:1

In several texts we found significant uses of words denoting God's "calling," both in the synoptics and Acts. We

---

[67]This seems to be the best explanation for Paul's use of *pōroō* (harden) at Rom 11:17, where Israel experiences hardening due to a failure to believe (10:21), a failure also called "their transgression" (11:11–12). Their rejection preceded their hardening. See also Eph 4:18.

[68]Schnackenburg, *The Gospel According to St. John*, 2:417.

discovered none in the fourth gospel, though we located two uses in other Johannine books. In 1Jn 3:1 the writer extols the great love the Father demonstrated to us. The evidence resides in our name: we are *called* children of God. This is no invitation (cf. Mt 22:14), but has a definite naming sense. Brown says, "Through God's love Christians are given a new (eternal) life and a new identity, and so they have a new name."[69] The writer focuses attention on the new status and position of believers in contrast both to their former state and to the heretics who are trying to mislead them. God has acknowledged them as his own.[70]

Revelation 17:14

The other interesting use of the concept of God's calling employs another crucial term as well—*eklektos* (chosen). The writer piles up descriptions of Jesus' followers. They are "called," "chosen," and "faithful," all collective substantives that clearly refer to the same group of people. We saw the concept of "chosen" applied to the Twelve (Jn 6:70; 13:18; 15:16, 19) and to local congregations (2Jn 1, 13). Here the term applies corporately where the entire body of believers consists of the "called ones" and the "chosen ones." Here is no synoptic distinction between called and chosen (Mt 22:14), but, rather, the standard, technical terminology for the church or the totality of believers, as the writer makes explicit by the third title, *pistoi*—faithful ones, or believers.

Yet, no further insight about these concepts emerges here. The standard use and understanding of the terms are assumed. The reader knows who are the "elect ones," just as the synoptists' readers understood this exact term at Mt 24:22, 24, 31; Mk 13:20, 22, 27; and Lk 18:7. Likewise, *klētoi* (called ones) is a technical term for believers.[71]

Revelation 3:5; 13:8; 17:8; 20:12, 15; 21:27

These verses have a common motif that seems to have a ring of election to it—they all refer to "the book of life." John

---

[69]R. E. Brown, *The Epistles of John*, AB (Garden City, NY: Doubleday, 1982), 388.

[70]See Marshall, *The Epistles of John*, 170, and W. Fohrer, *TDNT*, 8:344–45.

[71]Our development of the technical status and meaning of the various "calling" terms must await our investigation of Paul.

identifies the unsaved or worldlings as those whose names have *not* been written in the book of life from the creation of the world (Rev 17:8; cf. 13:8). Those who remain faithful to Jesus avoid having their names erased from the book of life (3:5). Having one's name inscribed in the book of life is the necessary criterion for escaping the lake of fire (20:12, 15) and for inhabiting the New Jerusalem (21:27). The data are consistent: the names of the saved appear in the book; not so for the damned.[72] The writer envisions a register of some kind in which people's names have been entered (before the world's founding, 17:8).

The image of such a book resists precise delimitation. In several places names can be erased from the book (Rev 3:5; cf. Ex 32:32–33). If we understand the image to teach that certain people are predestined (or even foreknown) to salvation, this phenomenon of erasure is most unsettling, if not fatal. Yet Caird, for one, sees references to the book of life as "one of the many ways in which John expresses his belief in predestination."[73] However, he must qualify this: "Yet the predestination in which John believes is a conditional predestination. A man cannot earn his right to have his name on the citizen roll, but he can forfeit it."[74] With such a qualification, Caird has redefined predestination in a novel way. It would be better if he called this something besides "predestination." This shows the problem of viewing the reference to the "book" in strict predestinarian terms. And yet, what are we to make of the phrase "from the creation of the world" (17:8)?

The best solution recognizes the entire concept of a "book" as metaphorical and discourages any pressing of its details. On one hand it points to God's eternal foreknowledge. He has always known who would be his people. They belong to him, just as items on an inventory belong to their owner. But the possibility of erasure and the inherent

---

[72]These data also conform to several New Testament parallels. Jesus told his disciples to "rejoice that your names are written in heaven" (Lk 10:20). Paul refers to fellow workers with him at Philippi as ones "whose names are in the book of life" (Php 4:3). The writer of Hebrews speaks of "the church of the firstborn, whose names are written in heaven" (12:23). There are Old Testament allusions to this idea too (see Ex 32:32; Ps 69:28).

[73]G. B. Caird, *A Commentary on the Revelation of St. John The Divine*, BNTC (London: A. & C. Black, 1966), 49.

[74]Ibid.

warnings surrounding 3:5 (and in fact the warnings, in different terms, in some of the other letters; cf. 2:5: "I will . . . remove your lampstand from its place"; 2:16: "I will soon come . . . and will fight against them with the sword of my mouth"; and 2:23) show the need for human response.

Local churches are motley collections of people. They often include unbelievers masquerading as true disciples. Jesus offers no assurance to these impostors. Only the truly saved, whose names remain in the book, will inherit God's blessings. All who would be on the register must come to God in faith and continue in obedience. Only "overcomers"—those who remain faithful to Christ—have their names permanently engraved on the register.[75]

The metaphor of the "book" stationed in heaven conveys confidence. A divine transaction has occurred for a person's name to be known and actually recorded in God's book. Certainly this elicits heavenly rejoicing (Lk 10:20). It means one belongs to God and has certainty of endless life in God's eternal kingdom. Yet we doubt that this image conveys predestination or election, unless we are also ready to allow that what God has *predestined* may not occur (if a name may be erased). In many ways the category "those whose names are written in the book" is simply another name for believers, and therefore synonymous with the "called, chosen and faithful" (Rev 17:14).

SUMMARY

We have found in the Johannine literature quite a variegated picture. John repeats some themes that we have observed in the synoptics and Acts, and adds several more. Yet in some areas that appear to parallel the synoptics, John's approach is quite different. His approach to Jesus goes in different directions than that of the synoptic Evangelists. When John comes to treating God's role in applying salva-

---

[75]It would be pressing the details of this image to assume that "erasure" of people's names means they have lost the salvation they once possessed. The "book" pictures those finally saved and ought not be allegorized. Walvoord fails to observe this, so he has to resort to unnecessary contortions to get around the unthinkable—loss of salvation. His "solution" is either that the erasure (3:5) is only hypothetical or that the book starts out with the names of all people which are then erased if they fail to believe in Christ (J. F. Walvoord, *The Revelation of Jesus Christ* (Chicago: Moody, 1966), 82.

tion, his approach and emphases move in directions markedly distinct from the Synoptic Gospels. What are John's specific thrusts?

John includes a strong dimension of *love* not discernible in the synoptics. Though the synoptists do call Jesus the *beloved* Son, John brings out God's love for people. God has universally demonstrated his love for *all* people in sending his Son (Jn 3:16). Love moved God to give his only Son to die (1Jn 4:10). God loves those to whom he has given salvation, and their unity among themselves ought to portray his love for them (Jn 17:23). For John, God's love, though personal and relational, is not elective in that God singled out certain ones to love. John does not identify God's love as the criterion by which some are included in his family (1Jn 4:9–11, 16, 19).

God *knows* his people, a theme also present in the synoptics. Jesus knows his sheep and they know him—a reciprocal, mutual knowledge that bears some similarity to the mutual love of the Father and Jesus (Jn 10:14, 27). Jesus also knows all about his disciples, what they are like and what they will do in the future. He knew all about Judas, and still selected him to be in his apostolic circle (13:11, 18). Nevertheless, whether the knowledge is intimate and relational or more on the cognitive level, John's uses never suggest a knowledge that we would identify as selective. To say Jesus knows his sheep is not to say Jesus chose his sheep, as is clear from the reciprocal nature of the knowing.

John does convey Jesus' selection of the Twelve through the use of the key verb *eklegomai*, "choose." In four places Jesus tells his disciples that he chose them. Twice Jesus affirms that he chose all twelve, including Judas, whom he specifically identifies as a devil (Jn 6:70; cf. 13:18). His use of the word *choose* coincides with the synoptists' accounts of Jesus' choosing or appointing the disciples to a task or role. In Judas' case part of his role was to fulfill Scripture (13:18). Thus Jesus could *know* all about Judas and still *choose* him: this is election to a task. This element of election finds explicit reference when Jesus assures the eleven that he *chose* them to go and produce lasting fruit (15:16, 19). Similarly, the appointment of John the Baptist to his role as the Messiah's forerunner is an election to a task (3:27). God has *given* to him this function or role.

As John identifies the Baptist as the friend, so he marks

Jesus as the Bridegroom, the one appointed Messiah. This is the task given to him (3:27). This "sent one" speaks God's words, possesses the Spirit without limit, and has received everything from the Father who loves him (3:34–35). But precisely who is this one whom God has sent? John calls him the *monogenēs*, the unique, one-of-a-kind Son who becomes God's agent of revelation. He uniquely reproduces God's character (1:14, 18) and exhibits God's love in dying for the world (3:16, 18; 1Jn 4:9). He is God's Holy One (Jn 6:69). In his life Jesus, this Son, totally conformed himself to God's will (4:34; 5:30; 6:38). He lived to accomplish God's will. Unlike the synoptists, John records no heavenly voices at Jesus' Baptism or Transfiguration (cf. Jn 1:29–34; 12:28–30) to affirm his election. John stresses Jesus' status as the *unique* Son and his commitment to the Father's will in his life.

When we move completely into the sphere of salvation, we find three final categories. John speaks of two local church assemblies in somewhat cryptic terms, as an "elect lady" and an "elect sister." He describes a corporate body as elect, without further comment or explanation. Yet, even that is significant. Very naturally John sees the assembly as chosen by God, much like Israel, God's chosen people.

In a few places John opens the window to give a glimpse of God's purposes in applying salvation. Whom does God really want to save? John answers: those who believe (5:21). God does not will to select out only some; God wills to save all who come to him in the manner he has prescribed, namely, through faith in his Son (cf., e.g., 3:16, 18, 36; 4:42, 53; 6:40, 47). God's will for salvation encompasses all who believe in Jesus, and he will raise them up for eternal life (6:38–40). God wills the salvation of all; he will drive away none who come to him (6:37).

Yet God does more than simply desire people to be saved; he has acted both to make salvation available and to enable people to apprehend it. John says that God *draws* people so that they come to Christ (6:44). In fact, apart from this "pull" no one can come. Upon investigation we discovered that this drawing is neither selective nor irresistible. Everyone (*pas*) who listens and learns from God comes to Jesus (6:45), though many people refuse such revelation. They will not believe.

Jesus said that by his crucifixion he would *draw* all people to himself (12:32). His death would make provision for the salvation of all. Jesus' self-sacrifice and God's love shown through Jesus comprise the *attraction*. Anyone may respond and be saved. "Everyone who looks to the Son and believes in him shall have eternal life" (6:40). God is exerting his "pull" upon people, but they must respond in faith to be saved.

God *gives* to Jesus those who exercise such faith. They are saved by virtue of his death, and he promised to raise them to eternal life at the Last Judgment (6:37, 39). Their destiny is sure, but—to repeat—a person's inclusion in this group that God gives depends upon his or her faith in Christ. These "given ones" are believers (17:2, 6, 9, 24), but God does not select some to be given while he rejects or bypasses others. Jesus' words bring spirit and life (6:63), and he calls people to seize the life he offers. Yet this cannot be based on human effort or initiative; people come to Christ because God enables them (6:65). However—and this is crucial—Jesus does not suggest this limits who may come. It simply puts things in perspective. God is the provider and enabler of salvation: "The Spirit gives life; the flesh counts for nothing" (6:63). God has done his part; he has opened the way of salvation. Jesus is drawing all people to himself. In response they either believe this message or they reject it, as 6:66–69 illustrates.

To reject Christ is a dangerous stance, for God may (and does) respond to people's persistent rejection of Christ by hardening their hearts so they cannot believe (12:37–40). For John, this is God's response to their rejection and unbelief; he does not choose some people to harden before they have any opportunity to believe. It is true, on the other hand, that a people may be blinded for the wholesale rejection of the gospel. Yet, even so, individuals may come to faith.

John uses several terms for believers that have a technical meaning. They are *called* children of God (1Jn 3:1) in the sense that God named or designated them as his own. They enjoy status as members of his family. Thus they are *the called* and the *chosen* ones (Rev 17:14). These important terms describe Christ's followers: God has called and chosen them. God has also inscribed their names in his "book of life" (Rev 3:5; 13:8; 17:8; 20:12, 15; 21:27). Again their status is affirmed. God knows all about them; they are his possession.

8

THE PAULINE LITERATURE

When we think about the topic of election, our minds naturally fasten upon the writings of the apostle Paul. Paul's teaching about election has inspired and challenged all who have striven to understand this issue. To attempt to explain the theology of election requires that we zero in on what Paul wrote about the topic. Paul employs election concepts and terminology more than any other New Testament writer. Some epistles, like Romans and 1 Corinthians, seem to feature these issues throughout. While election is virtually absent in some books (2 Corinthians, Philippians, and Philemon), most of the other Pauline writings contain some references to election issues. Even those books often considered "deutero-Pauline" cannot be differentiated from the acknowledged letters on the basis of how they employ election material.[1]

Since our topic does loom so large in Paul's writings, to survey the landscape is no simple task. We will follow the procedure of the previous chapters, organizing Paul's perspective on election around God's actions.

---

[1]Ephesians especially, but also the Pastorals, evidences a use of election vocabulary and theology that differs little from the expressions found in Romans or 1 Corinthians.

Obviously, before we can proceed at all, we need to establish the boundaries of our investigation: just what is the corpus we will call "Pauline"? Must we limit ourselves to the *Hauptbriefe* (the main four), or to a larger group of "undisputed letters of Paul"?[2] How much of a scholarly consensus do we require to acknowledge a letter as being from Paul?

We have concluded that all the letters that purport to be from Paul are sufficiently Pauline in character to provide, for our purposes, the essence of Paul's perspective on election issues. We shall, thus, sidestep the entire "deutero-Pauline" issue and perform our analyses on what the church has traditionally accepted as the letters of Paul. Though this may be an unpopular position in some circles, there is modern opinion that it is tenable. I believe it to be the correct one.

Concerning the disputed authorship of Ephesians, M. Barth says of those who deny Pauline origin,

> The evidence produced by them is neither strong nor harmonious enough to invalidate the judgment of tradition. Although it cannot be definitely proven that Ephesians is genuinely Pauline, nevertheless, it is still possible to uphold its authenticity.[3]

Barth then comes to this conclusion:

> In view of the insufficient linguistic and historical arguments, and of the prejudicial character of the theological reasons exhibited against Ephesians, it is advisable for the time being to still consider Paul its author.[4]

Even C. L. Mitton, who decides against Pauline authorship, concurs with its distinctively Pauline character.[5] Finally, in *Redating the New Testament*, John A. T. Robinson presents a convincing case and cites additional literature in support.[6]

---

[2]The precise members of this category differ among scholars. A common conclusion accepts only seven letters as genuine: Romans, 1 and 2 Corinthians, Galatians, Philippians, 1 Thessalonians, and Philemon. See, e.g., L. E. Keck, *Paul and His Letters* (Philadelphia: Fortress, 1988), 5–7.

[3]M. Barth, *Ephesians*, AB (Garden City, NY: Doubleday, 1974), 1:41.

[4]Ibid., 49.

[5]C. L. Mitton, *The Epistle to the Ephesians* (Oxford: University Press, 1951), 268–69, says, "Not only is it built up of largely Pauline materials, but it faithfully represents the Pauline message." And again, it is "so true to the spirit of Paul and his insight into the Gospel that it has deservedly been regarded as the quintessence of Paulinism."

[6]J. A. T. Robinson, *Redating the New Testament* (London: SCM, 1976), 62–64.

Unquestionably the issue is far more complex with the Pastoral Epistles. These letters to Timothy and Titus clearly differ from the letters written to churches. Many more scholars dispute their alleged Pauline authorship. Yet a recent commentator, a patristic scholar at that, after weighing the evidence and considering the arguments on both sides of the question, decided for their Pauline origin. J. N. D. Kelly writes:

> Taken in conjunction with the early external testimony to the letters, the relatively primitive situation they presuppose, and the mass of convincingly Pauline material they embody, it tips the scales perceptibly, in the judgment of the present editor, in favour of the traditional theory of authorship.[7]

Kelly warns that neither side can be dogmatic. Noting the likelihood that Paul made extensive use of an amanuensis in their composition, he observes, "Nevertheless they remain, in substance and spirit as in occasion, his work, and the present day Christian is justified in assuming that they enshrine his authentic message."[8] Again, after noting that Jeremias, Kelly, Moule, Reiche, Guthrie, and most Roman Catholic scholars accept the style of the Pastorals as Pauline, J. A. T. Robinson himself notes, "I believe it to be open to fewer difficulties than any theory that requires the letters to be pseudonymous, whether in whole or part."[9] E. E. Ellis's discussion of this issue in *Paul and His Recent Interpreters* merits careful attention.[10]

Thus our study will embrace the entire traditional Pauline corpus. We have been unable to distinguish between the "acknowledged" and the "deutero-Paulines" on the basis of how they present Paul's perspective on election issues. Indeed, we found more diversity among some of the "acknowledged" books than between, say, Romans and

---

[7]J. N. D. Kelly, *A Commentary on the Pastoral Epistles*, BNTC (London: A. & C. Black, 1963), 34.

[8]Ibid.

[9]Robinson, *Redating the New Testament*, 70. See, there, his documentation concerning the authors mentioned. We can add C. Spicq to the list of those favoring Pauline origin: *Saint Paul Les Epitres Pastorales* (Paris: Librairie Lecoffre, 1947).

[10]E. E. Ellis, *Paul and His Recent Interpreters* (Grand Rapids: Eerdmans, 1961), 49–57.

Ephesians. We will not presume to decide the issue of authorship, nor need we, since they are all sufficiently Pauline in character for our study.

GOD FOREKNOWS PEOPLE

The initial category we observe concerns God's fore-knowledge. We have already noted the use of this concept in Acts (2:23; 26:5), and later we will examine Peter's use (1Pe 1:2, 20; 2Pe 3:17). We argued that the basic sense of "to know beforehand" seems the best way to understand the Acts occurrences. The uses in 1 Peter will prove more complex. Paul uses the term twice, once to apply to the nation Israel and once to believers in Christ.

Romans 11:2

In 11:1 Paul poses a question—"Did God reject his people?"—that anticipates the response, "No!" Paul then reaffirms that response in 11:2. God did not reject his people *hon proegnō* (whom he foreknew). What people did God foreknow? Without doubt, the people here refers to physical, historical Israel. In 11:1 Paul affirmed his membership in ethnic Israel. The example of Elijah in 11:2–4 turns on there being believers within physical Israel, and 11:7 confirms Israel as a topic here in contrast to the elect. Even Paul's own belief in Christ confirms that God has not abandoned corporate Israel. Paul asserts that foreknowledge extends to a nation, but, clearly, the entire foreknown nation does not possess eternal salvation.

Several writers insist that *proginōskō* here (and in 8:29) means "election" rather than simply "foreknowledge." Cranfield takes it to refer "to the general election of the people as a whole."[11] However, this statement goes beyond

---

[11]C. E. B. Cranfield, *The Epistle to the Romans*, ICC, 2 vols. (Edinburgh: T. & T. Clark, 1975, 1979), 2:545. It is fascinating to see what Bultmann does with *proginōskō* in his article (*TDNT*, 1:715–16). He freely admits it usually means "to know beforehand" everywhere it is used outside of the NT. But then he asserts, "In the NT *proginōskein* is referred to God. His foreknowledge, however, is an election or foreordination of His people (R. 8:29; 11:2) or Christ (1 Pt. 1:20)" (ibid., 715). So, though the basic sense is "advance knowledge," Bultmann opts for a special NT sense of "election." On the other side, H. A. W. Meyer asserts, ". . . *proginōskein* never in the NT (not

the evidence, especially when *proginōskō* and *prognōsis* have the basic, face-value sense of prior knowledge that sources both within and outside the Bible amply attest.

Is there a so-called biblical use of the word *know*? Does Paul use *ginōskō* (know) and *proginōskō* (foreknow) in an active, elective sense? Does an alleged Old Testament sense of *yāda'* impose a conceptual framework upon the New Testament writers, particularly Paul, that points in this direction?

Significantly, when they attempt to describe this special elective sense in *know*, the various proponents can find very few Pauline examples. Murray lists only three: 1Co 8:3 ("the man who loves God is *known* by God"); Gal 4:8–9 ("are *known* by God"); and 2Ti 2:19 ("the Lord *knows* those who are his"). There seem to be no compelling arguments that any of these are elective. To these, E. D. Schmitz adds 1Co 13:12 ("Then I shall know even as also I have been *known*") to illustrate the Pauline use of "God's loving, electing knowledge of men."[12] However, again, the component of choice is very doubtful in this verse.[13]

Certainly we may grant in these contexts that God has a special relationship with his own people—he *knows* them in some special sense. But special knowledge does not equal election. Indeed, our discussion of *yāda'* in the Old Testament did not warrant the view that *to know* is inherently elective. And even if there were such an elective sense to *yāda'* , it is far from clear that Paul was aware of it, much less that he used it here. Thus I remain skeptical when people claim that in Paul's use of *proginōskō*, he probably means "to choose beforehand."[14] We find it wiser to stay with "foreknowledge" as the better meaning.

Here Paul asserts that God foreknew his people, the

---

even in Rom xi.2, 1Pe i.20) means anything else than *to know* beforehand" (*Critical and Exegetical Commentary on the New Testament. Epistle to the Romans*, 2 vols. [Edinburgh: T. & T. Clark, 1873, 1874], 2:93).

[12]E. D. Schmitz, *NIDNTT*, 2:400.

[13]As C. K. Barrett says, "Man's present knowledge will be done away not in the interests of ignorance but of fuller understanding" (*A Commentary on the First Epistle to the Corinthians*, BNTC [London: A. & C. Black, 1968], 307). Past election cannot be read into this text.

[14]Even Bultmann, who accepts the special elective usage, still admits that "this usage is the farthest from ordinary Greek and was later abandoned" (*TDNT*, 1:706).

nation Israel. As a people, they are objects of his prior knowledge. Certainly God has a special relationship with his people Israel. Foreknowledge is corporate, but not strictly salvific.[15] However, the existence of a saved remnant proves that God has not abandoned his foreknown people.

Romans 8:29

Paul addresses God's foreknowledge, not here of corporate Israel, but of the corporate body of Christians. Covering the grand scheme of redemption, Paul describes "the ones who love God" (8:28) as foreknown, predestined, called, justified, and glorified. Undoubtedly this context is salvific, as the string of terms shows. In this text God does not simply know a nation, many of whom may not enjoy his eternal salvation (11:2). God foreknows his own children: they love him and are called according to his purpose. They all possess salvation.

Again the debate rages about whether to take this as prescience only, or to see here God's active choice. W. Hendriksen takes *proginōskō* here to mean "divine active delight."[16] "It indicates that . . . God set his love on certain individuals, many still to be born, . . . electing them to everlasting life and glory."[17] Note that Hendriksen not only prefers an active elective sense for *proginōskō*, but also believes that here Paul teaches that God has chosen to save specific individuals.[18] On the other hand, although

---

[15]D. G. Johnson, "The Structure and Meaning of Romans 11," *CBQ* 46 (1984): 91–103, does assume that *proegnō* is salvific in its uses both in Ro 8:29 and here in 11:2. He argues that 11:2 begins the movement toward 11:26a when all Israel will be saved. But his case won't hold up. In the context of 11:1–7, clearly not all Israel attains salvation. Not until the eschaton does salvation come[s] to "all Israel."

[16]W. Hendriksen, *Exposition of Paul's Epistle to the Romans*, 2 vols. (Grand Rapids: Baker, 1980, 1981), 1:282.

[17]Ibid.

[18]W. Sanday and A. C. Headlam also cite Pss 1:6; 144(143):3; Hos 8:5; Am 3:2; and Mt 7:23 in support of what they call "the Biblical use of the word 'know,' which is very marked and clear" (*The Epistle to the Romans*, ICC, 5th ed. [Edinburgh: T. & T. Clark, 1902], 217). They go on to say, "In all these places the word means 'to take note of,' 'to fix the regard upon,' as a preliminary to selection for some especial purpose" (ibid.). This "electing" sense of *proginōskō* is also adopted by J. Murray, *The Epistle to the Romans*, NICNT, 2 vols. (Grand Rapids: Eerdmans, 1960, 1965), 1:315–18; J. Calvin, *The Epistles of Paul the Apostle to the Romans and to the Thessalonians*, eds. D. W.

Käsemann sees here the sense of election, he denies this means a pretemporal decree.[19]

This alleged elective sense to *proginōskō* raises many questions. Nor can we let stand Hendriksen's position that Paul here speaks of individuals. As we maintained above, the nature of God's pre-knowing must involve some special relationship. The Old Testament uses of *yāda'* (LXX uses *ginōskō*) in places such as Ge 18:19; Am 3:2; and Jer 1:5 make this evident.[20] Several NT uses of *ginōskō* provide confirmation (Mt 7:23; Jn 10:14; and 2Ti 2:19). As we discovered in our discussion of Ro 11:2, the component of choice is unlikely. And whatever else Paul is saying, his concern clearly lies with the corporate body of believers.

Taking the meaning as "prior knowledge" does not weaken the truth of God's election, particularly when this signifies the intimate knowledge that characterizes a special relationship. God elected and predetermined a destiny for his people in full *knowledge* of what they were, what they would be without his intervention, and, most significantly, what they would become as the result of his grace on their behalf. He knows them thoroughly, even before they existed as a people. He has brought them into being. This foreknown people—this corporate group—will enjoy all the advantages God has planned for them, as the succeeding terms in Ro 8:29–30 affirm. God knows this people—he has created this people—and for them alone he has carved out a glorious future.

---

and T. F. Torrance (Edinburgh: Oliver and Boyd, 1961), 317–18; L. Poellot, "The Doctrine of Predestination in Rom. 8:29–39," *Concordia Theological Monthly* 23 (1952): 345; E. B. Allo, "Versets 28–30 du chap. VIII *ad Rom.* (La question de la prédestination dans l'ép. aux Romains)," *Revue des Sciences Philosophiques et Théologiques* 7 (1913), 269, 272; B. Mayer, *Unter Gottes Heilsratschluss. Prädestination bei Paulus*, Forschung zur Bibel (Würzburg: Echter Verlag, 1974), 158; E. von Dobschütz, "Prädestination," *Theologische Studien und Kritiken* (1934), 10; K. Grayston, "The Doctrine of Election in Rom. 8,28–30," *Studia Evangelica*, ed. F. L. Cross, vol. 2, part 1 (1964), 583; and A. J. Martin, "The Sovereignty of Grace as Seen in Rom. 8:28–30," *BibSac* 99 (1942), 460–61.

[19]E. Käsemann, *Commentary on Romans* (Grand Rapids: Eerdmans, 1980), 244, 298. Likewise, K. Grayston sees Paul's use of *proginōskō* as elective, but says it "is used, by St. Paul at least, not to make a statement about pre-temporal eternity; but to assert with maximum force and brevity that God's choice is prior to any action or merit of ours" ("The Doctrine of Election in Romans 8, 28–30," 583).

[20]See our discussion in chapter 1.

GOD PURPOSES

A second divine activity that has elective significance for the biblical writers concerns God's purposes. We have seen this in our previous studies. Paul also predicates significant actions upon God's purposes. We have isolated, for our study, three sets of God's purposes: what he purposes concerning the plan of salvation, concerning events, and concerning his people:

God's Purposes and Will Concerning the Plan of Salvation

Romans 3:25

Paul uses the verb *protithenai* in all three of its NT occurrences. The middle voice can mean either, like the active, "to put or set forth" or "to purpose." Commentators are split as to which sense Paul intends in Ro 3:25.[21] The arguments for the sense of "purpose" seem to be slightly stronger. First, "purpose" is the natural and usual sense (see Ro 1:13 and Eph 1:9). Second, the NT writers, including Paul, repeatedly join God's purpose to salvific events (for example, Ac 11:23; 27:13; Ro 8:28; 9:11; Eph 1:11; 3:11; 2Ti 1:9; 3:10; 1Pe 1:20). Third, the related noun *prothesis* always means "purpose" apart from its use for the showbread in Heb 9:2.

In either case the context suggests an elective act of God in which he purpose (or set in action) a plan that Jesus would be a *hilastērion* (atoning sacrifice). God determined that Jesus should accomplish salvation, a salvation secured by faith. Paul asserts God's purpose to provide salvation or (taking the active sense) "to set forth" Christ to be *hilastērion*.[22]

---

[21]Those opting for the active "set forth" sense include: the NIV; BAGD: 722; J. D. G. Dunn, *Romans 1–8*, WBC (Dallas: Word, 1988), 170; Sanday and Headlam, *Epistle to the Romans*, 87; C. H. Dodd, *The Epistle of Paul to the Romans*, MNTC (London: Hodder & Stoughton, 1932), 55; and R. C. H. Lenski, *The Interpretation of St. Paul's Epistle to the Romans* (Columbus, Ohio: Lutheran Book Concern, 1936), 257–58. On the other side, opting for "purpose" are the NEB; M. Black, *Romans*, NCB (London: Oliphants, 1973), 68, who suggests: "proposed to Himself, purposed, designed and so 'ordained' (or 'foreordained')"; Hendriksen, *Epistle to the Romans*, 1:131; and Cranfield, *Epistle to the Romans*, 1:208–10.

[22]For an appraisal of the various positions and arguments for understanding *hilastērion*, see L. Morris, "The Meaning of *hilastērion* in Romans iii, 25,"

Romans 8:28

Paul describes the beneficiaries of God's working for good in two ways. They love God, and they are called according to (God's) purpose (*prothesis*). Paul depicts God's people as the "called ones." God called them on the basis of or through his own *purpose*. Calling, then, is purposeful or for a purpose. Put another way, God purposed to call them. As Barrett puts it, " 'Calling' is the realization in history of God's eternal *purpose*. It is here, in God's purpose, that the ultimate assurance of salvation rests."[23] Those who are called, then, reside squarely within the salvific purposes of God, as 8:29–30 will proceed to elaborate.

Romans 9:15, 18, 19

In 9:15 and 18 Paul predicates God's actions of showing mercy and hardening upon God's own determinative *will* (*thelō*). God's showing mercy or hardening appears to follow logically from his sovereign will. In 9:19 Paul poses a rhetorical question: "who resists [God's] *will*?" (*boulēma*). In other words, how can God hold people accountable when his own will ultimately determines what happens? In response Paul simply affirms God's autonomy in doing what he wants to do. There is no way to put God in the dock. Paul's use of the example of Pharaoh in 9:17 illustrates the principle that God acts sovereignly to accomplish his purposes. God raises up people and nations and uses them to further his objectives.

We get no teaching here that God has chosen specific individuals to whom to show mercy or to harden. In the context of Ro 9, as we will continue to see, Paul's concern is the elect people of God, a corporate entity. God has willed to

---

NTS 2 (1955): 33–43. He concludes that the term refers to "propitiation," the removal of God's wrath, rather than the mercy seat or Day of Atonement ceremonies (p. 43). See also D. Hill's discussion of this text in his *Greek Words and Hebrew Meanings* (Cambridge: University Press, 1967), 38–48. Hill's conclusions generally concur with those of Morris. Alternatively, among those who argue for the meaning "expiation," see L. Keck, *Paul and His Letters*, 37. Dunn, *Romans 1–8*, 171, wonders why these must remain polarized alternatives. He affirms that Jesus' death both averted God's wrath and provided the necessary sacrifice for sin.

[23]C. K. Barrett, *A Commentary on the Epistle to the Romans*, BNTC, 169.

show mercy to his people, to provide salvation; people cannot effect or procure their own salvation. Cranfield's important reminder confirms this analysis: "The assumption that Paul is here thinking of the ultimate destiny of the individual, of his final salvation or final ruin, is not justified by the text."[24] We discover the criterion for obtaining mercy later in Ro 9 and 10: faith. God calls those who come to him in faith, "my people." Conversely, he hardens those who reject him by hardening their hearts against him. He destines the first group for glory, the other for destruction. All this derives from the divine will, and, since he is God, no one can accuse him of being unjust for doing what he wills.

Romans 9:22

Paul bases God's wrath upon his will. Paul's point is not that God wills (or chooses) certain ones to suffer his wrath. Rather he confirms that God wills to display his wrath, either upon certain "vessels" (people) or through certain "instruments."[25] Later in this section Paul details why some experience God's wrath. To fail to believe puts one outside God's mercy. Romans 11:23 highlights the role of faith— Jews may reenter the people of God if they put away their unbelief. Paul teaches no rigid predestinarianism, but presents an open door to enter the body of believers. Hanson says, "We do not need to conclude that God previously chose them to be objects of his wrath; by their unbelief they chose themselves."[26]

1 Corinthians 1:21

Paul contends that God was pleased (*eudokēsen*) to save those who believe through the foolishness of the preached

---

[24]Cranfield, *Epistle to the Romans*, 2:489.

[25]Most commentators take *skeuē orgēs* (vessels of wrath) to mean that people are the recipients of God's wrath. A. T. Hanson, "Vessels of Wrath or Instruments of Wrath? Romans IX.22–3," *JTS* 32 (1981): 433–43, understands *skeuē* as instrument, rather than a passive vessel. He concludes, "Thus *skeuē orgēs* does not mean persons destined to be the recipients of God's anger, it means the instruments by which God's wrath is manifested" (441). He rejects any idea that Paul's concern here is with the eternal destiny of individuals.

[26]Ibid., 441. Dunn, *Romans 9–16*, concurs. He remarks, "Paul has no intention of engaging in a debate about election and judgment (far less about predestination and free will)" (567).

message. This is God's *chosen* method of operation: to present salvific truth via the foolish vehicle of preaching, and then to save those who believe it. *Eudokeō* has an elective sense,[27] but here Paul alludes to God's choice of a course of action, not a choice of individuals whom he will save.

Paul places the entire salvation complex under the auspices of God's determinative, though pleasurable, will. It pleased him to save a group of people through the gospel his messengers proclaimed. Paul does not say that God chose certain ones to save, or that God willed that only certain ones would believe the message and be saved. In fact, if Paul intends any emphasis, it would be on the side of human response. He does not say that God saves those whom he has chosen to believe, but rather that God has chosen that he save those who do believe. God has willed this to be the method for populating the eternal kingdom.

Galatians 1:4

Paul predicates Christ's death for sins upon the *thelēma* (will) of God. Specifically, salvation through Christ is *kata to thelēma*, a unique formulation, in which Paul employs *kata* (according to) instead of the more usual *dia* (through). F. F. Bruce suggests wider significance to this phrase than simply God's provision of salvation. The phrase "may imply not only that believers' deliverance from 'the present evil age' is in accordance with God's will but that such deliverance enables them to live in conformity with God's will."[28] Salvation's provision and implementation reside within the purposes of God.

Ephesians 1:9

Paul locates God's redemptive plan squarely within the purposive will of God. Though the content of God's will (*thelēma*) was formerly a mystery, now he purposes (*pro-tithēmi*) to make known this pleasurable will (*eudokia*) in

---

[27]See G. Schrenk (*TDNT*, 2:738–42) for a discussion of the elective nuances of *eudokeō*.

[28]F. F. Bruce, *The Epistle of Paul to the Galatians*, NIGTC (Grand Rapids: Eerdmans; Exeter: Paternoster, 1982), 76.

Christ. Again we find clear emphasis that salvation in Christ issues from God's causative, willful action.

Ephesians 1:11

In this text Paul employs several crucial terms, but for now we focus solely upon his use of *prothesis*, which again points to God's will. Paul asserts that the basis or motivation of predestination (*proorizō*) is the purpose of God. In other words, Paul bases an important element of salvation— predestination—on the purpose of God, in keeping with previous uses. In fact, here Paul asserts that all God does derives from the counsel of his will or plan which "seems intended to express emphatically the absolute self-determination of God."[29]

Colossians 1:27

Paul uses *thelō* to refer to God's definitive will or decision. God has willed, even decided, to reveal to his saints what are the riches of a glorious mystery among the Gentiles. God willed to provide the knowledge of salvation to Gentiles (so they might come to believe). Paul uses corporate language. These saints have come to see the light, for they are among the Gentiles to whom the revelation has come. As with the previous three verses, Paul does not imply that God willed specific ones to be saints.

1 Timothy 2:4

Partly in support of his exhortation to pray "for everyone" (2:1), Paul asserts that God "wants all men [*anthrōpous*] to be saved and to come to a knowledge of the truth." The goal of God's will (*thelō*) is that he save all. If we take the words *pantas anthrōpous* (all people) at their face value, then this is a unique use of "will." In all of Paul's other uses of *thelō*, what God wills will in fact occur. But clearly, not all people (each and every one) attain salvation, for Paul is no universalist (cf. Ro 2:5–16). So must we in some way weaken or alter the concept of salvation to that of protection or

---

[29]T. K. Abbott, *Epistles to the Ephesians and to the Colossians*, ICC (Edinburgh: T. & T. Clark, 1897), 21.

conservation?[30] Or ought we bifurcate, somehow, God's will so that what he wills in one sense is not what he decrees in another?

Both these options seem unlikely in this passage. Clearly the word *save* does have its salvific sense in this setting (note 1:15 and 2:5–7).[31] What is more, we have no evidence to posit that Paul envisioned two senses of God's will when he penned these words.

Nor will it do to suggest that "all men" means all types of people.[32] Concerning this kind of solution Kelly says, "All the subtle qualifications which have been proposed . . . are artificial and out of place."[33] Certainly God's love extends to all people, not merely to all types.

How, then, does Paul perceive God's will? In this context it must refer to what God wants, wishes, or desires, but does not command or determine. Apparently then, God's will (in this sense of wish or desire) is not always done.[34] This keeps 1Ti 2:4 in line with Paul's other statements that indeed some will perish.

God desires the salvation of every person, though not all attain it. God wills the salvation of all, not some specific group of individuals within the totality of humanity.

2 Timothy 1:9

Here the writer affirms that the ground, basis, or explanation for salvation resides not in works, but in God's

---

[30]This is what E. Simpson, *The Pastoral Epistles*, TNTC (London: Tyndale, 1954), 41–42, does. He removes this from a strict soteriological context and suggests a meaning for *sōzō* (save) as found in Mt 14:30; Jn 11:12; 12:27; cf. 1Ti 4:10, in which God is the Savior of all people.

[31]M. Dibelius and H. Conzelmann confirm this point, noting that the phrase "knowledge of the truth" "in the Pastorals is a formula for Christianity, viz., conversion to the Christian faith" (in *The Pastoral Epistles*, Hermeneia [Philadelphia: Fortress, 1972], 41).

[32]This is the position of some Reformed theologians like W. Hendriksen who says, "God desires *all* men—men from *every* rank and station, tribe and nation—to be saved" (*I and II Timothy and Titus*, [Grand Rapids: Baker, 1957], 97).

[33]J. N. D. Kelly, *Pastoral Epistles*, 62.

[34]R. A. Ward says, "The NT shows that God's will is not always done (Matt 6:10; 7:21; 12:50). The will of Jesus was not always done (Matt 23:37; Mark 7:24)" (*Commentary on 1 & 2 Timothy and Titus* [Waco, TX: Word, 1974], 45).

own purpose (*prothesis*) expressed in grace. God wills to save graciously. We find affirmation that Christians can attribute their saved status solely to God's purpose and grace.

God's Purposes and Will Concerning Events

Romans 15:32

Paul predicates his expected visit to the Roman Christians upon the important element of God's will (*thelēma*). Paul makes his plans while aware of a certain tentativeness about them; only a fool would deny that God sovereignly controls the events of the world (cf. Jas 4:13–16).

1 Corinthians 4:19

Paul states his plans to travel soon to Corinth, "if the Lord wills" (RSV) (*ean ho kyrios thelēsē*). Again Paul seems to echo James' advice (4:15). He recognizes that all human plans are contingent upon God's sovereign purposes. Paul plans his trip, but recognizes that God may overrule.

1 Corinthians 16:7

In discussing his personal plans, Paul tells his readers he hopes to spend time with them, if the Lord permits (*epitrepō*). This parallels the use at 4:19.

1 Thessalonians 3:3

Paul sent Timothy to encourage the Thessalonians so they would not be upset by the trials they were experiencing. In fact, he tells them, "we were destined for them". The use of *keimai* for "destine" corresponds to Luke's statement in Lk 2:34 that Jesus is destined to cause the fall and rising of many in Israel. Paul implies that the trials a Christian faces are not accidental nor the result of chance, but play a part in God's overall plan. Affliction goes with the territory of being a Christian and fulfills Jesus' words, "If they persecuted me, they will persecute you" (Jn 15:20). It is the destiny of Christians to follow in Jesus' footsteps. Yet Paul does not say here that God has specifically selected those who will follow this destiny.

God's Will Concerning His People

1 Thessalonians 4:3

In writing to the Thessalonian Christians Paul explains that it is God's will (*thelēma*) that they be holy; that they keep themselves from sexual immorality; that they take a spouse; and that they not defraud others. *Thelēma* describes what God desires or wishes for his people; he has called them to live in holiness (4:7). God's will may encompass more than the holiness of his people,[35] but certainly this is not God's determinative will. It expresses what he desires or wishes for his people. Whether or not they attain holiness depends on their obedience. This may match what we saw at 1Ti 2:4, where God desires the salvation of all people. Here Paul expresses what God desires, though certainly believers will not attain lives of perfect holiness in this age.

1 Thessalonians 5:18

Paul gives further instruction which depicts the "will of God in Christ Jesus" (RSV) for the Thessalonians. Again, this conveys what God desires or wishes from his people, namely, rejoicing, continual prayer, and constant thankfulness. God's will here is realized only to the extent that his people obey these entreaties.

GOD ELECTS

Paul affirms repeatedly that God is an electing God. Paul employs a reasonably large election vocabulary, and explains at various points his understanding of the nature of God's choosing.[36] Paul affirms that God also predestines, an action

---

[35]E. Best, *A Commentary on the First and Second Epistles to the Thessalonians*, BNTC (London: A. & C. Black, 1972), 159, argues that this paragraph does not exhaust the will of God for his people, but simply gives what God desires of his people in relation to sexual behavior. However F. F. Bruce responds that "the will of God for his people is not wider than their sanctification; his will is precisely that they should be holy, as he himself is holy (Lev 11:44, 45 etc; 1 Pet 1: 15, 16)" (Bruce, *1 & 2 Thessalonians*, WBC [Waco, TX: Word, 1982], 81–82).

[36]Paul employs the verb *eklegomai* (to choose, select) four of its twenty-two occurrences in the NT; *eklektos* (chosen), six of its twenty-two uses; and *eklogē*

we will discuss in the next section. Paul places God's act of choosing in three arenas: his choice of corporate Israel, his election of Christians, and his selection of angels. We will follow this order in our analyses.

God's Election of Corporate Israel

Romans 9:11

Paul affirms that God purposed to select Jacob above Esau. As God had named or counted Abraham's seed through Isaac (9:7), so now the line would run through Jacob, not Esau. This choice of Israel's lineage was a sovereign divine act, and not motivated by any specific acts or responses from the twins. This was God's sovereign choice of an individual, though we hasten to add that the issue here is not his personal salvation.[37] In reality, God made a corporate choice: he chose *Jacob and his offspring* to be his people rather than Esau and his descendants. As we noted above in our discussion of foreknowledge, in the section Ro 9–11 Paul struggles with the perplexing question, Has God rejected his *people*? God specifically chose Jacob, but not as an individual in isolation, nor for his personal salvation. Rather, Jacob became instrumental in tracing the ancestry of the *people* of Israel.

Romans 9:13

This verse parallels what we have just observed. The juxtaposition of "love" and "hate" surely bears elective significance.[38] Paul quotes Mal 1:2–3 to confirm the point he has been making in this section—God has chosen Jacob over against Esau. Is this the election of Jacob to salvation? In Mal 1:2–3 the prophet's point is not salvation, but rather God's choice of the nation Israel over Edom. Thus, Jacob and Esau represent their progeny. In Malachi the *nations* Israel and Edom are mentioned specifically. Cranfield confirms this

---

(choice), five of its seven uses, in addition to his use of words like *kleroō* (appoint) and *haireomai* (choose).

[37]See Sanday and Headlam, *Epistle to the Romans*, 245.

[38]E. Stauffer states that for Paul, "the love of God implies election" [*TDNT*, 1:49].

when he writes, "God has chosen Jacob and his descendants to stand in a positive relation to the fulfillment of His gracious purpose: He has left Esau and Edom outside this relationship."[39]

Käsemann, however, thinks Paul has wrenched quotes from the Old Testament (Ge 25:23; Mal 1:2–3) out of their original contexts and meanings. Thus Paul's meaning no longer concerns nations and their destinies, but the election and rejection of two persons elevated as types.[40] Arguing in different ways, J. Murray[41] and J. Piper[42] also contend for an individual interpretation.[43] However, their perception ignores the total context of Romans 9–11 in which Paul discusses the fate of corporate bodies—the Jews and Gentiles. Israel's present unbelief works to the advantage of Gentiles. Jews experience hardening *until* the full number of Gentiles find salvation (11:25). Throughout the passage the fate of Israel as a nation dominates Paul's thinking. Has God abandoned her (11:1)?[44]

---

[39]Cranfield, *Epistle to the Romans*, 2:480.

[40]Käsemann, *Commentary on Romans*, 264–65.

[41]Murray, *The Epistle to the Romans*, 2:21–24.

[42]J. Piper, *The Justification of God* (Grand Rapids: Baker, 1983), 45ff.

[43]Piper admits that the OT texts may be corporate, but he insists that they establish a *principle* of unmotivated, unconditional election, which then must be applied to the issue of the chapter expressed in 9:3: why so many Jews are unbelievers. Piper's answer is straightforward: because God has elected only some Jews to salvation and elected the rest to destruction (9:22–23) [*Jus ification*, 45–46]. One of the major flaws in Piper's book is that he treats Ro 9:1–23 in isolation from the entire treatise of Ro 9–11. Not only does he ignore the implications of "my people" in 9:25–26, but he fails to account for chapter 10 where Paul does give specific teaching about how salvation is apprehended—through faith. Furthermore, 11:26–28 must be read corporately and nationally. Thus Piper fails to consider the considerable evidence of the corporate nature of Paul's argument. Finally, as S. K. Williams notes in his review of Piper's book (*JBL* 1043 [1985]: 548–51), it is not likely that Paul would have expressed such personal anguish over the damnation of some fellow Jews (Ro 9:3), if as Piper alleges, God's name was being glorified thereby.

[44]F. Godet is firm in his conclusion: "In speaking of Jacob and Esau, either as men or nations, neither Genesis nor Malachi nor St. Paul have *eternal salvation* in view; the matter in question is the part they play regarded from the theocratic standpoint. . . ." (*Commentary on St. Paul's Epistle to the Romans*, 2 vols. [Edinburgh: T. & T. Clark, 1892], 2:152). J. Munck takes the references in Ro 9 to Isaac, Jacob, Esau, and Pharaoh to refer to peoples, not individuals (*Christ and Israel* [Philadelphia: Fortress, 1967], 45). Speaking of Ro 9–11 G. B. Stevens concludes: "(1) They treat, primarily, of the election of a people, not of the election of individuals. (2) They treat of election to a

We conclude that Paul affirms the divine election of Jacob and the physical nation Israel through him. Jacob's family becomes elect Israel in the national sense.

Romans 11:7

Though our insertion of this verse into the discussion may seem misplaced, this is the most appropriate setting to discuss God's hardening of the unbelieving Jews ("the rest"; *hoi loipoi*). Does this mean that God prevented the bulk of the Jews from believing the gospel? More likely Paul asserts that God confirmed them in their unbelief in response to their unwillingness to heed his appeals. In the context of Ro 9–11 Paul attributes Israel's failure to obtain salvation to her own rejection of the way of faith (see, for example, 9:30–32; 10:2–4, 16–21; 11:20). Paul identifies the root problems: Israel's stubbornness and unrepentant heart (cf. Ro 2:5). Nothing suggests that God, as a result of a prior elective choice, prevents any of his foreknown people (11:2), the Jews, from acquiring righteousness. This would be unthinkable. Paul expresses his personal anguish over the damnation of his fellow Jews who do not believe (9:3). Yet he does not attribute their state of unbelief to God's will or elective choice. This is no decree of election; namely, that a group of Jews cannot believe. Rather, it is God's response, perhaps provisional,[45] to those who will not believe.[46]

Romans 11:28

Paul speaks of Israel as a physical, historical nation. This nation is beloved (by God) because of the patriarchs and because God has chosen her. On the one hand, Israel's

---

historic function or mission, not of election to eternal destiny" (*Theology of the New Testament*, 2d ed. [Edinburgh: T. & T. Clark, 1911], 383–84). Finally, in this brief catalog, E. Best says of Ro 9–11: "It is never a question of the choice of individuals for eternal destiny but always of peoples and nations for historical service" (*First and Second Epistles to the Thessalonians*, 72). See also Dunn's explanation of the Malachi passage in *Romans 9–16*, 545–46.

[45]See Cranfield, *Epistle to the Romans*, 2:549.

[46]Barrett, *A Commentary on the Epistle to the Romans*, 210, disagrees. But there is other NT evidence to support this concept that God may respond to people's rejection of his message by confirming them in their rebellious state (e.g., Mt 13:11–17; Ro 1:24, 26, 28).

corporate rejection of the gospel caused her to forfeit salvation and become God's enemy. On the other hand, the nation's failure to believe the gospel has not negated her *corporate election* as the people of God. God chose and made promises to Israel's patriarchs; he will not abandon his call nor reject his people (11:2).

Election here is corporate and not specifically salvific. Barrett says, "They are the race whom God elected to be his peculiar people."[47]

Summary

From this brief look at these crucial chapters, one point emerges clearly. Paul's focus is upon God's selection of the nation Israel in its historic role, not upon specific individuals for eternal salvation. Even the choice of individuals like Jacob was for their tasks in God's historic program with his people, not their personal salvation.

God's Election of Christians

Romans 8:33

Paul identifies Christians, the recipients of God's redemptive acts in Christ (8:31–32), as "God's elect" (RSV). This substantival use of the adjective *eklektos* ("chosen") clearly represents an action: God has chosen these people. In neither this nor Paul's three other uses of this adjective (Col 3:12; 2Ti 2:10; Tit 1:1) does he specify a goal of God's choosing. They are not chosen *for* anything nor from among some larger group. We conclude that the use of *eklektos* places primary emphasis on the "chosenness" of the chosen ones, rather than on the specific action of selecting these ones from among the various alternatives. In a sense Paul assumes the choice, and then proceeds to speak about them as possessing the status of chosen ones. Finally we observe that the use is plural or corporate in nature. Paul lays stress upon the chosenness of God's people, not upon any idea of how specific ones came to be a part of that body.

---

[47]Barrett, *Epistle to the Romans*, 225.

Romans 11:5, 7

As God numbered 7000 faithful people during the time of Elijah, so now, Paul says, there is a remnant of believing Jews *kat' eklogēn charitos* (according to the election of grace). The remnant exists because of a gracious act of God's choosing. In distinction to the entire foreknown nation of Israel (11:2), a smaller group within that nation—the remnant—stands as the object of God's gracious choice. Paul describes God's choice of the remnant as gracious; that they attain righteousness rests solely on the grace of God, not human merit or worth. This corporate entity can thus be called "the election" (11:7).[48] This group gained what the entire nation was seeking—presumably righteousness or salvation (11:30). The rest of the nation failed in its quest because it pursued righteousness improperly (9:30–33).

1 Corinthians 1:27–28

Though the objects of God's choosing seem at first to be nonhuman, the context makes it clear that Paul is speaking of God's choice of people. Verses 18–31 of 1Co 1 form a discussion of salvation, and how it comes to certain people. Several features make this apparent: God saves those who believe (1:21); the "called" (1:24); "your call" (1:26); and being "in Christ Jesus" (1:30) who is "our righteousness, holiness and redemption."

What can we say about the objects of God's choosing in these verses? Paul says God has chosen the foolish things, the weak things, the lowly things and the despised things, and the things that are not. Though this may involve the choice of some out of a larger group, that is not what we usually mean by God's election. Here Paul wants to get

---

[48]Most people see the remnant as a corporate entity here. Käsemann says that *eklogē* "speaks in stereotyped fashion of the community of the elect . . ." (*Commentary on Romans*, 300). Barrett calls the remnant "a nation within a nation" (*Epistle to the Romans*, 209). Shrenk agrees (*TDNT*, 4:180–81). Murray dissents, insisting that the election in 11:5,7 "must refer to the particular election of individuals in distinction from the theocratic election referred to in 'his people' (vs. 1) and 'his people whom he foreknew' (vs. 2)" (*Epistle to the Romans*, 2:71). But Murray gives no evidence to support particular election here, nor is there any. The topic concerns a corporate body, a chosen remnant.

across to the misguided Corinthians that God's values were different from theirs, and that God often chooses what people reject. In fact, to accomplish his purposes God may choose the very things or people that humans despise. If we miss this point, we have to conclude that all the ones whom God has chosen are foolish, weak, low-born, and despised, and that no Christians are wise, strong, or of noble birth. As well, this would imply that *all* those in the former group are chosen (to salvation), and *none* from the latter. Surely Paul does not intend this. We infer that Christians as a corporate group are the objects of God's choice.[49] Paul does not assert that God has selected specific individuals to be saved.

1 Corinthians 8:3

This may be a pertinent text, or it may not, depending on how we interpret its meaning. Paul says that if anyone loves God, this "one [the person or God] is known by him [God or the person] (RSV)." In both cases either option can be defended grammatically and conceptually. The first option posits that if one loves God, then God knows that person. Support for this idea appears in several texts (1Co 13:12; Gal 4:9; 2Ti 2:19). The second option contends that if one loves God, then he or she knows God (cf. 1Jn 4:7).[50]

If we adopt the first option, then we have an example of God's knowledge of his people, a pervasive biblical idea. An impressive array of scholars defend this option, some even arguing that the "knowledge" here is elective.[51] Others

---

[49]Shrenk concurs that Paul here speaks of the election of the community, not of individuals (*TDNT* 4:175).

[50]G. Fee, *The First Epistle to the Corinthians*, NICNT (Grand Rapids: Eerdmans, 1987), 367–68, believes a few early Egyptian MSS (Clement, P[46]) best retain Paul's intention. They read: "If anyone loves, this one truly knows (or is known)." Fee argues that love for God does not really concern Paul in this context. Rather love toward other Christians dominates his thinking. Though Fee contends these two MSS alone preserve Paul's original wording, he fails to provide any textual critical defense, relying solely on intrinsic probability. In fact, the external MS evidence overwhelmingly supports the longer (traditional) texts.

[51]Barrett argues that "the context is the biblical doctrine of election and acceptance with God" (*First Epistle to the Corinthians*, 190–91). In Barrett's view Paul here expresses God's "initiative in taking knowledge of man, and acting on his behalf by sending his Son" (190). H. Conzelmann also opts for an elective sense here to the verb *ginōskō*, to know (*1 Corinthians*, Hermeneia

suggest Paul only affirms that God knows or acknowledges his people, without insisting that he has chosen who will be his people.[52] The NEB translates the verse, "If a man loves, he is *acknowledged* by God."

On the other hand, the second option has excellent contextual support, for 8:1–2 speaks of human knowing, as does the following discussion (see 8:4, 7, 10–11). Paul argues in response to the so-called knowledge of "the man who thinks he knows something" (8:2). He maintains that only when the person demonstrates love for God does he show that he really knows God. To know God is to love him, and we see later what Paul means by love (see 8:9–13 and 1Co 13). True knowledge of God results in love. This interpretation makes excellent sense of this passage and fares better than the first option.

Thus we remain unconvinced that here Paul teaches the election of individuals to salvation. Neither analysis of the verse in question warrants such a conclusion.

Ephesians 1:4

Here Paul states that God chose Christians in Christ before the creation of the world to be holy and blameless in his sight. The "chosen ones" designate the corporate group to whom Paul writes with himself (and presumably all Christians) included: God chose *us*. The focus is not on the selection of individuals, but the group of those chosen.[53] As Westcott notes, "*He chose us* (i.e. Christians as a body, v:3) for Himself out of the world)."[54] Paul specifies the timing of this choice—it was pretemporal, before the world was created. God made the choice "in him" (that is, "in Christ").

[Philadelphia: Fortress, 1975], 142), as do J. Héring (*The First Epistle of Saint Paul to the Corinthians* [London: Epworth, 1962], 68) and F. F. Bruce (*1, 2 Corinthians* [London: Oliphants, 1971], 79).

[52]So K. Grayston says, "The point of this remark is that our love for God, and not our vaunted gnosis, is a sign that he has acknowledged us as his People" ("The Doctrine of Election in Rom 8,28–30," 578).

[53]J. Armitage Robinson stresses the corporate nature of this election in his volume, *St. Paul's Epistle to the Ephesians*, 2d ed. (London: Macmillan, 1904), 23–27. At one point he says, "St Paul is dominated by the thought of the whole, and of God's purpose with the whole. It is a new Israel that Christ has founded, a People of privilege" (26–27).

[54]B. F. Westcott, *Epistle to the Ephesians* (London: Macmillan, 1906), 8.

In other words, Christ is the principal elected one, and God has chosen a corporate body to be *included in him*. J. K. S. Reid elaborates this conviction when he says, "As Himself the chosen, Christ is able to impart to those committed to Him and incorporated in Him the divine election. . . . God's choice of Him extends to those who are in Him."[55]

Others confirm this understanding too. K. Stendahl says, "Election in Christ strictly implies that Christ is the truly Elect. . . .The faithful become participants in His election."[56] H. Ridderbos notes that the church "was already united with the pre-existent Christ and thus chosen by God in him."[57] He goes on to speak of "the inclusion of the church in Christ, its corporate existence in him."[58] Mitton agrees. In speaking of "in Christ" he says,

> There is, however, in Paul's letters a third sense which has come to be regarded as the one most characteristic of him. In this sense it is used to express identification with Christ, with his death and with his risen life, as though Christ were a kind of corporate personality within which individual Christians and the Christian community as a whole may be included.[59]

And finally, M. Barth observes, "Election 'in Christ' must be understood as election of God's people. Only as members of that community do individuals share in the benefits of God's gracious choice."[60]

Election is the corporate choice of the church "in Christ." Before the foundation of the world God made his choice: those in Christ would be his people. Paul posits the goal of this election: in Christ the chosen ones would become holy and blameless. Election exists not for privilege, but to produce a holy people.

---

[55]Reid, "The Office of Christ in Predestination," *SJT* 1 (1948): 180. We do not agree with all Reid says in this article. In his view, "all therefore are predetermined to election" (182). This does not reflect Paul's perspective.

[56]K. Stendahl, "The Called and the Chosen. An Essay on Election," in *The Root of the Vine*, ed. A. Fridrichsen (London: Dacre, 1953), 68.

[57]H. Ridderbos, *Paul: An Outline of His Theology* (Grand Rapids: Eerdmans, 1975), 347.

[58]Ibid.

[59]C. L. Mitton, *Ephesians*, NCB (London: Oliphants, 1976), 46.

[60]M. Barth, *Ephesians*, 1:108.

Ephesians 1:11

Paul uses *kleroō* here in its sole occurrence in the New Testament. We probably find the basic meaning of this term from its cognates and Septuagintal uses: "choose by lot," "appoint by lot," "obtain an inheritance," and "be appropriated." Since God is the agent here, we may safely discard any idea of "lot." Probably Paul intends appropriation or choice, particularly in light of the clear parallel to 1:4. Thus, in Christ God appropriated (took hold of) a people to belong to him. Again the corporate sense predominates; as a body the church became God's possession or inheritance in Christ. God actively appropriated the church so it became his possession. Thus this verse closely parallels what Paul stated in 1:4. Both point to God's active choice of a group in Christ to belong to him and for whom he predestines a goal.

Colossians 3:12

Paul addresses his readers as "God's chosen people, holy and dearly loved." Christians as a group are chosen ones. The genitive *of God* can be either subjective (God has chosen them) or possessive (they are God's chosen ones). Probably not much separates these options. Paul's use of the substantive *chosen ones*, instead of the verb *to choose*, lays stress on the fact of their chosenness, rather than on the act of God's choosing. Since they are marked as God's chosen ones, these Christians ought to put on certain qualities in their lives, qualities that highlight their distinctiveness from the world.

1 Thessalonians 1:4

Calling his readers "brothers loved by God," Paul tells them he knows their election (*tēn eklogēn hymōn*). Surely that unpacks to mean "we know that God has chosen you." Paul's reason for this knowledge comes in 1:5: their ready reception of the gospel confirms their elect status. This refers to election to salvation. The object of God's choice is the corporate body of Christians at Thessalonica. There may be a hint of the purpose for their election in 1:6–10. At least Paul infers that the point of their election is not privilege, but responsibility. Election conveys the truth of God's initiative and grace. It focuses on the body God formed and the expectations he has for this people. When those who hear the message of the gospel respond to its call in faith, they establish their inclusion among the elect. Paul gives no hint that God chose specific individuals to respond to the gospel. He intends to remind the Thessalonian church that it enjoys the privilege and responsibility of being God's chosen ones.

2 Thessalonians 2:13

Paul expresses his obligation to give thanks for his readers because God chose them from the beginning for salvation through the sanctifying work of the Spirit and through belief in the truth. Here Paul uses the rare verb *haireomai*[61] for God's choice of the Thessalonian church. Paul utters a clear, unambiguous statement that God has chosen this particular group of Christian believers for the goal of their salvation. (No doubt Paul would say the same about every church.) In addition, Paul specifies the time in which God made this choice.[62] God's choice of the church was pretemporal. Paul appends two instruments. Salvation comes or is realized via two means: the sanctifying of the Holy Spirit, and the faith of the Thessalonians.

In summary, God pretemporally chose the church for salvation that is actualized by the work of the Spirit and the people's faith. In some way Paul makes election dependent on, or at least complementary to, the human exercise of faith. His words are not quite so strong as Peter's: "Make

---

[61]Paul employs this verb in two out of its three NT occurrences. In his other use at Php 1:22 he speaks of his own choice. It occurs a number of times in the LXX, translating several Hebrew words.

[62]This conclusion results from a textual critical decision in which we prefer *ap' archēs* (from the beginning) to the reading *aparchēn* (firstfruits). Though the manuscript evidence is fairly evenly divided, the intrinsic evidence seems to argue for the former. A temporal connection is common with the concept of choosing (cf. 1Co 2:7; Eph 1:4; Col 1:26; 2Ti 1:9). In addition, the idea of firstfruits is more difficult to conceive in the context: how could Paul consider the Thessalonians firstfruits? Thus I disagree with the opinion of the editors of the *UBS*, 3d ed. and Bruce (*1 & 2 Thessalonians*, 189–90) and concur with the opinion of E. Best (*First and Second Epistles to the Thessalonians*, 312–13), W. Hendriksen (*I–II Thessalonians* [Grand Rapids: Baker, 1955], 187), I. H. Marshall (*1 and 2 Thessalonians*, NCB [Grand Rapids: Eerdmans, 1983], 207), and L. Morris (*The First and Second Epistles to the Thessalonians*, NICNT [Grand Rapids: Eerdmans, 1959], 237, n: 48).

your calling and election sure. For if you do these things, you will never fall" (2Pe 1:10). Nevertheless, the same synergistic tension exists.

2 Timothy 2:10

The writer recognized a corporate group whom he calls the "elect ones" (*tous eklektous*). He affirms his willingness to endure suffering so that they might procure the salvation found in Christ Jesus. We discover two ways to understand the description of this group. First, this could be a presumptive description: some of the elect have not yet obtained salvation, and thus Paul labors to make it available to them. Hence in some way the classification "elect" may be applied to someone not yet a Christian, but who will become one through Paul's evangelistic efforts.[63] In this first interpretation, Paul envisions a group who were chosen for salvation. This might parallel Eph 1:4, though in 2Ti 2:10 we find no hint that the choice was pretemporal.

However, a second interpretation commends itself in light of the context of persevering. In this view, Paul speaks here of the "final salvation" attained only after a life of faithfulness to Christ. The author stresses this point in the saying that follows in 2:11–13 (note the conditional uses of *ei*, [if]). Living and reigning with Christ depend upon faithfulness to Christ in this life. So in 2:10 Paul envisions his own suffering as a model and inspiration for the elect who, by following his example, will attain final salvation—to live and reign with Christ. Paul sounds an urgent call for faithfulness and endurance on the part of the elect (just as Peter did: "Make your calling and election sure" [2Pe 1:10]). This makes better sense in the context. It is unlikely that we may speak of a group called the "elect" who in some way have already been chosen for that position prior to their acceptance of the gospel.

Titus 1:1

Again we meet two options. Paul's apostolic ministry has as its goal that the corporate body of the "elect ones"

---

[63]This view is defended by Kelly, *A Commentary on the Pastoral Epistles*, 178, and by Ward, *Commentary on 1 & 2 Timothy and Titus*, 165.

might either: (1) come initially to faith, i.e., salvation (see the first option discussed under 2Ti 2:10), or (2) have their faith (trust, reliance on God) strengthened. Though it might be difficult to separate these as motives for Paul's ministry, the second option makes better sense in the context. In the words of W. Hendriksen, Paul ministers ". . . in order to further or promote the reliance of God's chosen ones on him."[64] So in this verse Paul says he envisioned a corporate group who enjoyed the status "elect ones."

God's Election of Angels

1 Timothy 5:21

Paul makes his charge to Timothy in the presence of God, Christ Jesus, and the *elect* angels. Some angels enjoy the status of being elect or chosen. The point is not that God has chosen certain angels, but that some occupy the position or status of "chosen angels." These angels enjoy a special station before God. Perhaps these are God's faithful angels, the ones who did not join Satan's rebellion and lose their former state; they are the elect, in contrast to the fallen angels. Or the adjective *elect* might describe all angels. J. E. Huther argues this point: "Wiesinger rightly remarks that *eklektoi* is to be taken as a general epithet of all angels. . . . It is added in order to give greater solemnity to the form of adjuration."[65] In either case the emphasis is on their status, not on God's act of choosing specific angels.

GOD PREDESTINES

Paul uses the verb *proorizō* (predestine) in five of its six occurrences in the NT; it is a characteristically Pauline word.[66] In addition, in some uses the verbs *proetoimazō* and *tithēmi* portray God as the Predestiner. Paul's emphasis lies

---

[64]Hendriksen, *I and II Timothy and Titus*, 340. Ward, *1 & 2 Timothy and Titus*, 233, agrees.

[65]J. E. Huther, *Critical and Exegetical Commentary on the New Testament. The Pastoral Epistles* (Edinburgh: T. & T. Clark, 1881), 212.

[66]We saw Luke's use in Ac 4.28. It is rare outside the NT, occurring in Demosthenes 31, 4 (fourth century B.C.); Ignatius, *Ephesians*, inscr.; Heliodorus 7, 24, 4 (third century A.D.); Sopater, Rhet. (fifth century A.D.); in addition to secular papyri usage from the sixth century A.D. (BAGD, 709).

on Christians corporately and on the ultimate goals God has prepared for those who are his own. Paul concern in predestination is not *how* people become Christians nor *who* become Christians, but to describe *what* God has foreordained on behalf of those who *are* (or *will be*) Christians. Predestination pertains to God's causative action in marking out the present and future benefits and the priorities which accrue to those who are his children. In summary, God made prior arrangements for the present and future welfare of his own body. This is predestination.

Romans 8:29–30

Not only does Paul describe God's called ones (v. 28) as foreknown, but as those who are predestined to be conformed to the image of Christ. God marked out beforehand this destiny for his people. This conformation to Christ refers not only to the final transformation to occur at Christ's return, but also to the lifelong process of change that God effects in the lives of believers.[67] God determined that those in the foreknown group would become like Christ.[68] K. Grayston says it well: "Before we have raised a finger or uttered a cry, God has appointed our destiny for us."[69]

Romans 9:23

The basic surface structure affirms that "God beforehand prepared (*proētoimosen*) vessels of mercy for glory" (author's translation). The underlying meaning probably borders on

---

[67]This explanation is supported, among others, by Cranfield, *Epistle to the Romans*, 1:432; Käsemann, *Commentary on Romans*, 244; Dunn, *Romans 1–8*, 483; and Hendriksen, *Epistle to the Romans*, 1:283. Some commentators see only the final destiny here of being conformed to the image of Christ: e.g., Lenski, *Paul's Epistle to the Romans*, 561; Murray, *The Epistle to the Romans*, 1:319. The weight of the context of Ro 8 argues for a present as well as future application. Theologians call this process sanctification.

[68]Thus I disagree with K. L. Schmidt (*TDNT*, 5:452–56) who argues that when God is the subject of the verbs, there is no essential distinction between *proginōskō* (foreknow) and *proorizō* (predestine). Surely their occurrence in this string of five verbs argues for a distinction. Also the fact that "foreknow" is absolute whereas "predestine" has objects points to a distinction in meaning. God knows people, but he predetermines certain destinies for those he knows.

[69]Grayston, "The Doctrine of Election in Romans 8, 28–30," 583.

this thought: "God beforehand prepared that he glorify vessels who are the objects of his mercy." Paul identifies these vessels in 9:24: "us, whom he also called." He asserts, then, that God has effectively made advance preparation[70] for a goal—glorification—to which all his children will attain.

This definitely parallels what we find in Paul's uses of *proorizō* (predestine) in Eph 1:5–6, 11–12, where he specifically connects the goal of glory to the action of predestination. Paul does not say that God has chosen some (not others) for glory. Rather, he affirms that God has predetermined a goal for the called ones—the objects of his mercy. The question is not who will receive glory, but what God predestined for the chosen ones.

1 Corinthians 2:7

Here Paul asserts that God predestined (*proorizō*) wisdom for our glory. Wisdom (*sophia*) probably refers to God's eternal (formerly hidden) purpose to redeem sinful humankind through the sacrifice of Christ.[71] God's ultimate goal in predestining is that his people experience glory. God did not predetermine merely an abstract idea, but a plan of salvation that would result in glory for the people of God.[72]

Ephesians 1:5

Those he elected (1:4) God predestined in love to be adopted as his sons through (*dia*) Jesus Christ. He accomplishes this predestination in keeping with (or on the basis of) the good pleasure of his will (*kata eudokian tou thelēmatos autou*). Paul identifies God's pleasurable will as the impetus

---

[70]We need to disagree here with Munck (*Christ and Israel*, 68–69) who sees no pretemporal dimension to this verse. He limits the timing here to "actions of God within the range of history that Paul is able to survey: the period of Christ and the apostles."

[71]See Barrett, *First Epistle to the Corinthians*, 71, and Fee, *First Epistle to the Corinthians*, 104–7.

[72]The point is made also by Conzelmann, *1 Corinthians*, 62. In addition Robertson and Plummer say, "The 'wisdom' is 'Christ crucified' (i. 18–24), fore-ordained by God (Acts iv. 28; Eph. iii. 11) for the salvation of men" (*First Epistle of St. Paul to the Corinthians*, ICC [Edinburgh: T. & T. Clark, 1911], 38).

behind what God predetermined for his people. Predestination is not capricious, arbitrary, or accidental; rather it is purposeful and pleasurable. God has marked out or predetermined a goal for the ones chosen in Christ. He purposed to mark out for them the most desirable of all gifts: adoption into his family as his children.

Ephesians 1:11–12

Paul proposes another design in God's act of predestining. Predestination results in the praise of God's glory. God has determined beforehand that the body that becomes his inheritance will sing the praises of his glory. Clearly, this parallels a remote goal of predestination in 1:5–6: "to the praise of his glorious grace."

Ephesians 2:10

As in Ro 9:23, here Paul uses the verb *proetoimazō* (prepare beforehand) with obvious predestination overtones. The verse contains a grammatical ambiguity which, in the end, may not be so crucial for ascertaining its basic sense. The grammatical question is: Should we understand the relative pronoun *hois* to be a real dative or a dative of attraction? The real dative yields the sense: "God prepared us for 'which' [=good works]," supplying the direct object *us* from the context. Taking the dative case of the pronoun as a result of attraction yields: "God prepared 'which' [=good works]."

The second explanation is possible—that God actually determined the good works that his people would do.[73] However, the first—that God has prepared a people who will do good works—definitely makes better sense in the context. God has predetermined a state of affairs concerning those who belong to him. Being God's workmanship, his people are predestined, that is, prepared beforehand, to

---

[73]Calvin says, "What remains now for free-will, if all the good works which proceed from us are acknowledged to have been the gifts of the Spirit of God?" (*Commentaries on the Epistles of Paul to the Galatians and Ephesians* [Edinburgh: Calvin Translation Society, 1854], 229). F. Foulkes assumes a similar stance: "The nature and character of the works and the direction of the Christian's daily walk are predetermined" (*The Epistle of Paul to the Ephesians*, TNTC [London: Tyndale, 1963], 77).

accomplish good works. Experientially, of course, the two options are very close. God has so changed his people that they have the ability and the desire to do good works. However, to avoid the conclusion that God has premapped out all good works (a concept alien to Paul and which most scholars, in disagreement with Calvin, would find unacceptable), with no room for free will, we prefer the first option. Formerly "objects of wrath" (2:3), Christians can now perform good works because of the change God has brought about in their lives. Not only did God predetermine eternal glory for his people (Eph 1:5–6, 11–12), but also a present life doing good. In some ways this corresponds to what Paul declared in Ro 8:29 concerning the present process of conformity to Christ.

1 Thessalonians 5:9

Paul proclaims his confidence in his Christian readers (5:4), that they will be ready for Christ's Parousia. God "has placed" (tithēmi)[74] them not in a position where they will experience his wrath, but rather, where they will realize salvation. "God has appointed us" expresses Paul's point. God has determined for believers the glorious destiny of salvation, not wrath. This sense mimics Paul's uses of proorizō, pointing to the goal God has determined for his people. Yet Paul gives no hint that God has selected some for salvation and not others.

GOD APPOINTS

God's action of appointing has elective significance for Paul. Like other writers, Paul uses terminology indicating that God has explicitly designated certain individuals for definite roles or tasks. In distinction to the previous sections we have investigated, here Paul's focus is upon individuals, rather than corporate groups. His uses divide into three groups: the appointment of Jesus, Paul, and then other individuals.

---

[74]For the use of the middle of tithēmi here and for the construction, see Moulton-Turner, 55–56, and BDF, Sec. 316.1.

God Appoints Jesus

Romans 1:4

Paul says that Jesus was designated, decreed, or appointed (the verb is *horizō*) Son of God by his resurrection from the dead. Jesus did not become Son by his resurrection, but the resurrection marked out for him some new stature or status as the "Son of God in power," exalted for all to see.[75] Appropriately, Schmidt asks whether Jesus' appointment to something must not coincide with what "He already is from the beginning of the world, from all eternity in God's decree."[76] And yet Paul contends that in some sense Jesus became even more. Dunn observes that "in power" indicated "that Jesus' divine sonship (v 3) had been 'upgraded' or 'enhanced' by the resurrection."[77] In the words of Käsemann, "Jesus receives the dignity of divine sonship only with his exaltation and enthronement."[78]

Romans 3:25

Paul uses the verb *protithenai* in all its three NT occurrences. As noted above, this middle use can mean either "put, set forth" or "put forth a purpose or intention." As for the use here, opinions diverge.[79] In either case the context suggests an elective act of God in the sense that he has purposed or set in action a plan that Jesus would be a *hilastērion*. God determined that Jesus accomplish salvation— a salvation that people must apprehend by faith. Here is no choice of whom God will embrace in salvation, only the decision to provide it through Christ's death.

---

[75]See Sanday and Headlam, *Epistle to the Romans*, 7–8; Cranfield, *Epistle to the Romans*, 1:61–62; and Dunn, *Romans 1–8*, 13–14.

[76]Schmidt, *TDNT*, 1:453.

[77]Dunn, *Romans 1–8*, 14.

[78]Käsemann, *Commentary on Romans*, 12. Dunn says "the resurrection marked a decisive stage in Christ's divine Sonship—not as marking its beginning" (*Romans 1–8*, 23).

[79]See p. 165, note 21 above.

Romans 11:16

In Paul's use of "root" here, some see a reference to the Messiah.[80] Most commentators assume the "root" refers to the Jewish patriarch "and that Paul's meaning is that the unbelieving majority of the Jews are hallowed by their relation to the patriarchs."[81]

However, before we simply close the case, we must hear from J. Jocz. He argues that the common understanding contradicts the nature of God's sovereign election as totally unmotivated by anything in his people. Jocz makes the case that the root must be the Messiah, and that election has nothing to do with any national qualities of Israel or any "merits" of the patriarchs.[82] From Isaiah, Jocz argues that Christ is God's Chosen One, the "Root of Jesse" (Isa 11:10). In addition, Isa 53:2 is a messianic text in which the LXX translates the Hebrew *shōresh* by the Greek word meaning "root" (*hriza*). Thus the branches are those in Christ, to use the familiar Pauline expression. Though Jocz is probably wrong (Ro 11:28 provides confirmation that Paul has in mind the patriarchs), his view fits with the synoptic evidence of Christ as God's Chosen One.

Colossians 1:19

Here Paul's assertion could mean "all the fullness was pleased to dwell in Christ," or "God was pleased that all (his) fullness dwell in Christ."[83] The first requires a personali-

---

[80]Cranfield mentions that a few commentators also see in Paul's use of "first-fruit" in the previous clause a possible reference to Christ, in keeping with 1Co 15:20 (Cranfield, *Epistle to the Romans*, 2:564–65). This seems highly unlikely.

[81]Cranfield, *Epistle to the Romans*, 2:565.

[82]See J. Jocz, *A Theology of Election* (London: SPCK, 1958), 104ff.

[83]Commentators are divided. Those deciding for the first option include: C. F. D. Moule, *The Epistles of Paul to the Colossians and to Philemon*, CGTC (Cambridge: The University Press, 1968),70–71; E. Käsemann, *Essays on New Testament Themes*, SBT 41 (London: SCM, 1964), 157ff.; E. Lohse, *Colossians and Philemon*, Hermeneia (Philadelphia: Fortress, 1971), 56ff.; T. K. Abbott, *Epistles to the Ephesians and to the Colossians*, 218–19; et al. Those defending the second option include R. P. Martin, *Colossians and Philemon*, NCB (London: Oliphants, 1974), 59–60; J. B. Lightfoot, *St. Paul's Epistles to the Colossians and to Philemon*, 2d ed. (London: Macmillan, 1876), 158; Schrenk, *TDNT*, 2:741; Delling, *TDNT*, 6:303–4; E. Schweizer, *The Letter to the*

zation of the phrase "all the fullness" (*pan to plērōma*), while
the second requires that we supply the agent "God" from
the context. Against the first possibility, nowhere else does
Paul employ *plērōma* as a nonpersonal agent. It is more
difficult to propose that the *plērōma* experiences pleasure or
choosing/willing than to supply God as the agent of those
actions. With God as the agent the verb *eudokeō* conveys an
elective sense, meaning to "will, determine, or resolve."[84]
Paul uses this elective sense at 1Co 1:21 and Gal 1:15–16.

Paul here affirms something of Jesus' status, especially
his deity. As the result of God's definitive choice, Christ is
the "place" (*en autō*) where God in all his fullness chooses to
dwell.[85] God willed that Jesus be fully God, and, through
him, to reconcile people to himself.

2 Timothy 1:9

Paul affirms that God's salvation and call do not result
from the works people do, but issue from God's own
purpose and grace. He provided this grace of salvation in
Christ Jesus before time began (cf. Eph 1:4). God acted
graciously to elect Christ (and Christians in him) prior to
creation.

God Appoints Paul to His Role as Apostle

Romans 1:1

Paul describes himself as a man under divine "call" and
"appointment." Paul owes his apostolic position to these
acts of God. God set him apart (*aphorizō*) to be a preacher of
the gospel. Paul is an authoritative apostle because God has
chosen him for his role. Paul makes no explicit reference to
any choice to salvation, only appointment to apostleship, as
Calvin affirms:

> I do not agree with those who refer this call which Paul is
> describing to the eternal selection of God and interpret
> *separation* to mean either his separation from his mother's

Colossians (London: SPCK, 1982), 77; P. O'Brien, *Colossians, Philemon*, WBC
(Dallas: Word, 1982), 51–52; et al.

[84]BAGD, 319.

[85]O'Brien, *Colossians, Philemon*, 52.

womb, . . . or his election (referred to by Luke) to preach to the Gentiles.[86]

As Cranfield puts it, *"aphorismenos* refers . . . to God's consecration of him for his future task."[87] Here is election of an individual: the election of Paul to the task of apostleship.

Here and at 1Co 1:1 are the only places Paul uses *klētos* to apply to an individual (in both it is to refer to himself as a "called" apostle). This does not have the technical sense we see for the other *kalein* (call) paronyms (that is, the call to salvation). However, by a kind of extension of that technical sense, Paul uses the word *call* to describe God's activity of naming or designating him to be an apostle.

Romans 12:3

Speaking of his apostolic commission, Paul notes that God's grace was given to him. Käsemann notes that this is a stereotyped formula Paul uses to refer to his apostolate.[88] Paul speaks authoritatively to the Romans in his instructions because God chose to grace him with his apostolic role. Unquestionably this denotes a divine commission. The aorist tense of *dotheisēs* (was given) points to some specific occasion when Paul experienced God's grace. This probably corresponds to his explanation in Gal 1:15–16.

Romans 15:15–16

This statement parallels 12:3a: God has given Paul the grace of apostleship to proclaim the gospel among the Gentiles (also see 1:5). Paul's apostolic appointment to his ministry involves individual election to a task.

1 Corinthians 1:1

Paul bases his apostleship on the call of God. His use of *klētos* is clearly technical: Paul is a "called apostle."[89] Paul's

---

[86]Calvin, *Epistles of Paul to the Romans and to the Thessalonians,* 14.

[87]Cranfield, *Epistle to the Romans,* 1:53.

[88]See E. Käsemann, *Commentary on Romans,* 340. Most commentators agree, including Cranfield, *Epistle to the Romans,* 2:612; Murray, *Epistle to the Romans,* 2:117; and Barrett, *Epistle to the Romans,* 235.

[89]Conzelmann states that the "call" refers to the process of God's calling Paul on the Damascus Road (*1 Corinthians,* 20). Barrett, on the other hand,

status rests squarely on the will (*thelēma*) of God. His apostleship is a divine vocation.[90] He implies that any who reject his apostleship go against God's will, for Paul's call comes from God, not any human channel.

1 Corinthians 9:16–17

Here Paul expresses a sense of duty (even compulsion) to preach the gospel. Displaying a consciousness of a divine appointment, Paul says he has an *oikonomia*, an office entrusted to him, and he must discharge his responsibility. Barrett says, "The language recalls the appointment of imperial secretaries."[91]

1 Corinthians 15:10

Paul attributes his role as coming from God, specifically, the grace of God. God has graciously appointed Paul to be an apostle (15:9) and enables him to carry out his ministry of preaching.[92]

2 Corinthians 1:1

Again Paul predicates his apostleship upon the will (*thelēma*) of God. Paul believes his appointment to his role as apostle differed from the work of God that ushers all Christians into the Christian body. A special operation or act of the divine will appointed him to apostleship.[93]

---

suggests that Paul's reference might be more encompassing, including "the whole of Paul's apostolic activity" (*First Epistle to the Corinthians*, 30–31). Probably Conzelmann has a better grasp of the text here.

[90]Fee, *The First Epistle to the Corinthians*, 28–29.

[91]Barrett, *First Epistle to the Corinthians*, 189.

[92]J. Héring says Paul "owes his apostolic position, his perseverance in the work, the success of his preaching solely to the grace of God" (*The First Epistle of Saint Paul to the Corinthians* [London: Epworth, 1962], 162). Fee, *The First Epistle to the Corinthians*, 735, adds a crucial detail: ". . . although God's gracious gift of apostleship was the result of divine initiative, hence all of grace, nonetheless it required Paul's response."

[93]Surely C. K. Barrett, *The Second Epistle to the Corinthians*, BNTC (London: A. & C. Black, 1973), 54, goes beyond the evidence of the text when he says, "Paul had no choice about being an apostle and a preacher. . . ."

2 Corinthians 10:13

God has assigned (literally, measured out) the areas of ministry in which Paul works. Probably the primary sense of appointment here concerns Paul's apostolic ministry—God has measured out this task to him. In the context clearly Paul intends a reference to geography (v. 16). As a man under appointment, both his role and his itinerary derive from God.[94] God alone was responsible for both the extent and the success of his ministry. Thus Paul contrasted his ministry to that of others who were self-appointed and who boasted in themselves (v. 12).

Galatians 1:15

Paul lists a sequence of divine actions that explains his own salvation and commissioning to his apostolic ministry. In Paul's words, God "set apart" (aorist tense of *aphorizō*) Paul from his mother's womb; God "called" (aorist tense) Paul by his grace; and God "was pleased" (aorist of *eudokeō*) to reveal his Son in Paul so he might preach him among the Gentiles. We have Paul's clear statement that God chose and called him to his ministry.

Taking his main assertion first, Paul again uses *eudokeō*, "to be pleased," with the elective significance of God's pleasurable and effectual will. God chose that Paul receive revelation and in turn be an apostle to the Gentiles, an idea paralleled in Paul's speeches in Acts recorded by Luke (cf. Ac 22:10, 14; 26:16–18).

Paul's use of *aphorizō*, "to set apart," seems clearly to point to some idea of predestination. Paul claims that his commission came before his birth. Prior to his consciousness of God, or any ability to choose or respond, God acted to appoint him to his apostolic role. As F. F. Bruce puts it, "Before ever he was born, Paul means, God had his eye on him and set him apart for his apostolic ministry."[95] Consistent with his uses of *klētos* at Ro 1:1 and 1Co 1:1, here Paul

---

[94]R. P. Martin, *2 Corinthians*, WBC (Waco, TX: Word, 1986), 320, calls it an "assignment or a sphere of ministry." V. P. Furnish, *II Corinthians*, AB (Garden City, NY: Doubleday, 1984), 471, uses the word *jurisdiction* to capture the extent of God's appointment of Paul.
[95]Bruce, *Epistle of Paul to the Galatians*, 92.

uses a form of the verb *kaleō* (to call) to mark the historic realization and application of the divine appointment.

In the context of Gal 1:11–24 Paul underscores his apostolic commission and authority. He was appointed by God, not by other people. In v. 16 he isolates the purpose of that commission—to preach among the Gentiles. Yet only in a theological discussion can we separate Paul's apostolic appointment from his acquisition of salvation, as the Acts speeches show. In Paul's thinking, if God appointed him from birth to be an apostle, was he not also appointed to salvation? As he looked back, it was all God's doing. Paul never comes closer to asserting that God specifically chose an individual for salvation than he does in this personal defense. Nevertheless, the individual nature of this passage ought not be lost. This is his own testimony, and Paul does not extend his experience to others.

Ephesians 1:1

Paul again rests his apostleship on the outworking of the will (*thelēma*) of God (as in 1Co 1:1; 2Co 1:1; Col 1:1; and 2Ti 1:1). Paul did not deserve or nominate himself for his special position as apostle. Mitton observes, Paul "did not assume apostolic duties as his right. It was Christ who had sent him to fulfil them."[96]

Ephesians 3:7–8

God's grace was given (aorist tense) to Paul so that he might become an evangelist to the Gentiles (cf. 1Co 15:10). Paul recognizes that he owes his position as apostolic minister not to his own credentials, but to the mighty power of God graciously operating through him. He is a man under appointment.

Philippians 1:16

In this verse Paul explains that some brothers were preaching Christ out of motives of goodwill and love because they knew that Paul was *set* for the defense of the gospel.

---

[96]Mitton, *Ephesians*, 34.

Probably Paul uses the verb *keimai* (to set or put) in the sense of appoint (cf. Lk 2:34; 1Th 3:3).[97] R. P. Martin says, "*keimai* is a theological term, emphasizing that his appointment is a divine commission."[98]

Colossians 1:1

In a statement that agrees word for word with 2Co 1:1, Paul attributes his apostleship to God's will. This has an unmistakable elective sense to it. Lohse agrees: "The 'will' (*thelēma*) of God is the will which elects, which made Paul an apostle."[99]

1 Timothy 1:1; Titus 1:3

In both these texts Paul rests his apostleship upon the commission of God (*epitagē theou*). The language here is stronger than the more typical attribution of apostleship to God's will at the beginning of 1 and 2 Corinthians, Ephesians, Colossians, and 2 Timothy. J. N. D. Kelly says *epitagē* "connotes an order, and is often used of royal commands which must be obeyed."[100] God appointed Paul for his task, and he functions under divine orders. In Tit 1:3 Paul's commission embraces his apostolic role of preaching.

1 Timothy 1:12

Paul expresses thanks that Christ considered him faithful by appointing (the verb used is *tithēmi*) him for ministry. Again, Paul attributes his function as Christ's minister to divine appointment. This constitutes election to a ministry or task.

---

[97]Commentators concur: see G. Hawthorne, *Philippians*, WBC (Dallas: Word, 1983), 37; J. B. Lightfoot, *Epistle to the Philippians* (London: Macmillan, 1898), 89; W. Hendriksen, *A Commentary on the Epistle to the Philippians* (Grand Rapids: Baker, 1962), 72; and R. P. Martin, *Philippians*, NCB (Grand Rapids: Eerdmans, 1976), 74.

[98]Martin, ibid.

[99]Lohse, *Colossians and Philemon*, 6,n.10.

[100]Kelly, *Pastoral Epistles*, 40.

1 Timothy 2:7; 2 Timothy 1:11

Paul claims divine appointment (*tithēmi*) to be a herald, apostle, and teacher. Christ appointed Paul to his apostolic position.[101] As Kelly puts it, "Paul's ministerial status is due entirely to the divine initiative."[102]

2 Timothy 1:1

Following the exact formula of four previous epistolary introductions, Paul attributes his apostleship to the will (*thelēma*) of God. He presents God's will as the instrument through which God appointed him to his apostolic role or position.

God Appoints Individuals (Besides Paul) to a Position or Task

Romans 4:17

Paul quotes Ge 17:5 (LXX), where God tells Abraham he has appointed (*tithēmi*) him to be a father of many nations. God appointed or elected Abraham for this position or task. As we have just seen, this parallels Paul's other uses of this verb to designate his own apostolic appointment (1Ti 1:12; 2:7; and 2Ti 1:11).

Romans 9:11–13

In these verses Paul clarifies God's purpose in election. God did not base his choice of Jacob over Esau on any works either had done; he simply made a sovereign decision. God decided to appoint Jacob for his role. However, the context prevents any equation of this appointment with Jacob's personal salvation (though, of course, this does not deny his salvation). The quotation from Mal 1:2–3 confirms that Paul refers not to personal salvation but to God's choice of the nation Israel over Edom. Hence, Jacob and Esau represent their progeny. In tracing the ancestry of the Jews, Paul

---

[101]We posit Christ as the agent for these passive verbs on the basis of 1Ti 1:12.

[102]Kelly, *Pastoral Epistles*, 64.

asserts that God chose an individual—Jacob—for a specific mission or task, as he had chosen Isaac and Abraham before him.

Romans 9:17, 21

When he discusses the Egyptian pharaoh, Paul's concern is not his personal salvation. The discussion revolves around those God chooses to accomplish his purposes in the world. H. L. Ellison agrees: "Men are vessels or utensils. It is God's use of them and not their work for or against God that is under consideration."[103] Whether or not they (for example, the pharaoh) receive salvation is an issue separate from their selection for a task. Some chosen for an assignment will not receive salvation.[104] On the other side, others not chosen will be saved if God's wrath directs them to repentance and faith.[105]

Romans 12:6

Paul affirms that, like the gift or grace of apostleship (12:3), all spiritual gifts originate in the grace of God. He chooses to give gifts or ministries to specific individuals. This parallels election for a task or function, not election to salvation.

Romans 13:1

Paul exhorts his readers to submit themselves to the governing authorities, because all authorities have been appointed (the verb used is *tassō*) by God. God appoints governmental leaders to perform tasks on the earth. In a broad sense we could include this within the uses of election to a task or function, like the pharaoh's role.

---

[103]H. L. Ellison, *The Mystery of Israel. An Exposition of Romans 9–11* (Exeter: Paternoster, 1966), 53.

[104]Certainly Judas was in this category: chosen by Jesus for a task, yet finally a vessel for destruction. God certainly bears with and even uses people who have no use for him. He is patient with them in order to accomplish his purposes and make known his glory for the ultimate benefit of his people (9:23ff).

[105]Ellison, *The Mystery of Israel*, 54.

1 Corinthians 3:5

Paul argues that men like him and Apollos are God's servants performing the task or role that the Lord gave (*edōken*) or assigned to each one. Thus Paul defends God's appointment of these "apostles" to their tasks.

1 Corinthians 12:28

Using the verb *tithēmi* Paul affirms that God *appointed* people to exercise various ministries in the church and endowed them with the spiritual gifts necessary to perform these tasks. The appointees he specifically lists (though clearly the list is not exhaustive) include apostles, prophets, and teachers, followed by miracle-workers, healers, helpers, administrators, and those who speak in tongues. As with 12:11, God determined the ministries (and gifts) his people are to perform. God appoints all Christians to tasks in the congregation, a kind of election of individuals to roles or tasks.

Ephesians 4:7

In a vein similar to the previous verse Paul says that to each Christian grace was given (aorist of *didōmi*). The context makes clear that the "grace given" refers to spiritual gifts (4:8, 11). Christ has measured out or apportioned grace to each Christian as he saw fit (cf. Ro 12:6). This again is appointment to tasks or functions within the body of Christ.

GOD CALLS

Previously we simply mentioned Paul's technical use of the concept of "calling." Though the "calling" terms are common and have various senses throughout the New Testament, Paul characteristically uses the idea in a technical sense to specify the "call to be(come) a Christian." The NT employs two basic senses for the verb *kalein* (to call), the noun *klēsis* (calling), and the adjective *klētos* (called). The first is "name, designate, give a title to," as in the English, "We *called* her Sarah." The second is "summon, invite," as in,

"We *called* her, but she did not come."[106] In its technical sense, to "call" implies God's definitive designation or summons of a person to belong to God. God's calling of his people links his pretemporal choices and predeterminations for them on the one side, with his application of these goals and benefits on the other. The key to actualizing and appropriating God's choice and predestination is the *"call* to become a Christian."

Though this sense dominates, there are several nonsignificant uses of the various terms. One refers to corporate Israel and corresponds to the basic pattern of God's definitive action, though without the Christian connection. We will consider that one use first and then move to God's calling of Christians.

God Calls Corporate Israel

Romans 11:29

Employing what is probably the "naming"[107] sense (in distinction to the sense of "summons"), Paul says that God called Israel into existence and named her as his own. Paul asserts that God will not go back on or deny this call; the nation is his beloved people (11:28). His call is irrevocable. As Cranfield puts it, "By *hē klēsis* here we may understand God's calling of Israel to be His special people, to stand in a special relation to Himself, and to fulfill a special function in history."[108]

God Calls Christians

Romans 1:6–7

Here is the first of what we identified above as Paul's technical use of the concept of "calling." Using the adjective *klētos* (called), Paul identifies the Roman Christians as the *called* of Jesus Christ and the *called* saints. In both instances Paul employs the simple verbal adjective to indicate spe-

---

[106]These two basic senses can also be detected in secular Greek literature, the LXX, and early Christian writings.

[107]For a defense that the naming sense dominates Paul's uses, see W. W. Klein, "Paul's Use of *kalein*. A Proposal," *JETS* 27 (1984): 53–64.

[108]Cranfield, *Epistle to the Romans*, 2:581.

cifically that God (or Jesus) called these people to be Christians.[109]

In 1:7, as in 1Co 1:2, Paul identifies the readers as those who are "called holy." This may signify either of two senses: (1) God has designated them as saints, his holy ones; or (2) God has called them to be holy (where holiness is a goal to be reached). Probably we cannot separate completely the two, for Paul uses both ideas elsewhere. However, given the dominant use of "holy ones" as a synonym for Christians and the use here juxtaposed with 1:1, where Paul refers to his call to be an apostle, sense (1) is more likely. The readers can rest in the certainty that God has called them (to be his) holy ones. As Christians they enjoy that status.

Romans 8:28

Paul describes the beneficiaries of God's working for good in two ways. They love God, and they are the *called* according to God's purpose. God's people are "called ones"; the technical status of the term is indisputable. In addition, God called them on the basis of or through his own purpose. Their calling has identified them surely with God's salvific purpose, and, therefore, they can be sure that God will work out things for their good.[110] Barrett puts it this way: " 'Calling' is the realization in history of God's eternal *purpose*. It is here, in God's purpose, that the ultimate assurance of salvation rests."[111]

Some writers tend virtually to identify "calling" with election. However, considering the technical use dominant elsewhere in Paul, that position is not justified. "Calling" marks the point God applies salvation (or the status of being

---

[109]The genitive *of Jesus Christ* in 1:6 presents a problem, for usually genitives indicate either agent or recipient of the action and we find no parallel in Paul to identify Jesus as the agent who calls. We could take this as a unique use of Jesus as the "caller," and in fact Cranfield adopts this position (*Epistle to the Romans*, 1:68). If we insist on consistency then we will view the genitive as possessive—they are the called ones who belong to Jesus Christ (see the NIV and the Romans commentaries of Black, 38; Meyer, 1:54; Calvin, 18; Murray, 1:14; Barrett, 22; Sanday and Headlam, 12; Dunn, 1:19; Hendriksen, 1:46; as well as BDF, 98. With either option there is a divine agent who has called the Roman Christians.

[110]See Dodd, *The Epistle to the Romans*, 139–40.

[111]Barrett, *Epistle to the Romans*, 169.

a Christian) to a person. "The called" are the Christians. Although "the elect" are also Christians, it is erroneous to say that "call" equals "elect." They express different concepts.

Romans 8:30

In Paul's list of God's definitive actions, "calling" follows the pretemporal actions of "foreknow" and "predestine." It marks the point of reception of salvation for those embraced in the previous two actions. Dunn confirms that the verb *called* here "denotes divinely accomplished conversion."[112] Those called are then justified and glorified, the final two actions. Paul's emphasis falls upon assurance or security for the believers. He assures those called that God will complete their salvation in spite of all obstacles.

Romans 9:24–26

Paul provides some explanation of God's action of "calling," employing quotes from Hos 2:23 and 1:10 to confirm his case. In v. 24 Paul identifies those whom God calls: he calls from among the Jews and Gentiles. Those who become "my people" (v. 25) and "sons of the living God" (v. 26)—that is, those who attain salvation—do so because God calls both Jews and Gentiles. In the quote in v. 25 the use of the double accusative strongly suggests that the meaning of *call* is "name" or "designate." God names certain people as "my people" who formerly were not. In the act of calling they become God's people. This performative language communicates a distinct causative component. The quote in v. 26 confirms this naming sense. Because God's call causes them to become his people, others can justifiably "call" them "sons of the living God." They now enjoy the status "the called."

1 Corinthians 1:2

Paul describes the addressees of this letter as *klētois hagiois*, "called saints." The NIV translates this as "those . . .

---

[112]Dunn, *Romans 1–8*, 485.

called to be holy," and Calvin agrees.[113] Most commentators, however, prefer to understand the words to mean, in F. F. Bruce's words, "saints by divine calling."[114] More likely, at this beginning point in the letter, Paul wants to affirm the status of his readers, rather than issue a call to holiness. Though elsewhere Paul identifies holiness as the goal of God's call, that is not his point here. The readers are saints or God's holy people by virtue of God's call, just as Paul became an apostle because of God's call. God has labeled the Corinthians his "holy ones"; he has named them his own.

1 Corinthians 1:9

Using the aorist tense Paul asserts that God "called" the Corinthians into fellowship with Jesus Christ. The result or goal of God's call is *koinonia* with Christ. Barrett argues for a corporate sense of this *koinonia*. He remarks, correctly, "The sense would be that God has called you into the community—that is, the church—of Jesus Christ."[115] God's calling has placed them in his body. Through his call, God "is responsible for their very existence as a community of faith," says Fee.[116]

1 Corinthians 1:24

Paul preaches a message of the crucified Christ, a message that is a stumbling block to the Jews and appears as foolishness to Gentiles. However, to "the called" (*klētois*) among the Jews and Gentiles, Christ is the power and the wisdom of God.

In keeping with his other uses of the "calling" terms, here Paul stresses his readers' status as God's own "called ones." In contrast to the bulk of people who reject Christ, they have believed (v. 21), and God has acted to designate them as his people.

---

[113]J. Calvin, *The First Epistle of Paul the Apostle to the Corinthians* (Edinburgh: Oliver & Boyd, 1960), 22.

[114]Bruce, *1 and 2 Corinthians*, 30. Barrett renders the words "by divine call saints" (*First Epistle to the Corinthians*, 32). Conzelmann has "called to be saints" (*1 Corinthians*, 22). Finally, Fee says, "God's new people by divine calling" (*The First Epistle to the Corinthians*, 33).

[115]Barrett, *First Epistle to the Corinthians*, 40.

[116]Fee, *The First Epistle to the Corinthians*, 45.

1 Corinthians 1:26

In this text Paul emphasizes not the action of God's calling, but the state that has resulted from his call.[117] "Calling" (*klēsis*) is the present possession of Paul's readers: "Consider your *calling*." Paul asks the readers to think back to the time when they entered the state of being called ones. Not many were wise, influential, or well-born. Paul uses the technical meaning of "call": God designated them as Christians.

1 Corinthians 7:15–24

In this passage Paul repeatedly uses the verb *kalein* (to call) and in 7:20 also employs the noun *klēsis* (calling). Paul identifies the Lord or God as the agent who calls (vv. 17, 22). Indeed, each use of "call" is best understood with the divine agent. In v. 15 Paul attaches a goal to God's calling—peace. God called his people to live in peace, or peacefully.[118] In the remaining uses Paul simply attaches some attendant circumstance to the action of "call." Thus, God called the Corinthians while they were *in* some particular situation or circumstance (see vv. 18, 20, 21, 22, 24).

Since Paul specifies no goals or instruments in any of these latter uses, we may be tempted to conclude that they supply no further information about *kalein*. However, the absence of any further specifications is highly significant in this section. It provides convincing evidence that "call" indeed has technical status in Paul's uses. He could merely say, "You were called," and—omitting any instrument, goal, or even an agent in most uses—he could be sure his readers would understand his meaning. The "call" is clearly the "calling to be a Christian."

---

[117]Conzelmann (*1 Corinthians*, 49) disagrees, preferring to see in *klēsis* a reference to the act of calling rather than the state of being called. Though God's action is the basis, of course, Paul highlights here the resulting state, not the formative act.

[118]In defense of the goal orientation of the phrase "in peace" (*en eirēnē*) see Bruce (*1 and 2 Corinthians*, 70) and Barrett (*First Epistle to the Corinthians*, 166). C. F. D. Moule notes, ". . . the preposition may be used 'pregnantly': perhaps God has called you into a peace in which he wishes you to live" (*An Idiom Book of New Testament Greek*, 2d ed. [Cambridge: University Press, 1971], 79).

What about Paul's use of "calling" (*klēsis*) in v. 20? Is this the salvific, technical sense, the calling to be a Christian? Though some dissent, the answer must be no. In the context of each occurrence of the verb *to call* Paul lists the circumstances in which the Christians were when God called them to be Christians. These include circumcision, uncircumcision, slavery, and freedom. In this list of various situations, Paul includes *klēsis*. Here this must also refer to a secular vocation or state in life, and not the more common technical sense.[119] Paul's point is not that God calls people *to* a vocation or state, but that he calls people to salvation while they are *in a calling* (situation, circumstance).

Galatians 1:6

Paul depicts God as "the one who *called* you by the grace of Christ." Clearly the verb *kalein* has its Pauline technical status in this use: God is the one who calls people to salvation. The phrase *en chariti* (literally, "in grace") could be a goal or means, but the clear identification of grace as the instrument of calling in v. 15 argues for that sense here too.[120] Grace is the means by which God applied salvation to the readers when he called them, and the aorist tense probably harks back to the specific occasion of their conversion.

Galatians 5:8

Closely following the previous use, Paul describes God simply as "the one who calls you." Here the tense is present. Again the technical status is clear; the Galatians became— and continue to be—Christians because of God's action of designating them as his own people.

---

[119]Those who agree with us include Barrett, *First Epistle to the Corinthians*, 169; BAGD, 435–36; Fee, *The First Epistle to the Corinthians*, 314; and M. Barth, *Ephesians*, 2:453ff. In his *Biblical Doctrine of Work* (London: SCM, 1952), 36, A. Richardson disagrees.

[120]H. D. Betz disagrees with the instrumental sense and prefers a more local meaning—it is "a definition of the situation before God enjoyed by those who were called" (*Galatians*, Hermeneia [Philadelphia: Fortress, 1979], 48), parallel to such expressions as "in Christ" (Gal 1:22), "in peace" (1Co 7:15), or "in hope" (Eph 4:4). In either case, this does not affect our conclusion about the technical status of "calling" here.

Galatians 5:13

Paul tells his readers that God called them for the purpose or goal of freedom. When God named them as his saved ones, he intended that they enjoy freedom. Paul employs the technical sense of "call" to indicate the status the Galatians, having attained salvation, now possess.

Ephesians 1:18

Paul prays that his readers might know what is "the hope of his calling" (lit.). The underlying structure of this phrase can be recast as "God called you to a hope." Paul wants them to know experientially the hope to which God called them. The call (klēsis) to be a Christian is a call to live in hope. The noun *calling* shares the technical status of its fellow "call" words. Paul stipulates that hope ought to result from their new status as Christians.[121]

Ephesians 4:1, 4

In these verses Paul employs both the verb *to call* and the noun *calling*. In 4:1 Paul urges his readers to walk worthy of the calling to (or by) which God called them. God's call to be a Christian mandates a certain lifestyle. In 4:4 Paul tells them they were called to one hope of their calling. The calling of God carries with it hope; hope is part and parcel of the call to be a Christian. Unquestionably, both uses bear the technical meaning of "call." God calls people, and they become his. Consequently they have a calling. The *action* of God has resulted in a *state* for Christians. They have an obligation to live up to the demands or implications of this status.

Colossians 3:15

Paul tells his readers: "you were called to peace." When God called them, they assumed the responsibility to pursue peace within the body of Christ. *Kalein* (call) points to the time when they began the Christian life. Entering the

---

[121]Other outcomes or goals for the noun *klēsis* in Paul include hope (Eph 4:4); worthy living (Eph 4:1; 2Th 1:11); holiness (2Ti 1:9); and striving (Php 3:14). For the verb *kalein* Paul lists several other goals of God's calling.

Christian life included an obligation to emulate their name-
sake, Christ, letting his peace rule.

1 Thessalonians 2:12

With language matching that in Gal 1:6 and 5:8, Paul
describes God as the one who *calls* people into his kingdom
and glory. He urges his readers to walk worthy (cf. Eph 4:1)
of the God who calls (present tense). Since God named them
as his own, they have the duty to live up to the family name.
This is Paul's technical sense: God's calling results in access
to his kingdom and glory. E. Best proposes that the present
tense stresses "the continuous and effective call of God . . .
which can reassure his readers that they will attain to the
kingdom and glory even though their walk is not always
worthy of God."[122]

1 Thessalonians 4:7

Paul gives Christians a reason why they ought to pursue
holiness and shun immorality: God *called* us to holiness, not
to uncleanness. The goal God had in mind when he called
the Thessalonians was not uncleanness, but holiness. With
the "call to be a Christian" comes the obligation to live in
holiness.

1 Thessalonians 5:24

Here Paul describes God in very simple terms—he is *ho
kalōn* (the one who calls). Employing the technical sense of
God's call to salvation, Paul portrays God simply as the one
who appoints people to belong to him. Again the present
tense of the verb emphasizes the permanency of this
relationship.

2 Thessalonians 1:11

Paul prays that God might consider the Thessalonians
worthy of his *calling*. They exist in the state of "having been
called"; they have a *calling* (*klēsis*). Paul uses the technical

---

[122]Best, *A Commentary on the First and Second Epistles to the Thessalonians*,
108.

sense. God called them to be Christians, and thus they have a calling. Such a divine calling requires them to live and act in a manner that befits this status they enjoy. Again the naming sense helps our understanding. They possess God's calling (name) and must live up to it.

The call is not yet complete. Full salvation awaits Jesus' return and demands their faithful living until that event. Since they have a God who will aid them in their striving, Paul prays for the working of God's power in them. God's call has made them what they are. Now with his aid they must strive to be worthy.

2 Thessalonians 2:14

In 2:13 Paul explains why the Thessalonians ought to thank God constantly: God has brought them to salvation. In 2:14 he makes a rather complex assertion. Through the gospel message Paul preached, God *called* (aorist tense) the Thessalonians to a network of events: God's election, salvation, the Holy Spirit's sanctifying, and their faith. In the (preaching of the) gospel God summons people to faith, and he applies salvation when they believe the truth. The Holy Spirit sanctifies, the hearers exercise faith, and God grants salvation. This marks the point of God's call.

1 Timothy 6:12

Paul urges Timothy to "take hold of the eternal life to which you were *called* when you made your good confession in the presence of many witnesses." Some public occasion seems to be in view. Does *kalein* have its technical sense?[123] On one hand the meaning differs from the usual technical sense. Rather than being the initial point at which God designated Timothy to be a Christian, this appears to envision a summons to take up the demands and responsibilities of the Christian life as might occur at baptism. Is this, then, a nontechnical use of a public "call" that equals an affirmation of salvation? Yet, since the NT writers often closely identify (spiritual) salvation and its declaration in

---

[123]*Kalein* has some salvific sense here in light of the mention of eternal life. To this Timothy was called.

(physical) baptism,[124] this use of *kalein* might grow out of this natural connection. In the end it diverges little from the technical sense.[125] So we regard *kalein* here as the "call to be a Christian," but expressed as a summons publicly accepted or acknowledged at baptism.

2 Timothy 1:9

The author describes God as the one who *called* (aorist tense of *kalein*) [us] to a holy *calling* (*klēsis*). "Called to a holy calling" probably involves a Semitic redundancy and is equivalent to "called to a holy life." When applied by God, salvation carried the commitment to live a holy life (cf. 1Th 4:7). We cannot miss Paul's technical sense.

SUMMARY

We have covered much ground in the writings attributed to Paul. He, more than any other New Testament writer, addresses the issues that are germane to our investigation. Our analyses have uncovered various elements of Paul's view of God's election. The resulting picture is more comprehensive and detailed than for any other writer in the NT. Yet, we must also recognize that nowhere does Paul provide a detailed and systematic study of his perspective on election. His writings are mostly "occasional," written to respond to specific needs and crises in churches. We will piece together from a variety of places in his letters what Paul says about election. Overall our goal must be to let Paul be Paul, so that, in the interests of summarizing, we don't force him into our systems. Alas, how difficult that is after almost two thousand years of church history!

To begin, Paul affirms God's foreknowledge of his own people, both Israel as a nation and the body of Christians, the church. As to Israel, fore*knowledge* implies the special, knowing relationship God established with this people. This

---

[124]See, e.g., Ac 2:38; Ro 6:1–14; 1Pe 3:20–21.

[125]Kelly comes to this same conclusion when he says of baptism, "This above all was the occasion on which a Christian could be said to have accepted the call to eternal life" (*Pastoral Epistles*, 142). Those who agree include Dibelius and Conzelmann, *The Pastoral Epistles*, 88; W. Lock, *The Pastoral Epistles*, ICC (Edinburgh: T. & T. Clark, 1936), 71; and Ward, *1 & 2 Timothy and Titus*, 111.

knowledge is corporate—encompassing the entire nation—
but is not necessarily salvific. In addition *fore*knowledge
implies that God knew the dimensions and implications of
this relationship prior to their existence as a people.

Similarly, God foreknew the corporate body of Christians. As the chain in Ro 8:29–30 shows, God determined a
salvific destiny for his people in full knowledge of who they
were and what they would become as the result of his grace.
In none of Paul's uses is "choice" inherent in God's
foreknowledge of his people. The face-value sense of God's
prior knowledge conveys Paul's emphasis. "Knowledge"
means more than mere cognition or recognition, of course. It
connotes a special relationship. Yet it does not necessarily
imply "choice."

Paul affirms that he serves a purposing God. He asserts
that God's sovereign will determines whether human plans
will be realized. Likewise, God's will accounts for the trials
his people encounter. On the other hand, Paul depicts God's
will as the desires he has for his people (for example,
holiness, joy, prayer, and thankfulness)—desires they may
or may not fulfill.

Paul employs both these senses—what God mandates
and what God desires—when he explains God's will for the
salvation of his people. In the first place, God sovereignly
purposed to provide redemption through Christ's death.
That God calls Christians the people of God finds its basis in
his salvific purposes. His will also accounts for the revelation
of the knowledge of salvation to the Gentiles. God purposed
to show mercy and to grant salvation to his people—those
who come to him in faith—and to harden and reject for
punishment those who reject him. Paul expresses these
various purposes in binding terms. God determined them.

Yet, secondly, Paul also insists that God desires the
salvation of all people. If we understand correctly the import
of Paul's teaching, God's desire for the salvation of all will
not be realized. Not all people will attain salvation in the age
to come.

Paul contends that God chose angels, the nation Israel,
and the corporate body of Christians. In some sense faithful
angels enjoy the status of God's elect. Jacob and his
descendants, not Esau and his, comprise God's chosen and
beloved people. God will not abandon this call of the nation
Israel, though he will reject (and even harden) individual

Jews because of their unwillingness to believe the gospel of Jesus Christ. The election of Israel is distinct from the salvation of individual Israelites. Indeed, in distinction to the entire foreknown nation, the remnant—a smaller group within the nation—existed as the object of God's gracious choice. This remnant alone among the Jews obtained salvation, for they sought it correctly, by faith.

Analogous to God's choice of Israel, he also chose Christians, though for them election and salvation coincide. Before the creation of the world, God chose the church as a corporate group *in Christ*. As his body, the church finds its identity in Christ. Christ is God's Chosen One, and the church discovers its election by its incorporation in him. God's pretemporal choice becomes evident when people accept the gospel. Election finds concrete expression and is obvious to others when people believe. This takes place through some combination of the Holy Spirit's sanctifying work and human faith (2Th 2:13), though Paul never spells out precisely the details of this synergism. Election naturally leads to responsibility and service. The elect will attain final salvation as those who persevere through life's trials.

God has not only chosen a people, but he has predestined certain benefits and outcomes for them. For Paul predestination involves what God predetermined for the elect. It portrays God's causative action to determine beforehand the benefits of salvation for believers in Christ. These include present and future conformity to Christ's image, glory, adoption into God's family, being among those who praise God's glory, and the capacity to do good works. God has determined that his people enjoy his eschatological salvation, not the wrath he pours out upon unbelievers.

To accomplish his various purposes in the world God has appointed individuals to certain roles and tasks. Jesus' career to accomplish redemption by dying on the cross resulted from God's purpose and appointment. God pleasurably determined that the fullness of the deity dwell in Christ. God appointed him to his special status as powerful Son of God by his resurrection and exaltation.

Paul himself was a man under appointment. He repeatedly insists that God appointed him to his role as apostle to proclaim the message of salvation. His gracious commission as an apostle rested upon God's specific choice. Paul's authority with the churches derived neither from himself nor

others, but from God alone. God chose to reveal himself to
Paul and in turn to set him apart for his apostolic responsibility. In Paul's thinking he was a "marked man," even prior to
his birth. God chose him for salvation and service.

Besides Jesus and himself, Paul recognized that God
chose or appointed other individuals to perform specific
ministries or functions. God appointed Abraham to be the
father of many nations. He chose Jacob over Esau for his role
as patriarch and pharaoh for his part in releasing Israel from
Egypt. God chose Apollos to function as a servant for the
Corinthian church. God selects Christians for ministries by
giving them various spiritual gifts. God appoints governing
authorities to rule nations.

Paul establishes a distinct technical sense to the various
words he uses for "calling." God brought Israel into
existence and called her to be his own people. In the act of
that "call" Israel became God's people. For Christians,
"calling" marks that point when God applies to them
salvation or the status of belonging to God. It denotes the
fulfillment in present time of God's pretemporal foreknowledge and predestination. As performative language, "calling" specifies the divine act when God names or designates
people from among Jews and Gentiles to become his own
people. God calls Christians to be saints; he has labeled them
his holy ones. Having defined this technical meaning for the
"calling" words, Paul uses the description "the called
(ones)" to be synonymous with saints or Christians. Since
Christians are people whom God called, they have an
obligation (a calling) to live up to the implications of their
status. These responsibilities include holiness, peace, freedom, and hope.

9

HEBREWS

The purpose of the unknown author of Hebrews lay in convincing the readers of the superiority of the way of Jesus Christ to head off their defection back to Judaism. Since the writer stresses their need to persevere, he does not devote much space at all to election themes. Only Christ himself merits much consideration as one whom God appointed. The terms we have encountered for the election of believers are largely missing. I will categorize the meager texts and discuss the author's treatment of Christ at the end of the chapter.

GOD DETERMINES DATES

Hebrews 4:7

The author says that God set or appointed (*horizō*) a certain day to be Today. Five of the eight uses of *horizō* in the New Testament specify God's appointing Jesus to some position. The use here mirrors the use of this verb in Ac 17:26, where, as we saw, God determined times and boundaries for nations. So here God definitively determines a date.

GOD'S APPOINTMENT OF INDIVIDUALS

Hebrews 5:4

No one confers upon himself the office of high priest. Someone occupies the position only when God *calls* (*kalein*) him to it. God appointed Aaron; this is the proper pattern. This call, a divine act of appointment, grants the status or office of high priest. This supports the performative naming sense for *kalein*: God's call in fact caused Aaron to assume that position. At God's call he became high priest.

GOD'S ROLE IN APPLYING SALVATION

The first with more than a single entry, this category specifically relates to our central concern—salvation. Three texts make use of the concept of "call," so we will consider them together, and then return to the final text.

Hebrews 3:1

The writer addresses his exhortation to his "holy brothers, who share in the heavenly *calling*" (*klēsis*). This noun occurs nine times in Paul's writings, here, and then in 2Pe 1:10. Without doubt it is a technical term for the "calling to be a Christian." In this text the author characterizes this calling as "heavenly." F. F. Bruce remarks that their calling "marks them out as citizens of a realm not circumscribed by the conditions of earthly life."[1] What exactly might this mean for our understanding of the Christian calling?

"Calling" usually has some relation attached to it, often location, or instrument. God calls Christians *to* something or *by means of* something.[2] This analysis proves helpful in understanding the description "heavenly" here.[3] It presents several options, however. First, we may take "heavenly" to indicate the place or goal to which Christians have been called. If a place, then does the author mean that God called

---

[1]F. F. Bruce, *Commentary on the Epistle to the Hebrews*, NICNT (Grand Rapids: Eerdmans, 1964), 55.

[2]See W. W. Klein, "Paul's Use of *kalein*. A Proposal," *JETS* 27 (1984): 55ff. See 55, n.7.

[3]Other uses of "heavenly" in Hebrews describe the heavenly gift (6:4), sanctuary (8:5), things (9:23), country (11:16), and Jerusalem (12:22).

Christians to reside in heaven?[4] Indeed, in this context he exhorts the readers to persevere to receive the eternal rest God has in store for them. Second, the author may intend that we understand "heavenly" to be the reality that orders their present conduct. Their calling has the goal that they live "heavenly" lives according to God's real and superior values. Adopting this sense D. Guthrie says that if a calling is heavenly, "it must mean a vocation which has a spiritual and not a material direction."[5] Third, if a calling is heavenly, it originates in heaven, and the focus may be on its source in God. The call comes from or through God.

It is difficult to decide which nuance the author intended. Certainly, like the third, the first two options also presume God issued the call; he is its source. Indeed, that is consistent with Paul's uses of the term *calling* (*klēsis*). And surely "heavenly" conveys more than simply origin or instrument. We dare not exclude either the heavenly goal or the present goal for living in light of this entire epistle. B. F. Westcott said, "The Christian's "calling" is heavenly . . . as being a calling to a life fulfilled in heaven, in the spiritual realm."[6] God *calls* the Christian to a life characterized by heavenly values *and* to an eternal inheritance.

Hebrews 9:15

Jesus mediates a new covenant so "the ones who have been called" (*hoi keklēmenoi*) may receive the promise of the eternal inheritance. Instead of using the verbal adjective *klētoi* for the "called ones" (cf. Ro 1:6; 1Co 1:24; Jude 1; Rev 17:14), the author employs the perfect participle of the verb *kalein* (to call). Perhaps this underscores their settled status: they *are* the ones God has called. Without question *kalein* has its technical meaning here. Independent of any elaboration the author designates believers in Christ as "those who are called." J. Moffatt said, "The *keklēmenoi* are the faithful People."[7]

---

[4]The idea of a place may find support at 9:15 where the author uses the verb *kalein* (call) in connection with the promise of an eternal inheritance.

[5]D. Guthrie, *The Letter to the Hebrews* (Leicester: Inter-Varsity, 1983), 97.

[6]B. F. Westcott, *The Epistle to the Hebrews*, 3d ed. (London: Macmillan, 1920), 74.

[7]J. Moffatt, *Epistle to the Hebrews*, ICC (Edinburgh: T. &. T. Clark, 1924), 127.

In Heb 1:2 the writer asserts that God appointed the Son to be heir of all things. The heir (*klēronomon*) receives the inheritance (*klēronomian*). But though the Son is heir, he mediates the new covenant so the ones whom God called receive a share in the inheritance. Moreover, 6:17 affirms Christians to be heirs of God's promise. This suggests some parallel to the "in Christ" concept so prominent in Paul's writings. Christians acquire an inheritance only because of their association with the Son.

Hebrews 11:18

Here the verb *kalein* occurs with a sense other than its technical meaning of "call to be a Christian." In fact, the writer uses *kalein* here in a quote from the Septuagint version of Ge 21:12. Translators render the literal "in Isaac your seed will be *called*" in various ways: "It is through Isaac that your offspring will be *reckoned*" (NIV); "Through the line of Isaac your posterity shall be *traced*"; and "Through Isaac shall your descendants be *named*" (RSV). The naming sense certainly captures the sense of *kalein* here.[8]

GOD'S APPOINTMENT OF CHRIST

This grouping contains the most entries, as we might expect in this document. Even so, the development is not extensive, and the author employs some terms we have not encountered before. He shows little interest in explaining any doctrine of Christ's election. Statements concerning Christ's appointment occur incidentally in the author's development of his major themes.

Hebrews 1:2

At the beginning of his argument that Jesus is the superior agent of revelation, the author asserts that God *appointed* (*tithēmi*) the Son to be heir of all things.[9] The use of

---

[8]Guthrie, *Letter to the Hebrews*, 236, and Westcott, *Epistle to the Hebrews*, 368, agree.

[9]This is the first incidence of the inheritance motif in Hebrews, though we have already mentioned it in connection with 9:15. Besides these it occurs at 6:12, 17; 10:36; and 11:8.

the aorist tense of *tithemi* raises an initial question of the timing of this appointment. Was there an investiture at some point, or is this simply language that expresses some relationship between the Father and Son? J. Moffatt allows for either, saying, "Probably it describes a pre-temporal act, or rather a relationship which belongs to the eternal order."[10] However, more likely the aorist represents a timeless state, and does not envision some investiture ceremony.[11] In the eternal relationship between Father and Son, "heir" in some manner expresses that Christ will receive "all things" from the Father in eternity. Guthrie also argues against some past appointment when he says,

> It is the present reality of the appointment that the writer is concerned about, and not about when it was made. Indeed, it is clear that the writer wants us to understand that there was never a time when the Son was not the heir.[12]

Since Christ is appointed heir, he can mediate his inheritance to sharers of the new covenant, as we noted concerning 9:15. P. E. Hughes's comment is apropos:

> Christ is the heir of *all* things precisely because God has only *one* Son and *one* heir. . . . In short, apart from Christ there is no sonship and heirship. Those therefore who desire to enjoy the privileges of the sons and heirs of God can do so only as by faith they are found *in Christ*.[13]

Again *tithēmi* occurs with elective significance. The Son is God's Appointed One. At this point his appointment as heir focuses on his status with God. In the next verse, 1:3, we see his mission to accomplish redemption.

Hebrews 1:5; 5:5

The author conveys the idea of God's appointment of Jesus through his Septuagint quotes of Ps 2:7 and 2Sa 7:14. In

---

[10]Moffatt, *Epistle to the Hebrews*, 5.

[11]However, we did argue that Jesus' baptism constituted a kind of investiture (or better, ordination) for his public ministry. But this was no pretemporal event. Further, it is not likely that the author of Hebrews refers to Jesus' baptism here.

[12]Guthrie, *The Letter to the Hebrews*, 64–65.

[13]P. E. Hughes, *A Commentary on the Epistle to the Hebrews* (Grand Rapids: Eerdmans, 1977), 39; his emphasis.

1:5 the writer argues that God never used such language of angels. However, the words apply *par excellence* to the Son. No angel enjoys the place or status of Jesus: he is the Son of God. The psalmist (David or perhaps one of his successors) confidently proclaimed that the king was the Lord's anointed. Eventually, the text was applied to the Messiah (Ps 17:26), the Davidic successor whom God would raise up to overthrow the yoke of the oppressors. We considered the strong possibility that an allusion to Ps 2:7 also lies behind the heavenly voice at Jesus' baptism (Mk 1:11, par.). The use of the same text at Ac 13:33 shows that the early church made the connection to Jesus early in its theologizing.

Again, in citing Ps 2:7 in these two places, the author does not identify some time or event in history when the Father begat the Son, any more than "firstborn" (Col 1:15; cf. Ps 89:27) means that Jesus was "born" or only came into existence at some point. Psalm 2:7 probably celebrated an annual coronation festival of the king. He did not first become king "today." The Hebrews author highlights Jesus' status as the Son in 1:5. His appointment displays his position; alone he holds the rank of Son of God. In 5:5 his status as Son underscores his appointment to be high priest. The God who affirms Christ as his Son also affirms him to be high priest.

Hebrews 5:10

In Heb 5 the writer employs another term to express Christ's appointment to the high priesthood. Using a *hapax legomenon*, he says that God *designated* (*prosagoreuō*) Christ to be a Melchizedekian high priest. Having said that God must appoint one to the high priesthood (5:4), the author affirms that, in fact, God did so specify Jesus. Westcott says, "The word *prosagoreuein* expresses the formal and solemn ascription of the title to Him to whom it belongs ('addressed as,' 'styled')."[14] This comment certainly fits the sense of the verb *kalein* in 5:4: "He must be *called* by God." Jesus was so *called*; he was *designated* high priest by God. Thus the author asserts that God named or appointed Jesus to the position of high priest in the order of Melchizedek. The aorist tense of

---

[14]Westcott, *Epistle to the Hebrews*, 132.

prosagoreuō is probably timeless. The focus is not on when he was named high priest, but that his appointment comes from God himself.

Hebrews 7:28; 8:3

In 7:28 the author uses an elliptical construction which declares, after we reconstruct it, that the oath *appointed* (*kathistēmi*) the Son. Certainly God made this oath (7:20–22). In contrast to the weak, sinful, and mortal human priests simply appointed by law, God appointed the Son to his Melchizedekian priestly role with his own oath. In 8:3 the author adds that like his human counterparts Jesus the High Priest was *appointed* (*kathistēmi*) to offer sacrifices. These two uses of this verb fall under the sense which A. Oepke defines as "to set in an elevated position, in an office," "to install."[15] This common meaning occurs throughout Greek literature.[16] It implies causality, to cause someone to be something. God acted definitively to designate the Son as high priest.

Hebrews 10:9–10

The author affirms that God's will (*thelēma*) set the agenda for Jesus' death by which Christians have been sanctified. This echoes the role of God's will (*boulē*) behind the plan of redemption through Jesus' death (Ac 2:23; 4:28). It may match even more the Johannine statements of Jesus' consuming commitment to do the Father's will (*thelēma*) (Jn 4:34; 5:30; and 6:38).

SUMMARY

Election concepts do not have much place in the Epistle to the Hebrews. In fact, apart from some clear statements of God's appointment of Jesus, we are hard-pressed to discover much treatment of election themes. We found only sporadic use of terms which other writers employ with elective significance. The author uses *horizō* (determine) for God's determination of a date: he sets a day as Today (4:7). This is

---

[15]A. Oepke, *TDNT*, 3:444.
[16]The verb *kathistēmi* also occurs with the meaning "appoint" in its other use in Hebrews (5:1). See also Tit 1:5.

definitive, divine action, but not elective. We likewise discover a statement of God's definitive will and purpose (6:17), but not in the sphere of the application of salvation. We do find a mention of God's appointment of human high priests (5:4). God planned to call or designate men to this position. This may mirror our Old Testament findings of God's selection of individuals for tasks. This use of *kalein* (call) at 5:4 does reflect the "naming" sense of this verb. God caused men to become high priests by his act of calling.

We do find some examples that involve God's role in applying salvation to people, though none that speak in terms of God's choosing. Several texts confirm the technical status of "calling" terms. Christians share in a heavenly calling (*klēsis*, 3:1), meaning that God has designated people to be his own such that they become "heavenly" and "heaven-bound." He calls them to values and a destination that are heavenly. Only the "called" (*kalein*) receive (9:15) this eternal inheritance. Without question the "called" are Christians, for Christ has mediated this promised inheritance to them via the new covenant. More support for the "naming" sense of "call" occurs in 11:18, quoting Ge 21:12 (LXX)—in Isaac your seed will be called. However, salvation is not the topic here.

The author uses three different verbs and a familiar Old Testament quote to assert that God appointed Jesus to his position. God appointed (using *tithēmi*) the Son heir of all things (1:2). The aorist tense is timeless; this appointment expresses an eternal relationship between Father and Son. In 1:5 the author celebrates this relationship with a quote from Ps 2:7. Alone, Jesus holds the rank of Son of God. These relational concepts expressed in 1:2 and 5 remind us of the Johannine use of *monogenēs* (one and only) and perhaps *agapētos* (beloved) in the synoptic accounts of Jesus' Baptism and Transfiguration. Jesus enjoys a special status and relationship with God; he has no peers as the unique, beloved Son. For the author of Hebrews the Father is responsible for the status and privileges that the Son enjoys. In their eternal relationship, the Father is the "appointer."

God also *appointed* Jesus to the role of high priest in the order of Melchizedek. The author employs two verbs to convey this concept: *prosagoreuō* (designate, 5:10) and *kathistēmi* (appoint, 7:28). Both convey definitive action. God's act of appointment determined the position Jesus holds as high priest. Yet Jesus was no unwilling conscript. He desired to accomplish God's will by coming to earth to become a sacrifice (10:9–10). To express the position of the Son as the one who would become the sacrifice, the author confirms that Jesus was under God's appointment to his priestly role.

The writer does not employ the term *elect* in its more recognizable forms. But his presentation of the Son certainly suggests that we recognize the Son as God's Elect One as much as if he had used the more "standard" election/predestination terminology we encountered elsewhere. Jesus the Son was under divine appointment, both in his status as the only Son and in his role as high priest. In this latter capacity we see a familiar ingredient of the election of individuals—election to a task. However, Jesus is more; his "election" concerns "being" as well as "doing." This resembles the data from the gospels. In his being Jesus is the beloved, unique Son. As to his mission, he accomplishes God's will as the Chosen One, to seek and to save lost sinners. And in his being and doing, Christians fit in.

How can the "called" have claim to the promised inheritance (Heb 9:15), when Christ is the rightful heir (1:2)? Paul's answer is that they are in Christ. As a corporate body Christians are in Christ and therefore claim their inheritance in him. The writer of Hebrews shares this understanding. There is no other way, for he is the only Son, and he is heir of all things. As the Son, he was qualified by divine appointment to accomplish redemption. Believers in him receive the blessings only he could obtain.

10

THE EPISTLES OF JAMES, PETER, AND JUDE

In this chapter we consider the four remaining epistles in the New Testament. In keeping with my methodology I will appraise the documents separately to appreciate their unique perspectives. Most of the data for this chapter comes from 1 Peter, where the author engages election issues extensively. The four epistles outline five categories that are pertinent for our enterprise. I have discovered no new groupings. However, one category, described in previous chapters as "God Applies Salvation," is more unified in these four epistles. The entries here concern God's "calling," and thus we could classify them more simply as "God Calls People," understanding that the call is not an invitation, but a definitive act of naming.

JAMES

God's Will in the Circumstances of Life

I have divided the texts that deal with God's will into two groups: this first groups concerns events, and the next more directly speaks to the issue of salvation. We find a text from James in each category; 1 Peter has several texts in the former, and 2 Peter one text in the latter. In our study of the

Acts we found several texts speaking of God's role in determining events or states of affairs, and two specifically of God's will in the circumstances of Paul's ministry (Ac 18:21; 21:14).

James 4:15

James directs one of his rebukes against people who arrogantly plan for the future without thought of a sovereign God. They plan their agendas and calendars with not even the slightest acknowledgment of their human limitations and frailty. James advises his readers to be conscious of God's sovereign control over all contingencies in the world. He says that all Christian plans ought to include the proviso, *ean ho kyrios thelēsē* (if the Lord wills).[1] Obviously James does not intend this to be a "knock on wood" magic charm, as if merely uttering this formula or writing D.V. would have some automatic effect. Rather, James shares a common conviction (recall Ac 18:21)[2] that God's will is sovereign and may at any time supplant the most carefully laid plans. As two proverbs put it: "The lot is cast into the lap, but its every decision is from the LORD" (16:33), and "In his heart a man plans his course, but the LORD determines his steps" (16:9). James affirms a fundamental belief in the sovereign God. When God sets in motion his decretive will, nothing stands in its way.

God's Will in Providing Salvation

James 1:18

James predicates what God did in giving birth (to Christians) on God's will (*boulomai*). In the previous text

---

[1]The actual phrase, "if the Lord wills," is not found in the Old Testament, though many commentators show its extensive Greco-Roman background. Most noteworthy are M. Dibelius, *James*, Hermeneia (Philadelphia: Fortress, 1976), 233–34; S. Laws, *A Commentary on the Epistle of James*, BNTC (London: A. & C. Black, 1980), 192; J. B. Mayor, *The Epistle of St. James* (London: Macmillan, 1910), 151–52; and J. H. Ropes, *Epistle of James*, ICC (Edinburgh: T. & T. Clark, 1916), 279. Laws observes, "It is clear that the formula played a 'tough wood' role in popular superstitution" (*Epistle of James*, 192).

[2]For examples of other Christian uses see, Ro 1:10; 1Co 4:19; 16:7; Php 2:19; Heb 6:3; and Ignatius, *Ephesians* 20:1.

James expressed God's will by using the verb *thelō* (4:15). In fact, he uses both terms to indicate human volition (*thelō*: 2:20; and *boulomai*: 3:4; 4:4). Any conclusions about the nature of this action cannot be based on the choice of one verb over the other.[3] The text conveys the idea that God definitively determined a course of action. This expresses not merely his plan, wish, or desire, but decretive volition.

God willed (NIV: "he chose"), James says, to bring us forth as his regenerated and redeemed people.[4] His will was to bring into existence or give birth to a new entity or creation. As Dibelius puts it, "Here the divine will to provide salvation is stressed."[5] We can trace the existence of a saved people only to the benevolent will of God. Adamson says, "In contrast to man's 'desire,' which begets spiritual death (1:13ff.), God's deliberate purposive will is gracious, choosing to initiate and to beget new spiritual life."[6] James does not intimate that God selected some people for spiritual birth and not others.[7] He affirms God's choice or purpose in providing salvation—in bringing the people of God into existence—not the choice of who will be among those saved. There is a clear component of corporateness here. God's will "births" a people. He willed to save a people.

God Calls People to Salvation

James 2:7

In this section James berates his readers for showing favoritism to the rich. He appeals to their common sense. Using a rhetorical question that expects a positive response,

---

[3]L. E. Elliott-Binns, "James I.18: Creation or Redemption?" *NTS* 3 (1957), is certainly correct: "By the time when the Epistle was written any emphasis on *boulomai* as denoting deliberate purpose as distinct from *thelō* seems to have broken down" (149).

[4]That "bring us forth" refers to redemption is the view adopted by virtually all commentators: J. B. Adamson, *The Epistle of James*, NICNT (Grand Rapids: Eerdmans, 1976), 76–77; P. Davids, *The Epistle of James*, NIGNT (Grand Rapids: Eerdmans, 1982), 89; Dibelius, *James*, 104–5; Laws, *Epistle of James*, 78; C. L. Mitton, *The Epistle of James* (London: Marshall, Morgan & Scott, 1966), 56; Ropes, *Epistle of James*, 166; and R. V. G. Tasker, *James*, TNTC (London: Tyndale, 1956), 49.

[5]Dibelius, *James*, 103.

[6]Adamson, *Epistle of James*, 76.

[7]Mitton also warns against seeing predestination here (*Epistle of James*, 56).

James asks, "Are these rich not slandering the good name by which you are *called*?" It makes no sense, James pleads, to favor the rich; they are the ones who slander your Lord!

We are interested in the use of *epikaleō*, which can mean either "to appeal to someone,"[8] or "to name." The naming sense, literally "to call a name upon" is very common in the Septuagint.[9] Davids observes that the "phrase 'to call a name upon one' is a septuagintalism, indicating possession or relationship, particularly relationship to God."[10]

There can be no doubt that here James intends the naming sense. *Whose* name the recipients bear is debatable. To whom do they belong? The name could be "Christian" (Ac 11:26),[11] or simply "Jesus."[12] Quite possibly the entire formula, "the good name that was called upon you," may allude to Christian baptism, the point at which they publicly identified with the name of Jesus (or Christ).[13]

Much is at stake here. To bear the name of Christ proclaims a fundamental change in a person's being. The title may not simply be dismissed. It is no superficial label only on the surface. These believers have come under the ownership of the Lord, and they bear his name. He has granted them great status and privilege when he conferred his name on them. Thus, to curry favor with people who slander their Lord makes no sense.

We see further confirmation of the naming sense to "call" words. James bases a point of argument on the meaning of *epikaleō*. One way of explaining what happens when a person becomes a Christian is to say that Jesus' name was *called* upon him or her. To be called a Christian is to be named one of Christ's own.

---

[8]See Ac 25:11–12, 25; 26:32; 28:19; 2Co 1:23.

[9]See, e.g., Ge 48:16; Nu 21:3; Dt 28:10; 2Ch 7:14; Isa 4:1; 43:7; Jer 14:9; Am 9:12.

[10]Davids, *Epistle of James*, 113.

[11]Adamson, *Epistle of James*, defends this (112–13).

[12]Davids, *Epistle of James*, prefers "Jesus."

[13]A baptismal connection is defended by the following in their James commentaries: Adamson, 112–13; Davids, 113; Laws, 105; Mayor, 89; and Tasker, 60.

God's Election of People

James 2:5

James has a second argument why Christians ought not show favoritism to the rich. Again expecting a yes answer, James asks the question, "Has God not *chosen* those who are poor in the eyes of the world to be rich in faith and to inherit the kingdom?" Using *eklegomai* (choose) James affirms God's choice of the economically poor. Thus, he argues, if his readers are to favor anyone, it ought to be the poor, not the rich. Our interest, again, is not in James' main point, but what he says to make it. What does he mean in saying that God *chose* (aorist tense) the poor as rich in faith and heirs of the kingdom he promised to those who love him?

One explanation proposes that this refers to God's pretemporal election, either of the poor as a class or of individual poor people. Various texts in the Old Testament point to God's special concern for the poor and needy (for example, Pss 9:18; 12:5; 70:5). Hence, some argue, not only does God sympathize with the plight of oppressed people, but he has acted to assure that they become rich in the world to come. This accounts for the observed phenomenon that the poor more readily embrace the gospel. It is, as Mitton says, "the result of the deliberate strategy of God."[14]

However, many problems immediately arise if we adopt this sense. Unquestionably, God has not chosen *all* the poor, for many reject the gospel. And clearly God has chosen *some* rich. To hold a meaning for *eklegomai* (choose) that requires such qualifications evacuates the phrase "God chose the poor" of its meaning. Is this only a general strategy? God has elected poor people, in general, though there are many exceptions—not all the poor are elected and indeed some of the rich are.

Another possibility sees God's choice as not pretemporal but historical.[15] As God chose Abraham and Israel to accomplish his purposes, so God chooses "to make especially the poor and humble in Israel citizens of the king-

---

[14]Mitton, *The Epistle of James*, 85.

[15]This line is argued by older theologians G. B. Stevens, *The Theology of the New Testament*, 2d ed. (Edinburgh: T. & T. Clark, 1911), 286; and W. Beyschlag, *New Testament Theology*, 2 vols., 2d ed. (Edinburgh: T. & T. Clark, 1899), 1:351.

dom."[16] However, this has not avoided the problems of the previous view. Still, not all the poor Israelites are saved, nor are all rich Gentiles excluded.

A third option views this statement as a proverbial expression that captures the historical makeup of the early church. Since most of the early Christians were poor, they correctly perceived that God had chosen the poor. Those adopting this perspective understand the statement "God chose the poor" descriptively rather than prescriptively. This describes their situation; it does not prescribe whom God will elect to salvation. To say that "God chose the poor" prescribes God's method, and results in the problems of the previous options. The statement does not define how election works (namely, God chooses the poor) as much as it describes the state of the church. It consists of poor people who have been chosen by God.

It is important to register here the "ethos" of the word *poor* in biblical literature. We observed above that many Old Testament texts intimate that the poor and needy have a special place in God's heart. Often God recounts his special concern for their welfare (for example, Dt 15:7–9; Pss 41:1; 69:33; 82:3–4; 140:12; Pr 14:31). Further, *poor* eventually came to be synonymous with "pious" or "devout." This development is pronounced in the intertestamental and rabbinic literature.[17] Matthew's version of the beatitude "blessed are the poor *in spirit*" (Mt 5:3) shows that *poor* was taking on a spiritual dimension in Christian thinking. If the sense of the word has at least some component of "devout" in James' mind, then his question could be paraphrased thus: "Has not God chosen the poor in spirit, those who are willing to obey me and depend on me rather than on their own resources (as the rich do)?"

We conclude that our third option, with this "spiritual" understanding of poor, best explains the author's intention. Surely he cannot have meant that *all* economically poor and that *no* rich will attain to God's kingdom.[18] Rather this seems to be a descriptive statement of the makeup of the church.

---

[16]Beyschlag, *New Testament Theology*, 1:351.

[17]Davids cites numerous sources to defend this point (*Epistle of James*, 111). See also E. Bammel, *TDNT*, 6: 895–98; and Mitton, *Epistle of James*, 86.

[18]The Gospel tradition speaks of Joseph of Arimathea as a rich man (Mt 27:57; Mk 15:43).

Probably due to their disadvantageous circumstances, the poor more readily admitted their need and turned to the hope held out in the gospel of Christ. They were more readily "poor in spirit" because they lived in poverty. And so they embraced the Christian message and came to love God. James says that God promised the kingdom to those who love him. We doubt, along with most interpreters, that James here teaches a pretemporal election of certain people—the poor, not the rich—to salvation. Rather, James teaches a principle: it is outrageous to ignore the poor and exalt the rich when: (1) the church consists, by and large, of poor people; and (2) the poor are far more likely to be won to the faith.

Can we learn anything about election in Jas 2:5? Not the pretemporal choice of some individuals or a group to be saved. Rather, election appears to be a term that describes the status of these believers—they are chosen ones. Though the world considers them poor, their poverty makes them objects of God's care. God considers the poor to be blessed (Lk 6:20; cf. Mt 5:3). They love God and thus inherit the kingdom. Election here does not prescribe who will come to believe; it describes those who are "believers in our glorious Lord Jesus Christ" (2:1).

Summary

We have isolated in James only four texts that employ terms or concepts that we have identified as elective in nature. The first affirms God's sovereign will that is the ultimate determiner of events (4:15). No plans come to fruition unless God so wills. James affirmed that God willed to provide salvation, bringing the people of God into existence (1:18). These saved people bear the name of the Lord (2:7). They have entered into an intimate relation with Christ so they can be called by his name. Not only did God give them birth and call the name of Jesus upon them, but he chose them (2:5). James' (mostly) poor readers (5:1–11) owe their inheritance in God's kingdom, not to wealth or their own doing in any way, but only to God's choice. Since they are God's chosen ones, he has turned their poverty to riches.

1 PETER

In 1 Peter we meet an epistle that devotes much attention to the theme of election, especially for a book of its size. We will follow the same order of categories presented for James, though 1 Peter omits one found in James and adds another.

God's Will in the Circumstances of Life

1 Peter 2:15

In this first of four references to the will (*thelēma*) of God, Peter informs his readers what that will is. Nevertheless, we cannot be sure precisely what he meant, for the Greek particle *houtos* can point either forward or backward. If it points forward, then the following clause elaborates the content of God's will: by doing good to silence the ignorance of foolish men.[19] But if it points backward, then the previous statement contains God's will: being obedient to authorities (2:13–14).[20] One commentator, E. Best, argues that *houtos* points *both* forward and backward,[21] and this may the wisest option. Even Hort argues that the final phrase of 2:15 is in apposition to "the will of God" and explains these words.[22] This comes very close to what Best says.

Thus Peter defines what God desires or wishes, not what he decretively wills or sovereignly puts into effect. When Christians properly submit to authorities, they are doing good and keeping in step with God's intentions for them. In 4:2 Peter again holds up the "will of God" as a goal of the Christian's conduct. Peter sets "doing the will of God" in opposition to living "for evil human desires."

---

[19]The following reflect this option: NIV, RSV, NEB, UBS , C. Bigg, *Epistles of St. Peter and St. Jude*, ICC (Edinburgh: T. & T. Clark, 1902), 141, and R. C. H. Lenski, *Epistles of St. Peter, St. John and St. Jude* (Minneapolis: Augsburg, 1966), 111–12.

[20]F. J. A. Hort, *The First Epistle of Peter I.1–II.17* (London: Macmillan, 1898), 143, is the classic defender of this "retrospective" position. His supporters include J. N. D. Kelly, *A Commentary on the Epistles of Peter and Jude*, BNTC (London: Black, 1969), 110 and F. W. Beare, *The First Epistle of Peter* (Oxford: Blackwell, 1970), 143.

[21]E. Best, *1 Peter*, NCB (London: Oliphants, 1971), 115.

[22]Hort, *First Epistle of Peter*, 143.

1 Peter 3:17; 4:19

In these other uses of *thelēma* (will) of God in 1 Peter, the writer admits that God's will may will (*thelō*) that Christians experience suffering even though their actions have been only good. Doing good is always God's will, even when it induces suffering. Doing evil is never good, even when it avoids suffering. So God's will operates in the affairs of his people. When they encounter suffering, this does not mean that God has abandoned them to their persecutors. His will possibly (Peter uses the optative mood—*theloi*) includes the suffering of his people.

We find no uses of God's will that impinge on the topic of salvation, as we did in James. Thus we move on to the next topic of God's call.

God Calls People to Salvation

Peter employs the verb *kalein* (call) six times in the epistle. In five of these instances Christians are the objects of the action of calling. Three times Peter speaks (explicitly) of God as the one who called Christians. Twice Christians are simply the ones who were called. All five uses confirm the technical status of this term in 1 Peter.

1 Peter 1:15

Peter appeals to his readers to be holy in all their conduct since "he who *called*" them is holy. The aorist tense of this participle points to the time in their experience when God called the readers. Ones whom God called ought to exhibit the character of the one who called them. W. Grudem calls it "a calling to live with God and to be like him."[23] This first use strongly suggests that *kalein* (to call) is a technical term for "call to be Christians." It is not possible to determine whether the sense of "call" is "invite" or "name." We detect, however, a strong hint of the naming sense in the exhortation to holiness. "To name" suggests to impart character or status. One names what one owns or is responsible for. A name often reflects aspiration or (hoped

---

[23]W. Grudem, *1 Peter*, TNTC (Leicester: Inter-Varsity; Grand Rapids: Eerdmans, 1988), 79.

for) character. In his appeal for holy conduct Peter appeals to Christians to live up to the name they bear. The holy God called them; they bear responsibility to live up to his character and aspirations for them. "God called you" is a way of saying "God saved you" or "God granted you the status (or name) Christian." Kelly says, "As a result of his calling . . . He has made them His own."[24]

1 Peter 2:9

In this text Peter uses two crucial concepts, choosing and calling, though at this point we consider only the latter. As in 1:15 the author reminds his readers that they are a *called* people. One of God's purposes is "that you may declare the praises of him who called you out of darkness into his wonderful light." Again the technical status of *kalein* is confirmed,[25] for, as in 1:15, Peter identifies God simply as the "one who called you." The aorist tense points to a past event. Elliott suggests a naming sense for *kalein* here, and he is probably right. He says,

> Here those people who believe in Jesus the elect messianic Stone of God are named with the body of God's elect and holy nation: His Royal Residence, His Body of Priests.[26]

In his mercy God has brought into existence a people. Once they lived in darkness but now exult in his wonderful light. As the string of descriptive terms in the first part of the verse shows, God's call has resulted in a drastic change of allegiance and status for the called ones. So much has changed; they owe so much to God. Their response can only be one of praise.

1 Peter 2:21

The author assures his readers who are slaves (2:18) that it is commendable to endure suffering for doing good (2:20).

---

[24]Kelly, *Epistles of Peter and Jude*, 69.

[25]Kelly notes concerning this use of *kalein*: "The verb 'call' (*kalein*) is the technical term in both LXX and NT for God's saving initiative" (*Epistles of Peter and Jude*, 100). See also J. H. Elliott, *The Elect and the Holy. An Exegetical Examination of 1 Peter 2:4–10*, Suppl. *NovT* 12 (Leiden: Brill, 1966), 44.

[26]Elliott, *Elect and Holy*, 221.

Giving the reason (*gar*) for what he has just said, Peter adds, "to this you were *called*." Here *kalein* (call) refers not so much to the act of applying salvation (though it definitely assumes it), but to the goal, outworking, or implication of the change to the status of Christian.[27] A person who has been "called to be a Christian" is also called to suffer and endure. In many ways what Peter says here parallels his discussion of God's will in 2:15 and 3:17. To be called (to be a Christian) demands that one submit to the outworking of God's will in one's life. This is an essential aspect of the call to be a Christian. Best says of these Christians, "They are given a new dignity and a new destiny, viz., to suffer."[28]

1 Peter 3:9

Here the language almost exactly follows 2:21, though *hoti* (because) replaces the *gar* (for). Peter says, "Because to this you were *called*." The term *this* could either refer backward or forward. If backward, then Peter asserts that God called them to repay evil and insults with blessing. If it points forward, then God called them to inherit a blessing. Probably the second alternative is preferable. In either case, we have another claim, similar to 2:21, of the goal or purpose to which God has called Christians. Being named a Christian conveyed an expectation for how they lived, even in suffering.

1 Peter 5:10

Along with 1:15 and 2:9, this text identifies God as "the one who *called*" (*ho kalesas*). Again, the aorist tense probably refers back to some occasion when they entered into possession of "eternal glory." To say that God called them to glory means that at some point God granted them the status or position of "saved." The sense could be either "name" or "summons." The "naming" sense fits well if the phrase "in Christ" goes with "called" rather than "glory," as it most

---

[27]The conception "God called you to . . ." is common in the Pauline literature. See, e.g., 1Co 1:9; Gal 5:13; Col 3:15; 1Th 2:12; 4:7; 2Th 2:14; and 1Ti 6:12.

[28]Best, *1 Peter*, 119.

likely does.[29] Christians, very simply, are in Christ (5:14), and those in Christ ought to display a certain type of behavior (3:16). Their calling, then, is in Christ. Christians gain their standing, their status, and their name in Christ. When God made them Christians, he called them (to be) in Christ. In any case the term *kalein* has undeniable technical status for Peter; it means God has applied salvation to them.

God's Choice of Christ

Many English versions employ some equivalent of the word *chosen* three times to describe Christ. Two different Greek words lie beneath this translation.

1 Peter 1:20

Referring to Christ, Peter asserts on the one hand that he was *foreknown* (*proginōskō*) before the foundation of the world and on the other hand that he was revealed in these last times because of those who believe. For the Greek word *proginōskō* (which we literally translate "foreknow"), the NIV, GNB, and PHILLIPS have "chosen"; the RSV has "destined"; and the NEB, "predestined." How ought we to understand that Christ was foreknown (perfect tense) and was revealed (aorist)? Why do these translators opt for giving *proginōskō* such a predestinarian emphasis? Are they justified?

The meaning of the verb *proginōskō* is much debated. In its only other use in the Petrine writings, it denotes simple prior knowledge (2Pe 3:17), also its meaning at Ac 26:5. The two Pauline occurrences (Ro 8:29; 11:2) close out the uses. Peter uses the noun *prognōsis* (foreknowledge) as the basis for Christians' election in 1Pe 1:2. However, in 1:2, the juxtaposition of "election" and "foreknowledge" casts doubt about their synonymity. Can foreknowledge really be the same as "choosing" in light of 1:2?

As we have already noted, many versions and commen-

---

[29]Although Bigg (*Epistles of St. Peter and St. Jude*, 195) prefers to attach "in Christ" to "glory," most interpreters prefer "called in Christ" (e.g., Best, *1 Peter*, 173; Beare, *First Epistle of Peter*, 206; and Kelly, *Epistles of Peter and Jude*, 212). In 1 Peter the concept of glory is identified with Christ, though the connections vary and are at times loose (1:7, 21; 4:11, 13; 5:1, 4). In none of these do we find the concept of glory in Christ per se.

tators do think so,[30] though most actually defend the interpretation "foreordain" rather than "choose." Peter affirms, then, that God marked out Jesus' redemptive career for him. One is left to wonder, though, if the author meant to convey the notion of "predestine," why he didn't employ a verb that would more obviously convey that idea. Why would he use *proginōskō* to mean *prohorizō* when, as the use at 2Pe 3:17 shows, *proginōskō* normally means "prior knowledge"?

If we start by assuming the face-value sense of "foreknow," then what would Peter mean? Before creation Christ was foreknown; in the last times he has been revealed. "Foreknow" is both cognitive and relational, but for the preincarnate Jesus, it is also hidden from human view. Now the Incarnation has made Christ and his mission visible and public for all to see. God knew Christ prior to creation, and that loving relationship of mutual knowing describes his state and status throughout history (perfect tense). However, in these last days God has uncovered what had been mostly hidden to humans.

We argue this makes very good sense, but can be even more refined. The verses 1 Pe 1:10–12 are a parallel to 1:20. Salvation was a mystery into which the prophets diligently searched. Yet a full explanation never came to them, not even to angels. God certainly knew all along what his intentions and actions would be, though he only gave hints to the prophets. That describes God's foreknowledge.

We observed a parallel to this in the use of *prognōsis* in Ac 2:23. In our discussion of this text we suggested the possible link to prophecy.[31] Jesus' crucifixion was according to God's plan and foreknowledge, which he had (roughly)

---

[30]Kelly, though admitting that the literal meaning of *proginōskō* is "foreknown," says, "We have already noticed (see on i.2) that for him God's foreknowledge includes His creative will and determination" (*Epistles of Peter and Jude*, 76). Best, *1 Peter*, also assumes that *proginōskō* means destined here. Beare adds his support: "That Christ is 'foreknown' means that His work in the world was ordained of God, that the fulfillment of God's purpose for the world was destined to be accomplished through Him, through His sacrifice of himself" (*First Epistle of Peter*, 106). Hort finds in the uses of *proginōskō* referring to persons "that in them *proginōskō* means virtually prerecognition, previous designation to a position or function" (*First Epistle of Peter*, 80). Finally, Grudem, *1 Peter*, 85, gives three arguments to defend that foreknowledge was really predetermination.

[31]See pp. 118–19.

revealed to his prophets. God had prior knowledge of Christ's career. In fact, he determined the events in his life (Ac 2:23; 4:28; 13:29). Here, by using *proginōskō*, Peter wishes to draw special attention to prior *knowledge* more than prior determination.

So we seem to have two defensible options. Peter's sense might be that God predetermined Christ's career in eternity, and now he has revealed or worked it out in history. This is true, and can be defended from other texts. However, to posit it for this text forces an unnatural meaning on *proginōskō*.

The other option springs from the natural sense of *proginōskō* as "know beforehand." When we connect God's foreknowledge of Christ with the plan of redemption, we cannot deny the factor of prior determination. However, we bring that understanding of Jesus' role to this text. It is not inherent in this text which affirms Jesus as the "foreknown one." The one who was foreknown by God came to earth to accomplish the redemptive mission marked out for him.

1 Peter 2:4, 6

In 1Pe 2:4–10 the author develops the theme of the corporate people of God using a variety of images. One picture, the "spiritual house," portrays stones built together on the cornerstone, Jesus. Peter affirms Jesus to be the living Stone, rejected by men, chosen by God and precious. The specific terms *chosen* and *precious*, derive from an Old Testament source, Isa 28:16, which Peter adopts from the Septuagint (1Pe 2:6). The Septuagint employs the term *eklektos* (chosen) for the Hebrew *bōhan*, which usually means trial or proving.[32] Peter latches on to this Septuagint sense: Jesus is the *chosen* and precious cornerstone. If we ask, "Who chose Jesus?" the answer must be God, though we ought not press the movement from description to action. Jesus is both; he is "choice" (as "precious" also emphasizes), and God chose him. Jesus Christ is God's Chosen One.[33]

Peter sees the prophecy of Isa 28:16 fulfilled in Christ. He is the elect and precious cornerstone that God has placed

---

[32]In fact, *bōhan* is translated by *dokimazō* fourteen times in the LXX.

[33]Beare (*First Epistle of Peter*, 122) says that *eklekton* carries the double sense of "choice" and "chosen." Hort agrees (*First Epistle of Peter*, 107).

in Zion.[34] The rabbis also interpreted the "stone" messianically. Kelly observes:

> In rabbinical exegesis the stone was paraphrased as "the mighty king, heroic and terrible," i.e. the Messiah, whom Yahweh would establish in Sion and in whom the righteous might confidently place their trust.[35]

This status of Christ prepares for the exhortations to follow. Peter begins by affirming that Jesus, in spite of his suffering and rejection, is God's elect and precious Stone. Then he tells the readers that they are stones (2:5) and they are chosen (2:9). Therefore, they may confidently follow in Jesus' footsteps (2:21), knowing that the experience of suffering is not incompatible with their election. If Jesus, God's chosen and precious Stone, faced suffering, certainly it may be within God's will for believers to suffer too (2:21; 3:17; 4:19).

God's Election of People

In this final category we locate several texts in which Peter addresses his readers using terms and concepts that are elective in character. While we find only one text from this category in James and 2 Peter, we discover five in 1 Peter. God's election of a people is a significant issue in this letter.

1 Peter 1:1–2

The salutation to 1 Peter employs two of our key elective terms, *eklektos* (elect) and *prognōsis* (foreknowledge). The Greek structure of this opening sentence seems straightforward. However, it contains several ambiguities that make certainty about its interpretation extremely difficult. We can describe the situation as follows. Peter, the apostle of Jesus Christ, pens his letter to the "elect ones" who are strangers. Alternatively, he writes to the "chosen strangers," since *eklektois* (chosen) can function either as a substantive or adjective. As in 1Pe 2:4, 6 concerning Christ, here "chosen" can focus either on God's act of choosing them or on their

---

[34]Isaiah the prophet warned the people that their confidence lay not in military might or political alliances, but in God who was Israel's true strength.

[35]Kelly, *Epistles of Peter and Jude*, 89.

status as special or choice "chosen ones." After listing the various locations of their dispersion, Peter adds three prepositional phrases using *kata* (according to), *en* (in, through) and *eis* (for, to). Where to attach each of these phrases is another problem, and the options are several. A simplified diagram of 1Pe 1:1, 2 will clarify our discussion:

> Peter an apostle   to the *elect*, the strangers dispersed in Pontus, Galatia, Cappadocia, Asia, and Bithynia
>
> (1) *according to* the foreknowledge of God the Father
>
> (2) *through* the sanctifying work of the Spirit
>
> (3) *for* obedience to and sprinkling of the blood of   Jesus Christ

The diagram illustrates that the three prepositional phrases could all attach to the same word (or words) or to different ones. We need not solve all the interpretive problems of this passage, only enough to help us comprehend what Peter says about election.

The prepositional phrases

There are several possibilities for attaching the three phrases. All three could qualify the term *elect*. Thus election is based on or grounded in God's foreknowledge, it is accomplished through the Spirit's sanctifying work, and its goal is obedience to Jesus and the sprinkling of his blood.[36] Alternatively, all three phrases could attach to the entire salutation—to Peter's apostleship, to the strangers' election,

---

[36]Some take all three phrases with "elect": Bigg, *Epistles of St. Peter and St. Jude*, 90–92; Kelly, *Epistles of Peter and Jude*, 42–43; and Schrenk, *TDNT*, 4:190.

and to the grace and peace he prays for them. The phrases express the context of who Peter is, what his role is, the work of the gospel, and the state of the readers. The entire complex occurs in accordance with God's foreknowledge, through the Spirit's sanctifying, and for obedience to Christ.[37]

Without introducing any further elements to the discussion, we can draw conclusions. Beare is correct in observing that the intervention of eight words into the text following *eklektois* (elect) makes it very unlikely that Peter intended the phrases to attach directly and only to this term.[38] These three phrases define and describe, not solely their election, but also all that Peter and his readers are. Peter's apostleship, his readers' dispersion, and their election—all come within the scope of the Father's foreknowledge, the Spirit's sanctifying and the salvation secured by faith in Christ and his salvific work. They all function and flourish in the context of a concerted Trinitarian effort.[39]

The key words

In addition to understanding the structure of these verses, we must discuss both *eklektos* (elect) and *prognōsis* (foreknowledge). We noted above that we can regard "elect" here either as a substantive ("the elect ones") or as an adjective describing the readers ("elect strangers").[40] However, our conclusions about election do not depend upon settling this minor point.

Peter applies the category of election to the recipients of the letter. This is standard, technical terminology to refer to the people of God, and we stress *people* here, since Peter uses "election" corporately. Miller rightly says of Peter's readers:

---

[37]Commentators who apply the phrases in this wider sense include: Lenski, *Epistles of St. Peter, St John and St Jude*, 24–25; Beare, *First Epistle of Peter*, 75; and E. G. Selwyn, *The First Epistle of Peter* (London: Macmillan, 1946), 119. Of course, there are several permutations of these that attach only one or two phrases with different words, but these are less likely.

[38]Beare, *First Epistle of Peter*, 75.

[39]W. Grudem, *1 Peter*, 50–52, confirms this analysis.

[40]The NIV clearly takes the former option: "To God's elect, strangers" (cf. GNB: "God's chosen people"), while the commentaries of Bigg (90), Beare (74), and Lenski (21) defend the use of *eklektos* as an adjective modifying "strangers."

"God has chosen them as he had chosen Israel, and called them into being as a people just as he had called Israel out of Egypt."[41] In addition, here Peter stresses not so much God's action of choosing this body as he does their chosenness. Peter uses the adjective *chosen* rather than the verb *eklegesthai* (choose). We conclude, therefore, that he focuses on their status as chosen ones.[42] They may be strangers or refugees in this world, but they are God's elect. They enjoy a position that only God can confer. They belong to a chosen people.

As we noted at 1:20, *prognōsis* has generated much debate. Does it mean simply "foreknowledge" or does it have the stronger sense of "foreordination"? The KJV, NIV, and PHILLIPS translate it here as "foreknowledge." On the other side the RSV has "destined" and the NEB and GNB have "purpose" to indicate a stronger sense. In our discussion of 1:20 we concluded that the face-value sense of "prior knowledge" does make good sense. Yet in the context of the discussion of Jesus' salvific mission, there is probably justification for seeing a stronger sense of prior determination.

Indeed, many scholars argue for more than simple prior knowledge here at 1:2 as well.[43] They infer this stronger, elective sense from the use of *yāda* (know) in the Old Testament. Yet in the extant uses of both the verb *to foreknow* and the noun *foreknowledge* outside the New Testament, simple prescience or prior knowledge prevails. However,

---

[41]D. G. Miller, "Deliverance and Destiny. Salvation in First Peter," *Int* 9 (1955): 415. Hort also sees the sense of *eklektois* in 1:1 as a body. He says, "That St. Peter is here following the O.T. idea in its idea of a chosen people, not merely an assemblage of chosen men, is a natural inference from ii.9f., where *genos eklekton*, 'an elect or chosen race,' is one of the phrases taken directly from II Isa xliii.20" (Hort, *First Epistle of Peter*, 14). Interestingly, Hort goes on to insist that this corporate concept does not exclude individual election but can argue only an inference here: "The individual relation to God implies individual election" (ibid.). But he does not defend this "implication." Surely here Peter only knows of the choice body. Bigg adds his voice: "Elect, in fact, means simply Christian. What the apostle is thinking of is corporate citizenship among the elect people . . ." (Bigg, *Epistles of St. Peter and St. Jude*, 90).
[42]Beare takes *eklektois* to mean "choice" or "select." Thus, "The 'sojourners of Dispersion' are choice souls, rare spirits, picked warriors . . ." (Beare, *First Epistle of Peter*, 74). He bases his conclusions on papyri usage.
[43]Those in this group include Bigg (*Epistles of St. Peter and St. Jude*, 92), Kelly (*Epistles of Peter and Jude*, 42–43), Hort (*First Epistle of Peter*, 19–20), and Bultmann (*TDNT*, 1:715–16).

when interpreters start with the assumption that "God knows Israel" equals "God chooses Israel," they see in Peter's use here God's "effective choice,"[44] his "previous designation," or "previous recognition."[45]

Kelly's explanation of "foreknowledge" as "previous choice" seems unlikely in this context, as Peter has already employed the concept of "choice" in his description of the recipients as "chosen ones." The likely options are either (1) the face-value, "foreknowledge," or (2) previous designation, "foreordination."

We doubt there is sufficient warrant simply to dismiss the face-value and commonly attested meaning of "prior knowledge" (found at Ac 26:5 and 2Pe 3:17). Even if God's knowledge of his people implies a special relation with them, this does not necessarily imply that foreknowledge includes a component of choice or predestination.

In light of what we concluded above about the prepositional phrases, we can see some contextual argument for a stronger sense to "foreknowledge." Peter involves all three persons in the divine Trinity, and since the Spirit and Jesus have active roles, probably the Father's role is more than cognitive. But this ought not be pressed into too strong predestinarian terms in the absence of any other evidence. This "prior knowledge" might consist of God's providential care over them[46] or "an eternal intention to bless."[47] Grudem sees it as God's "knowing people with a personal, loving, fatherly knowledge."[48]

The readers' situation as *chosen refugees* has not escaped that active and concerned knowledge of God. He has always known about them and has been at work to secure their well-being. However, Peter does not base God's choice of some to be Christians on his foreknowledge, whether it be the alleged strong sense of foreordination or the face-value sense of prior knowledge (as of eventual faith). Both miss the mark of this passage.

Rather Peter affirms that believers are God's chosen

---

[44]Kelly, *Epistles of Peter and Jude,* 43.

[45]Hort, *First Epistle of Peter,* 19.

[46]Beare, *First Epistle of Peter,* 76.

[47]D. E. Hiebert, "Designation of the Readers in 1 Peter 1:1–2," *BibSac* 137 (1980): 71.

[48]Grudem, *1 Peter,* 50.

ones and that the Father's eternal knowledge encompasses them in all their circumstances. Likewise, the Spirit is doing its sanctifying work, such that they have come to obey Christ for salvation through his shed blood. They owe all they are and have to God's doing; indeed, they enjoy a "choice" position as God's people.

1 Peter 2:8

Following the stone metaphor that described Jesus in 2:4, Peter cites various Old Testament texts in 2:6–8. In 2:7–8 he picks up the idea of "rejected by men" from 2:4, and in 2:8a he cites Isa 8:14 to show that people stumble and fall over the stone that is Christ. Then in 2:8b Peter evaluates this phenomenon of stumbling or falling. Peter says two things. First, these unbelievers (*apistousin*, 2:7) stumble because they disobey the (Christian) message. It is best to take "message" (*tō logō*) with "disobey" rather than with "stumble."[49] Certainty is not possible, but the natural meanings of the words suggest that to disobey the message makes better sense. Most commentaries and versions agree. Hence the writer defines "unbelief" as disobedience of the message. Bigg says the concepts "are closely connected and here practically equivalent, because disobedience is the outward expression of disbelief."[50]

The participle *apeithountes* (disobey) is circumstantial, probably indicating reason or cause. They stumble *because* of their disobedience (as in NIV, RSV, NASB, and GNB). So, Peter attributes stumbling over (or rejecting) Christ to disobedience. As 2:7 makes clear, there are only two groups of people. Christ is the "continental divide" that separates one group (believers) from the other group (unbelievers). As Peter states in 2:8, obedience to the word is critical.[51]

Peter adds further clarification: "which is also what they were destined for." The key question here is, What is the antecedent to the word *which*? To what were these unbe-

---

[49]Lenski (*Epistles of St. Peter, St. John and St. Jude*, 97–98) takes *logos* to refer to Jesus the *Word* in the clause "they stumble against the word."

[50]Bigg, *Epistles of St. Peter and St. Jude*, 132.

[51]Schrenk says it well: "What is said is that everything depends upon whether one is willing or not to believe in Christ and to obey Him" (Schrenk, *TDNT*, 4:191).

lievers destined or appointed (*tithēmi*)? We have already noted the strong elective sense in some uses of this verb, where it means "to appoint."[52] There are two possible interpretations here. Either unbelievers were appointed to stumble (because they disobey the message), or they were appointed to disobey.[53]

In his article on *tithēmi* C. Maurer argues for the second option, that God ordained some to take offense at the word.[54] So also Kelly says, "Just as in 1:2 he represents his readers marked out by God for salvation, so here he envisages their adversaries as predestined to destruction." Kelly adds, though, that "the personal decision of the individual is involved."[55] But to make God in some way responsible for the disobedience of the wicked cuts against the context of 2:4–8 we have discussed so far. An unwillingness to believe and obey is the explicitly stated cause of the stumbling of these people. To foist ultimate responsibility onto God imports an alien concept into this passage.

Then, to what are they appointed? The first option provides the better answer.[56] God has ordained that, for those who will not believe in Christ, this Stone becomes for them a stumbling block. No salvation exists apart from Christ—this is God's predestined plan. God has determined that Jesus will be a stumbling block to those who reject the Christian message. Jesus is either precious or a pitfall. If a person rejects Christ, God has appointed that he will stumble. Bigg explains,

[52]For example, see Ac 1:7; 13:47; 20:28; Heb 1:2; 1Ti 1:12; 2:7; 2Ti 1:11; Jn 15:16.

[53]Grudem, *1 Peter*, 107, has a third option, that unbelievers were appointed *both* to stumble *and* to disobey. He defends this interpretation.

[54]C. Maurer, *TDNT*, 7:152–58.

[55]Kelly, *Epistles of Peter and Jude*, 94. Grudem, *1 Peter*, 108, concludes that "God has *established* (or 'destined') the rebellious to stumbling and disobedience." In an excursus Grudem defends that "all disobedience which tragically does persist to the end of life (and thus into eternity) has been 'destined' by God" (109).

[56]Agreement with our position comes in the commentaries of Bigg (133), Lenski (98), and Best (106). Beare appears at first to agree and says as much, but then moves to a hybrid position that combines both options (126). For Beare both the fact of their unbelief and their fate of reprobation were determined by God. Yet after Beare says, ". . . it is the stumbling that is foreordained, rather than the unbelief which yields to it" (126), it is difficult to see why or how he moves to combine both options.

The sense, therefore, is "they disobey, and for that reason stumble"; "because they disobey, God ordains that they shall stumble." Their disobedience is not ordained, the penalty of their disobedience is.[57]

The stumbling may refer to punishment—the retribution God has appointed for those who disobey the message (cf. 1Th 5:9). This destiny is not negotiable. God has determined the two destinies for people. If people will not accept the Gospel message, their punishment is sure. We deny that this text teaches that God has appointed some people to unbelief.[58]

1 Peter 2:9

After arguing for the central role of Christ as the "chosen and precious cornerstone" (2:4, 6), Peter, in 2:9, applies a series of corporate terms to this new people of God. They are a *genos* (race, people), a *hierateuma* (priesthood), an *ethnos* (nation), and a *laos* (people). There can be no doubt that Peter pictures the church in corporate terms. In our study of the Old Testament concept of election we noticed the many corporate terms routinely applied to Israel.[59] For Peter the church has taken over the position Israel lost. The church is the new people of God.

Peter first uses the phrase *genos eklekton* (chosen people, or race). This description seems to derive from the end of Isa 43:20 (LXX), which promises God's blessing to *to genos mou to eklekton* (my chosen race). The word *genos* (race) occurs twenty times in the New Testament, nine of those in Acts and six in Paul's letters. Often it is used of people who share an ancestor, who are related by blood.[60] Peter applies this Old Testament imagery that signified Israel to the body of Christians. Christians are now God's chosen people.[61]

---

[57]Bigg, *Epistles of St. Peter and St. Jude*, 133.

[58]For an opposing defense that Peter does teach predestination to unbelief, see Grudem, *1 Peter*, 106–10. J. Piper, *The Justification of God* (Grand Rapids: Baker, 1983), adopts this same stance on the basis of Romans 9:1–23.

[59]We cited such terms as *people, flock, house, congregation,* and *vine.*

[60]So, see Ac 7:13: Joseph's *family*; 7:19: our *people*; 13:26: *children* of Abraham; 17:28–29: his [God's] *offspring*; 2Co 11:26: my own *countrymen*; Php 3:5: the *people* of Israel; Rev 22:16: *offspring* of David.

[61]See Beare, *First Epistle of Peter*, 129, and Elliott, *Elect and Holy*, 225.

More than a new race, they are *eklektos* (a *chosen* race). Once again we find the emphasis on their status as chosen rather than on the action of God's choice. The descriptive metaphors that follow underscore this conclusion. The obvious parallel to and dependence on the description of Christ, the Stone, provide further confirmation. Christ is the Chosen Stone; the church is the chosen race. Peter pictures Christ as the cornerstone (2:4, 6). Christ provides the basis or support for this new house (2:5) and race.[62] Elliott draws the parallel in this way: "They who believe in Jesus as the Elect and Precious One of God are gathered together as the Elect and Precious People."[63]

Thus we find Peter applying the Old Testament description of the elect Israel to the Christian body of believers. In contrast to the unbelievers who trip over Jesus, these readers have come to believe. And these believers, as they come to place their faith in Christ, enter into an elect body or people. For Israel, physical descent from Abraham and Jacob furnished the entrance into the elect nation. Now faith in Jesus is the criterion. Though we would employ more inclusive language, we cannot help but agree with Stevens' point: "Men of any nation who will heed his word and receive his Son become part of the elect race, the royal priesthood, the holy nation (ii:9)."[64] As Christ is God's elect Son, so the church is God's elect people. The focus is upon the church's chosenness; she is a choice people.

1 Peter 5:13

"She who is in Babylon, chosen together with you, sends you her greetings, and so does my son Mark." So the author concludes his letter, after he adds a final greeting and word of peace. The word the NIV translates "chosen together

---

[62]Schrenk, *TDNT*, 4:190.

[63]Elliott, *Elect and Holy*, 222. He argues in his book for the parallelism between 2:4 and 2:9, and that the structure of 2:4–10 deriving from this parallelism presents through the theme of election the character of the eschatological people of God. He says, "In support of this theme a Christological complex containing a statement concerning Jesus as the Elect Stone (vv. 6–8) was combined with a group of Old Testament passages describing the believing community as the Elect People of God (vv. 9–10)" (145).

[64]Stevens, *Theology of New Testament*, 296–97.

with you" is *syneklektē*, a *hapax legomenon*, but one that is close to *eklektos*. The prefix *syn* makes this an election or chosenness that is shared *with* others. But who is this chosen *she* who is in Babylon? Actually there are two questions here: (1) is "she" a literal woman or a metaphor of the church? and (2) do we take the city as literal Babylon or as a symbol for Rome? Though we cannot be certain, it seems that the second option is preferable for both questions.

First "she" is very probably the local church from which Peter writes. The gender of the word *ekklēsia* (church) is feminine, and it would be natural to refer to it simply as "she." Other female metaphors like bride of Christ (Eph 5:22–33; Rev 19:7–8; 21:2–3; 22:17) make this more understandable. If this were a literal woman, or even Peter's wife,[65] we would expect a more specific description.

The case becomes stronger if Babylon is also symbolic. Scholars have found virtually no evidence to commend the literal Babylon option. There is no tradition that Peter, Mark, or Silvanus ever visited Babylon, whereas a Roman connection, especially for Peter, is both strong and early. In both Revelation and the writings of the Jewish apocalyptists Babylon stood for Rome.[66] Christians viewed Rome as the capital of the pagan world—as Babylon was of the ancient world. Thus if Peter wrote this letter from Rome, it is easy to see how he could simply refer to his congregation as "she in Babylon." This would parallel the personification of the church as a "chosen lady" and "chosen sister" in 2Jn 1 and 13.[67] So Peter also personifies the local community of believers and describes it as elect.

Summary

Peter's understanding of election moves from the choice of Christ to a chosen people to an elect congregation. Jesus enjoys the status of being God's chosen and precious Stone (2:4, 6), the cornerstone of the spiritual house God is

---

[65]See Bigg, *Epistles of St. Peter and St. Jude*, 77–78.

[66]See Rev 14:8; 16:19–18:24; 2Ba 11:1–2; 67:7; 2Es 3:1–2, 28; and Sib 5:143, 157ff.

[67]Commentators agreeing that this is a metaphor of a Roman church include Best (177–79), Beare (209–10), Kelly (218–19), Selwyn (243, 303–5), and Lenski (231).

building. God elected him to his role as Messiah; God placed him in Zion to perform his salvific mission as Lamb of God (1:19). He is God's Chosen One to perform his task of redemption. God and Christ enjoyed a relationship of mutual knowing prior to the world's creation (1:20). God knew, planned, and purposed all along what he would do in and through Christ. And what God so foreknew, he has now accomplished.

God applies this salvation secured by Christ only to those who believe. Peter portrays such believers as those whom God called. To be called or named as belonging to God carries the obligation to live up to the character of God himself (holiness, 1:15). Their status and destiny have changed; to be called is to move from darkness to light (2:9) and to share God's glory (5:10). God may also call them to share Christ's experience of suffering (2:21; 3:9). Peter clearly uses "calling" with technical meaning. To say "God called you" means God saved you or granted you the position (name) of Christian. Calling represents membership in the people of God.

God not only called a people, but he chose them. Peter clearly applies the title "chosen" to the corporate body of all believers. So he calls his readers the chosen ones (1:1) whom God has foreknown (1:2). In appealing to God's foreknowledge, Peter did not say God chose some to save, nor even that God chose those whose eventual faith he foresaw. Rather Peter uses it expansively to refer to himself and his Christian readers, and all they are. The Godhead has been actively at work on behalf of the people of God. God has a special, knowing relation with them, and his intentions have always been for their well-being.

Peter perceived the church as the people of God who had taken over the special status and position formerly held by Israel. Now Christians are God's chosen race (2:9). Their special status as elect derives only from their relation to the Chosen Stone, Christ. In fact, he is a stone that trips unbelievers; he divides humanity. If people reject the salvation proffered in Christ, God has appointed that they stumble, a probable reference to the punishment God has in store for the wicked (2:8).

What is true of the universal church is true of local congregations. So if the body or people of God is chosen, a local assembly can also be elect. Indeed, Peter refers to a local

Roman congregation as "she who is. . . chosen" (5:13). The status or position of chosen also applies to the local, corporate body of believers.

Election in 1 Peter is primarily a status or position. Jesus is the precious and chosen cornerstone. The church is the chosen race. To be called means God has granted a person a new position, and it is indeed a choice one. The people enjoy a position as chosen. We find no hint of the selection of some individuals to be saved. The only individual elected is Christ, the One appointed to his task as redeemer.

Though we did find references to God's will in 1 Peter, they concern God's desire or wish for how he would have his people act (2:15; 4:2). Or, God may will (in a determinative sense) his people to suffer (3:17; 4:19), but they must continue their virtuous conduct knowing that God has not forsaken them. The choice of who realizes salvation is not linked to God's will in 1 Peter.

2 PETER

We have selected five texts in 2 Peter to consider. They divide into four categories, ones we previously encountered in James and 1 Peter. This epistle of 2 Peter omits the nonsalvific category of God's will in life's circumstances.

God's Will for People's Salvation

2 Peter 3:9

In 3:3ff. the author responds to the scoffers who raise doubts about the reality of the *Parousia*—the Lord's coming (3:4), also called the Day of the Lord (3:10). Peter[68] counters that Jesus' coming is "delayed" because God wills to exercise patience. In effect he makes two statements about God's will: the Lord does not *will* that any perish, but (the Lord *wills*) that all come to repentance.[69] The verb that expresses what

---

[68]Of course, Petrine authorship of 2 Peter is widely doubted. We have evaluated the two epistles attributed to Peter separately. Our findings, therefore, do not depend on settling this question. For a defense of Petrine authorship see M. Green, *The Second Epistle General of Peter and the General Epistle of Jude* (London: Tyndale, 1968). In defense of pseudonymity see R. Bauckham, *Jude, 2 Peter*, WBC (Waco, TX: Word, 1983).

[69]Various texts that express God's will that people repent and not perish include Eze 18:23, 32; 33:11; Ac 17:30; Ro 2:4; 1Ti 2:4; 1 Clem 8:5 ("Wishing

God wills is *boulomai*, used here in the present tense. We saw this verb in Mt 11:27 and Lk 10:22 where the Son reveals God to whomever he wills. God's will moved him to provide salvation (Jas 1:18). The Holy Spirit distributes gifts as he wills (1Co 12:11). We gain the impression of distinct purpose, considered volition. Hebrews 6:17 underscores how fixed God's will can be.

The context makes clear that the author fully expects some people will in fact perish and meet destruction (2:7), even though this goes contrary to God's will. We must conclude, then, that this statement of God's will is not what we have called his determinative or decretive will. This text affirms what God really desires and purposes, but the implementation of which he does not enforce. Whether an individual person perishes or repents does not depend on what God wills, for God wills *all* (*pantas*) to repent. An individual's fate must depend on other factors.

Without question, one factor inherent in the meaning of *metanoia* (repentance) is the willingness of the sinner to turn from sin to God. Certainly God desires such repentance, though many exercise their wills to reject salvation.[70] The use of *boulomai* indicates premeditated volition. It is doubtful Peter believes God wills something not possible. The text must imply that God desires all people to escape destruction and to repent. That some fail to attain what God wills must, therefore, be attributed to them, not God.

---

all his beloved therefore to partake of repentance, he hath established it by his almighty will"); and Eusebius, *HE* 5:1:46.

[70]R. J. Bauckham, *Jude, 2 Peter*, 313, limits the force of *pantas* (all) to *hymas* (you), Peter's readers. God is being patient with the readers, giving them time to repent. But surely they are Christians. What have they to repent of? Bauckham responds, "No doubt repentance from those sins into which some of them have been enticed by the false teachers (2:14, 18; 3:17) is especially in mind" (ibid.). Bauckham here misses the point of the entire section. Peter's discussion concerns the scoffers, and God's destruction of ungodly people and the universe. God delays his fury, but not merely so Christians can repent, though we dare not dismiss the sins of believers. Much more likely God patiently stays the judgment so more people can escape "destruction of ungodly men" (3:7). We admit that Peter does have a word for his Christian readers here, especially beginning at 3:11. But to them he urges a holy lifestyle rather than repentance. The principle of 3:9, though certainly applicable to Christians, extends to all people. God wills all to repent; he wills that none perish. Eventually Bauckham does come to admit that the principle of 3:9 can be applied more widely beyond the Christian readers addressed here (314).

God Calls People to Salvation

God's calling had an important place in 1 Peter, occurring in five texts. In 2 Peter the concept occurs twice, again with the same technical sense of the call to salvation.

2 Peter 1:3

Peter says that his readers have all they need for life and godliness "through the [or, our] knowledge of him who *called* us by his own glory and goodness." The technical status of this use is clear-cut. The aorist tense points to that occasion when God applied salvation to them.[71] This use corresponds to those at 1Pe 1:15; 2:9; and 5:10. However, here Peter identifies Christ rather than God as the one who calls Christians. Though it is more common in the New Testament to see God as the agent of calling, there are a very few scattered references to Christ as caller (see Ro 1:6; Mt 9:13, par.). In the end deciding between God or Christ as the agent is not crucial to our understanding of the use of *kalein*.[72] Only a divine agent, God or Christ, is qualified to call a person a Christian.

2 Peter 1:10

At the end of his appeal (starting in 1:5: "make every effort . . ."), Peter urges his readers to be diligent to make sure "your calling and election" (*hymōn tēn klēsin kai eklogēsn*). In this exhortation we find two key words, but here we only consider the first one—*klēsis* (calling). The term usually means summons or invitation, though there are some instances outside the New Testament of the sense of name or naming. It occurs eleven times in the New Testament but

---

[71]This seems preferable to Kelly's view that the calling here is Christ's call to his disciples (Kelly, *Epistles of Peter and Jude*, 300–301). The context of 1:3–11 concerns the *readers'* apprehension of and growth in salvation. The incontestable reference to a salvific calling (*klēsis*) in 1:10 appears to clinch the case.

[72]Most commentators do prefer to take Christ as the one who called. See Bigg (253–54); Bauckham (178); Green (*Second Peter and Jude*, 63); J. B. Mayor (*The Epistle of St. Jude and the Second Epistle of St. Peter* [London: Macmillan, 1910], 85; and Kelly (300–301). Lenski, *Epistles of St. Peter, St. John and St. Jude*, prefers to interpret God as the caller, consistent with 1Pe 2:9 (258–59).

only twice outside of Paul's letters: Heb 3:1 and 2Pe 1:10. As we might expect, its technical status comes through. It means the calling to salvation in Christ.

This appeal presents a fascinating juxtaposition of definitive divine acts—"calling" and "election"—and necessary human responses. Peter accents the human response with the aorist imperative verb *spoudasate*: "Be diligent," or "Be all the more eager" (NIV). It sounds a note of urgency: do it *now*. They should "continue to make" (*poieisthai*), a present middle infinitive. The middle voice focuses on the need for the readers' cooperation—"make for yourselves"—while the present tense underscores the need for constant action. God's calling and election must continually be made *sure* (*bebaios*). Bauckham mentions that this word had a legal sense of "ratified" or "guaranteed."[73]

Peter's objective is not that his readers might have a *feeling* of assurance of their salvation, but that they might *have it for sure*. He argues from the catalog of qualities in 1:5–7 "that the ethical fruits of the Christian faith are objectively necessary for the attainment of final salvation."[74]

I must hasten to say that this in no way rests salvation on their ability to produce these qualities listed in 1:5–7. Peter has confirmed that Christ has called his readers (1:3), and that they have been cleansed from their past sins (1:9). And certainly calling and election are divine acts. Yet Peter shows the emptiness of a profession that bears no fruit. If one is truly "called," then he or she will do these things. It is consistent Christian paranaesis to exhort believers to "become what you are." Thus if one possesses the Christian "calling," he or she will produce the appropriate Christian evidences. Naturally, then, Peter urges them to do it. "Calling" is not a mere label that some people come to adopt. Calling embodies a change of status, yes, and also a change of values and lifestyle. To be called is to be a new person; this is Peter's claim. So unless these Christian virtues now *characterize* a person's life, there is no surety that the calling and election are authentic.

---

[73]Bauckham, *Jude, 2 Peter.*
[74]Ibid., 190.

God's Choice of Christ

2 Peter 1:17

In his defense of the historical basis for the Christian message, Peter quotes the voice from heaven at Jesus' Transfiguration. Peter claims he was an eyewitness of this event; he heard the voice. The word order of the quotation differs from that in Mt 17:5 and Mk 9:7, but the meaning is the same.[75] Peter's words are closest to Mt 17:5 in that he includes the phrase about God's being well pleased, absent from Mk 9:7 and Lk 9:35. Where Matthew has "in whom I am well pleased," Peter says, "with him I am well pleased," again, with no shift in meaning. Two final changes from the synoptic tradition are Peter's omission of the synoptists' "Hear him" and Peter's insertion of an additional *mou* (my) with *agapētos* (beloved). The effect is to make *agapētos* function as a second title: "This is my Son, my beloved one."[76]

Because our comments here closely parallel the discussion in the synoptics, they can be brief. We can make a good case that the use of "Son" is an allusion to Ps 2:7, which was being interpreted messianically by Jews in the first century.[77] In the psalm the king celebrates his enthronement. So Jesus enjoys God's appointment to his messianic role because he is God's Son. Bauckham says, ". . . *because* Jesus was already God's Son, he has appointed him to be his vicegerent."[78]

In addition to identifying Jesus as Son, the heavenly voice validates Jesus as "my beloved one." Two ways of understanding this term stand out as more likely than other options. It may correlate with the Hebrew *yehîd*, "my only one" (cf. Ge 22:2, 12, 16), and then read closely with the

---

[75]I accept the reading of UBS, 3d ed. The majority text reading is identical to the quotation in the synoptic accounts. But this is a sure sign of scribal assimilation. If these were Peter's original words the change would be difficult to explain.

[76]For an extensive discussion of the structure of this citation as compared to the synoptic accounts, see Bauckham, *Jude, 2 Peter*, 204–12. He includes a section on the various theories to account for the use and meaning of *agapētos* in the baptismal and transfiguration accounts (207–9).

[77]J. A. T. Robinson, *St. Paul's Epistle to the Ephesians*, 2d ed. (London: Macmillan, 1904), 229–33, defends the view that "the Beloved" was a messianic title.

[78]Bauckham, *Jude, 2 Peter*, 220.

previous "Son." This would make it almost synonymous with *monogenēs* (only, unique) meaning something like, "this is my unique son." Or *agapētos* (beloved) might be based on *beḥîrî*, "my chosen," as in Isa 42:1, and then read with the following phrase, " . . . my chosen one whom I have set my favor on."

The verb *eudokein* (to be well pleased) adds a final elective component to the citation. This is not simply a statement of God's pleasure in his Son, but a statement of electing favor. Bauckham echoes the conclusions we drew in our prior evaluations of this verb when he says it "carries the special sense of God's *electing* good pleasure."[79]

Jesus was on a mission from God. The words "Son," "beloved," and "I am well pleased" draw attention to Jesus' status as God's specially Chosen One. Alone he enjoys the status of beloved Son, and God confirmed this status to him and the three disciples on the mount. God set his elective favor on his unique Son and sent him on his redemptive mission.

God's Election of People

2 Peter 1:10

Peter urged his readers to make sure not only their "calling," but also their "election," (*eklogē*). In the Greek text one article governs both "calling" and "election" as if the author intended to contemplate the actions together. We have seen that *klēsis* is a technical term for the action of God in applying salvation or in naming a person as belonging to God. It points to an action in a person's life—the time when God names that one a Christian. Now, what about *eklogē*? When does that occur, and does Peter give any hints here about what it is?

The basic sense of the word involves an act of selection, either by people or God. Peter provides no elaboration, neither about the timing[80] nor nature of this election. We can

---

[79]Ibid.

[80]On the basis of other data, Green (*Second Peter and Jude*, 74) declares, "Chronologically speaking, of course, *election* precedes *calling* (cf. Rom. viii:30). There is nothing arbitrary or unfair about it. Christ is the Elect One. Election is in Christ. Outside Him is ruin." Green is probably right about his conclusions, but nothing in 2Pe 1 places the election of the reader in Christ

only assume it bears the consistent sense of God's selection of his people, certainly a sense that fits well here. Peter urges his readers to live in keeping with the position they occupy—both called and chosen. Not only did God name them to be his people, but they are also his chosen ones. Peter holds them accountable to give evidence in their lives that will confirm this status they enjoy. As with "calling," obedience establishes "election," as Peter spells out further in 1:5–7.

Having said this, I must make one final observation. Peter's use of "election" in this way suggests he does not understand it in a pretemporal or predetermined sense. Election implies that these Christians enjoy the status of God's chosen ones. However, only a life of faithfulness demonstrates the validity of its application to individuals. Election describes the readers' status as Christians. It does not point, in 2 Peter, to a choice to mark out some from before the foundation of the world (contrast Eph 1:4).

Summary

We can divide our findings between what the author says about Jesus, and the salvation he came to secure for his people. Peter quotes from the tradition of Jesus' transfiguration to affirm Jesus as God's Chosen One, the beloved Son upon whom God has set his elective favor (1:17). The heavenly voice affirmed Jesus as one God sent to accomplish his messianic mission.

Concerning people Peter says several things. First, God wills that none perish but all come to repent of their sins and attain salvation (3:9). Since some perish we must assume that this will of God is not entirely accomplished. Therefore, whether a specific individual obtains salvation is not solely dependent upon what God wills, for he wills all to repent. Repentance depends upon the operation of the human will; a person must will to repent for God's will to be done.

Second, Peter says that God calls people. Initially Peter attributes that calling to Christ (1:3). Christians are who they are because of Christ's call. This call gives them their

---

the Elect One, nor does Peter establish that election precedes calling. In 2Pe 1:10 he puts calling before election! Peter is not concerned to make these points.

position. Thus Peter says that Christians have a calling (1:10). They must then confirm the validity of this title in their experience. Peter follows the dominant technical New Testament sense of "calling." To be called a Christian means not merely the change of name or title, but of nature. Hence the values and lifestyle of a person with the Christian "calling" will reflect godly virtues (for example, those in 1:5–7).

The same is true, thirdly, of the "election" that characterizes God's people (1:10). A life of obedience validates the reality of the status of God's chosen ones. The proof that people really belong to the body of those whom God has chosen lies in their exhibition of godliness.

JUDE

The epistle of Jude closely parallels 2 Peter and yet the one instance of a verse significant for our study does not match a Petrine text. In v. 1 Jude identifies his addressees as "those who are the loved by God the Father and kept for [or, by] Jesus Christ, called ones." This literal translation is too wooden to stand. Probably the NIV captures the sense well: "To those who have been called, who are loved by God the Father and kept by Jesus Christ."[81]

Again there can be no doubt that this verbal adjective *klētos* (called) shares the technical status of its partners *kalein* (to call) and *klēsis* (calling). For Paul to specify people as Christians, it was sufficient to use the designation *klētoi*, the called ones (Ro 1:6; 8:28; 1Co 1:24). We discovered this same meaning in Rev 17:14. This differs from the sense at Mt 22:14, where, in Jesus' words, not all the called are chosen. Paul also employs *klētos* to refer to his call to apostleship (Ro 1:1; 1Co 1:1).

Jude's use exhibits the technical salvific sense. His readers are Christians; hence they are "the called." And as Jude affirms, they are *loved*, and they are *kept*. That is the position of all God's called ones.[82]

---

[81]This basic approach is also followed by Bauckham (19), Bigg (324), Kelly (242–43), and Lenski (605).

[82]Bauckham argues that the title *klētoi* was transferred to Christians from Old Testament Israel through such texts as Isa 41:9; 42:6; 48:12, 15; 49:1; 54:6; and Hos 11:1. Compare CD 2,9; 4,4 from Qumran; 1 Clem, inscr.; Barn 4:13–14; and Sib 8:92 (Bauckham, *Jude, 2 Peter*, 26–27).

III

CONCLUSIONS

The preceding analyses have ranged over the entire corpus of the New Testament. A major goal was to perceive the unique perspectives and emphases of individual authors, and our perception determined how we approached the text. Now we need to distill these findings and draw some deductions about the early church's understanding of election issues (as reflected in the New Testament canon). We must be careful that in the interests of synthesis we do not miss the individual authors' unique emphases. Nonetheless, I believe we have detected some broad patterns that pervade the New Testament. Indeed, some of our conclusions from the New Testament data fall into line with views of election we detected in the Old Testament and other Jewish literature. First we will assess the nature of election. Then we follow several conclusions that touch on various other aspects of election that we have investigated: God's call, foreknowledge, predestination, and will. At appropriate points I will propose what I believe might be some valid implications of these conclusions for the church today.

1
THE CORPORATE NATURE OF ELECTION TO SALVATION

Corresponding to the evidence in the Old Testament, the New Testament writers present election from two basic perspectives—corporate and individual. I conclude, first of all, that the New Testament writers address salvific election in primarily, if not exclusively, corporate terms. In others words, God has chosen an elect body to save. Election to salvation applies to the church, God's chosen body. Though God previously chose Israel, she forfeited her position and the blessings God had offered because she failed to live up to the conditions of God's covenant with her.

For Paul, Israel still enjoys her election in a national or ethnic sense (Ro 11:28–29). God will not reject his people (11:2). Paul retained the Old Testament and Jewish teaching that affirmed Israel as God's chosen people (cf. 9:11, 13). However, now God has chosen a new eschatological people—the church. Several New Testament writers insist that the church has inherited many of the terms, categories, and promises that God once gave to Israel.[1] The Christian church now enjoys the unique position of "chosen people." P. Jewett puts it well in commenting on Jesus' warning to unbelieving Jews in Mt 21:43:

> If the church is the "nation" that inherits the kingdom belonging to Israel, then the church must inherit the election belonging to Israel. As Israel was, so the church now is the elect community.[2]

Only those who exercise saving faith in Christ inherit the blessing of eternal life (Ro 9:6, 30–32; 10:9, 16, 20–21). Paul insists that faith was always the criterion for salvation. Though the *nation* Israel enjoyed status as elect, in fact, only the remnant who believed was truly saved (Ro 11:5, 7). Jesus placed emphasis upon the need for belief or faith. The Jews could not count on their status as Abraham's children. The church, as the company of those who believe in Christ, constitutes the people of God and likewise the elect.

Our study of the New Testament documents demands that we view election to salvation corporately. We found in the synoptics, John, Peter, James, and Paul evidence that God has chosen a people—a community. Plural language dominates election texts. Though we might view some of these as references to a collection of elect individuals, many

---

[1]See, e.g., Gal 6:16 (the church as the new Israel has supplanted old Israel); Php 3:3 (we are the circumcision); Ro 9:25 (Gentiles called "my people"); Ro 2:28 (being a Jew is a matter of an inward condition); Ro 11:17–24 (Gentiles grafted into the people of God); and 1Pe 2:9–10 (the church is a chosen race).

[2]Paul Jewett, *Election and Predestination* (Grand Rapids: Eerdmans, 1985), 32–33.

of the texts must be viewed in communal terms. This creates the overwhelming impression—in keeping with the Old Testament pattern of a chosen people—that God has chosen the church as a body rather than the specific individuals who populate that body. The author of 2 John, in calling two local churches "the chosen lady" (v. 1) and "your chosen sister" (v. 13), highlights this conviction of the chosenness of the body of Christ.

Paul affirms that the total body of Christians was chosen "in Christ" before the world's creation (Eph 1:4, 11). This raises the interesting phenomenon of the "in Christ" formula that pervades Paul's writings.[3] And even beyond the use of that phrase, Paul understands the church as a community that is in some sense incorporated into Christ.[4] Sanders says, "Christians really are one body and Spirit with Christ."[5] Similarly, E. Best observes:

> The phrase "members of Christ" suggests a very close identity between Christ and the community of believers; if they are his members, then together they form him. The Church, or the community of believers, is thus identical with Christ; the Church is Christ.[6]

Thus, if the Christian body was chosen in Christ, the church acquires her election from the fact of Christ's election (see Lk 9:35; 1Pe 2:4–6).[7] A. Richardson puts it this way: "If

---

[3]The phrase is especially pervasive in Ephesians. In fact, J. A. Allan, "The 'in Christ' Formula in Ephesians," *NTS* 5 (1959): 54–62, thinks the formula is too pervasive in Ephesians and uses this to argue against its Pauline authorship. Though we find his case unconvincing, that issue lies beyond our concerns here.

[4]Paul presses this union with Christ on an individual level too. Essentially, Paul equates the salvation experience with being "baptized into Christ Jesus" (Ro 6:3). In addition, "our old self was crucified with him" and "we died with Christ" (6:6, 8). Paul affirms, "I have been crucified with Christ" (Gal 2:20).

[5]E. P. Sanders, *Paul and Palestinian Judaism* (London: SCM, 1977), 237.

[6]E. Best, *One Body in Christ* (London: SPCK, 1955), 78. We need to clarify Best's position. He believes that the body is a metaphor. The church is like the body of Christ; it is "not really and ontologically the Body of Christ" (100).

[7]See also Lk 22:22; Jn 1:34, v.l.; 12:32–33; 13:19, 27–28; 18:32; Ac 2:23; 3:18; 4:27; 13:27. We discovered numerous texts that affirm that Christ was chosen or predestined by God for his salvific task. Not only do the baptismal and transfiguration accounts make this point explicit, but it finds expression throughout the New Testament, as our previous studies demonstrated.

Christians are 'the elect,' it is because they are 'in Christ,' because they are baptized into the person of him who alone may with complete propriety be called the Elect of God."[8]

In our study of the Old Testament we discerned the pattern that God chose Abraham and his seed to be his chosen nation. Correspondingly, God chose Christ and those "in Him" to be his chosen people. God's free and sovereign electing grace has chosen the community of those "in Christ." Christ is God's Chosen One, and the church is chosen in him.

This brings us to consider the whole construct of "corporate solidarity" that is so foreign to our Western thinking. In his book *The New Testament World*, Bruce Malina argues persuasively that the first-century Mediterranean person did not share or comprehend our idea of an individual.[9] Malina is convinced that instead of being individualistic, in the world of the New Testament, people were what he calls "dyadic." That is, they conceived of themselves in relation to others, not as separate entities. Thus they did not view people in terms of their specific qualities as individuals, but rather the qualities of their family, village, city, or nation. This sheds light on Paul's presentation of the church as incorporated into Christ. It helps explain the numerous corporate metaphors employed to describe the church—body of Christ,[10] house (temple), bride, people of God, and "in Christ." Christians find their identity as members of this inclusive organism.[11]

---

[8]A. Richardson, *An Introduction to the Theology of the New Testament* (London: SCM, 1958), 279. K. Stendahl echoes this point: "Election in Christ strictly implies that Christ is the truly Elect, as the beloved Son in whom God is well pleased. The faithful become participants in His election" ("The Called and the Chosen. An Essay on Election," in *The Root of the Vine*, ed. by A. Fridrichsen (London: Dacre, 1953), 68).

[9]B. Malina, *The New Testament World* (Atlanta: John Knox, 1981). See especially his chapter 3, "The First-Century Personality: The Individual and the Group," 51–70.

[10]Though he seems to prefer another option, F. F. Bruce, "The Logic of the Damascus Road," *Scottish Evangelical Theological Society Bulletin*, 2:10, suggests that the "Hebrew concept of 'corporate personality' " might be the origin of Paul's presentation of the church as the body of Christ.

[11]D. E. H. Whitely, *The Theology of St. Paul* (Oxford: Blackwell, 1964), 45, goes so far as to say, "It is one of the main contentions of this book that many of St. Paul's fundamental doctrines can be properly understood only if we realize that he took for granted the presupposition of human solidarity." This perspective is certainly not limited to Paul. R. Schnackenberg argues for

Thus, though individualism dominates our thinking, it would have been very foreign to the world of the writers of the New Testament.[12] They would approach the basic theological issues from a corporate frame of reference, which is precisely what we discovered in our analyses.[13] Our exegeses of many Pauline texts clearly demonstrated Paul's view of the corporate solidarity of the human race. A review of several key texts will suffice to drive home this point.[14]

Romans 5:12–21 reveals that Paul routinely views people corporately. In 5:12 Paul bases his case on the reality that all sinned (*pantes hēmarton*). Clearly all people did not individually commit an act of sin at the time that Adam disobeyed. Nor is Paul saying that we all inherit a sinful nature as a result of Adam's act.[15] The best explanation is that Paul here views the human race corporately. What Adam did, we all did. In their corporate solidarity with Adam, all people participated in his sin.

This feature of Adam's role as head of a race—the one whose act affected his entire corporate group—becomes the

---

a strong corporate sense of salvation in the Johannine literature (*The Gospel According to St. John*, 3 vols. (New York: Herder and Herder; London: Burns & Oates, 1968) 3:206–17). He observes, "The community is not only firmly based on Jesus—it has its permanent existential centre of being in him" (212).

[12]It is also foreign to other non-Western cultures today. In a chapter entitled "Corporate Personality: Ancient Israel and Africa," in *The Challenge of Black Theology in South Africa*, ed. B. Moore (Atlanta: John Knox, 1974), B. Goba argues for a strong sense of corporate personality in African culture based on kinship. There is a relational cohesion that transcends individual wishes and feelings. He observes that an individual is completely part of a community. "The individual depends on the corporate group" (68). "A man's existence is a corporate existence" (ibid.). In this article Goba decries the breakdown of this sense of solidarity in black South Africa due to the influences of Western materialism and capitalism that stress individualism.

[13]See, e.g., M. Barth, *The People of God*, JSNT Suppl. 5 (Sheffield: JSOT, 1983), 13.

[14]Clearly, Paul's writings are the dominant source here. But in his commentary on John, R. Schnackenberg (*The Gospel According to St. John*, 3:441, n. 10) quotes approvingly a statement of E. Schweizer: "Independently of Paul and using a completely different terminology, the gospel here [John 15.1–8, the vine and branches metaphor] provides a view in which Christ includes all believers as a 'corporate personality' within himself" (E. Schweizer, "Der Kirkenbegriff in Evangelium und den Briefen des Johannes," *Neotestamentica* [Zürich/Stuttgart: Zwingli Verlag, 1963], 260).

[15]For a comprehensive discussion of the various interpretive options, see C.E.B. Cranfield, *The Epistle to the Romans*, ICC, 1:274–81.

point of comparison ("type"; Greek *typos*) to another Representative, Christ (5:14). Paul repeats the paradigm of one person's act affecting an entire group several times in the passage (see 5:15, 16, 17, 18, and 19). Whatever else we may say about the passage (and our concern here is not with its total exegesis), clearly Paul is employing some concept of corporate solidarity. He does not view people as isolated or independent individuals. Apart from our knowledge or consent, when Adam sinned we all sinned.[16]

C. H. Dodd agrees that the correct understanding of Ro 5:12–21 must recognize in Paul's thinking "the ancient concept of solidarity."[17] Citing the situation concerning Achan, Dodd remarks, "the moral unit was the community (clan, tribe, or city), rather than the individual."[18] Nygren concurs: "Paul does not think of humanity as a chance gathering of individuals, . . . [but] as an organic unity, a single body under a single head."[19] Dodd adds, "Adam is a name which stands to him for the 'corporate personality' of mankind, and a new 'corporate personality' is created in Christ."[20]

We detect the corporate union of Christ and his body in other places in Paul's writings. He says, "So in Christ we

---

[16]J. Dunn, *Romans 1–8*, WBC, 272–74, dismisses the concept of "corporate personality" here. In fact, he views it as a hindrance to understanding Paul's meaning. Yet he provides little support for his rejection. He simply admits that "the link between the 'one' and the 'all' is not explained" (273), and goes on to assert confidently that "the 'all' are not simply subsumed within the 'one' " (ibid.). He believes that Paul uses the verb *hēmarton* to denote specific sinful acts. He fails to appreciate the corporate perspective in which the entire race acts in its ancestor, as our following discussion reveals.

[17]C. H. Dodd, *The Epistle of Paul to the Romans*, MNTC (London: Hodder & Stoughton, 1932), 79–80.

[18]Ibid.

[19]A. Nygren, *Commentary on Romans*, trans. C. C. Rasmussen (London: SCM, 1952), 213.

[20]Dodd, *Epistle of Paul to the Romans*, 80. In chapter 1, on the Old Testament understanding of election, we discussed H. Wheeler Robinson's concept of "corporate personality." In *The Christian Doctrine of Man* (Edinburgh: T. & T. Clark, 1913), where he considers Ro 5:12ff., he sees very naturally the "distinct thought of Adam as the 'corporate personality' of the race over against Christ as the corporate personality of His body, the Church" (21). R. Shedd, in *Man in Community* (London: Epworth, 1958), comments on Ro 5:12ff. and 1Co 15:21–22: "It is Adam's position as the archetypal head of the race, which he embodies as a corporate personality, that makes his rebellion against God the revolt of his group" (108).

who are many form one body, and each member belongs to all the others" (Ro 12:5). Christ died, and yet that means that all who are in Him also died (2Co 5:14–17). Christ is the promised Seed, and Christians receive the promised blessings by their inclusion in him (Gal 3:16). A. Oepke sums it up this way:

> The first and second Adam are progenitors initiating two races of men. Each implies a whole world, an order of life or death. Each includes his adherents in and under himself. . . . By baptism believers are removed from the sphere of the first Adam, which is that of sin and death, into the sphere of the second Adam, which is that of righteousness and life. . . . At root is the view of Christ as a universal personality.[21]

In 1Co 15:22 Paul says, "in Adam all die," again affirming the corporateness of the human race. B. Schneider views vv. 20–22 as an example of Paul's embracing the principle of corporate personality.[22] He argues that Paul appeals to "the parallel of Adam as the corporate personality of the first creation with Christ as the firstfruits (*aparchē*) and corporate personality of the new creation. . . ."[23] E. Best puts the matter in concise terms: ". . . Christ is the head of a new race who are 'solid' with him: his actions affect them; he passes on righteousness and life to them."[24]

IMPLICATIONS OF A CORPORATE VIEW OF ELECTION

The implications of "corporate solidarity" are penetrating for Paul's presentation of God's election to salvation. We

---

[21]A. Oepke, *TDNT*, 2:542.

[22]Schneider, "The Corporate Meaning and Background of 1Cor 15, 45b— O ESCHATOS ADAM EIS PNEUMA ZOIOPOIOUN," *CBQ* 29 (1967): 450–67.

[23]Ibid., 451. Schneider goes on to say, "Such a corporate-person meaning for *o anthropos, ha' adam* in Gen 2,7 and also here in [1Co 15] v. 45 by reason of the whole argument in vv. 42–46 is the only natural one" (457).

[24]Best, *One Body in Christ*, 36. Best rightly points out errors to be avoided in understanding the corporate personality concept (22–23). Surely we must avoid any concept that the body expresses Christ's personality. Similarly, Christians do not lose their own personalities in being incorporated into Christ; nor are their personalities fused with Christ's. Christ and his members have their separate existences; their relationship is not mystical.

are convinced that election is essentially corporate. Paul has *not* conceived of election in terms markedly different from the election of Israel. We would not expect him to. In fact, the concepts are quite parallel. As Israel became God's chosen people when God chose Abraham, so the church finds her election in solidarity with Christ and his election. All the church has and is she achieves in Christ. The church is not a collection of individuals who decide to affiliate with Christ or become Christian. As Conzelmann puts it, "[the church] is constituted by God's act of election."[25] Thus the church is God's elect body; Christians are the "elect ones." We can hardly put the matter more precisely than Shedd:

> This election does not have individual emphasis in Paul, any more than it did for Israel in the Old Testament or the Early Jewish period. Rather, it implies a covenant-relationship through which God chooses for Himself a whole people. This collectivism is of supreme importance for the understanding of the implications of "election in Christ."[26]

The New Testament does know of the election of individuals to tasks or ministries. But when the issue concerns God's choice for salvation, he has chosen a community—the body of Christ, the church.

Some might object: "How can you have an elect body apart from the specific selection of who will be in that body?" However, that objection imposes modern (and Western) categories upon the New Testament data. Further, such an objection seeks to impress upon the biblical authors a kind of logic that is foreign to their thinking. Their perspective is corporate, and they find no need to ask this question. Individuals find their election in being part of the elect body of Christ. To enter that body requires faith—a trust in God that involves a commitment of one's will and life to the way of Christ. The New Testament writers do not cite election as the underlying reason or cause why some individuals believe, or its lack as the explanation why others do not.

This changes the focus for theological discussion of election. Rather than "God chose *me*," we need to stress

---

[25]H. Conzelmann, *An Outline of the Theology of the New Testament* (London: SCM, 1969), 42.
[26]Shedd, *Man in Community*, 133.

"God chose *us*." A corporate understanding of election reveals the error in an individualistic "maverick Christianity." All believers find their identity as one of God's chosen ones through participation and incorporation in the body of Christ. An individual finds "chosenness" "in Christ." The New Testament knows of no "lone ranger" Christians out on their own. God has chosen a people, and we must seek our identity in our affiliation with his church.

Christians today need to recapture the reality of the church as an organism. It is not a montage of individuals. No believer in Christ should feel or become isolated. Christians are members of one another. For Paul this is a basic and established *fact*, not a goal.

Christian security rests not in an individualistic "God chose me," but in the reality that by faith "I am a member of his chosen body." Membership in the body of Christ provides security, for we know that God has chosen us in Christ before the foundation of the world (Eph 1:4).

Today we wistfully talk about unity—it would be nice, but it is totally out of the question. If believers genuinely form an organism—the body of Christ—chosen in him before the foundation of the world, then unity and the demonstration of mutual love for one another must be a priority. These show the truthfulness of this reality. For most of the world looking at us, our claims are too often self-deceiving mirages.

An understanding of salvific election as corporate also shifts the focus of many debates about election. Some of these debates may be beside the point. The debates often center on the issue by asking: Has God chosen specific individuals to save, and, if so, was it on the basis of foreseen faith or simply a matter of God's sovereign will? We have concluded that this question does not trouble the biblical writers. God has chosen to save a people, and in New Testament language that people is the church. In the old covenant a person entered the chosen nation of Israel through natural birth. In the new covenant a person enters the chosen body, the church, through the new birth. To exercise faith in Christ is to enter into his body and become one of the "chosen ones."

The New Testament writers simply do not entertain the issue of whether God has selected specific individuals to become members of that body. The body is chosen; one enters that body through faith in Christ. If anything, we have seen in our exegesis of the appropriate texts in the New Testament the emphasis upon the universal availability of the gospel. To exercise faith seems possible for all. God holds people responsible and accountable for accepting or rejecting the gospel. The invitation goes out to all, as if anyone could respond. We have seen face-value statements that God wills that none perish, all come to repentance, and all people enter salvation. The New Testament writers affirm that Christ identified with his human creatures and made provision for their salvation by instituting a new community in himself. People must accept Christ's work on their behalf to enter this fellowship. Shedd says,

> This involves the free choice of the individual without any violation of the corporate predestination and election of the whole People. While the original decree of God assures the existence of the whole Community (Eph 1:14), the gospel is preached and must be believed for the election to find its historical fulfillment (Ro 10:8–21).[27]

These data present an impressive case that election is not God's choice of a restricted number of individuals whom he wills to save, but the description of that corporate body which, in Christ, he is saving. God has covenanted to save his people through their identification with Jesus, his beloved and elect Son. To become a member of that chosen people requires faith in the gospel. Anyone who believes may enter into this elect nation. To make election restrictive is to limit God's boundless mercy. As Paul put it, "For God has bound all men over to disobedience so that he may have mercy on them all" (Ro 11:32). God gives people the freedom to rebel and to reject him. He may respond to their continued rejection by hardening them in their sinfulness. But God shows mercy in all his dealings with his creatures and does not cast away those who come to him in faith (Jn 6:37).

In the context of Ro 9–11 Paul does not maintain that some individual Jews or Gentiles could not come to God in faith because God had not elected them. In fact, in 10:21 Paul quotes Isaiah, who says, "All day long I have held out my hands to a disobedient and obstinate people" (Isa 65:2). If these unbelieving Israelites (in both Isaiah's and Paul's

---

[27]Ibid., 178.

times) were simply nonelect, why do Isaiah and Paul express such anguish? But more, in the Isaiah text *God is speaking*! Why does God make so impassioned an appeal if the ultimate explanation for their unbelief was that he had not chosen them for salvation? No, for God, Isaiah, and Paul, the plea makes more sense if the issue here is the need for faith, not a lack of election.

Though Paul does not envision the salvation of all persons, he does view God's mercy as universally available. In our concern for evangelizing we never need to resolve whether people are elect or not, and, therefore, whether or not they can respond to the gospel. Election is not a prior selection by God that excludes nonchosen individuals from salvation. God has chosen a people in Christ, but individuals must decide whether or not to accept God's salvation and so enter that body (Ro 10:13). God has given his people a task— to be his agents in advancing the kingdom of God in the world. As we share the gospel of the kingdom, we give people the opportunity to believe in Christ and thus to become members of God's elect people.

Some further practical results of this corporate solidarity in election merit brief consideration here. Clearly the modern church has lost the sense of group responsibility for our actions. Our "lone ranger" approach to Christianity leaves individual believers the freedom to "do their own thing," even when it involves sin. A conviction of corporate accountability has all but disappeared. What would happen today if God judged each sin against the body as he did Ananias and Sapphira in Acts 5? Perhaps he is. As a result of the Corinthians' sin against the "body" (that is, the church; 1Co 11:29), God judged them with sickness and death.[28] What plagues is God inflicting upon his people today in response to the sins of modern Achans (Jos 7)? Goba cites a Zulu proverb, *Zifa ngamvunye*, which he translates, "When one individual has done wrong, the rest of the group to which he belongs is responsible."[29] We have allowed cultural values like individualism to blind us to our obligation to maintain the purity of the body.[30] We have lost the sense of

[28]G. Fee, *The First Epistle to the Corinthians*, NICNT, 563–64.

[29]B. Goba, "Corporate Personality: Ancient Israel and Africa," in *The Challenge of Black Theology in South Africa*, 68.

[30]See R. Bellah, et al., *Habits of the Heart* (New York: Harper & Row, 1985) for their assessment of how individualism has become one of the dominant cultural values in the United States.

"belongingness" that ought to characterize members of Christ's body.

We ought to celebrate the rites of baptism and the Lord's Supper with a greater sense of their significance in affirming our corporate solidarity. In Ro 6:2–6 Paul attests that baptism celebrates the believers' incorporation into Christ, into the body that the Holy Spirit spawned (1Co 12:13; see Gal 3:27; Eph 4:4–5). Likewise the Lord's Supper celebrates and proclaims the unity of the body. One loaf symbolizes one body (1Co 10:16b–17). Paul reminded the Corinthians to discern the body of Christ (the church) when they ate the bread and drank the cup (1Co 11:23–29).[31] Participation in the Eucharist ought to heighten our sense of corporateness. In commemorating Jesus' death for us we affirm the covenant that makes us the people of God. These church ordinances or sacraments ought to help us recapture the *koinonia* that asserts "we, who are many, are one body" (1Co 10:17).

2

INDIVIDUAL ELECTION TO A TASK

The New Testament writers follow in the footsteps of their Old Testament predecessors in speaking of God's appointment of individuals to perform tasks, functions, or ministries in his service.[32] Not only did God chose the church to be his people; he also chose specific individuals to carry out his purposes in and for that body and in the world. We may conveniently divide the evidence into several categories: God's choice of Christ; Jesus' choice of the twelve apostles; Paul's appointment as an apostle; and God's choice of other individuals.

---

[31]For an excellent discussion of this passage and its pointed implications for today's church, see G. Fee, *The First Epistle to the Corinthians*, 545–64.

[32]The New Testament writers use election terms to speak of God's choice of the patriarchs of the nation Israel. See, e.g., Ac 13:17; Ro 4:17; 9:11–13; Heb 5:4.

THE ELECTION OF CHRIST

A wide range of texts throughout the New Testament identifies Jesus as God's Chosen or Appointed One. God selected him to accomplish his redemptive role in the world. We saw this mainly in the four gospels.[33] Confirmation came from the Acts,[34] the writer of Hebrews,[35] Peter,[36] and Paul.[37] The New Testament writers assure their readers that Jesus was the promised Messiah, the One God appointed to usher in the kingdom. In a baptismal text God says, "You are my Son, whom I love; with you I am well pleased" (Lk 3:22). Then in the Transfiguration account he continues, "This is my Son whom I have chosen; listen to him" (Lk 9:35). The parallel between these texts and the assertion about the servant in Isa 42:1 is striking: "Here is my servant, whom I uphold, my chosen one in whom I delight; I will put my Spirit on him and he will bring justice to the nations" (cf. Lk 4:18; Mt 12:15–21).

The Evangelists portray Jesus as conscious of his own special appointment by God. Jesus applies to himself the messianic prophecy of Isa 61:1–2 (Lk 4:18–21).[38] He is conscious that God specially selected him to accomplish his will on earth. Unquestionably he was "sent" to fulfill God's purpose.[39] So Jesus applies Ps 118:22 to himself: "The stone the builders rejected has become the capstone" (Lk 20:17–

[33]Matthew's pervasive and well-known motif of prophetic fulfillment signifies his view that Jesus' advent and career were divinely planned and executed. That Jesus fulfills so many Old Testament prophecies proves he is the predicted and long-awaited Messiah. For Matthew this means Jesus is God's Elect One. Mark begins his gospel by quoting Mal 3:1 and Isa 40:3 to show the prediction of John the Baptist to prepare the way for the Messiah (Mk 1:2; as does Lk 3:4–6 and Mt 3:3). Jesus comes according to God's prophetic plan. In his infancy narrative Luke includes prophecies of Zechariah and Simeon to show Jesus as the one promised to bring salvation to all people (Lk 1:68–79; 2:29–32). John identifies Jesus as God's unique Son (e.g., Jn 1:14, 18).

[34]See, e.g., Ac 2:23; 3:20; 10:42; 17:31.

[35]See, e.g., Heb 1:2, 5; 3:2; 5:5, 10; 7:28; 8:3.

[36]See, e.g., 1Pe 2:4, 6; 2Pe 1:17.

[37]Ro 1:4; 3:25; Col 1:19; 2Ti 1:9.

[38]W. W. Klein, "The Sermon at Nazareth (Luke 4:14–22)," in *Christian Freedom: Essays in Honor of Vernon C. Grounds,* ed. K. W. M. Wozniak and S. J. Grenz (Lanham, Md.: University Press of America, 1986).

[39]John's Gospel seems to stress this aspect. See, e.g., Jn 7:33; 8:16, 18, 26, 29, 38, 42; 12:44–45; 17:3, 8, 18, 21, 23, 25.

18). He accepts his role as one who will divide people. He understands that God predestined his mission on earth (Lk 24:26–27). To accomplish his mission he willingly submits his will to that of his Father (Jn 4:34; 5:30; 6:38).

Without question, Jesus' election was functional. That is, God chose him for a mission or task. Surely his election was not salvific in the sense that he was chosen to be saved. His assignment was certainly salvific: to live as a man and by his death and resurrection to secure salvation for all who trust in him. He was the only Person qualified to take on this mission. God chose him to accomplish that task on the earth.

THE ELECTION OF THE TWELVE APOSTLES

In the gospel accounts Jesus uses elective language in the choice of his apostles. Beyond that, Jesus "appoints" the Seventy-two (or Seventy) for ministry (Lk 10:1).[40] We may conclude on the basis of our previous analyses that this election or appointment is also functional. Jesus chose disciples or apostles to carry out various ministries or functions. Though it may seem difficult to separate the issues of appointment to salvation and appointment to tasks here, we insist that the evidence demands it.

A crucial factor to assess here is Jesus' selection of Judas to be among his group of twelve apostles. Unquestionably Judas shared the election of the other eleven (Lk 6:13; Jn 6:70). After Judas' suicide the disciples felt compelled to replace him with another whom God had also chosen (Ac 1:24). Yet Judas was a traitor, a devil. It cannot be that Judas was "elect to salvation." His election was to a task or function. We see no reason why he could not have come to faith in Christ, yet apparently he did not.

To what task was Judas chosen? Perhaps Jesus had hopes for him as he had for the others. Perhaps Judas had abilities that God could have used had he come to faith. John adds another perspective: Judas fulfills the prophecy of Ps 41:9 about a betrayer (Jn 13:18). Though Judas willingly betrayed Jesus, his treacherous act was foreseen (though not

---

[40] In Greek usage the word here, *anadeiknymi*, frequently referred to persons appointed to a public office or position (cf. Josephus, *Ant*, 20:227; Da 1:11; 2Mc 9:23, 25; et al.).

predetermined) by God. Jesus chose him so he could freely act out his deceit.

Thus we conclude that Jesus selected individuals for the tasks or ministries they would perform for him. Jesus' choice of disciples was not so that they would (be able to) believe. Rather, he appointed them for service. This individual election is for service, not for salvation.

THE ELECTION OF PAUL

Paul repeatedly expressed his conviction that he was a man under divine appointment. At the start of virtually all the letters attributed to him, Paul asserts that he is an apostle because of the will of God. God set him apart, called and appointed him, made him a steward, and gave him the grace of his position as apostle. Our studies showed the functional nature of these assertions. As Jesus appointed his disciples to their tasks, so God chose and appointed Paul to his role as apostle. His individual election was also election to a task, not to salvation.

What about Gal 1:15? Isn't this one text that blurs any distinction between appointment to salvation and appointment to a task? We argued that the primary focus of Paul's argument in Gal 1 is his position and authority as an apostle. His salvation, though prominent in the background, is not the primary concern here. Paul understands that God had in mind all along to use him as an ambassador of the gospel. As he looks back on his life, he perceives how his Jewish heritage and training uniquely prepared him for his role as preacher. He could see how God had specially set him apart for his eventual ministry. In the fullness of God's timing the divine, pleasurable will thrust the reality of Jesus upon Paul's attention. All these were necessary steps so Paul could function in the vocation God chose for him.

Does all this mean that Paul had no choice but to become a believer in Jesus? Did God's revelation of the gospel to Paul imply that Paul could not have responded as most of his fellow Jews did? Could not Paul have acted as did Judas and rejected God's choice? Manifestly, Paul never envisions these as possibilities; he simply exults in the awareness of God's gracious choice. Would we expect a murderer-turned-apostle to contemplate the option that he could have spurned God's grace? In his autobiographical musings, his conversion and appointment as an apostle were inextricably integrated. He owed all he was to God's grace.

Thus we must hesitate before building a theology of "God's choice of individuals to salvation" on this unique, autobiographical (and isolated) text. Admittedly, this text provides some basis for individual election to salvation. Nevertheless, Paul's overwhelming perspective is corporate.

THE ELECTION OF OTHER CHRISTIANS

According to various New Testament writers God chooses other individuals to perform tasks in his service. The functional or task orientation of these texts seems clear. Paul identifies God's choice of Pharaoh (Ro 9:17, 21) and government officials (13:1). Presumably these chosen agents may or may not believe in or consciously seek to serve God, reminding us of Judas. God appoints elders for the local church (Ac 20:28). He calls missionaries to spread the gospel (Ac 13:2; 16:10). God gives spiritual gifts to his children so they may function in ministry (Ro 12:6; 1Co 12:28; Eph 4:7).

These texts confirm the previous conclusions about God's selection of individuals: God chooses individuals to perform tasks. Individual election is election to a task.

IMPLICATIONS FOR INDIVIDUAL ELECTION
TO MINISTRY

What implications might this perspective on individual election have for ministries today? It would be difficult to argue that God has repealed what Paul said about the government in Ro 13:1. Christians today ought to view government officials as having divine sanction when they are fulfilling God's purposes for them.[41] Many studies have considered the obligations Christians have to be exemplary citizens, working for the good of human society as well as for the good of the kingdom of God. We cannot consider this

---

[41]We cannot enter into the complex of issues involved here. Jesus commanded that people are to render to God what is his due, and to government what is its due (Mt 22:21). There are times when governments attempt to infringe upon territory that belongs only to God. When such a conflict of loyalties confronts a Christian, the proper response is, of course, to obey God and not the government (cf. Ac 4:18–20).

huge topic here, especially since this is a rather minor aspect of our study. It does confirm, however, that God authorizes rulers who function as his ambassadors.

These varied texts that focus on the election of individuals lead to a simply stated but amazing conclusion: God uses people to accomplish his purposes in the world. First he started with Jesus Christ, the divine Son. His chosen task was to redeem lost humanity. The beloved and chosen Son attained salvation for believers; he accomplished the mission God set before him. While on this earth, Jesus chose apostles to serve him in spreading the Good News of the kingdom. Though many other options were open to the omnipotent God, he decided to select a few Galileans, and then others, to work with him to reach sinners.

Later came the time to select further missionaries and another apostle named Paul to spread the kingdom message through the founding of churches in the Roman world. Again, God chose individuals to bear the Good News. Those local churches came to have leaders, and, according to Luke, Paul assured the Ephesian elders that God participated in their selection as such (Ac 20:28). And beyond leaders, individual believers possess spiritual gifts as the result of God's wishes and desires, not their own. God chose the way Christians would best function in his church.

If nothing else, these insights elevate the task of ministry today. We readily acknowledge that God continues to give spiritual gifts for ministry. This suggests that God has chosen individuals to serve him. To engage in ministry using the capacities God has supplied fulfills the divine call. To sit on the sidelines of ministry as an unproductive onlooker robs individual election of its significance. The texts declaring God's choice of individuals for ministry are abundant and diverse. We may not simply banish them to a former era. As God chose Peter, Phoebe, Matthew, and Lydia to serve him in the first century, so he chooses women and men today. Of all the ways God could use to accomplish the spread of his kingdom today, he still chooses individuals.

As Christ's followers today, we must affirm with confidence our individual giftedness. And beyond that, we must all become involved in the service of our King. God has called us to be his people and has given us important roles to play. If all Christians have spiritual gifts, then all are "elect to a task." To opt out of ministry is an affront to God, who has called and equipped his people for service.

3
GOD'S CALL TO SALVATION

God not only chose the church to be his own people, he achieved that act of ownership through his "call." Though we encounter several nontechnical uses of the concept of "call" (as in Jesus' statement, "many are called, but few are chosen"), the dominant technical sense makes clear that the "called ones" are those "called to be Christians." The "called" are the saints, the faithful, the believers, the church, Christians (Ro 1:6; 1Co 1:24; Jude 1; and Rev 17:14). All the foreknown and predestined ones are also called (Ro 8:29–30). Those who love God are the ones called (8:28).

Our study has suggested that the sense of "to give a name" captures the nuance of this technical sense of "call." By the act of calling, those who were once not God's people become the people of God (Ro 9:24–26; 1Pe 2:9). "To name" better grasps this performative function of the action of calling than does the translation "to invite," though at times the two senses are difficult to separate.[42] Elsewhere we have defended this point in more detail.[43] In the action of calling, then, God names or appoints people to be his own. As God called Israel out from the nations to be his unique race, now he calls a new people into existence from among the inhabitants of the world—both Jews and Gentiles (Ro 9:24–26). Through God's election and his covenant, Israel became God's "son" (Ex 4:22–23; Hos 11:1; 1:10). Under the new covenant God calls Christians his sons and daughters (2Co 6:18; Gal 4:7; Ro 8:15; 9:26).

Since God called Christians to become his people, Paul can speak of them as "the called" (Ro 1:6; 8:28; 1Co 1:24) or "called saints" (Ro 1:7; 1Co 1:2). In addition he specifies that

---

[42]The two senses merge when the invitation or summons is viewed as "effectual." Nevertheless, "to name" captures a crucial component of meaning for these terms.

[43]W. W. Klein, "Paul's Use of *kalein*. A Proposal," *JETS* 27 (1984): 53–64.

Christians have a "calling" (for example, 1Co 1:26; Eph 4:1,4; Php 3:14; 2Th 1:11; 2Ti 1:9). The status of being called God's people entails the obligation to live and act in a manner that befits that calling. This includes living in hope, in a worthy manner, in holiness, and suitable striving.[44]

We have seen how this performative sense dominates Paul's uses. "Calling" is his technical term, but this sense also occurs in the other New Testament writers. In Acts Luke recognizes that when people "cross over the line" in repentance and baptism to receive forgiveness and become Christians, the divine activity involved is the call of God (Ac 2:39). John affirms that God has called us his children (1 Jn 3:1; Rev 17:14). The writer of Hebrews uses Pauline-sounding terminology in speaking of Christians as "the called" (Heb 9:15) who share in a heavenly "calling" (Heb 3:1). James speaks of the "name by which you are called" (RSV) (Jas 2:7). Peter's language also closely parallels Paul's technical sense: God is the one who called Christians (1Pe 1:15; 2:9; 5:10; 2Pe 1:3); God called them to a specific kind of life (1Pe 2:21; 3:9); and Christians possess a "calling" (2Pe 1:10).

Since people individually respond to the gospel to become Christians, is God's "call" an action performed upon individuals? The evidence of the New Testament suggests that calling, like election, is primarily corporate in its orientation. The "call of God" brings into existence a people who have an obligation to exhibit God's character in their actions. Richardson agrees:

> Broadly speaking there is no emphasis at all in the New Testament upon the individual's call, and certainly no suggestion that he ought to hear voices or undergo emotional experiences. The fact is that *klēsis* is a social conception and it is significant that except in the special case of Paul in Rom 1:1 and 1Cor 1:1 the word *klētos* is never found in the singular. Christians are corporately "the called" and corporately "the elect" and they are these things because they are one body in Christ, the Elect One.[45]

---

[44]This list is not exhaustive in Paul's writings, but comes out of the previous selection of examples. To these we could add other goals to which God calls Christians including: fellowship with Christ (1Co 1:9), peace (1Co 7:15; Col 3:15), freedom (Gal 5:13), hope (Eph 4:4), God's kingdom and glory (1Th 2:12; 2Th 2:14), salvation (2Th 2:14), and eternal life (1Ti 6:12).

[45]A. Richardson, *An Introduction to the Theology of the New Testament*, 274.

However, in 1Co 7:17–24 Paul asks each individual in the Corinthian congregation to recall the situation in life when God called him or her. God applies salvation to people individually. Each person has a "call" as a part of the called body. Each person has a responsibility to promote, for example, the holiness of the entire body by his or her personal holiness. As with election, individuals can exult in the call of God. Nevertheless, to repeat, the New Testament writers stress the corporate call. The elect body of Christ is also the body that God called into fellowship with his Son Jesus Christ our Lord (1Co 1:9). Corporate language dominates the New Testament theology of "calling."

IMPLICATIONS OF THE CALL OF GOD

God's call of those "who were not a people" to become "the people of God" adds more gravity to the corporate nature of election that we reviewed above. Those whom God calls he appropriates as members of his chosen people. The implications of our corporateness as believers that we considered above find added emphasis here in the call of God. However, since a "calling" comes to each believer at the point of conversion, Christians have, individually, the obligation to live out the implications of their new status in Christ.

Do Christians today sense that they have a calling—an assignment from Christ himself? Alas, such a sense of mission is all too rare. Because they have not experienced some mystical "missionary call," many Western Christians assume that God wants them to pursue a successful and self-centered life in suburbia. We have seen that because God calls all Christians (to be) the people of God, they all possess a calling. That implies an active quest of a character and lifestyle that befits the people who belong to God. It means earnestly pursuing lives of holiness, peace, freedom, and hope, as well as working to promote God's kingdom in the world. God calls Christians to identify with his people and to advance his values. This is a vital calling for the Christian community. We can only convince the world that God is really alive and in us if it can see the church actively pursuing God's agenda rather than its own selfish one.

4

GOD'S FOREKNOWLEDGE

In their discussion of soteriology the New Testament writers devote relatively little space to God's foreknowledge. In our analyses we concluded that the basic, face-value sense of "advance knowledge" best captures the sense of the noun *prognōsis*. Similarly, "to know beforehand" best decodes the verb *proginōskō*. This sense is unquestioned in the uses prior to and following the New Testament, and it fits best the few nonsalvific instances in the New Testament (Ac 26:5; 2Pe 3:17). Thus, God foreknew the course of Christ's redemptive career (Ac 2:23; 1Pe 1:20) as he did Israel's history (Ro 11:2). Likewise, God foreknew Christians (Ro 8:29; 1Pe 1:2).

This is not to say that God's knowledge of his Christ or of his people is mere cognition or recognition. More than merely acknowledging them or knowing information about them, God's knowledge implies a special, loving relationship. Nevertheless, such knowledge, even when it is *fore*knowledge, is not equivalent to choice. Paul understands and uses the various words that signify choice. Thus, foreknowledge emphasizes prescience, not selection.

The New Testament writers speak of God's specific foreknowledge of only one individual—Jesus Christ. Not only did Christ's life on earth take place according to God's set purpose, but also in keeping with his full knowledge (Ac 2:23). Luke makes a distinction between what God determined or willed concerning Christ (Ac 4:28; 13:29; Lk 22:22, par.), and what was a matter of his prior knowledge. He affirms both; they are not different ways of saying the same thing. Though God knew in advance precisely what would happen to his beloved Son, he still set in motion the plan of redemption.

Two corporate groups are portrayed as "foreknown." First, Paul assures the Romans that God will never reject his foreknown people Israel. In spite of their present wholesale rejection of the gospel of Jesus, God has not annulled his loving concern nor his promises for his ancient people. Our analyses demonstrated no reason to forsake the well-attested sense of "prior knowledge." Of course, this conveys all the ramifications of that special knowing relationship God shares with his people alone. Some insist that this prior knowledge is not pretemporal, but harks back only to "the previous history of the people of Israel in Abraham."[46] However, in keeping with the preponderance of *pre-* terms that do imply God's pretemporal activities, we must disagree. In any case, as with the uses concerning Christ, we find Paul distinguishing between God's choice and his foreknowledge of Israel.

Second, God foreknew Christians. In 1 Peter 1:2 the author distinguishes election from foreknowledge when asserting that God's chosen people are *kata prognōsin* (according to foreknowledge). Paul refers to believers as those who were foreknown (Ro 8:29). As with the other items in the chain of actions in Ro 8:29–30, the corporate body of Christians is the object of God's prior knowledge. It is a special and loving knowledge of relationship,[47] but the temporal prefix *fore*—casts the knowledge into the past. We concluded that it is impossible to speak very confidently about a "loving relationship" prior to the existence of one of the partners in the relationship. To say God had a "loving relationship" with his people in eternity past leaves many unanswered questions. Yet God's omniscience includes knowledge of the future—all its contingencies and eventualities. Then it makes sense to conclude that God possessed prior knowledge of his people, who they were and what they would become in Christ. For these foreknown ones God predestined conformity to Christ (Ro 8:29). Paul distinguishes foreknowledge from election (Ro 8:33).

5

GOD'S PREDESTINATION

The New Testament writers present God as one who predetermines events and outcomes. We detected this in several arenas. First, apart from our central concerns, we found affirmation that God determines events or affairs in the world (Ac 1:7; 14:27; 15:7; 17:26; Heb 4:7). Second, but in

---

[46]See, e.g., W. Beyschlag, *New Testament Theology*, 2d ed., 2 vols., trans. N. Buchanan (Edinburgh: T. & T. Clark, 1899), 2:111.

[47]In speaking of his disciples Jesus affirmed, "I *know* my sheep" (Jn 10:14, 27). In contrast, Jesus identified those who will be excluded from the future kingdom with this indictment: "I never knew you" (Mt 7:23; cf. 25:12).

a parallel vein, God determined stumbling for those who reject Christ (1Pe 2:8). More to the point, God marked out beforehand or predestined Jesus' career on this earth, especially the events surrounding his death. This may be very close to God's foreknowledge, since human responsibility for Jesus' death is specially affirmed (Mt 26:24, par.; Ac 2:23). God did not force Judas or the Jewish leaders to commit their sins. However, analogous to our findings concerning God's election of Christ, clearly his salvific career was predestined.

God predestined certain goals for his people. We insist this is the central point of predestination, not the selection of who will become his people. For those he foreknew (those in Christ), God predetermined certain benefits and privileges. Essentially these favors consist of the blessings of his eschatological salvation (1Th 5:9), though they include present conformity to Christ's image (Ro 8:29–30) and the capacity to do good works (Eph 2:10). Future glory is certain for the body of Christ (Ro 9:33; 1Co 2:7; Eph 1:11–12), for God had adopted believers into his family (Eph 1:5). These favors are definite for those in Christ; God has predestined them.

IMPLICATIONS OF GOD'S FOREKNOWLEDGE AND PREDESTINATION

These affirmations ought to excite the heart of every believer in Christ. God has entered into a loving relationship with his people. In his omniscience he has always known who they are, and in eternity past determined for them a grand and glorious future. God determined for his people his glorious salvation and all it entails, both now and into the future of eternity. Apart from any merit or attractiveness on their part, he destined for them great blessings and benefits. They alone comprise the ones he knows, and they alone enjoy the supreme privilege of knowing God.

These doctrines ought to give confidence to Christians today. Paul asserts that God has predetermined that believers will do good works. In addition God has resolved that they will become conformed to the image of Christ. Living lives that please God is not an impossible dream. God has given us the capacity to become like Christ and to perform the good works he desires.

In addition to present confidence in God's activity in their lives, Christians have the certainty of enjoying God's eschatological salvation. Though sin has resulted in a present diminished glory (Ro 3:23), God determined to restore his glory to his people. They will bear Christ's character and enjoy the glory of fellowship with God forever. These are not mere desires or wishes of weak though hopeful mortals. The omnipotent God predestined them. They are certain.

6

THE PLACE OF GOD'S WILL

The New Testament writers present God's will or purpose in two distinct senses. Being the sovereign and omnipotent One, God wills some things in a fiat or determinative way. For one, God decided to provide salvation (Jas 1:18). Paul credits many aspects of salvation to this divine and sovereign will. God's purpose supplies the foundation for his "calling" (Ro 8:28). God's will accounts for salvation itself (for example, 1Co 1:21; Gal 1:4; Eph 1:9; 2Ti 1:9). He displays mercy, hardens, and exercises his wrath—all in keeping with his purposes. What God predestined occurs because of the will of God (Eph 1:11). In what we might call a weaker sense of God's determinative will, he may allow suffering to befall his children, as he did in Jesus' life (1Pe 3:17; 4:19). Certainly he could prevent such suffering if he desired. In a reverse kind of way, several New Testament texts affirm that though people are free and should make their plans, such plans ought always to recognize the sovereign will of God. God always remains free to overrule or negate such human decisions (for example, Ac 18:21; Jas 4:15; Ro 15:32; 1Co 4:19; 16:7).

In a second broad category we found texts that present what God desires but does not choose to determine. While expressing what God wants or prefers, these passages leave the outcome contingent upon other factors—usually human response or obedience. The petition "Your will be done on earth as it is in heaven" (Mt 6:10) appears to fall in this class. Although Christians pray for God's will on earth, in fact, it is not always accomplished. In quoting from Hos 6:6 Jesus specifies God's will: "I desire mercy, not sacrifice" (Mt 9:13; 12:7). Alas, often people fail to demonstrate mercy and so thwart God's desire. Jesus fervently desired the Jews of his day to repent and find refuge in him, but they were not willing (Mt 23:37; Lk 13:34). God desires (and even makes possible) a life of holiness, sexual purity (1Th 4:3), and doing good (1Pe 2:15) for his children, though they sometimes disobey. God's will for his people includes their continual joy, prayer, and thanksgiving (1Th 5:16–18). The life of self-sacrifice has as its goal the performance of the good, acceptable, and perfect will of God (Ro 12:2). Unquestionably, Christians do not always fulfill God's will.

Both Peter and Paul affirm that God desires the salvation of all people; it is not God's will that anyone perish (1Ti 2:4; 2Pe 3:9). Yet the New Testament writers are clear that people who fail to believe in Christ will perish in their sins. These various texts express what God desires or wills, but which will not necessarily be achieved.

At times, of course, it may be difficult to put a specific text in one of the above two categories. An example might be Mt 18:14 where Jesus says that the Father is not willing that any of these little ones be lost. Does this express God's determinative will such that all the little ones find eventual reclamation and thus salvation, or simply God's fervent desire, which may or may not be accomplished (cf. Jn 6:38–40)? To resolve this theological conundrum lies beyond the purposes of this section. However, the text does help to illustrate the two broad categories and what is at stake.

When it comes to the provision of salvation and the determination of its benefits and blessings, the language of the New Testament writers is commanding. God decreed in his sovereign will to provide for salvation, and then he set Jesus on a course to secure it through his human life, death, and resurrection (Heb 10:9–10). He purposed to extend mercy to his people and to harden and punish unbelievers. He predestined or predetermined what believers will enjoy by virtue of their position in Christ. We may trace salvation and all that it entails solely to the pleasurable will of God.

God's will does not determine the specific individuals who will receive that salvation. The language of "willing" embraces all, not a select number. God's will is not restrictive; he wills all to be saved. Yet people can procure salvation only on God's terms. Though Jesus desires to reveal God to all, only those who come to him in faith find God and the salvation he offers. That some fail to find salvation can be attributed only to their unwillingness to believe—to their preference for their own way rather than God's. If God desires salvation for all, he wills (in the stronger sense) to give life to those who believe. These are not incompatible. They place the initiative with God for providing salvation and the obligation with people to receive it on God's terms—faith in Christ. God has done more than merely provide salvation; he "draws" people (Jn 6:44) so they come to Christ. In fact, people come to Christ because God enables them (Jn 6:65). However, these actions of drawing and enablement are neither selective (only some are chosen for it), nor are they irresistible. Jesus' crucifixion was God's means of drawing all people to Christ (Jn 12:32). It was God's provision for their salvation. All may respond to God's overture, but they must do so by placing their trust in Christ. Since God draws all via the Cross, and he desires that all repent of their sins and find salvation, it is not God's will that determines precisely which individuals will find salvation. Though God surely has always known who they will be, and though he chose them as a body in Christ, individuals must repent and believe for God's will to be done.

IMPLICATIONS OF GOD'S WILL

The various components of the salvation God has provided for his people find their source in the decretive will of God. God decided to send his beloved Son to secure atonement for people. It pleased God to grant salvation to his people. God will accomplish his purposes for his people and for those who reject his salvation. Nothing can thwart his loving purposes which he will accomplish for his own. This ought be a source of comfort and assurance to believers. Paul put it succinctly: "And we know that in all things God works for the good of those who love him, who have been called according to his purpose" (Ro 8:28). Rarely (if ever) can we answer the haunting "why" questions in the midst of the "all things"—the tests of faith. Yet even severe and unexplainable suffering does not indicate a believer lies outside the scope of God's purposes.

Returning to the topic of evangelism, we know from the biblical texts that God desires the salvation of people. When

Christians engage in sharing the gospel, they join with God in a task that is at the core of his purposes for the people he created. Christ died so all people might come to salvation. As John put it, "He is the atoning sacrifice for our sins, and not only for ours but also for the sins of the whole world" (1Jn 2:2). It is too easy for the church today to become indifferent to the task of world evangelization. It *matters* whether or not believers share the gospel—across the hall, across their back fences, and across the oceans. People need to hear the gospel presented in a culturally appropriate and understandable way (that presents it as really "good news"), so they may respond. Though we cannot (nor does God) coerce people to believe, we must present the message of salvation to them so they may make a responsible decision. God desires salvation for all, but he will only grant it to those who place their trust in Christ. "And how can they believe in the one of whom they have not heard? And how can they hear without someone preaching to them?" (Ro 10:14).

We cannot view evangelism as an option. Faith in Christ is the only way people can be reconciled to God. In bringing the gospel to people we gladden the heart of God, for we become colaborers with him in accomplishing what he really wants.

Our studies led to a further listing of things God *desires* in his people. These are contingent upon our obedience. Like ancient Israel, we will enjoy or forfeit God's blessing depending on our obedience. For people whom God has so abundantly graced, it only makes sense for them to aspire to be and do what pleases him. Today Christians need to face this duty to obey. We find "believers" today asserting their own wills against God's. No matter that God has asserted his desire for the holiness or sexual purity of his people, professed Christians blatantly disregard God's will and act as they please.

Instead of doing the "good" that God has enabled and called them to do, God's people often selfishly seek only their own interests. God desires people who are thankful and joyful. What he too often finds are disgruntled complainers who do not perceive how blessed and prosperous they are. If he should allow adversity to purify or deepen their faith, they question his love or his wisdom. Instead of prayerful and trusting children, he finds arrogant "know-it-alls" who think they are self-sufficient and independent.

We must give serious thought to our understanding of God and his will. Do we truly love God? To love God is to keep his commands, according to Jesus (Jn 14:15; 15:14). In fact, John defies a person to say he knows or lives in God if he does not keep God's commands (1Jn 2:3–6; 3:10, 24). We dare not treat God's will with impunity. Paul reminded the Corinthians, "But if we judged ourselves, we would not come under judgment" (1Co 11:31). There is no reason to incur God's judgment. However, we must repent of our sin and follow God's will. If we dismiss God's will, we invite his discipline. John insisted that God's commands are not burdensome (1Jn 5:3). Jesus assured his followers that his burden is light (Mt 11:30). May we, with the Psalmists, delight ourselves in doing God's will.[48]

---

[48]See, e.g., Pss 1:2; 112:1; 119:16, 24, 47, 70, 77, 143, 174.

BIBLIOGRAPHY

Abbott, T. K. *Epistles to the Ephesians and to the Colossians*. Edinburgh: T. & T. Clark, 1897.

Adamson, J. B. *The Epistle of James*. NICNT. Grand Rapids: Eerdmans, 1976.

Aland, K. *Synopsis Quattuor Evangelium*. 4th ed. Stuttgart: Württembergische Bibelanstalt, 1967.

Aland, K., et al., eds. *The Greek New Testament*. 3d ed. United Bible Societies, 1966, 1968, 1975, 1983.

Allan, J. A. "The 'In Christ' Formula in Ephesians." *NTS* 5 (1959): 54–62.

_____. "The Will of God: In Paul." *ExpT* 72 (1961): 142–45.

Allen, L. C. "The Old Testament Background of (ΠΡΟ) 'ΟΡΙΖΕΙΝ in the New Testament." *NTS* 17 (1970): 104–8.

Allen, W. C. *Gospel According to St. Matthew*. ICC. Edinburgh: T. & T. Clark, 1907.

Baird, J. A. "A Pragmatic Approach to Parable Exegesis: Some New Evidence on Mark 4:11, 33–34." *JBL* 76 (1957): 201–7.

Bammel, E. "πτωχός." *TDNT* 6 (1968): 888–915.

Barrett, C. K. *A Commentary on the Epistle to the Romans*. BNTC. London: A. & C. Black, 1957.

_____. *A Commentary on the First Epistle to the Corinthians*. London: A. & C. Black, 1968.

_____. *The Second Epistle to the Corinthians*. BNTC. Black, 1973.

_____. *The Gospel According to St. John*, 2d ed. London : SPCK, 1978.

Barth, K. *The Epistle to the Romans*. Translated from 6th ed. by E. C. Hoskyns. London: Oxford University Press, 1933.

_____. *Church Dogmatics*. II, 2. Edited by G. W. Bromiley and T. F. Torrance. Edinburgh: T. &. T. Clark, 1957.

Barth, M. *Ephesians*. 2 vols. Garden City, N.Y.: Doubleday, 1974.

_____. *The People of God*. JSNT Supplement Series, 5. Sheffield: JSOT, 1983.

Basinger, D., and R. Basinger, eds. *Predestination and Free Will*. Downers Grove, Ill.: InterVarsity, 1986.

Bauckham, R. J. *Jude, 2 Peter*. WBC. Waco, Tex.: Word, 1983.

Bauer, W. *A Greek-English Lexicon of the New Testament and Other Early Christian Literature*. Translated by W. F. Arndt and F. W. Gingrich; 2d ed. revised and augmented by F. W. Gingrich and F. W. Danker. Chicago: University of Chicago Press, 1957, 1979.

Beare, F. W. *The First Epistle of Peter*. 3d ed. Oxford: Blackwell, 1970.

_____. *The Gospel According to Matthew*. Oxford: Blackwell, 1981.

Beasley-Murray, G. R. *The Book of Revelation*. NCB. London: Oliphants, 1974.

————. "The Righteousness of God in the History of Israel and the Nations: Romans 9–11." *Review and Expositor* 73 (1976): 437–50.

Becker, U. "Hard, Hardened," *NIDNTT* 2 (1976): 153–56.

Beckwith, I. T. *The Apocalypse of John.* Grand Rapids: Baker, 1967. Reprint of 1919 ed.

Behm, J. "ἄμπελος." *TDNT* 1 (1964): 342–43.

Beitenhard, H. "Please—εὐδοκέω, εὐδοκία." *NIDNTT* 2 (1976): 817–20.

Berkouwer, G. C. *The Triumph of Grace in the Theology of Karl Barth.* London: Paternoster, 1956.

————. *Divine Election: Studies in Dogmatics.* Grand Rapids: Eerdmans, 1960.

Bertram, "νήπιος." *TDNT* 4 (1967): 912–23.

Best, E. *One Body in Christ.* London: SPCK, 1955.

————. "1 Peter II 4–10—A Reconsideration." *NovT* 11 (1969): 270–93.

————. *1 Peter.* NCB. London: Oliphants, 1971.

————. *A Commentary on the First and Second Epistles to the Thessalonians.* London: A. & C. Black, 1972. BNTC.

Betz, H. D. *Galatians.* Hermeneia. Philadelphia: Fortress, 1979.

Beyschlag, W. *New Testament Theology.* Translated by N. Buchanan. 2 vols. Edinburgh: T. & T. Clark, 1899.

Bigg, C. *Epistles of St. Peter and St. Jude.* ICC. Edinburgh: T. & T. Clark, 1902.

Black, M. "The Interpretation of Romans viii 28." In *Neotestamentica et Patristica* (for Oscar Cullmann). Supplements to *NovT.* Vol. 6. Leiden: Brill, 1962.

————. *Romans.* NCB. London: Oliphants, 1973.

Blass, F., and A. Debrunner. *A Greek Grammar of the New Testament and other Early Christian Literature.* Translation and revision of the 9–10th ed. by R. W. Funk. Cambridge: University Press, 1961.

Blevins, J. L. "The Christology of Mark." *Review and Expositor* 75 (1978): 505–17.

Boobyer, G. H. "St. Mark and the Transfiguration." *JTS* 41 (1940): 119–40.

Botterweck, G. J., and H. Ringgren, eds. *TDOT.* Vol. 2. Rev. ed. Grand Rapids: Eerdmans, 1977.

Bowen, C. R. "Love in the Fourth Gospel." *JR* 13 (1933): 39–49.

Braun, H. *Qumran und das Neue Testament.* 2 vols. Tübingen: J. C. B. Mohr, 1966.

————. "ποιέω." *TDNT* 6 (1968): 458–84.

Brooke, A. E. *Johannine Epistles.* ICC. Edinburgh: T. & T. Clark, 1912.

Brosché, F. *Luther on Predestination.* Uppsala: Uppsala University Press, 1978.

Brown, C., ed. *New International Dictionary of New Testament Theology.* 3 vols. Exeter: Paternoster; Grand Rapids: Zondervan, 1975–78.

Brown, R. E. *The Gospel According to John*. AB. 2 vols. Garden City, N.Y.: Doubleday, 1966, 1970.

————. *The Epistles of John*. AB. Garden City, N.Y.: Doubleday, 1982.

Bruce, A. B. *St. Paul's Conception of Christianity*. Edinburgh: T. & T. Clark, 1894.

Bruce, F. F. *The Acts of the Apostles*. London: Tyndale, 1951.

————. *Commentary on the Book of the Acts*. Grand Rapids: Eerdmans, 1956.

————. *Commentary on the Epistle to the Hebrews*. NICNT. London: Marshall, Morgan & Scott, 1964.

————. *1 and 2 Corinthians*. London: Oliphants, 1971.

————. *The Epistle of Paul to the Galatians*. Exeter: Paternoster, 1982.

————. *1 & 2 Thessalonians*. Waco, Tex.: Word, 1982.

Büchsel, F. "κεῖμαι." *TDNT* 3 (1965): 654.

————. "μονογενής." *TDNT* 4 (1967): 737–41.

Bultmann, R. *Theology of the New Testament*. 2 vols. London: SCM, 1952, 1955.

————. "ἔλεος, ἐλεέω." *TDNT* 2 (1964): 477–85.

————. "γινώσκω, γνῶσις, ἐπιγνώσκω, ἐπίγνωσις, προγινώσκω, πρόγνωσις." *TDNT* 1 (1964): 689–716.

————. *The Gospel of John. A Commentary*. Oxford: Blackwell, 1971.

————. *The Johannine Epistles*. Hermeneia. Philadelphia: Fortress, 1973.

Burkitt, F. C. "On Matthew XI. 27, Luke X. 22." *JTS* 12 (1911): 296–97.

Burrows, M. *The Dead Sea Scrolls*. New York: Viking, 1955.

Burton, E. D. W. *The Epistle to the Galatians*. ICC. Edinburgh: T. & T. Clark, 1921.

Caird, G. B. "The Will of God: In the Fourth Gospel." *ExpT* 72 (1961): 115–17.

————. *A Commentary on the Revelation of St. John the Divine*. London: A. & C. Black, 1966.

————. *The Gospel of St. Luke*. London: A. & C. Black, 1968.

————. "Son by Appointment." In *The New Testament Age*. Vol. 1 (Bo Reicke *Festschrift*). Edited by W. C. Weinrich. Macon, Ga.: Mercer University Press, 1984.

Calvin, J. *Commentaries on the Epistles of Paul to the Galatians and Ephesians*. Translated by W. Pringle. Edinburgh: Calvin Translation Society, 1854.

————. *The Gospel According to St. John, 1–10*. Edinburgh, London: Oliver & Boyd, 1959.

————. *The First Epistle of Paul the Apostle to the Corinthians*. Translated by J. W. Fraser. Edited by D. W. Torrance and T. F. Torrance. Edinburgh: Oliver & Boyd, 1960.

————. *The Gospel According to St. John 11–21 and the First Epistle of John*. Edinburgh and London: Oliver & Boyd, 1961.

————. *The Epistles of Paul the Apostle to the Romans and to the Thessalonians*. Translated by R. Mackenzie. Edited by D. W. and T. F. Torrance. Edinburgh: Oliver & Boyd, 1961.

————. *The Epistle of Paul the Apostle to the Hebrews and the First and Second Epistles of St. Peter*. Translated by W. B. Johnston. Edinburgh: Oliver & Boyd, 1963.

Carson, D. A. "Predestination and Responsibility." Ph.D. diss., University of Cambridge, 1975.

————. *Divine Sovereignty and Human Responsibility*. Atlanta: John Knox; London: Marshall, Morgan & Scott, 1981.

Charles, R. H. *The Book of Enoch*. Oxford: Clarendon, 1893.

Charles, R. H., ed. *The Apocrypha and Pseudepigrapha of the Old Testament*. 2 vols. Oxford: Clarendon, 1913.

Charlesworth, J. H., ed. *The Old Testament Pseudepigrapha*. Vol. 1: *Apocalyptic Literature and Testaments*. Garden City, N.Y.: Doubleday, 1983.

Clarke, F. Stuart. "Christocentric Developments in the Reformed Doctrine of Predestination." *Churchman* 98 (1984): 229–45.

Clements, R. E. "Deuteronomy and the Jerusalem Cult Tradition." *Vetus Testamentum* 15 (1965): 300–12.

Coenen, L. "Call." *NIDNTT* 1 (1975): 271–76.

————. "Elect, choose—ἐκλέγομαι, et al." *NIDNTT* 1 (1975): 536–43.

Conzelmann, H. *An Outline of the Theology of the New Testament*. Translated by J. Bowden. London: SCM, 1969.

————. *1 Corinthians*. Hermeneia. Translated by J. W. Leitch. Philadelphia: Fortress, 1975.

Cope, O. Lamar. *Matthew: A Scribe Trained for the Kingdom of Heaven*. CBQ Monograph Series, No. 5. Washington, D.C.: The Catholic Biblical Association of America, 1976.

Cranfield, C. E. B. "St. Mark 4.1–34." *SJT* 5 (1952): 49–66.

————. "St. Mark 13. Part I." *SJT* 6 (1953): 189–96; 287–303.

————. "St. Mark 13. Part I, II." *SJT* 7 (1954): 284–303.

————. "The Baptism of Our Lord—A Study of St. Mark 1.9–11." *SJT* 8 (1955): 53–63.

————. *The Gospel According to Saint Mark*. Cambridge: University Press, 1959.

————. "ΜΕΤΡΟΝ ΠΙΣΤΕΩΣ in Romans XII. 3." NTS 8 (1962): 345–51.

————. "Romans 8.28." *SJT* 19 (1966): 204–15.

————. *The Epistle to the Romans*. ICC. 2 vols. Edinburgh: T. & T. Clark, 1975, 1979.

Creed, J. M. *The Gospel According to St. Luke*. London: Macmillan, 1942.

Daane, James. *The Freedom of God*. Grand Rapids: Eerdmans, 1973.

Dahms, J. V. "The Johannine Use of Monogenes Reconsidered." *NTS* 29 (1983): 222–32.

Davids, P. H. *The Epistle of James*. Exeter: Paternoster, 1982.

Davies, P. R. *The Damascus Covenant*. Sheffield: JSOT, 1982.

Davies, W. D. " 'Knowledge' in the Dead Sea Scrolls and Matthew 11:25–30." *HTR* 46 (1953): 113–39.

De Kruijf, Th. C. "The Glory of the Only Son (John 1.14)." In *Studies in John* (Sevenster *Festschrift*). Suppl. to *NovT* 24. Leiden: Brill, 1970.

de la Potterie, I. "οἶδα et γινώσκω. Λεσ δεθχ μοδεσ δε λα ψονναισσανψε δανσ λε βθατριϡμε ϡωανγιλε." *Bib* 40 (1959): 709–25.

Delling, G. "πλήρωμα." *TDNT* 6 (1968): 298–305.

———. "ἐπιταγή." *TDNT* 8 (1972): 36–37.

———. "τάσσω." *TDNT* 8 (1972): 27–31.

De Lorenzi, L., ed. *Die Israelfrage Nach Röm 9–11*. Rome: Abtei von St. Paul vor den Mauern, 1977.

Dibelius, M. *James*. Hermeneia. Philadelphia: Fortress, 1976.

Dibelius, M., and H. Conzelmann. *The Pastoral Epistles*. Hermeneia. Philadelphia: Fortress, 1972.

Dodd, C. H. *The Epistle of Paul to the Romans*. London: Hodder & Stoughton, 1932.

Dombkowski Hopkins, D. "The Qumran Community and I Q Hodayot: A Reassessment." *Revue de Qumran* 10 (1981): 323–64.

Donfried, K. P. "The Allegory of the Ten Virgins (Matthew 25:1–13) as a Summary of Matthean Theology." *JBL* 93 (1974): 415–28.

Dunn, J. D. G. *Romans*. 2 vols. Dallas, Tex.: Word, 1988.

Eakin, F. E. "Spiritual Obduracy and Parable Purpose." In *The Use of the Old Testament in the New and Other Essays*. (Stinespring *Festschrift*). Edited by J. M. Efird. Durham, N.C.: Duke University, 1972.

Eissfeldt, O. "The Ebed-Jahwe in Isaiah xl.–lv. in the Light of the Israelite Conceptions of the Community and the Individual, the Ideal and the Real." *ExpT* 44 (1933): 261–68.

Elliott, J. H. *The Elect and the Holy. An Exegetical Examination of 1 Peter 2:4–10*. Suppl. *NovT* 12. Leiden: Brill, 1966.

Elliott-Binns, L. E. "James I.18: Creation or Redemption?" *NTS* 3 (1957): 148–61.

Ellis, E. E. *The Gospel of Luke*. NCC. London: Nelson, 1966.

Ellison, H. L. *The Mystery of Israel: An Exposition of Romans 9–11*. Exeter: Paternoster, 1966.

Esser, H.-H. "Mercy, Compassion." *NIDNTT* 2 (1976): 593–98.

Evans, C. A. "A Note on the Function of Isaiah, VI, 9–10 in Mark, IV." *RB* 88 (1981): 234–35.

———. "The Function of Isaiah 6.9–10 in Mark and John." *NovT* 24 (1982): 124–38.

Fee, G. D. *The First Epistle to the Corinthians*. NICNT. Grand Rapids: Eerdmans, 1987.

Filson, Floyd V. *A Commentary on the Gospel According to Matthew*. London: A. & C. Black, 1960.

Fitzmyer, J. A. "The Aramaic 'Elect of God' Text From Qumran Cave IV." *CBQ* 27 (1965): 348–72.

―――――. "'Peace Upon Earth Among Men of His Good Will' (Lk 2:14)." In *Essays on the Semitic Background of the New Testament*. London: Geoffrey Chapman, 1971.

Foakes-Jackson, F. J. *The Acts of the Apostles*. London: Hodder & Stoughton, 1931.

Foerster, W. "κθριοσ, κθρία, et al." *TDNT* 3 (1965): 1039–98.

Fohrer, W., E. Lohse, and E. Schweizer. "yῐów." *TDNT* 8 (1972): 340–92.

Ford, J. M. "The Parable of the Foolish Scholars (Matthew xxv 1–13)," *NovT* 9 (1967): 107–23.

Fornberg, T. *An Early Church in a Pluralistic Society. A Study of 2 Peter*. Lund, Sweden: Gleerup, 1977.

Foulkes, F. *The Epistles of Paul to the Ephesians*. TNTC. London: Tyndale, 1963.

Freedman, H., and M. Simon, eds. *Midrash Rabbah: Esther and Song of Songs*. London: Soncino, 1939.

Friedrich, G., ed. *Theologishes Wörterbuch zum Neuen Testament*. Band X/2: Literaturnachträge. Stuttgart: Verlag W. Kohlhammer, 1979.

Furnish, V. P. *II Corinthians*. AB. Garden City, N.Y.: Doubleday, 1984.

Gerhardsson, Birger. "The Seven Parables in Matthew XIII." *NTS* 19 (1972): 16–37.

―――――. "The Matthaean Version of the Lord's Prayer (Matthew 6:9b–13): Some Observations." In *The New Testament Age*. Vol. 1 (Bo Reicke *Festschrift*). Edited by W. C. Weinrich. Macon, Ga.: Mercer University Press, 1984.

Goba, Bonganjalo. "Corporate Personality: Ancient Israel and Africa." In *The Challenge of Black Theology in South Africa*. Edited by B. Moore. Atlanta: John Knox, 1974.

Godet, F. *Commentary on St. Paul's Epistle to the Romans*. Translated by A. Cusin. 2 vols. Edinburgh: T. & T. Clark, 1892.

Goppelt, L. *Apostolic and Post-Apostolic Times*. London: A. & C. Black, 1970.

Gould, E. *Gospel According to St. Mark*. Edinburgh: T. & T. Clark, 1896.

Grant, F. C. *Ancient Judaism and the New Testament*. Edinburgh & London: Oliver & Boyd, 1960.

Grayston, K. "The Doctrine of Election in Romans 8, 28–30." In *Studia Evangelica*. Edited by F. L. Cross. Vol. 2, part 1. Berlin: Akademie-Verlag, 1964.

Green, M. *The Second Epistle General of Peter and the General Epistle of Jude*. TNTC. London: Tyndale, 1968.

Grindel, J. "Matthew 12, 18–21." *CBQ* 29 (1967): 110–15.

Grudem, W. *1 Peter*. Leicester: Inter-Varsity; Grand Rapids: Eerdmans, 1988.

Gundry, R. H. *The Use of the Old Testament in St. Matthew's Gospel.* Suppl. to *NovT,* 18. Leiden: Brill, 1967.

_____. *Soma in Biblical Theology with Emphasis on Pauline Anthropology.* SNTS Monograph Series, 29. Cambridge: University Press, 1976.

_____. *Matthew: A Commentary on His Literary and Theological Art.* Grand Rapids: Eerdmans, 1982.

Günther, W., and H.-G. Link, "Love—ἀγαπάω, et al." *NIDNTT* 2 (1976): 538–47.

Guthrie, D. *The Letter to the Hebrews.* Leicester: Inter-Varsity, 1983.

Haenchen, E. *The Acts of the Apostles.* Oxford: Blackwell, 1971.

Hagner, D. A. *Hebrews.* San Francisco: Harper & Row, 1983.

Hanson, A. T. "Vessels of Wrath or Instruments of Wrath? Romans IX. 22–3." *JTS* 32 (1981): 433–43.

Harnack, A. *The Acts of the Apostles.* London: Williams & Norgate, 1909.

Hauck, F. "κοινωνός, et al." *TDNT* 3 (1965): 797–809.

Hawthorne, G. F. *Philippians.* Waco, Tex.: Word, 1983.

Hebblethwaite, B. L. "Some Reflections on Predestination, Providence, and Divine Foreknowledge." *Religious Studies* 15 (1979): 433–48.

Helfgott, B. W. *The Doctrine of Election in Tannaitic Literature.* New York: Columbia University King's Crown, 1954.

Hendriksen, W. *I—II Thessalonians.* Grand Rapids: Baker, 1955.

_____. *I and II Timothy and Titus.* Grand Rapids: Baker, 1957.

_____. *A Commentary on the Epistle to the Philippians.* Grand Rapids: Baker, 1962.

_____. *Ephesians.* Grand Rapids: Baker, 1967.

_____. *A Commentary on Galatians.* Grand Rapids: Baker, 1968.

_____. *The Gospel of Matthew.* Grand Rapids: Baker, 1973.

_____. *The Gospel of Mark.* Grand Rapids: Baker, 1976.

_____. *The Gospel of Luke.* Grand Rapids: Baker, 1978.

_____. *Exposition of Paul's Epistle to the Romans.* 2 vols. Grand Rapids: Baker, 1980, 1981.

Héring, J. *The First Epistle of Saint Paul to the Corinthians.* Translated by A. W. Heathcote and P. J. Allcock. London: Epworth, 1962.

_____. *The Epistle to the Hebrews.* London: Epworth, 1970.

Hiebert, D. E. "Designation of the Readers in 1 Peter 1:1–2." *BibSac* 137 (1980): 64–75.

Hill, D. *Greek Words and Hebrew Meanings.* Cambridge: University Press, 1967.

_____. *The Gospel of Matthew.* NCB. London: Oliphants, 1972.

_____. "On the Use and Meaning of Hosea VI:6 in Matthew's Gospel." *NTS* 24 (1978): 107–19.

_____. "Son and Servant: An Essay on Matthean Christology." *JSNT* 6 (1980): 2–16.

Hodge, C. *An Exposition of the Second Epistle to the Corinthians.* Grand Rapids: Eerdmans, 1953.

Holm-Nielsen, S. *Hodayot. Psalms From Qumran*. Aarhus, Norway: Universitetsforlaget, 1960.

Hooker, M. D. *The Son of Man in Mark*. London: SPCK, 1967.

Hort, F. J. A. *The First Epistle of Peter I:1–II:17*. London: Macmillan, 1898.

Hughes, P. E. *Paul's Second Epistle to the Corinthians*. NICNT. Grand Rapids: Eerdmans, 1961.

——————. *A Commentary on the Epistle to the Hebrews*. Grand Rapids: Eerdmans, 1977.

Hunter, A. M. "Crux Criticarum—Matthew XI.25–30—A Re-appraisal." *NTS* 8 (1961–62): 241–49.

Huther, J. E. *Critical and Exegetical Commentary on the New Testament: The Pastoral Epistles*. Edited by H. A. W. Meyer. Edinburgh: T. & T. Clark, 1881.

Jacobs, P., and H. Krienke. "Foreknowledge, Providence, Predestination." *NIDNTT* 1 (1975): 692–97.

Jenni, E., and C. Westermann. *Theologisches Handwörterbuch zum Alten Testament*. 2 vols. 3d ed. München: Chr. Kaiser Verlag, 1978.

——————. *The Parables of Jesus*. New York: Scribner, 1963.

——————. "θύρα." *TDNT* 3 (1965): 173–80.

——————. "λίθος." *TDNT* 4 (1967): 268–80.

——————. "νύμφη, νυμφίος." *TDNT* 4 (1967): 1099–1106.

——————. "παῖς θεοῦ." *TDNT* 5 (1967): 654–717.

——————. "ποίμην, ποίμνιον." *TDNT* 6 (1968): 499–502.

——————. "πολλοί." *TDNT* 6 (1968): 536–45.

Jewett, P. K. *Election and Predestination*. Grand Rapids: Eerdmans, 1985.

Jocz, Jakób. *A Theology of Election*. London: SPCK, 1958.

Johnson, D. G. "The Structure and Meaning of Romans 11." *CBQ* 46 (1984): 91–103.

Johnson, S. E. *A Commentary on the Gospel According to St. Mark*. BNTC. London: A. & C. Black, 1960.

Johnston, G. "The Will of God: In 1 Peter and 1 John." *ExpT* 72 (1961): 237–40.

Jones, A. "God's Choice: Its Nature and Consequences." *Scripture* 13 (1961): 35–43.

Joüon, P. "Les verbes ΒΟΥΛΟΜΑΙ and ΘΕΛΩ dans le Nouveau Testament." *Recherches de Science Religieuse* 30 (1940): 227–38.

Käsemann, E. *Essays on New Testament Themes*. SBT 41. London: SCM, 1964.

——————. *Commentary on Romans*. Translated and edited by G. W. Bromiley. Grand Rapids: Eerdmans, 1980.

Keck, L. E. *Paul and His Letters*. 2d ed. Philadelphia: Fortress, 1988.

Kelly, J. N. D. *A Commentary on the Pastoral Epistles*. BNTC. London: A. & C. Black, 1969.

——————. *A Commentary on the Epistles of Peter ad Jude*. London: A. & C. Black, 1969.

Kingsbury, J. D. *The Parables in Matthew 13*. London: SPCK, 1963.

————. *Matthew: Structure, Christology, Kingdom*. Philadelphia: Fortress, 1975.

Kirkland, J. R. "The Earliest Understanding of Jesus' Use of Parables: Mark IV:10–12 in Context." *NovT* 19 (1977): 1–21.

Kittel, G., and G. Friedrich, eds. *Theological Dictionary of the New Testament*. 10 vols. Grand Rapids: Eerdmans, 1964–76.

Klein, W. W. "Paul's Use of *kalein*: A Proposal." *JETS* 27 (1984): 53–64.

————. "The Sermon at Nazareth (Luke 4:14–22)." In *Christian Freedom: Essays in Honor of Vernon C. Grounds*. Edited by K. W. M. Wozniak and S. J. Grenz. Lanham, Md.: University Press of America, 1986.

Kuhn, K. G. *Konkordanz zu den Qumrantexten*. Göttingen: Vandenhoeck und Ruprecht, 1960.

————. "Nachträge zur *Konkordanz zu den Qumrantexten*." *Revue de Qumran* 4 (1963): 163–234.

Kümmel, W. G. *Introduction to the New Testament*. London: SCM, 1966.

————. *The Theology of the New Testament*. Translated by J. E. Steely. London: SCM, 1974.

Lacocque, A. *But As for Me*. Atlanta: John Knox, 1979.

Ladd, G. E. *A Commentary on the Revelation of John*. Grand Rapids: Eerdmans, 1972.

Lake, Kirsopp, and H. J. Cadbury. *The Beginnings of Christianity*. Part I, the Acts of the Apostles. Edited by F. J. Foakes-Jackson and K. Lake. Vol. 4. English Translation and Commentary. London: Macmillan, 1933.

Lane, W. L. *The Gospel According to Mark*. NICNT. Grand Rapids: Eerdmans, 1974.

Laws, S. *A Commentary on the Epistle of James*. BNTC. London: A. & C. Black, 1980.

Leaney, A. R. C. *A Commentary on the Gospel According to Luke*. BNTC. London: A. & C. Black, 1958.

Lees, R. "Corporate Personality: A Fiction." *The London Quarterly and Holborn Review*. Vol. 175—Sixth Series, Vol. 19 (1950): 335–37.

Lenski, R. C. H. *The Interpretation of St. Paul's Epistle to the Romans*. Columbus, Ohio: Lutheran Book Concern, 1936.

————. *Epistles of St. Peter, St. John and St. Jude*. Minneapolis: Augsburg, 1966.

Lewis, T. W. "' . . . And if he shrinks back' (Heb. X.38b)." *NTS* 22 (1976): 88–94.

Liddell, H. G., and R. Scott. *A Greek-English Lexicon*. Revised and augmented by H. S. Jones and R. McKenzie. Oxford: Clarendon, 1940.

Lightfoot, J. B. *St. Paul's Epistle to the Philippians*. London: Macmillan, 1898.

Lignée, H. "Concordance de I Q Genesis Apocryphon." Revue de Qumran 1 (1958): 163–86.

Lindars, B. New Testament Apologetic. London: SCM, 1961.

————. The Gospel of John. London: Oliphants, 1972.

Lock, W. The Pastoral Epistles. Edinburgh: T. & T. Clark, 1936.

Lohse, E. Colossians and Philemon. Hermeneia. Philadelphia: Fortress, 1971.

Malherbe, A. J. "Christology in Luke–Acts." Restoration Quarterly 2 (1958): 62–66; 115–27.

Malina, B. J. The New Testament World. Atlanta: John Knox, 1981.

Mánek, J. "Fishers of Men." NovT 2 (1958): 138–41.

Manson, T. W. The Sayings of Jesus. London: SCM, 1937.

————. "The Argument From Prophecy." JTS 46 (1945): 129–36.

Manson, W. The Gospel of Luke. London: Hodder & Stoughton, 1930.

Marshall, I. H. "The Divine Sonship of Jesus." Int 21 (1967): 87–103.

————. The Gospel of Luke. Grand Rapids: Eerdmans, 1978. NICTC.

————. The Epistles of John. Grand Rapids: Eerdmans, 1978. NICNT.

————. The Acts of the Apostles. Leicester: Inter-Varsity, 1980. TNTC.

————. 1 and 2 Thessalonians. Grand Rapids: Eerdmans, 1983. NCB.

Martin, R. P. Colossians and Philemon. London: Oliphants, 1974. NCB.

————. Philippians. Grand Rapids: Eerdmans, 1976, 1980.

————. 2 Corinthians. Waco, Tex.: Word, 1986.

Marxsen, William. Mark The Evangelist. Translated by James Boyce, et al. Nashville: Abingdon, 1969.

Maurer, C. "τίθημι." TDNT 8 (1972): 152–58.

May, H. G., and B. M. Metzger, eds. The New Oxford Annotated Bible with the Apocrypha (RSV). New York: Oxford University Press, 1973, 1977.

Mayor, J. B. The Epistle of St. Jude and the Second Epistle of St. Peter. London: Macmillan, 1907.

————. The Epistle of St. James. London: Macmillan, 1910.

Ménard, J. E. "Pais theou as Messianic Title in the Book of Acts." CBQ 19 (1957): 83–92.

Mendenhall, G. E. "The Relation of the Individual to Political Society in Ancient Israel." In Biblical Studies in Memory of H. C. Allemann. Edited by J. M. Myers, et al. Locust Valley, N.Y.: Augustin, 1960.

Merrill, E. H. Qumran and Predestination. Leiden: Brill, 1975.

Meyer, H. A. W. Critical and Exegetical Commentary on the New Testament. Epistle to the Romans. 2 vols. Edinburgh: T. & T. Clark, 1873, 1874.

————. The Epistle to the Ephesians and the Epistle to Philemon. Translated, revised, and edited by W. P. Dickson. Edinburgh: T. & T. Clark, 1895.

Michaelis, W. "προχειρίζω." TDNT 6 (1968): 862–64.

Michaels, J. R. "'Eschatology in 1 Peter III.17," NTS 13 (1967): 394–401.

Michel, O. "οἶκος, οἰκία." *TDNT* 5 (1967): 119–34.

_____. "ναός." *TDNT* 4 (1967): 880–90.

Milik, J. T. *Ten Years of Discovery in the Wilderness of Judea.* Translated by J. Strugnell. London: SCM, 1959.

Miller, Donald G. "Deliverance and Destiny. Salvation in First Peter." *Int* 9 (1955): 413–25.

Milligan, G. *The Theology of the Epistle to the Hebrews.* Edinburgh: T. & T. Clark, 1899.

Mitton, C. L. *The Gospel According to St. Mark.* London: Epworth, 1957.

_____. "The Will of God: In the Synoptic Tradition of the Words of Jesus." *ExpT* 72 (1960): 68–71.

_____. *The Epistle of James.* London: Marshall, Morgan & Scott, 1966.

_____. *Ephesians.* London: Oliphants, 1976.

Moffatt, J. *Epistle to the Hebrews.* Edinburgh: T. & T. Clark, 1924. ICC.

Moody, D. "God's Only Son: The Translation of John 3:16 in the Revised Standard Version." *JBL* 72 (1953): 213–19.

Morris, L. *The First & Second Epistles to the Thessalonians.* Grand Rapids: Eerdmans, 1959. NICNT.

_____. *The Gospel According to John.* Grand Rapids: Eerdmans, 1971. NICNT.

_____. *The Gospel According to St. Luke.* TNT. London: Inter-Varsity, 1974.

Moule, C. F. D. *The Epistles of Paul to the Colossians and to Philemon.* Cambridge: University Press, 1968. CGTC.

_____. "Mark 4:1–20 Yet Once More," in *Neotestamentica et Semitica.* Edited by E. E. Ellis and Max Wilcox (Matthew Black *Festschrift*). Edinburgh: T. & T. Clark, 1969.

_____. *An Idiom Book of New Testament Greek.* 2d ed. Cambridge: University Press, 1971.

Moulton, J. H. *A Grammar of New Testament Greek.* Vol. 3, "Syntax," by N. Turner. Edinburgh: T. & T. Clark, 1963.

Mounce, R. H. *The Book of Revelation.* Grand Rapids: Eerdmans, 1977.

Müller, D. "Disciple, et al.—μαξητής, μανξάνω." *NIDNTT* 1 (1976): 483–90.

_____. "Will, purpose." *NIDNTT* 3 (1978): 1015–23.

Munck, J. *Christ and Israel.* Philadelphia: Fortress, 1967.

_____. *The Acts of the Apostles.* AB. Garden City, N.Y.: Doubleday, 1967.

Murray, J. *The Epistle to the Romans.* NICNT. 2 vols. Grand Rapids: Eerdmans, 1960, 1965.

Neil, W. *The Acts of the Apostles.* NCB. London: Oliphants, 1973.

Nestle-Aland, et al., eds. *Novum Testament Graece.* 26th ed. Stuttgart: Deutsche Bibelstiftung, 1979.

Neusner, J. "The Use of Later Rabbinic Evidence for the Study of First-Century Pharisaism." In *Approaches to Ancient Judaism* I. Edited by W. S. Green. Missoula: Scholars, 1978.

Nordholt, G. "Elect, choose—αἱρέομαι, et al." *NIDNTT* 1 (1976): 533–35.

Nygren, A. *Commentary on Romans*. Translated by C. C. Rasmussen. London: SCM, 1952.

O'Brien, P. *Colossians, Philemon*. Waco, Tex.: Word, 1982.

O'Neill, J. C. *The Theology of Acts in Its Historical Setting*. London: SPCK, 1961.

Oepke, A. "ἔλκω." *TDNT* 2 (1964): 503–4.

―――――. "ἐν. " *TDNT* 2 (1964): 537–43.

―――――. "καθίστημι." *TDNT* 3 (1965): 444–46.

Pannenberg, W. *Human Nature, Election, and History*. Philadelphia: Westminster, 1977.

Paterson, Robert M. "The Doctrine of Election." *Colloquium* 1 (1964–65): 211–18.

Peisker, C. H., and C. Brown. "Open—ἀνοίγω, et al." *NIDNTT* 2 (1976): 726–29.

Pinto de Oliveira, C.-J. "Le verbe ΔΙΔΟΝΑΙ comme expression des rapports du père et du fils dans le IVe Evangile." *Revue des Sciences Philosophiques et Théologiques* 49 (1965): 81–104.

Piper, J. *The Justification of God*. Grand Rapids: Baker, 1983.

Plummer, A. *Pastoral Epistles*. The Expositor's Bible. London: Hodder & Stoughton, 1891.

―――――. *Gospel According to Luke*. Edinburgh: T. & T. Clark, 1896.

Porter, J. R. "The Legal Aspects of the Concept of 'Corporate Personality' in the Old Testament." *Vetus Testamentum* 15 (1965): 361–80.

Procksch, O., and K. G. Kuhn, "ἅγιος." *TDNT* 1 (1964): 88–110.

Quell, G., and E. Stauffer. "ἀγαπάω, ἀγάπη, ἀγαπητόσς." *TDNT* 1 (1964): 21–55.

Reicke, Bo. *The Epistles of James, Peter, and Jude*. AB. Garden City, N.Y.: Doubleday, 1964.

Rengstorf, K. H. "δώδεκα." *TDNT* 2 (1964): 321–28.

―――――. "μανθάνω." *TDNT* 4 (1967): 390–413.

Reynolds, S. M. "The Supreme Importance of the Doctrine of Election and the Eternal Security of the Elect as Taught in the Gospel of John." *WTJ* 28 (1965–66): 38–41.

Richardson, A. *An Introduction to the Theology of the New Testament*. London: SCM, 1958.

Ridderbos, H. *The Epistle of Paul to the Churches of Galatia*. NICNT. Grand Rapids: Eerdmans, 1956.

―――――. *Paul: An Outline of His Theology*. Translated by J. R. DeWitt. Grand Rapids: Eerdmans, 1975.

Roberts, R. L. "The Rendering 'Only Begotten' in John 3:16." *Restoration Quarterly* 16 (1973): 2–22.

Robertson, A., and A. Plummer. *First Epistle of St Paul to the Corinthians.* Edinburgh: T. & T. Clark, 1911.

Robinson, H. W. *The Christian Doctrine of Man.* Edinburgh: T. & T. Clark, 1913.

_____. "Hebrew Psychology." In *The People and the Book.* Edited by A. S. Peake. Oxford: Clarendon, 1925.

_____. *The Cross of the Servant.* London: SCM, 1926.

_____. "The Social Life of the Psalmists." In *The Psalmists: essays on their religious experience and teaching, their social background and their place in the development of Hebrew psalmody.* London: Oxford University Press, 1926.

_____. *Corporate Personality in Ancient Israel.* Philadelphia: Fortress, 1964. (This book incorporates two of H. W. Robinson's articles previously published: "The Hebrew Conception of Corporate Personality," in *Werden und Wesen des Alten Testaments,* edited by P. Volz et al. ["Beihefte zur Zeitschrift für die Alttestamentliche Wissenschaft," 66. Berlin: Töpelmann, 1936; and "The Group and the Individual in Israel," in *The Individual in East and West,* edited by E. R. Hughes, Oxford: University Press, 1937.)

Robinson, J. A. *St. Paul's Epistle to the Ephesians.* 2d ed. London: Macmillan, 1904.

Robinson, J. A. T. *The Body.* London: SCM, 1952.

Rogerson, J. W. *Anthropology and the Old Testament.* Oxford: Blackwell, 1978.

_____. "The Hebrew Conception of Corporate Personality: A Reexamination." *JTS* 21 (1970): 1–16.

Ropes, J. H. *Epistle of James.* Edinburgh: T. & T. Clark, 1916.

Rowley, H. H. *The Biblical Doctrine of Election.* London: Lutterworth, 1950.

Russell, D. S. *The Method and Message of Jewish Apocalyptic.* London: SCM, 1964.

Sabbe, M. "Can Matthew 11, 27 and Luke 10, 22 Be Called a Johannine Logion?" In *Logia.* Edited by J. Delobel. Leuven, Belgium: University Press, 1982.

Sabourin, L. " 'Connaître les mystères du royaume' (Mt 13, 11)." In *Studia Hierosolymitana* (P. B. Bagatti *Festschrift*). Jerusalem: Franciscan Printing Press, 1975.

Sanday, W., and A. C. Headlam. *The Epistle to the Romans.* 5th ed. Edinburgh: T. & T. Clark, 1902.

Sanders, E. P. *Paul and Palestinian Judaism.* London: SCM, 1977.

Sanders, J. A. "The Ethic of Election in Luke's Great Banquet Parable." In *Essays in Old Testament Ethics.* Edited by J. L. Crenshaw and J. T. Wallis. New York: KTAV, 1974.

Schechter, S. *Some Aspects of Rabbinic Theology.* London: A. & C. Black, 1909.

Schlier, H. "ἀναδείκνυμι." *TDNT* 2 (1964): 30.

298   BIBLIOGRAPHY

──────. "αἱρετίζω." TDNT 1 (1964): 184.

Schmidt, K. L. "καλέω, κλῆσις, κλητός, ἐπικαλέω, προσκαλέω."
    TDNT 3 (1965): 487–501.

──────. "ἐκκλησία." TDNT 3 (1965): 501–36.

──────. "ὁρίζω, ἀφορίζω, προορίζω." TDNT V (1967): 452–56.

Schmidt, K. L., and M. A. Schmidt. "πωρόω." TDNT 5 (1967): 1022–28.

Schmitz, E. D. "Knowledge—γινώσκω, et al." NIDNTT 2 (1976): 392–
    406.

Schnackenburg, R. The Gospel According to St. John. 3 vols. New York:
    Herder and Herder; London: Burns & Oates, 1968, 1980, 1982.

Schneider, B. "The Corporate Meaning and Background of 1 Cor 15,
    45b—O ESCHATOS ADAM EIS PNEUMA ZOIOPOIOUN." CBQ
    29 (1967): 450–67.

Schneider, H. " 'The Word Was Made Flesh.' An Analysis of the
    Theology of Revelation in the Fourth Gospel." CBQ 31 (1969):
    344–56.

Schottroff, W. "jd." THAT 1 (1978): 682–702.

Schrenk, G. "γράφω." TDNT 1 (1964): 742–49.

──────. "βούλομαι, βουλή, βούλημα." TDNT 1 (1964): 629–37.

──────. "εὐδοκέω, εὐδοκία." TDNT 2 (1964): 738–51.

──────. "θέλω, θέλημα." TDNT 3 (1965): 44–62.

──────. "ἱεράτευμα." TDNT 3 (1965): 249–51.

Schrenk, G., and G. Quell. "ἐκλέγομαι, ἐκλογή, ἐκλεκτός." TDNT 4
    (1967): 144–92.

Schweizer, E. Church Order in the New Testament. London: SCM, 1961.

──────. The Letter to the Colossians. Translated by A. Chester. London:
    SPCK, 1976; ET 1982.

──────. The Good News According to Matthew. London: SPCK, 1976.

──────. "σῶμα." TDNT 7 (1971): 1024–94.

──────. The Good News According to Mark. London: SPCK, 1971.

──────. "Dying and Rising With Christ." NTS 14 (1967): 1–14.

──────. Neotestamentica. Zürich/Stuttgart: Zwingli Verlag, 1963.

Seebass, H., et al. "bāchar." TDOT 2 (1977): 73–87.

Seebass, H., and C. Brown. "Holy—ἅγιος." NIDNTT 2 (1976): 224–32.

Seesemann, H. "οἶδα." TDNT 5 (1967): 116–19.

Selwyn, E. G. The First Epistle of Peter. London: Macmillan, 1946.

Senft, Chr. "L'élection d'Israël et la justification (Romains 9 á 11)." In
    L'Evangile, hier et aujourd'hui (Festschrift for F.-J. Leenhardt).
    Genève: Labor et Fides, 1968.

Shedd, R. P. Man in Community. London: Epworth, 1958.

Simpson, E. The Pastoral Epistles. London: Tyndale, 1954. TNTC.

Smith, C. W. F. "Fishers of Men. Footnotes on a Gospel Figure." HTR
    52 (1959): 187–203.

Spicq, C. Saint Paul Les Epitres Pastorales. Paris: Librairie Lecoffre, 1947.

Stählin, G. "προσκόπτω, et al." TDNT 6 (1968): 745–58.

Stauffer, E. New Testament Theology. Translated by J. Marsh. London:
    SCM, 1955.

Stegner, W. R. "Romans 9:6–29—A Midrash." *JSNT* 22 (1984): 37–52.

Stendhal, K. *The School of St. Matthew.* Lund, Sweden: Gleerup, n.d.

———. "The Called and the Chosen. An Essay on Election." In *The Root of the Vine.* Edited by A. Fridrichsen. London: Dacre, 1953.

Stevens, G. B. *The Theology of the New Testament.* 2d ed. Edinburgh: T. & T. Clark, 1911.

Storms, C. S. *Chosen for Life: An Introductory Guide to the Doctrine of Divine Election.* Grand Rapids: Baker, 1987.

Stott, J. R. W. *The Epistles of John.* London: Tyndale, 1964.

Strathmann, H., and R. Meyer. "λαός." *TDNT* 4 (1967): 29–57.

Sutcliffe, E. F. "Many Are Called But Few Are Chosen." *ITQ* 28 (1961): 126–31.

Swete, H. B. *The Gospel According to St. Mark.* London: Macmillan, 1909.

Talbert, C. H. *Reading Luke.* New York: Crossroad, 1984.

Tasker, R. V. G. *James.* London: Tyndale, 1956. TNTC.

Taylor, F. J. "The Will of God: In the Epistle to the Hebrews." *ExpT* 72 (1961): 167–69.

Taylor, V. *The Gospel According to St. Mark.* 2d ed. London: Macmillan, 1966.

Thompson, G. H. P. "Called–Proved–Obedient: A Study in the Baptism and Temptation Narratives of Matthew and Luke." *JTS* n.s. 11 (1960): 1–12.

Thornwell, James H. *Election and Reprobation.* Philadelphia: Presbyterian and Reformed, 1961. Reprint of 1870 ed.

Tiede, D. L. *Prophecy and History in Luke–Acts.* Philadelphia: Fortress, 1980.

Torrey, C. C. " 'When I Am Lifted Up From the Earth,' John 12:32." *JBL* 51 (1932): 320–22.

Turner, C. H. "Ο ΤΙΟΨ ΜΟΤ Ο ΑΓΑΠΗΤΟΨ." *JTS* 27 (1926): 113–29.

Urbach, E. E. *The Sages. Their Concepts and Beliefs.* Translated by I. Abrahams. Jerusalem: Magnes, Hebrew University, 1979.

Van Elderen, B. "The Purpose of the Parables According to Matthew 13:10–17." In *New Dimensions in New Testament Study.* Edited by R. Longenecker and M. Tenney. Grand Rapids: Zondervan, 1974.

von Iersel, B. M. F. *"Der Sohn" in den Synoptischen Jesusworten.* Suppl. to *NovT.* 3. Leiden: Brill, 1961.

Vermes, G. *The Dead Sea Scrolls in English.* Harmondsworth: Penguin, 1962.

von Balthasar, H. *The Theology of Karl Barth.* New York: Holt, Rinehart and Winston, 1971.

Vriezen, Th. C. *An Outline of Old Testament Theology.* 2d ed. Oxford: Blackwell, 1970.

Wace, H., ed. *Holy Bible. Apocrypha.* 2 vols. London: John Murray, 1888.

Wallis, G., et al. *"ahabh." TDOT* 1 (1974): 99–117.

Walvoord, J. F. *The Revelation of Jesus Christ.* Chicago: Moody, 1966.

Ward, R. A. *Commentary on 1 & 2 Timothy & Titus.* Waco, Tex.: Word, 1974.

Warfield, B. B. *Calvin and Augustine.* Edited by S. G. Craig. Philadelphia: Presbyterian and Reformed, 1956.

Weiss, B. *Biblical Theology of the New Testament.* 2 vols. Translated by D. Eaton. Edinburgh: T. & T. Clark, n.d.

Westcott, B. F. *The Epistle to the Hebrews.* 3d ed. London: Macmillan, 1920.

————. *Epistle to the Ephesians.* London: Macmillan, 1906.

————. *The Epistles of St. John.* London: Macmillan, 1909.

Whiteley, D. E. H. *The Theology of St. Paul.* Oxford: Blackwell, 1964.

Wildberger, H. *"bḥr." THAT* 1 (1978): 275–300.

Williams, S. K. Review of *Justification of God* , by J. Piper. *JBL* 104/3 (1985): 548–51.

Womack, M. M. "The Elect Lady." *Restoration Quarterly* 1 (1957): 67–70.

Wright, G. E. *The Old Testament Against Its Environment.* London: SCM, 1957.

INDEX

Aaron, 27, 54, 214
Abraham, 25, 27, 29, 31, 32, 33, 55, 56, 133, 173, 197, 198, 212, 226, 244, 258, 260, 264, 278
Abram, *See* Abraham.
Achan, 37, 262, 267
Acts of the Apostles, 63, 92, 96, 99, 104–23, 124, 131, 132, 142, 151, 154, 223, 225, 243
  on corporate election, 107–11, 267
  on God's call, 113–14, 275
  on God's determination of events, 104–7
  on God's foreknowledge, 118–19, 161, 233, 234, 235, 277, 279
  on God's will, 280
  on individual election, 111–17, 272, 273
    by Christ, 107, 112–13, 115, 122
    of Christ, 117, 118–20, 123, 218, 219, 269
    of patriarchs, 113
    of Paul, 115–17, 194, 195
  on predestination, 109–11, 278
  on salvation, 107–8, 110, 113, 114, 121–22, 165
Adam, 261, 262, 263
Adamson, J. B., 224
Amoraitic literature, 57
Amos, 108, 133, 164
  election of, 27
  on election of Israel, 29, 31
  on God's knowledge of his people, 87
  on individual election, 27
  on purpose of election, 34

Ananias, 115, 116, 117, 267
Angels, 86, 218
  election of, 173, 184, 210
Apocalypse, 124, 245
Apocrypha, 215 *See also* specific works.
Apollos, 212
Apostles, 268, 270–71, 273
  Acts on, 107, 112–13, 115, 122
  John on, 128, 129–32, 152, 155
  Paul on, 199
  synoptics on, 65, 90–92, 103 *See also* individual apostles.
Aquinas, Thomas, 19
Arminians, 19, 20, 21
Arminius, J., 19
Augustine, 19

2 Ba, 54, 55
Babylon metaphor, 244–45
Baird, J.A., 75
Baptism, 123, 209, 225, 268
  of Christ, 92–95, 96, 97, 103, 135, 156, 218, 220, 269
Barnabas, 108, 110, 113–14, 116, 122
Barrett, C. K., 130, 139–40, 141, 143, 150, 166, 176, 201, 203
Barth, K., 19
Barth, M., 159, 180
1 Baruch, 54
Bauckham, R.J., 250, 251, 252
Beare, F.W., 238
Beatitudes, 227
Best, E., 37, 39, 207, 229, 259, 263
Bethsaida, 82
Bietenhard, H., 94

Bigg, C., 241, 242–43
Blessings, The, 49, 51
Book of Jubilees, 55, 56, 70
Bride metaphor, 245
Brown, R. E., 128, 150
Bruce, F. F., 105, 106, 109, 110, 113, 168, 194, 203
Bultmann, R., 30–31, 144
Burrows, M., 50

Cadbury, H. J., 105
Caird, G. B., 146, 153
Calvary, 98, 118
Calvin, J., 19, 132, 137, 140, 143, 188, 191–92, 203
Calvinists, 19, 20, 21
Capernaum, 82
Carson, D.A., 58
Charles, R.H., 54
Christians, 65, 121
  corporate election of, 110, 259–60, 264–65
    John on, 178
    Paul on, 173, 176–84, 212
    Peter on, 182–83
  election of Christ and, 219, 221
  God's call to, 222, 274–75, 276
    Hebrews on, 214–16
    James on, 224–25
    Jude on, 254
    Paul on, 200–209, 212
    Peter on, 230–33, 246, 247, 249–50
  God's foreknowledge of, 163, 210, 233, 277, 278, 279–80
  God's role in events and, 171, 223, 229–30
  God's will and, 171, 280, 281, 283–84
  individual election and, 199, 272–74
  poverty and, 227
  predestination and, 185, 188, 279–80

1 Chronicles, 27, 96
2 Chronicles, 27
Church, 58, 120, 136, 145, 211
  corporate election and, 21, 180, 243, 244, 245, 246, 247, 258, 259–60, 264, 265, 267, 268
  God's call and, 274
  individual election and, 199
  metaphors for, 245
  the poor and, 227–28
  understanding of election in, 257
Circumcision, 205
Colossians, 218
  on election of Christ, 190–91
  on election of Christians, 176, 181
  on election of Paul, 195, 196
  on God's call, 206–7
  on salvation, 169
Commentary on Micah, 47
Commentary on Psalm 37, 51
Community Rule, 47, 48, 51
Conzelmann, H., 264
Corinthian people, 178, 267, 268, 276, 284
  God's call to, 203, 204
1 Corinthians, 158, 248, 254, 268
  on corporate election, 263, 267
  on election of Christ, 191
  on election of Christians, 177–79
  on election of Paul, 192–93, 194, 195, 196
  on God's call, 201, 202–5, 215, 274, 275, 276
  on God's foreknowledge, 162, 279
  on God's role in events, 171
  on God's will, 280, 284

on individual election, 199, 272
on predestination, 186
on salvation, 167–68
2 Corinthians, 151, 158
on corporate election, 263
on election of Paul, 193–94, 195, 196
Cornelius, 112, 119
Corporate election, 21, 257–68
Acts on, 107–11, 267
in Apocrypha and Pseude-pigrapha, 54–56
Christ and, *See* Jesus Christ.
of Christians, *See* Christians.
Church and, *See* Church.
of Gentiles, 107, 108–9, 110–11, 114, 174, 227, 266
God's foreknowledge and, 163, 164
implications of, 263–68
of Israel, *See* Israel.
James on, 108, 236, 258
Jews and, 107, 108, 266
John on, 258, 266
OT on, 33, 35–36, 51, 108, 259, 260
Paul on, *See* Paul; Pauline literature.
Peter on, *See* Peter; 1 Peter; 2 Peter.
predestination and, 109–11, 181, 239, 240, 242, 278
of priests, 35, 51
Qumran on, 50–51, 52
Rabbinic writings on, 59–60
salvation and, *See* Salvation.
synoptics on, 107, 258 *See also* specific gospels.
Corporate personality, 40–42, 262 *See also* Corporate solidarity.
Corporate salvation, 257–68

Corporate solidarity, 36–40, 260–64
Cranfield, C. E. B., 75–76, 93–94, 161, 167, 173–74, 192, 200
Creed, J. M., 86, 100
Crucifixion, 100, 144–45, 148, 156–57, 282
as God's will, 99, 120, 123
God's foreknowledge of, 118–19, 234
predestination and, 211

Daane, J., 36
Damascus Document, 47, 49, 51
Daniel, 37, 92
David, 26, 38, 42, 218
election of, 27, 31, 32, 54
Davidic dynasty, 35
Davids, P. H., 225
Day of Atonement, 37, 42
Day of the Lord, *See* Parousia.
Dead Sea Scrolls, 49, 53
Delling, G., 109
Deuteronomic code, 27–28, 29
Deuteronomy
on corporate solidarity, 37
on election of Israel, 20, 28, 29–30, 33, 34, 124
on the poor, 227
on salvation, 70
Deutero-Pauline books, 158, 160
Dibelius, M., 105, 224
Dodd, C. H., 39, 262
Dunn, J. D. G., 189, 202

Ecclesiasticus, *See* Sirach.
Edom, 173, 174, 197
Egypt, 29, 212, 239
Eissfeldt, O., 36
Eli, 27
Elijah, 161, 177
Elliott, J. H., 231, 244
Ellis, E. E., 78, 160
Ellison, H. L., 198

Ephesians, 20, 159, 161, 268
    on Church, 136
    on election of Christ, 191
    on election of Christians,
        179–81, 183, 265
    on election of Paul, 195,
        196
    on God's call, 206, 207, 275
    on God's foreknowledge,
        279
    on God's will, 280
    on individual election, 199,
        272
    on predestination, 186–88
    on salvation, 165, 168–69
Ephesus, 122
Ephisian people, 106
Epistles, 222–54 *See also* spe-
    cific epistles.
Esau, 173, 174, 197, 210, 212
Eschatological Midrashim, *See*
    Florilegium.
1 Esdras, 92
2 Esdras, 55
Ethiopic Book of Enoch, 54,
    55, 56
Evans, C. A., 75, 149
Exodus, 58, 153
    on corporate solidarity, 37,
        38
    on election of Israel, 28, 31
    on God's call, 274
    on purpose of election, 33,
        34
Exodus, The, 29
Exodus Rabba, 58
Explanatory formula, 76
Ezekiel, 27, 29, 35, 38

Female metaphors, 244–45
Fitzmyer, J. A., 85–86
Florilegium, 51
Free will, 45, 47, 48, 49, 50,
    63, 146, 150 *See also* Pre-
    destination.

Galatian people, 205, 206

Galatians, 268
    on church, 136
    on election of Christ, 191
    on election of Christians,
        178, 263
    on election of Paul, 79, 192,
        194–95, 271
    on God's call, 205–6, 207
    on God's foreknowledge,
        162
    on God's will, 280
Genesis, 26, 133, 174, 216,
    251
    on corporate solidarity, 37,
        40
    on election of Israel, 31, 33
    on God's foreknowledge,
        164
    on individual election, 197
Gentiles, 106, 121, 122, 145
    corporate election of, 107,
        108–9, 110–11, 114,
        174, 227, 266
    God's call to, 202, 203, 274
    God's will and, 169, 210
    Paul and, 115–16, 192, 194,
        195
Gibeonites, 38, 42
Goba, B., 267
God
    determination of dates by,
        213, 219
    election by, see Corporate
        election; Individual
        election
    knowledge of his people
        and, 87–90, 127–28
    love of, 32–33, 124–26, 155,
        156, 157
    predestination by *See* Pre-
        destination.
    purpose of, 165–72
    role of in events, 104–7,
        171, 222–23, 229–30
    role of in salvation
        Hebrews on, 214–16
        James on, 223–25

John on, 136–57
Paul on, 165–71
Peter on, 230–33, 247–50
synoptics on, 70–87 *See
    also* God's call; God's
    foreknowledge; God's
    will.
God's call, 199–209, 257, 274–
    76
  Acts on, 113–114, 275
  Hebrews on, 214–16, 250,
    275
  James on, 224–25, 275
  John on, 151–52, 275
  Jude on, 254
  Paul on, 199–209, 212, 214,
    215, 216, 274–75
  Peter on, 214, 230–33, 246,
    247, 249–50, 275
  predestination and, 200–202
  to Christians, *See* Chris-
    tians.
  to Israel, 200, 212, 274
  to Jews, 202, 203, 274
  to mission, 113–14 *See also*
    Salvation.
God's foreknowledge, 177,
    257, 277–78
  Acts on, 118–19, 161, 233,
    234, 235, 277, 279
  of Christ, 278, 279
  of Christians, 163, 210, 233,
    277, 278, 279–80
  implications of, 279–80
  of Israel, 161, 163, 177,
    209–11, 277–78
  Paul on, 161–64, 202, 209–
    11, 277, 278
  Peter on, 118, 161, 233–35,
    236–38, 239–40, 246,
    277, 278
    predestination and, 279
  Qumran on, 49
God's will, 257
  concerning circumstances,
    222–23, 229–30
  concerning events, 171

concerning his people, 172
implications of, 282–84
place of, 280–84
salvation and, 80–87, 136–
    39, 165–71, 223–24,
    247–48, 280
Grayston, K., 185
Grudem, W., 230, 240
Gundry, R., 70
Guthrie, D., 160, 215, 217

Haenchen, E., 105
Haggai, 27, 96
Hanson, A.T., 167
Hauptbriefe , 159
Hebrews, 63, 96, 99, 133, 134,
    213–21
  on election of Christ, 213,
    216–19, 220–21, 269
  on God's call, 214–16, 250,
    275
  on God's determination of
    dates, 213, 219
  on God's will, 248, 281
  on individual election, 214,
    220
  on predestination, 221, 278
  on salvation, 214–16, 220
Helfgott, B. W., 58–59
Hendriksen, W., 84, 97, 163,
    164, 184
Hill, D., 68, 71, 81, 88, 93
Hodge, C., 19
Hort, J. A., 229
Hosea
  on corporate solidarity, 37,
    38
  on election of Israel, 32
  on God's call, 202, 274
  on God's will, 280
  on salvation, 70, 71, 81
Hughes, P. E., 217
Hunter, A. M., 82, 83
Huther, J. E., 184
Hymns, 49
Hymn Scroll, 47, 48

Individual election, 21, 268–74
  Acts on, *See* Acts of the
    Apostles.
  Apocrypha and Pseudepig-
    rapha on, 53–54
  Christ and, *See* Jesus
    Christ.
  Christians and, 199, 272–74
  Church and, 199
  God's foreknowledge and,
    163–64
  Hebrews on, 214, 220
  implications of, 272–74
  John on, 128–32
  of kings, 27–28, 34, 42, 43,
    54
  OT on, 27–28, 32, 33, 34,
    35–36, 42, 43, 113,
    220, 268
  of overseers, 115
  of patriarchs, 34, 42, 113,
    122
  Paul on, *See* Paul; Pauline
    literature.
  Peter on, 112
  predestination and, 271
  of priests, 34, 42, 43, 219,
    220
  of prophets, 34, 42, 199
  Qumran on, 50–51, 52
  Rabbinic writings on, 59, 60
  salvation and, 91, 113, 114,
    197, 198, 212
  synoptics on, 91 *See also*
    specific gospels
Infancy narrative, 85
Introductory formula, 76, 78
Isaac, 25, 133, 198, 216
Isaiah, 26, 108, 116, 190, 243,
    252, 269
  on corporate election, 36,
    266–67
  on corporate solidarity, 37,
    38
  election of, 32
  on election of Israel, 43

prophecy in, 92, 93, 94, 96,
    149, 150, 151, 235, 241
  on salvation, 73, 74, 76, 77,
    78, 79, 86
Israel, 99–101, 113, 171, 212
  corporate election of, 20,
    21, 111, 265
    Apocrypha and Pseude-
      pigrapha on, 54–56
    John on, 124, 156
    OT on, 20, 25, 28–34,
      35–36, 42–43, 243,
      244
    Paul on, 173–76, 264
    Peter on, 239, 240
    Qumran on, 51
    Rabbinic writings on, 58–
      60
  corporate solidarity in, 37–
    38
  displaced by church, 58,
    243, 244, 246
  God's call to, 200, 212, 274
  God's foreknowledge of,
    161, 163, 177, 209–11,
    277–78
  God's will and, 283
  salvation of, 71, 197, 258
  special place of poor in,
    226–27 *See also* Jews.

Jacob, 25, 27, 44, 54, 55, 56,
    173, 174, 197, 198, 210,
    212, 244
James, 63, 142, 171, 222–28,
    248
  on corporate election, 108,
    236, 258
  on God's call, 224–25, 275
  on God's role in events,
    171, 222–23
  on God's will, 280
  on individual election, 226–
    28, 228
  on salvation, 223–25, 227,
    228

Jeremiah, 133, 142, 164
  on corporate solidarity, 37, 38
  election of, 27, 32, 54
  on election of Israel, 31
Jeremias, J., 93, 101, 160
Jerusalem, 53
Jesus Christ, 65, 102, 104, 116, 172, 177, 184, 199, 210, 254
  call of, 200, 201, 215, 249
  corporate election and, 259–60, 262–63, 265, 266, 267, 268
    Paul on, 179–80, 181, 183
    Peter on, 236, 237, 238, 239, 241, 242, 243, 244, 247
  election of, 20, 268, 269–70, 273
    Acts on, 117, 118–20, 123, 218, 219, 269
    Hebrews on, 213, 216–19, 220–21, 269
    John on, 219, 270
    Paul on, 119, 188, 189–91, 269
    Peter on, 118, 119, 233–36, 245, 247, 251–52, 253, 269
    prefigured in OT, 93, 95–96
    synoptics on, 92–101, 118 *See also* specific gospels.
  God's call and, 203, 205, 206, 208, 225, 274, 276
  on God's determination of events, 105
  on God's election of his people, 66, 67, 68, 69
  God's foreknowledge of, 278, 279
  on God's knowledge of his people, 87–90
  God's love and, 124, 125, 126
  on God's role in salvation, 71–79, 80, 81, 82–85
  God's will and, 280–82, 283, 284
  individual election by
    of apostles, *See* Apostles.
    of John the Baptist, 128–29, 155
    of Paul, 196, 197, 271
  knowledge of his people, 127–28
  predestination and, 186, 188, 221, 233, 234, 235, 270, 279
  role of in events, 171
  role of in salvation
    James on, 228
    John on, 139–54, 155–57
    Paul on, 165, 168, 169
    Peter on, 232–33, 247
  task of, 132–36 *See also* Baptism; Crucifixion; Transfiguration
Jewett, P., 258
Jews, 116, 145, 197, 251
  corporate election and, 107, 108, 266
  divisions over Christ among, 100
  God's call to, 202, 203, 274
  God's will and, 281
  predestination and, 49–50
  rejection of Christ by
    Acts on, 108, 109, 110, 121–22
    John on, 137, 138, 142, 143, 144, 148–49, 150–51
    Paul on, 174, 175, 211
    synoptics on, 68, 69, 82, 83, 85, 102
  salvation and, 52, 167 *See also* Israel.
Jocz, J., 190
Joel, 108

Johannine literature, 63, 104, 124–57, 164, 220
  on church, 135, 145
  on corporate election, 258, 266
  on election of apostles, 112
  on election of Christ, 219, 270
  on God's call, 275
  on God's knowledge of his people, 127–28
  on God's love, 124–26, 155, 157
  on God's role in events, 171
  on God's will, 281, 282, 284
  on individual election, 128–32
  on salvation, 136–57
  on task of Christ, 132–36
    See also 1 John; 2 John; Revelation.
1 John, 157
  on election of Christians, 178
  on God's call, 151–52, 275
  on God's love, 155, 156
  on God's will, 283, 284
2 John, 131, 136, 259
John the Baptist, 128–29, 155
Joseph, 99
Josephus, 92, 133
Joshua, 26, 37, 267
Judas, 99, 112, 122, 128, 129–31, 132, 155, 270–71, 272, 279
Jude, 63, 215, 254, 274
Judgement Day, 80, 87–88, 90, 138, 139, 157
Judges, 26, 28, 133

Kasemann, E., 164, 174, 189, 192
Kelly, J. N. D., 160, 170, 231, 240, 242
Kerygma, 72

Kings, 27–28, 34, 42, 43, 54, 56
1 Kings, 27
Kingsbury, J. D., 74, 94
Kirkland, J. R., 76
Korah, 27, 37
Korazin, 82

Lake, K., 105
Lane, W. L., 76
Last Supper, 98
Levites, 27, 35
Leviticus, 33, 37, 38
Lévy-Bruhl, 40
Liddell, H. G., 112
Lindars, B., 126, 140, 142, 147
Lord's Prayer, 80–81
Lord's Supper, 268
Luke, 65, 102, 131, 143, 146, 152, 196, 248, 251
  on corporate election, 111, 259
  on election by Christ, 90, 91–92, 103, 112, 270
  on election of Christ, 92–95, 97–101, 103, 118, 119, 269–70
  on God's election of his people, 65–66, 67
  on God's foreknowledge, 277
  on God's knowledge of his people, 89–90
  on God's will, 281
  on individual election, 128, 129, 132, 228, 273
  on salvation, 71–79, 81–84, 85
  on task of Christ, 133, 135
    See also Acts of the Apostles.
Luther, M., 19
Lydia, 114, 123, 273

2 Maccabees, 55, 92
Macedonians, 114

Malachi, 173, 174, 197
  on corporate solidarity, 37,
    38
  on election of Israel, 32
  on individual election, 27
Malchus, 142
Malina, B., 260
Man in Community , 37, 39
Manson, T. W., 70
Manual of Discipline, *See*
  Community Rule.
Mark, 110, 143, 152, 245, 251
  on election by Christ, 90,
    91, 103, 107
  on election of Christ, 92–
    95, 97–99, 100, 119,
    120
  on God's election of his
    people, 66–67
  on individual election, 128,
    129, 132
  on salvation, 71–79
Marshall, I., 77
Mary, 99
Matthew, 101, 102, 121, 131,
    143, 146, 152, 164, 248,
    251, 254
  on corporate election, 258
  on election by Christ, 90,
    107
  election of, 273
  on election of Christ, 92–
    99, 100, 103, 119, 120,
    269
  on God's determination of
    events, 106
  on God's election of his
    people, 66–69
  on God's foreknowledge,
    279
  on God's knowledge of his
    people, 87–89
  on God's will, 280, 281, 284
  on individual election, 128,
    129, 228
  on the poor, 227
  on salvation, 70–85

Maurer, C., 242
Melchizedek, 218, 219, 220
Mendenhall, G. E., 40, 41
Merrill, E., 47, 48, 49
Micah, 38, 86
Miller, D. G., 238–39
Mitton, C. L., 159, 180, 195,
    226
Moffatt, J., 215, 217
Monogenes , 133–35
Morris, L., 140, 143, 145, 149
Moses, 27, 31, 32, 53
Moule, C. F. D., 77, 78, 160
Muller, D., 81–82, 83–84
Murray, J., 162, 174

Nehemiah, 27, 33, 37, 113
Neil, W., 110
Neusner, J., 57
New Testament, 20–21, 45,
    58, 63
  on corporate salvation, 257–
    68
  on God's foreknowledge,
    277–78
  on God's will, 280–84
  on individual election, 268–
    74
  on predestination, 278–80
  See also specific books
    of.
New Testament World, The ,
    260
Numbers, 27, 34, 37
Numbers Rabba, 58
Nygren, A., 39

Oepke, A., 142, 219, 263
Old Testament, 25–44, 63,
    109, 110, 162, 174, 235,
    239, 241, 257
  compared to Qumran, 50,
    52
  compared to Rabbinic writ-
    ings, 60
  compared to synoptics, 91

on corporate election, 33, 35–36, 51, 108, 259, 260
on corporate salvation, 257, 258
on corporate solidarity, 36–40
election of Christ prefigured in, 93, 95–96
on election of Israel, 20, 25, 28–34, 35–36, 42–43, 243, 244
on election purpose, 33–35
on God's foreknowledge, 164
on God's love, 32–33, 124
on individual election, 27–28, 32, 33, 34, 35–36, 42, 43, 113, 220, 268
on the poor, 226, 227
on salvation, 70 *See also* specific books of.
Olivet Discourse, 65
One Body in Christ , 39

Pannenberg, W., 36
Parable of the Lost Sheep, 84–85
Parable of the Tenants, 68
Parable of the Ten Virgins, 88–89
Parable of the Two Sons, 68
Parable of the Wedding Banquet, 67–68, 101–2
Parables, 72–79 *See also* specific parables.
Parousia, 66, 67, 101, 188, 247
Pastoral epistles, 160
Patriarchs, 34, 42, 55, 56, 113, 122, 175, 176, 190
Paul, 121, 142, 221, 268
    on corporate election, 108, 109, 110, 111
    election of, 20, 80, 113–14, 115–17, 122–23, 188, 191–97, 223, 268, 271–72, 273

on election of Christ, 119
on God's determination of events, 105, 106–7
on individual election, 113, 115
Jews' foreknowledge of, 118
    See also Pauline literature.
Paul and His Recent Interpreters , 160
Pauline literature, 63, 69, 79, 120, 158–212, 233, 243, 250, 254
    on corporate election, 179–80, 181, 183, 258, 259, 260, 261–64, 265, 266–67
    on corporate salvation, 258
    on election of angels, 173, 184, 210
    on election of Christ, 188, 189–91, 269
    on election of Christians, 173, 176–84, 212
    on election of Israel, 173–76, 264
    on God's call, 199–209, 212, 214, 215, 216, 274–75
    on God's foreknowledge, 161–64, 202, 209–11, 277, 278
    on God's purposes, 165–72
    on God's will, 280
    on individual election, 188–99, 191–97
    on predestination, 167, 169, 172–73, 181, 184–88, 200, 202, 211, 279
    on salvation, 165–71, 182, 183 *See also* Paul; specific works.
Pelagius, 19
Pesikta Rabbati, 58
Peter, 121, 136, 142, 148, 150
    on corporate election, 107, 108, 258
    election of, 273

on election of Christ, 118, 119, 269
on God's determination of events, 105–6
on individual election, 112
See also 1 Peter; 2 Peter
1 Peter, 20, 21, 222, 229–45, 249
on church, 136
on corporate election, 235, 236–47, 259
on election of Christ, 233–36, 245, 247
on God's call, 230–33, 246, 247, 275
on God's foreknowledge, 118, 161, 233–35, 236–38, 239–40, 246, 277, 278
on God's role in events, 229–30
on God's will, 280, 281
on predestination, 233, 234, 235, 239, 240, 242, 279
on salvation, 165, 230–33
2 Peter, 115, 222, 247–54
on corporate election, 236, 252–54
on election of Christ, 251–252, 253
on election of Christians, 182–83
on God's call, 214, 249–50, 275
on God's election of his people, 69
on God's foreknowledge, 118, 161, 233, 234, 277
on God's will, 281
on predestination, 253
on salvation, 247–50
Pharaoh, 166, 197, 272
Pharisees, 71
Christ's disputes with, 69, 85, 95
neglect of God's will by, 81

rejection of Christ by, 68, 72, 151
Philippi, 114
Philippians, 115, 158, 195–96, 275
Phoebe, 273
Piper, J., 174
Pisidian Antioch, 108
Plato, 142
Plummer, A., 77–78
Porter, J. R., 40, 41–42
Predestination, 45, 46, 49, 50, 63, 172–73, 181–84, 211, 253, 257, 278–80
Acts on, 109–11, 278
Christ and, 186, 188, 221, 233, 234, 235, 270, 279
corporate election and, 109–11, 278
God's call and, 200–202
God's foreknowledge and, 279
Hebrews on, 221, 278
implications of, 279–80
individual election and, 271
Jews and, 49–50
Paul on, 167, 169, 172–73, 181, 184–88, 200, 202, 211, 279
Peter on, 233, 234, 235, 239, 240, 242, 253, 279
salvation and, 141, 142, 149, 153–54, 167–69, 186, 188
Priests, 219
corporate election of, 35, 51
corporate solidarity and, 37
individual election of, 34, 42, 43, 219, 220
rejection of Christ by, 68
Prophets, 34, 42, 199
Proverbs, 26, 33, 227
Psalms, 26, 92, 93, 133, 218, 251, 269
on corporate solidarity, 38
on election of Israel, 28

on individual election, 27, 28, 113
on the poor, 226, 227
prophecy in, 270
Psalms of Solomon, 55, 70, 218
Pseudepigrapha, 53–56 *See also* specific works.
Purpose of election, 33–35

Quell, G., 33
Qumran, 45–52, 53, 59, 60, 85 *See also* specific documents in.

Rabbinic writings, 57–60, 85 *See also* specific works.
Rawlinson, 55
Red Sea parting, 58
Reiche, B., 160
Reid, J. K. S., 180
Relating the New Testament , 159
Rest of Esther, 54
Resurrection, 140–41, 189
Revelation, 69, 157, 254
  on church, 136
  on God's call, 215, 274, 275
  on God's love, 126
  metaphor in, 245
  on salvation, 152–54
Richardson, A., 259–60, 275
Ridderbos, H., 39, 180
Robinson, H. W., 38, 39, 41
Robinson, J. A. T., 159
Rogerson, J. W., 40, 41
Romans, 69, 117, 151, 158, 160, 254, 280
  on baptism, 268
  on corporate election, 258, 261, 262, 263, 266, 267
  on election of Christ, 189–90
  on election of Christians, 176–77
  on election of Israel, 44, 173–76

on election of Paul, 79, 191–92, 194
on God's call, 200–202, 215, 274
on God's foreknowledge, 163–64, 210, 277, 278, 279
on God's role in events, 171
on God's will, 280, 281, 282, 283
on individual election, 197–98
on predestination, 185–86, 187, 188
on salvation, 165–67, 169, 258
Rowley, H. H., 33–34
Ruth, 38

Sadducees, 68
Saints, 169, 201, 202–3, 212, 274
Salvation, 63
  Acts on, 107–8, 110, 113, 114, 121–22, 165
  Apocrypha and Pseudepigrapha on, 54–56
  as separate from election, 44
  Christ and, *See* Jesus Christ.
  corporate election and, 54–56, 107–8, 110, 141–42, 182, 183, 210, 211, 257–68
  free will and, 48
  God's call and, 201, 202, 205, 208, 274–76
  God's role in, *See* God.
  God's will and, 80–87, 136–39, 165–71, 223–24, 247–48, 280
  Hebrews on, 214–16, 220
  individual election and, 91, 113, 114, 197, 198, 212
  of Israel, 71, 197, 258

James on, 223–25, 227, 228
Jews and, 52, 167
John on, 136–57
Paul on, *See* Pauline litera-
    ture.
Peter on, 165, 230–33, 247–
    50
predestination and, 141,
    142, 149, 153–54, 167–
    69, 186, 188
Qumran on, 48, 51, 52
Revelation on, 152–54
synoptics on, 70–87, 91,
    102 *See also* specific
    gospel.
the poor and, 227
1 Samuel, 26
on corporate election, 35
on corporate solidarity, 38
on individual election, 27
2 Samuel, 217
on corporate solidarity, 38
on election of Israel, 31, 33
on individual election, 27
Sanders, E. P., 47, 48, 49, 50,
    54–55, 57, 59, 60, 259
Sapphira, 267
Satan, 130, 144, 184
Saul
election of, 27, 35, 43
sins of, 38–39, 42
Schechter, S., 58
Schlier, H., 92
Schmidt, K. L., 108, 189
Schmitz, E. D., 88, 162
Schnackenburg, R., 127, 134–
    35, 145–46, 151
Schneider, B., 263
Schrenk, G., 115
Schweizer, E., 84, 93, 95
Scott, R., 112
Seesemann, H., 89
Septuagint, 85, 92, 96, 115,
    133, 134, 142, 164, 190,
    197, 216, 225, 235, 243
Sermon on the Mount, 88
Shedd, R. P., 37, 39, 264, 266

Shepherd metaphor, 37–38,
    127
Sifre, 58
Silas, 142
Silvanus, 245
Simeon, 99, 100
Sirach, 53, 54, 70, 85
Solomon, 33, 54
Stendahl, K., 180
Stevens, G. B., 244
Stone metaphor, 235–36, 241,
    242, 243, 244, 245–46,
    247, 269
Sutcliffe, E. F., 69
Swete, H. B., 98
Synoptic Gospels, 63, 65–103,
    104, 124, 132, 137, 143,
    151, 190, 220
compared to Acts, 120, 123
compared to John, 139,
    154–55, 156
on corporate election, 107,
    258
on election by Christ, 90–
    92
on election of Christ, 92–
    101, 118
on God's election of his
    people, 65–69
on God's knowledge of his
    people, 87–90
on salvation, 70–87, 91, 102
    See also specific gos-
    pels.
Syrian Antioch, 110

Tannaitic literature, 57
Temple, The, 53
Thanksgiving Hymns, 46, 47,
    48
Thelema , 135
Thessalonian people, 171, 207,
    208
1 Thessalonians, 196, 243
on election of Christians,
    181–82
on God's call, 207, 209

on God's foreknowledge,
279
on God's role in events,
171
on God's will, 172, 281
on predestination, 188
2 Thessalonians, 211
on election of Christians,
182–83
on God's call, 207–8, 275
Thessalonica, 181
Timothy, 160, 171, 208 *See
also* 1 Timothy; 2 Tim-
othy
1 Timothy
on election of angels, 184
on election of Paul, 196–97
on God's call, 208–9
on God's determination of
events, 106
on God's will, 172, 281
on salvation, 169–70
2 Timothy, 164
on election of Christ, 191
on election of Christians,
176, 178, 183
on election of Paul, 195,
196, 197

on God's call, 275
on God's will, 280
on salvation, 165, 170–71
Tithing, 38
Titus, 115, 160
on election of Christians,
176, 183–84
on election of Paul, 196
Tobit, 54
Transfiguration, 92, 96, 97,
135, 156, 220, 251, 269

Urbach, E. E., 59

Vine metaphor, 38, 131
Vriezen, Th. C., 40

Wallis, G., 32–33
Warfield, B. B., 19
War Scroll, 46, 47, 51
Westcott, B. F., 179, 215, 218
Wiesinger, 184
Wisdom of Solomon, 54, 70
Wright, G. E., 25

Zechariah, 133
Zerubbabel, 27